RACISM AND CULTURAL STUDIES

New Americanists A Series Edited by Donald E. Pease

E. San Juan Jr.

RACISM and CULTURAL STUDIES

Critiques of Multiculturalist Ideology and

the Politics of Difference

Duke University Press   Durham and London   2002

© 2002 Duke University Press

All rights reserved.

Printed in the United States of America

on acid-free paper ∞

Designed by C. H. Westmoreland

Typeset in Times Roman with Meta display

by Keystone Typesetting, Inc.

*Library of Congress Cataloging-in-
Publication Data*

San Juan, E. (Epifanio), Jr.

Racism and cultural studies : critiques of

multiculturalist ideology and the politics of

difference / E. San Juan Jr.

p. cm. — (New Americanists)

Includes bibliographical references and index.

ISBN 0–8223–2851–8 (cloth : alk. paper)

ISBN 0–8223–2866–6 (pbk. : alk. paper)

1. Racism. 2. Multiculturalism. 3. Ethnicity.

4. Culture — Study and teaching. I. Title.

II. Series.

HT1521.S2716 2002

305.8 — dc21   200104056

FOR DELIA, KARIN, AND ERIC

Perhaps you wonder how we know of you [Mumia Abu-Jamal, African American political prisoner in Pennsylvania] . . . and why it is that we extend this long bridge which goes from the mountains of the Mexican southeast to the prison of Pennsylvania which has imprisoned you unjustly. . . .

I could tell you that, for the powerful of Mexico and the government, to be indigenous, or to look indigenous, is reason for disdain, abhorrence, distrust and hatred. The racism which now floods the palaces of Power in Mexico goes to the extreme of carrying out a war of extermination, genocide, against millions of indigenous. I am sure that you will find similarities with what the Power in the United States does with the so-called "people of color" (African American, Chicanos, Puerto Ricans, Asians, Northamerican Indians, and any other people who do not have the insipid color of money). . . .

And with this bridge goes pieces of salutes and hugs for Leonard Peltier (who is in the prison at Leavenworth, Kansas), and for the more than 100 political prisoners in the USA who are the victims of injustice, stupidity and authoritarianism. . . . The powerful in North America carried out a "military intelligence" study . . . so that they might be able to violate justice and reason, to assault history and lose the truth, and that you and Leonard Peltier and many others would be silenced (and I remember your own words, "They not only want my death, they want my silence"). . . .

We salute you and may justice and truth find their place.

—— FROM THE MOUNTAINS OF THE MEXICAN SOUTHEAST,

    SUBCOMANDANTE INSURGENTE MARCOS

    MEXICO, APRIL 1999

The philosophers have only interpreted the world, in various ways; the point, however, is to change it.

—— ANONYMOUS MORO WOMAN GUERILLA

    FIGHTER IN MINDANAO, PHILIPPINES,

    CIRCA DECEMBER 2000

Contents

Acknowledgments

Every work is always the temporary outcome of a social process in which countless individuals find themselves complicit without their knowing it. Lest someone mistake this for my disavowing responsibility for what follows, I hasten to say that all errors are ascribable to me insofar as the author is an overdetermined site/agency of writing. In any case, we all belong to multiple communities that form as a result of complex articulations of historical and social forces, with their specific contingencies and durations. I would like to refer here to these conjunctures made up of individuals who may be credited for whatever virtues and strengths the book may possess; any inadequacies can be explained but not dismissed by my own situation and history. But I can assure readers that the persons named below are real, not postmodern simulacras or ludic impersonations.

The initial impetus for this work I owe to Donald Pease (Dartmouth College), a dynamic and creative scholar-teacher, whose stewardship of the "new Americanists" is a sign of fresh invigorating impulses sweeping American Studies and Cultural Studies in general. I am grateful to the solidarity of the following intellectuals who have been invaluable in manifold ways: Alan Wald, Evelyn Hu-DeHart, Peter McLaren, Sam Noumoff, Robert Dombroski, David Palumbo-Liu, Arif Dirlik, David Roediger, Manning Marable, Barbara Harlow, and Nancy and Norman Chance. Dean Paul Wong of the University of Michigan and Michael Martin, Chair of the Department of Ethnic Studies, Bowling Green State University, have given generous assistance. For stimulation and support, I am thankful to Csaba Polony, Dick Bennett, Neil Lazarus, Patrick Hogan, Kenneth Bauzon, Jorshinelle Sonza, Charlie Veric, Sarah Raymundo, Renato Asa, Delfin Tolentino Jr., William Boelhower, Michael Löwy, Ping-Hui Liao, M. Keith Booker, Anne Lacsamana, Jeff Cabusao, and many others too numerous to mention. I am grateful to Representative Velma Veloria of the Washington State House of Representatives and Phil Tajitsu Nash, Esq., of *Asian Week* for their support. I wish to acknowledge the help of my comrades in the Philippines: Bienvenido Lumbera, President Francisco Nemenzo of the University of the Philippines, Judy Taguiwalo, Joseph Lim, Roland Simbulan, Elmer Ordoñez, Fe and Roger Mangahas, Tomas Talledo, Soledad Reyes, Lulu Torres, and Sister Mary John Mananzan.

I also want to thank the editorial staff of Duke University Press, in particular Reynolds Smith, Sharon P. Torian, and Leigh Anne Couch, for their professional expertise and encouragement. Parts of the materials reworked into this book, now thoroughly revised and modified, first appeared in the following journals to whose publishers and editors I am grateful: *Left Curve, The CEA Critic, Diliman Review, College Literature, Mediations, Gramma, Explorations in Ethnic Studies, Against the Current, Pretexts, Danyag, Dialogue and Initiative, The Connecticut Review, The Arkansas Quarterly,* and *Nature Society and Thought.*

Without the friendship of the three indispensable persons to whom I dedicate this book, I would not have been able to carry out this project among many others, so may this be a humble gesture of recognizing their contribution.

Introduction

We make the world in which we live. So far we've made it a racist world.
But surely such a world is not worthy of man as we dream of him and want
him to be. — Richard Wright, *White Man, Listen!*

At the threshold of this new millennium, we encounter once again
W. E. B. Du Bois's "problem of the color line," but this time in more
duplicitous and seductive guises. No doubt racism as practice/ideology
has undergone a tortuous metamorphosis in the twentieth century. But
what has not changed, and has instead become more egregious, is the
existence of a determinate racial polity called the United States of
America. Exploring the space of this polity is bound to be hazardous
fieldwork, attended by false leads, traumas, tantalizing risks, and shocks
of misrecognition. Cognizant of this prospect, our goal remains rational
comprehension of the fields of social power and symbolic violence
(Bourdieu 1991), a research project oriented toward transformative
praxis. Before crossing the borderlines of what/who is included and
what/who is excluded in these fields, we need a historicizing vantage
point to delineate the contours of the social topology and chart the
landscape of collective representations, beliefs, and practices encom-
passed by the interface of racism and contemporary cultural studies.

One instructive message of the "signs of the times" may be captured
in the nexus between the United States — the only "superpower" left in
the "New World Order" — and its former colony in Southeast Asia, the
Philippines. The transition from the last to this new century marks the
centenary of the conquest of the Philippines by the military force of the
"colossus of the North," as the Latino insurgents put it. The Filipino-
American War of 1899–1902 was an inordinately barbaric war, the

"first Vietnam," with profound consequences still felt today. However, most textbooks devote only a paragraph, if anything at all, to this period — a crucial stage in the construction of the American national identity. More than one million Filipinos died, more than eight thousand invading soldiers perished, for the sake of vindicating "Manifest Destiny" (Constantino 1975; Miller 1982). Carey McWilliams editorialized in *The Nation*: "Mark Twain was right — the Philippines were our first real temptation to play the imperial role overseas. . . . It took three years and cost as much in lives and effort as the whole war with Spain, before the islands were sufficiently pacified so that we could guide the natives in ways of our own choosing" (1973, 548). Unrelenting pacification continues up to this day.

At that time President McKinley did not know where the islands were, but he was not deterred. With missionary hubris, he justified in 1899 the forcible annexation of the Philippines to a delegation of Methodist Church leaders: since the natives were "unfit for self-government, . . . there was nothing left for [the United States] to do but to take them all, . . . and uplift and civilize and Christianize them" (Schirmer and Shalom 1987, 22). Samples of those natives who would be uplifted by the Puritan work ethic and gradualist self-help were exhibited in the St. Louis Exposition of 1904, one of a series of industrial fairs designed to project the United States as the worthy successor to the European imperial powers.

From the beginning, it was a thoroughly racialized war of conquest. The rhetoric and discourse of that "civilizing mission," which had earlier legitimized the unrelenting genocide against the Native Americans, slavery of Africans, and violence against the Mexicans, continued up to the time, in the first two decades of the twentieth century, when thousands of Filipinos were recruited for the Hawaiian sugar plantations with the barring of Asian (Chinese and Japanese) migrant labor. I survey the relevant scenarios in chapters 1 through 3. Objects of McKinley's policy called "Benevolent Assimilation," which was not so benignly implemented, Filipinos became the new "nationals" who were neither citizens nor aliens, but rather an amalgam of sorts — postcolonial hybrids *avant le lettre*! Completely taken by surprise, these naive "Indios" suffered attacks by white vigilantes in Yakima Valley, Washington, and throughout the entire West Coast in the twenties and thirties.

This learning ordeal instigated Carlos Bulosan (1995), the organic intellectual of this expatriate generation, to confess that it was a crime to be a Filipino in America.

One of the scandalous but still little known incidents of the U.S. campaign to pacify the islands was the defection of more than a dozen African American soldiers to the side of the "enemy," the revolutionary army of the first Philippine Republic. Soldiers fresh from the onslaught against the Plains Indians considered the Filipinos savages and "niggers" who needed taming and domestication; reservation-like hamlets had to be set up to cut short a ferocious guerilla war that was becoming indefensible. I interpose here a reminder that the famous *Plessy v. Ferguson* judgment occurred in 1896, two years before the outbreak of the Spanish-American War. The system of apartheid — not to be altered for half a century — was finally given its juridical imprimatur.

Quite a number of notable public figures — William Jennings Bryan, Andrew Carnegie, William James, Mark Twain, and William Dean Howells, among others — vehemently opposed the carnage. One of the most significant protests was the anti-imperialist resolution of the Black Citizens of Boston published in the *Boston Post* of 18 July 1899, which reads in part: "Resolved, That, while the rights of colored citizens in the south, sacredly guaranteed them by the amendment of the Constitution, are shamefully disregarded; and, while the frequent lynchings of negroes who are denied a civilized trial are a reproach to Republican government, the duty of the president and country is to reform these crying domestic wrongs and not to attempt the civilization of alien peoples by powder and shot." Calling attention to the gap between the idealized representation of democracy in foreign adventure and its actual realpolitik conduct in the heartland exposes the true character of the expanding nation-state as a racialized monopoly-capitalist formation, constructed on the basis of racial segregation, hierarchy, and repression. As the Black Radical Congress (2001) recently stated, "Racist violence was fundamental to the creation of the United States." While "Manifest Destiny," the proclaimed messianic mission with its accompanying myth of "the promised land," and the terror of white supremacy may appear incompatible from a larger historical perspective, that apparent incongruity may be grasped as itself the condition of possibility for the gestation of a neocolonizing imperium. Imperial hegemony orchestrates the spatiotemporal valences of race, class, gender, sexuality, and nationality in the carnivalesque terrain of market globalization.

A review of the geopolitical formation of the United States demonstrates a clear racial, not simply ethnic, pattern of constituting the national identity and the commonality it invokes. As revisionist historians have shown, the U.S. racial order springs from a politics of exploitation and containment encompassing inter alia colonialism, apartheid, racial segregation, xenophobia, ethnic cleansing, and genocide. It evolved from four key conjunctures that mark the genealogy of the social field of power and its logic of division: first, the suppression of the aboriginal inhabitants (Native Americans) for the exploitation of land and natural resources; second, the institutionalization of slavery and the post–Civil War segregation; third, the conquest of territory from the Mexicans, Spaniards (Puerto Rico, Cuba, the Philippines, Guam), and Hawaiians, together with the colonization of Mexicans, Filipinos, Puerto Ricans; and, fourth, the subordination of Asian labor (Kolko 1976; Goldfield 1997). This racial genealogy of the empire followed the logic of capital accumulation by expanding the market for industrial goods and securing sources of raw materials and, in particular, the prime commodity for exchange and maximizing of surplus value: cheap labor power. This confirms the enduring relevance of Oliver Cromwell Cox's proposition that "racial exploitation is merely one aspect of the problem of the proletarianization of labor, regardless of the color of the laborer. Hence racial antagonism is essentially political-class conflict" (A. Reed 2001, 27).

Gradually, however, the shaping of the racial polity is blurred by the official enshrinement of immigration as the foundational event of nationhood (see chapters 1 and 2). It also served as the allegorical script through which other major social anxieties and antinomies are translated. Establishment rituals still rehearse the doxa that the United States is a "nation of immigrants," with the obvious exception of the Native Americans. This received truism has been consecrated by erudite scholars, among them Oscar Handlin, Nathan Glazer, Patrick Moynihan, Alejandro Portes, and recycled by numerous "multicultural" textbooks. Handlin's *Race and Nationality in American Life* (1957), to cite one example, reiterates the centrality of immigration in the continous reappropriation of the primordial matrix of national subjecthood: white supremacy as "Manifest Destiny" and the U.S. national-security state as the prime defender of Western civilization threatened by dark-skinned terrorists and rogue states.

One of the conjunctural events confirming the value of issues surrounding immigration was the controversy sparked by Proposition 187 in California. This involved the denial of social services to undocumented workers and residents of Mexican descent. It should be mentioned here that more than half a million arrests and deportations of "undocumented" persons take place annually; between one and eight million Mexicans are thought to reside illegally in the United States (Cashmore 1988). After a thorough exposure of the political, economic, and ideological agenda promoted by the advocates of the proposition, the Los Angeles-based Labor/Community Strategy Center pointed out that the real issue centers on the causes of the "decline of people's living standards and the growing disintegration of our society that is rooted in the out-of-control 'free market' system" (1994, 4). The center stressed W. E. B. Du Bois's insight that behind the great problem of the "color line" is "the fact that so many civilized persons are willing to live in comfort even if the price of this is the poverty, ignorance and disease of the majority of their fellowmen." Hence, across class, nationality, and gender boundaries, a racist *habitus* (Bourdieu 1999) operationalized through various instrumentalities continues to fuel today's anti-immigrant hysteria. After reviewing the differential treatment and incorporation of people of color that configured the racial polity, the center concluded that "we are a continent founded on genocide [of the indigenous peoples] in the name of colonization, read immigration."

Multiculturalist Interlude

In the context of restrictive and selective immigration laws, the problem of cultural ethos has become the major site of racial categorization and conflict. (I address this field of contestation in chapters 4 and 5.) The ideal of cultural diversity implies that there is a normative standard — call it the "American Way of Life," the "common culture," the "Great Books," the canon, civic or republican nationalism — compared to which the other ways (not real alternatives) are alien, weird, menacing. Some people become problems by the simple fact of their bodily existence. With the demise of the welfare state, the Self/Other binary persists as the integrating paradigm that underpins token programs of multiculturalism with all their infinite permutations. One hypothetical question may be posed here: Could this multiculturalist strategy of peacefully managing differences have prevented the 1992 Los Angeles riot if it had been deployed earlier? Is multiculturalism a reformist tactic for carrying out those infamous neoliberal goals of stabilization, deregulation, and privatization that have caused untold misery for millions?

Multiculturalism is celebrated today as the antiphony to the fall of the "Evil Empire" and the triumph of the free market, the performative self, and unlimited shopping for all. Ishmael Reed (1998), among the multiliterati, has trumpeted the virtues of "America: The Multinational Society." The rubric "multinational" is meant to vindicate the thought of Du Bois, the proponents of La Raza Unida, and the theories of internal colonialism. Ironically, however, Reed declares somewhat naively that "the United States is unique in the world: The world is here" in New York City, Los Angeles, and so on. Reed, I suspect, does not mean that the problems of the underdeveloped and dependent societies have come in to plague American cities. With this figure of subsumption or synecdochic linkage, the imperial center reasserts a privileged role in the world — all the margins, the absent Others, are redeemed in a sanitized, uniform space where cultural differences dissolve or are sorted out into their proper niches in the ranking of national values and priorities. Multicultural USA reigns over all.

We are now supposed to accept a fait accompli: plural cultures or ethnicities coexisting peacefully, without serious contestation, in a free play of monads in "the best of all possible worlds." No longer a melting pot but a salad bowl, a smorgasbord of cultures, our society subsists on the mass consumption of variegated and heterogeneous lifestyles. There is of course a majoritarian consensual culture — tune in to the six o'clock news — to which we add any number of diverse particulars, thus proving that our principle of tolerance can accommodate those formerly excluded or ignored. Even recusant denizens can be invited to the Mall of America. Why not? It is a bazaar for anyone who can buy, although it may turn out that your particular goods are not as valuable or significant as mine. Assorted postcolonialists and postmodernists are accessories to this pluralizing scheme. Whether formulated in terms of modernity, communitarian togetherness, representative democracy, or individual self-fulfillment, the old belief in "our civilizing mission" endures despite claims of charity, patriotic compassion, liberal latitude, respect for cultural diversity, and so on. The aim of the cultural literacy movement espoused by E. D. Hirsch, for example, and by business-oriented distance and "general education" programs, is to reproduce the competitive entrepreneurial self, now assuredly more sophisticated and cosmopolitan, founded on centuries-old strategies of domestication and devaluation of "Others." Updated and streamlined, "Manifest Destiny" marches on.

On closer scrutiny, this bureaucratic mechanism of inclusion — what Herbert Marcuse once called "repressive desublimation" — is a mode of appropriation: it fetishizes and commodifies others. The self-arrogating universal swallows the unsuspecting particulars in a grand hegemonic compromise. Indeed, retrograde versions of multiculturalism celebrate in order to fossilize differences and thus assimilate "others" into a fictive gathering that flattens class, race, and nationality contradictions. Other versions grant cultural autonomy but hide or ignore structural inequalities under the umbrella of a refurbished humanist cosmopolitanism. And so the noisy border-crossers like Guillermo Gomez Peña or Coco Fusco, our most provocative agitprop artists, are constantly reminded that to gain full citizenship, unambiguous rules must be obeyed: proficiency in English is mandatory, assimilation of certain procedures and rituals assumed, and so on and so forth.

Cultural pluralism first broached in the twenties by Horace Kallen has been retooled for the imperatives and exigencies of the "New World Order." What the current multiculturalist orthodoxy (of left or right varieties) elides, however, is the history of the struggles of people of color — both those within the metropolis and in the far-flung outposts of finance capital. While the political armies of racial supremacy were defeated in World War II, the practices of the capitalist nation-states continue to reproduce the domination and subordination of racialized populations in covert and subtle ways. The citizen-subject, citizenship as self-ownership with the right to buy and sell (that is, alienate one's own labor-power), demonstrates the universalizing virtue of the liberal nation-state. Citizenship remains defined by the categories that govern the public sphere and the marketplace, categories denominating race, geopolitical location, gender, nationality, sexuality, and so on (Peller 1995). While globalization may render national boundaries porous, the U.S. nation-state continues to institutionalize social differences in national structures of enfranchisement, property law, and therefore of exploitation by class, race, sexuality, gender, and so on. As Stephen Steinberg has tirelessly argued, "The essence of racial oppression [in the United States] — our grand apartheid — is a racial division of labor, a system of occupational segregation" (2000, 64). The racial polity is a thoroughly nationalized machine for reproducing racial hierarchy anchored to and intensified by class antagonism.

Culture as ethnic distinction then reinforces the legitimacy of the racial polity. Opposed to those who insist on conformity to a monolithic pattern of conduct, I am for the recognition of the integrity and value of peoples' cultures and life-forms and for their collective right to exist and flourish. But how can this recognition of multiplicity and autonomous singularities be universalized? It cannot happen as long as the global logic of corporate accumulation determines the everyday life of people on this planet. To lay the groundwork for a genuine popular-democratic esteem for cultural differences, class divisions must be abolished first with the socialization of productive property and the equalization of competencies. Power relations need to be overhauled according to egalitarian principles. Multiculturalism, as long as it is conceived within the existing framework of the racial polity, of a hegemonic order founded on class inequality, cannot offer the means to realize justice, fairness, and recognition of peoples' singular identities and worth. We need to be critical of this easy way out of the present crisis. The multiculturalist respect for the Other's individuality, according to Slavoj Žižek (1997), is the very form of asserting one's own superiority. This paradox underlies multiculturalism as, in fact, the authentic "cultural logic of multinational" or globalized capitalism. So I am afraid the terror of racism will be with us in this new millenium as long as the conditions that produce and reproduce class relations, in effect the material armature of the racial polity, remain the sine qua non for the reproduction and legitimation of the dominant social structures and institutional practices of our everyday lives.

Unbeknownst to many, fierce race war — a sublimation of the class struggle — rages on around us. With the propagation of the Murray-

Herrnstein notion of genetically defined intelligence, we are once more bombarded with arguments for white supremacy first systematized by Comte Joseph de Gobineau in his infamous *Essay on the Inequality of the Human Races* (1853–1855) and later elaborated by Social Darwinism, eugenics, and pragmatic utilitarianism. Presumably invented by Immanuel Kant (borrowing from Linnaeus, Buffon, Blumenbach), the scientific concept of race acquired a teleological cast and became naturalized — even though the intent was to provide "a regulative principle of reason" to adjudicate ideas of monogenesis and polygenesis, the origin of physical characteristics, and so on (Bernasconi 2001). But what Blumenbach accomplished in 1795, namely, the five-race taxonomy of humanity, was significant. According to Stephen Jay Gould, Blumenbach "changed the geometry of human order from a geographically based model without explicit ranking to a hierarchy of worth, oddly based upon perceived beauty, and fanning out in two directions from a Caucasian ideal" (1996, 260). This hierarchy of implied worth emanates from a principle of division of the social field, conjugating space by evolutionary time and ascribing supremacy to the colonizing powers that have been preoccupied, beginning from the fourteenth century, in partitioning the planet into geopolitical real estate, including its inhabitants. The latest manifestation of Kant's "regulative principle" of racialization is, in my view, the theory of "common culture" whose essence is the glorification of the heritage of Western civilization. It informs all philosophies and policies that legislate a scheme of general education for everyone based on a narrative of development framed by the classics of the Western canon, from Aristotle to Rorty and Lacan.

Multiculturalism in its diverse modalities has indeed become the official policy designed to solve racism and ethnic conflicts in the North. Contextualized in the history of transnational capitalism, however, multiculturalism tends to occlude, if not cancel out, the material conditions of racist practices and institutions. It conceals not only the problematic of domination and subordination but also reconstitutes this social relation in a political economy of difference where privatized sensibilities and sensoriums become the chief organs of consumerist experience. The performative self fragments the public sphere into self-replicating monadic entities equipped with customized survival kits. In short, neoliberal multiculturalism idealizes individualist pluralism as the ideology of the "free market" and its competitive utilitarian ethos. Chapters 4 and 5 and the afterword strive to anatomize the problematic of multiculturalism and uncover its theoretical ambiguities and ideological implications. I aim to foreground the social context of the contemporary "culture wars" and craft a historical-materialist perspective toward discrepant language games and discordant performances of groups. My intent is basically exploratory and heuristic, hoping thereby to provoke all-sided discussions of substantive issues involving people of color in a participatory democratic arena.

In the last few decades, the vogue for civil society may have succeeded in foreclosing any radical political initiative critical of consumerism and the "society of the spectacle." Contra statist Soviet communism, civil-society ideologues extolled the virtues of the unregulated marketplace. They lauded private, voluntary associations in quest of affirming flexible chameleonic identities. In effect, this cult of civil society, like the fetish of ethnicity, serves only to excuse the predatory practices of property owners. As Ellen Meiksins Wood acutely diagnosed, the obsessive valorization of civil society conceptualized "away the problem of capitalism, by disaggregating society into fragments, with no overarching power structure, no totalizing unity, no systemic coercions — in other words, no capitalist system, with its expansionary drive and its capacity to penetrate every aspect of social life" (1995, 245). In truth, civil society proves itself equivalent to the class-divided racial polity that "makes man a commodity whilst making him believe that he is free" (Edelman 1979, 112). Even the institution of the family, Patricia Hill Collins (2001) points out, has been mobilized to contain any dissent against racial hierarchy, "the constructed and masked power dynamics of race and class."

Interrogating Cultural Studies

The themes and leitmotifs converging in these zones of engagement — the United States as a racial polity, the ideology of multiculturalism, and the question of identity in a disenchanted world — occupy center stage in the new field of institutional teaching/research known as contemporary Cultural Studies. I take as a point of departure my previous inquiries in *Racial Formations/Critical Transformations*, *Hegemony and*

Strategies of Transgression, and *Beyond Postcolonial Theory* concerning the articulation of race, class, gender, and nationality in the socio-historical complex of the United States as a racialized socioeconomic formation (Baron 1985; Omi and Winant 1986; Mills 1999). Associated with this complex articulation are all the nodal arguments in the current "culture wars" that I survey and gloss in chapters 5 through 8: citizenship, recognition of differences, canon revision, political correctness (now dubbed the "rococo Marxism" of the polymorphously perverse), ethnicity, immigration, social redistribution, nation-state violence, and diaspora.

In the midst of the rightist resurgence, the initially counterdisciplinary trend of Cultural Studies enters the scene, together with the phenomenal rise in prestige of academic postcolonial studies. One begins to sympathize with the partisans of suspicion and methodical doubt. Controversies surrounding Raymond Williams and Frantz Fanon, tied up with the question of "the model-minority myth," cannot be avoided in the period bracketed by the Los Angeles uprising of 1992 and the 1999 "Battle of Seattle" against the World Trade Organization (WTO), the International Monetary Fund (IMF), and the World Bank (WB). Without intending to, I provide an unfashionable "third-world" point of view on these disputes and debates (chapters 7 and 8 and the afterword), which continue to engage scholars, public intellectuals, bureaucrats, and conscienticious citizens around the world. What is perhaps unconventional for many, threatening for some, and anathema to others may be my attempt to utilize historical-materialist principles in questioning orthodoxies and Establishment wisdom in these matters, hoping that fresh insights and uncompromising diagnosis on top of visionary proposals can be gleaned from this intervention.

Ideally, theory and practice should coincide, if not dovetail. My commentary on ideology and cultural practices presupposes an array of facts and statistics that can only be selectively referred to here, citations that should dispel any suspicion that I have illicitly psychologized socio-historical data, or allegorized them in an eclectic postmodernist fashion when I invoke certain philosophical aperçus from the rich tradition of dialectical-materialist criticism and speculation. If history is what hurts, then only the callous or insensitive can escape it. What I need to reaffirm here is the imperative to organize in a wide-ranging historical overview the mutable contingencies of quotidian life that would remain incomprehensible without a double analytic-synthesizing orientation and transformative motivation. My framework of intelligibility remains, as always, the historical-materialist one in which complex, ever altering social relations of production and reproduction interact with a constellation of beliefs and practices woven in manifold, overdetermined lifeforms. It is this synergy of social production/reproduction relations (analogous to Williams's organizing principle of cultural formations; see chapter 8) that Georg Lukács considers the special area of investigation for cultural critics, a field comprised of the differentiated totalities of human experience embedded in historically specific, evolving social modalities of existence. Of decisive importance are the mediations between particular and universal, as Lukács reminds us: "Only in this context, which sees the isolated facts of social life as aspects of the historical process and integrates them into a totality, can knowledge of the facts hope to become knowledge of reality" (Lukács 1971, 22). One example of a sociopolitical totality that I investigate in chapter 3 and in the afterword is the Asian American situation, its real-life contradictions and imaginary resolutions, and its refraction in the lived experiences of Chinese and Filipino groups.

"Need is the mother of thought," Ernst Bloch writes; and the need to create order out of chaos seems the most urgent and desperate. Uneven development of imperialism, or finance capital on the rampage, serves as the condition of possibility of postcolonial discourse. With the rise of merchant capital, incompatible modes of production with varying temporalities and "superstructural" effects — the aftermath of colonial domination — have since then reconfigured the planet. In the late nineteenth and early twentieth centuries, finance capital overlapping with previous modes of political and economic mechanisms drastically compressed time and space, thereby amalgamating a variety of social formations linked to the center as the measure of modernity coeval with technological progress. Postmodernities have finally arrived. If modernity inheres in the discovery of the future as "an open, unbuilt site never visited before, but a place reachable and constructible" (Therborn 1995, 126), then the postmodernist concentration on the ephemeral present and the pleasures of the instant sacrifices time to the stasis of abstract space — the space of commodity exchange, circulation of money, and accumulation of capital.

Pretexts and Alibis

Theories of modernization/developmentalism arose to lend coherence to the bewildering ensemble of pastiches and bricolage. After World War II and especially during U.S. counterinsurgency actions in Korea, Vietnam, and Central America, the accelerated migration of former colonial subjects to the metropoles and the unremitting Western intervention in the peripheries, together with the refinement of technologies of communication, heightened the spectacle of wild exchanges. We behold heterogeneous languages and syncretic life-forms coexisting with conspicuous mass consumerism that rapidly spread from Europe and North America to the rest of the world. From this perspective, we can view postcolonial thought as a version of late modernity that offers an explanatory formula for the mixture and multilayering of forms from an alienated position, bereft of any self-critical reflexiveness.

Situated in this conjunctural grid, postcolonial theory may be read as a symptom of "third-world" intellectuals' behavior as they try to claim a niche for themselves in the transnational production of knowledge. It is a quest for identity and status by deracinated, stranded intellectuals removed from the everyday struggles of peasants, women, workers, indigenes, and the middle strata. Instead of revolution, postcolonialism opts for a place within the global marketplace in which official policies of multiculturalism allow localized identities based on ethnic/racial markers to flourish. This is due not only to the class origin and determination of diasporic intellectuals as such but also to the shift in the alignments of nation-states in the world system (the collapse of the Soviet Union; the failure of bourgeois-democratic projects of reform, not to speak of national-liberation struggles, in the peripheries; the neoconservative resurgence in North America and the rise of neofascist regimes in Europe) and the attenuation of radical, left-wing movements in the metropolitan centers (for Taiwan, see Liao 1999).

Complicit with the racial polity, Establishment postcolonial criticism now celebrates hybridity, ambivalence, and shifting or fluid identities.

Its vocation compels it to reject foundational categories such as the Cartesian ego and ancillary notions of progress, history, revolution. Otherness becomes fetishized, displaced from the political economy of asymmetrical center-periphery relations. Notions of syncretism and interstitiality may be read as allegorical ciphers gesturing to a colonial heritage that erases history, the record of popular democratic revolutions, and any cognitive grasp of social linkages and the practice of collective resistance. We are no longer involved with structural changes in the mode of production and property/power relations. Instead of political economy and the totality of social relations, culture becomes for postcolonial critics a magic paradigm for illuminating complex social transformations affecting individual sensibilities and group actions.

Originally emerging from the poststructuralist controversies of the sixties, mainstream postcolonial theory offered a critique of Eurocentric discourse and imperial practice. In a larger context, it evolved as a parasitic excrescence of anticommunist Cold War politics. By the end of the century, it has degenerated into an apologia for neoconservative free marketeers and other reactionary social programs. Its logic of deconstructive critique has now led to its subsumption in an idealist epistemology that displaced concepts of class and nation, replacing them with byzantine if not obsessive musings on atomistic identity. Although it may not have completely succumbed to endorsing end-of-ideology and end-of-history nostrums, postcolonial critics objectively serve an anti-revolutionary function in their denunciation of Marxism and other "totalizing" modes of analysis and historical critique. In valorizing a Disneyland multiculturalism, postcolonial theory fits perfectly the needs of global finance capitalism even as it claims to address and solve problems of racial and ethnic conflicts plaguing the borderlands traversing both geopolitical center and margins. Postcolonialism then proves itself as the ideology of globalized capitalism — precisely because it does not know that it is, that is, in spite of and because of this ignorance. It offers a metaphysics of legitimation for those groups who stand to benefit from the predatory economics of uneven development, namely, transnational corporations and their compradors, including their retinue of postcolonial rationalizers. A critique of postcolonial thought and its grounding in the logic of commodity exchange is sketched in chapter 7 (see San Juan 1998a).

To shift from the internal colonies to the territorial possessions is a tactical maneuver that can disclose starkly the inner workings of the racial polity. I want to avoid the pleasures of "epistemological vertigo" by invoking the proscribed but latent, aborted epic of Filipino revolutionary nationalism. Mocked by self-aggrandizing ludic scholars, Filipino aspirations for self-determination after 1900 materialized first as an assault against white supremacy and later as peasant insurrections against the class hegemony of the U.S. elite and its native lackeys. Its objective was to win genuine sovereignty. Since I traced this counter-hegemonic plot in my book *After Postcolonialism*, I will confine myself here to commenting briefly on the Filipino presence in the United States, with my reflections on the plight of the Filipino diaspora reserved for the afterword.

Who are these "brown brothers" addressed by William Howard Taft at the turn of the century? Ever since the 1904 St. Louis Exposition when Igorots (tribal mountain groups) from the new possessions called "the Philippine Islands" were exhibited to the public, the Filipino image has always served the Anglo-Saxon "civilizing mission." Distinct from other Asians, Filipinos experienced the full impact of U.S. military and then civil governance first as "wards" of the government's Bureau of Indian Affairs. Unlike the Chinese and Japanese stereotypes, this new enigma was interpreted within the framework of U.S. genocidal aggression against the indigenous Indians and the Mexican "bandidos" who challenged the incursions of monopoly capital. The dark-skinned Filipinos also fitted the emergent apartheid system of the post-Reconstruction period. Styles of representing the colonized Other resonated with the ideological shifts in the flexibly administered hegemonic rule over the "internal colonies," including islands thousands of miles away from the North American continent.

At first viewed as wild savages, the Filipino "racial type" shifted from the African stereotype to a more classic Orientalized template: guerillas resisting U.S. pacification appeared wily, devious, incapable of domestication. Eventually, disciplinary regulation and tutelage by proxy were devised for the unruly childlike subjects. Anthropological knowledge was supplemented by the ideological state apparatuses of jurisprudence, the penal system, the annual census, health surveys, and more quantifying forms of surveillance that accompanied the military conquest. Representations can reveal and hide at the same time, depending on our hermeneutic techniques. The photographs of primitive types gathered by the colonial bureaucracy in the first three decades of U.S. rule were gradually replaced by the spectacle of rowdy migrant workers on strike in Hawai'i, California, and Washington in the thirties. The "oversexed" Filipino depicted in the media was attacked and stigmatized, then driven out or forced underground, labeled as a pariah or troublemaker. With the sacrifices of Filipinos for the U.S. empire in World War II, the Filipino portrait changed into the successfully Americanized native—until its latest metamorphosis into the alternating "good" and "bad" Filipino during and after the Cold War era. The representation of an "inscrutable" subaltern like the Filipino is governed by what Roland Barthes (1981) calls the "studium" of a taxonomic machine with a predictable code, while the "punctum" of the Filipino image, the zone of ambiguity or uncertainty, reveals a gap open for articulating what is hidden or repressed: the national-popular protagonist on the edge of market civilization.

Now the largest segment (more than three million) in the Asian American category, Filipinos in this racial polity have been tokenized in practically every discourse and text devoted to immigrant populations. As noted earlier, the violent subjugation of the Philippines and its revolutionary army after the brief Spanish-American War established the background for the disintegrated, vacillating, even schizoid, character of the Filipino community here. Certain historical specificities of the Filipino physiognomy distinguish it from other Asians, particularly the neocolonial subservience of the native comprador/feudal elite and the relentless Americanization of its citizens that we witness today. Not to be forgotten is the long and durable history of plebeian, grassroots opposition to U.S. rule. Its subsumption in the homogenizing rubric "Asian American" inflicts violence on that history. In chapter 3 and the afterword (as well as in my other writings), I speculate on the emergence of Filipino revolutionary agency as the antithesis to "Manifest Destiny" and as a delayed riposte to the genocidal drive of white supremacy.

U.S. "exceptionalism" continues to be belied by the neocolonial status of the Philippines, its only territorial possession in Asia acquired at the expense of more than one million Filipino lives. The balance-sheet of U.S. colonial domination in the Philippines (as well as in Puerto

Rico and Hawai'i) has irrevocably damaged its self-proclaimed role as the paragon of Western virtues and its claim as exemplary leader of the "free world." No amount of learned apologetics or refined casuistry can expunge the historical record (Jones 1970).

Where are we now? In the last three years, millions of Filipinos have protested against the IMF/WB and the WTO and their complicity with the current regime's policies of deregulation, liberalization, and privatization that have caused untold misery and havoc in people's lives. At least three decades of IMF-dictated "structural adjustment programs" have kept the Philippines indebted (the debt now exceeds $52 billion), economically depressed, and inveterately dependent. From 1972 to 1986, the Marcos family and cronies looted $10 billion of the imposed loans from the WB since 1962; now the Filipino people are obliged to pay with 40 percent of the national budget, depleting resources needed for social services, education, and rural development programs. The neocolonial economy continues to serve as a dumping ground for industrial goods and speculative finance capital, as a source of raw and semiprocessed materials, but more crucially as a reservoir of dirt-cheap labor.

The Philippines has one of the lowest wage levels in all of Asia: an eight- to twelve-hour day of labor costs only five dollars, hence eight million Filipinos, Overseas Contract Workers (OCW), leave for the Middle East, Europe, Hong Kong, Singapore, Japan, and all parts of the world — an unimpeded exodus of Filipino bodies. Unemployment in the country stands at 40 percent, with most workers exploited as contractual or part-time labor. The unrelenting immiseration of the countryside and the heavy taxation of low- and middle-income Filipinos contrast with the tax incentives offered to big business and foreign monopolies tied to local subcontractors. The Philippines offers a bonanza for multinational corporations and shady foreign speculators since the comprador regimes from Marcos to Aquino, Ramos, Estrada, and Arroyo have served well as factotums of the world's managerial corporate elite.

More starkly unconscionable is the return of U.S. military power after the scrapping of the huge Clark Air Force Base and Subic Naval Base in 1992 — two of the most strategic springboards for U.S. imperialist aggression in Asia and the Middle East. After an absence of eight years, approximately three thousand American soldiers held exercises in the Philippines in February 2000, courtesy of the infamous Visiting

Forces Agreement (VFA) signed between the two governments. What is the VFA? The VFA essentially revives the RP (Republic of the Philippines)-U.S. Military Bases Agreement by allowing U.S. military forces to use various parts of the country as staging grounds for foreign-policy operations and worldwide interventions. By granting extraterritorial rights to the neocolonial master, the VFA makes a mockery of Philippine sovereignty. U.S. military actions make the Philippines complicit in global schemes of imposing exploitative agendas on various nation-states, not sovereign states but really dependent neofeudal territories. Underdeveloped by the stranglehold of U.S. military, economic, and political instrumentalities — primarily mediated through the WB-IMF conditionalities and reconfirmed by the scandalous VFA on the basis of which U.S. troops can be deployed anywhere in the islands and wreak havoc on Filipino citizens with impunity — even after gaining independence in 1946, the Philippines has become the world's leading supplier of migrant workers (Sison 1999). Incredibly the majority of American Studies scholars who claim to be in the vanguard of progressive or radical movements are completely ignorant of the VFA, not to speak of other horrendous interventions by the U.S. government in the affairs of nominally independent countries in Asia, Africa, and Latin America. Responsibility and accountability should ideally be first in the agenda of popular democratic transformation. But of course this is only a telltale sign of the dark times we have to live through, and hopefully beyond.

What Is to Be Done?

We now confront the actuality of globalization, or neoimperialism, in this new interregnum between epochal crises. The end of the Cold War witnessed the rise of a market triumphalism that promised to realign powers, nations, and constituencies throughout the world for the sake of greater profitability. Transnational finance capital distinguished by the multiculturalist ethos of globalized corporations seems to dominate everywhere, wrecking if not making permeable the boundaries of nation-states and drastically altering norms of social life and international relations. Although passports, IMF strictures, tariffs, and customs checkpoints abound, we are told that we now inherit a borderless world. Is this a new mystification, a virtual reality inducing mass euphoria and narcissistic fantasies?

Mesmerized by the miracle of electronic telecommunication, we surmise that cultures — tastes, values, lifestyles — are being reformed, transmuted, and altered in ways that seem to transvalue the meaning and content of modernity (Featherstone 1990). Heterodox thinkers devoted to the production of scientific knowledge of human relations, in particular the changes in the content and form of late-modern sociality, now face this formidable challenge of trying to grasp the contours of the new objective reality surrounding us. In both humanities and the social sciences, old paradigms and frameworks of explanation confront experiences that seem to disprove or escape them. The most serious problems involving racism, ethnic conflicts, nationality disputes, economic deprivation, environmental damage, migrant workers, trade in women's bodies, drugs, and so on — symptoms of social decay and the deep reification of social relations — seem to multiply and accumulate, demanding interpretation and new methods of elucidation. Postmodernism has interrogated and cast doubt on the validity of scientific method and instrumental reason, part of the legacy of the European Enlightenment (McLaren and Farahmandpur 2000). If we want to advance the cause of mutual understanding and justice based on the appreciation of differences and respect for the equal worth of peoples, do we need to abandon what are called "metanarratives" of emancipation, progress, and national liberation — for me, allegories of the reciprocal interchange between humans and the natural world — that have been profoundly implicated in the colonial and imperial adventures of European capitalism?

My response may be condensed in a simple statement: the majority of the problems brought about by the accelerated globalization of corporate greed and its immanent contradictions can be solved only by the popular-democratic struggles of working people, peasants, women, indigenous communities, and other victims of neoliberal imperialism. Barbarism or socialism? Either one or the other — we have to make the choice. Critiques of the destructive tenets of neoliberalism are urgent: unlimited market rule, cutback of public expenditures, deregulation, privatization, abolition of the idea of the public good (Bruin 1996). I happened to glance at a recent issue of the *Chronicle of Higher Education* featuring a one-page advertisement for Hungrymind.com that read: WE'RE ASKING THE BEST MINDS IN ACADEMIA TO JOIN ANOTHER VENERABLE INSTITUTION. IT'S CALLED CAPITALISM. I glance at this side by side with the lead article of *Newsweek* (24 April) entitled "The 2.1 Trillion Market Tumble." The Dow fell 22.6 percent in October 1987; the fall of NASDAQ by 25.3 percent two weeks ago is described as "sickening," a nausea that bottles of Pepto-Bismol will not chase away so easily. Despite this symptom of the general systemic crisis, left-leaning liberals refer to this as the end of the bull market, resigned to the eternity of the business cycle and the intransigence of the law of value.

Against the advice of postcolonial theorists, stock market price fluctuation is one fragmentary phenomenon in the metropolitan centers that we need to link with the lives of masses of people around the world. Anomie and alienation in a market-dominated milieu require a rigorous "cognitive mapping" in order to renarrativize the play of heterogeneous forces and connect them into a dynamic multitiered totality (Jameson 2000). In the reconstruction of a new political subject antithetical to the anomic consumer, it is necessary to be extremely sensitive to the victims of political subjugation; otherwise, the privileges of the old hegemonic bloc will be reinstated. Moreover, we need to heed Pierre Bourdieu's advice to intellectuals who have grown cynical about the possibility of overhauling seemingly fixed "structures of feeling" (to recall Williams's concept) or bodily beliefs sedimented in the routines of everyday life and resistant to the injunctions of utilitarian individualism. The violence of the universal proclaimed from Washington, Paris, Berlin, London, and Tokyo operates in insidious ways worse than the demonized fundamentalist bogey:

> Scientific rationalism — the rationalism of the mathematical models which inspire the policy of the IMF or the WB, that of the law firms, great juridical multinationals which impose the traditions of American law on the whole planet, that of rational-action theories, etc. — is both the expression and the justification of Western arrogance, which leads people to act as if they had the monopoly of reason and could set themselves up as world policemen, in other words as self-appointed

holders of the monopoly of legitimate violence, capable of applying the force of arms in the service of universal justice. (Bourdieu 1998, 19–20)

It is precisely the violence of this "universal justice" that has driven millions of indigenous communities in Mexico to join the Zapatista National Liberation Front (Ellwood 1998) and has jailed thousands of progressive activists in the racial polity. Of those still manacled, Mumia Abu-Jamal demands urgent succor. Mumia, an award-winning African American journalist, has been falsely charged of murder. He now faces an imminent threat of execution after the Pennsylvania Supreme Court upheld his trumped-up 1982 conviction (Bloom 1999). Of the one million five hundred prisoners in the United States, the majority are people of color. And of those in death row, 40 percent are African Americans who together comprise only 11 percent of the total U.S. population. Through the criminal justice system, and now more privatized prisons, the racial polity exercises selective terror and violence on minority groups who have been traditionally victimized by the organs of the state and civil society. Genocide, entailed by white supremacy (Ignatiev 1994), underwrites the utopia of unlimited consumption and puritanical meritocracy.

I express here a view that may outrage guardians of the hegemonic dispensation resting on received disciplinary boundaries — perhaps evidence that despite modifications on the surface, the deep structures of habitual thought and feeling remain entrenched. But what are progressive teachers for, asked James Baldwin, if not to disturb the peace? While critical of the doxa of modernizing progress (courtesy of the IMF/World Bank and World Trade Organization), I should also state here that I do not count myself as one of those postmodernist skeptics who believe that everything is a manifestation of pure power, discourse or textuality, arbitrary and pragmatic social constructions whose truth-claims cannot be adjudicated. After all, reality is what hurts. But, in spite of the odds, millions victimized every day are up in arms, mounting the next attacks on the fortresses of the transnational corporate elite.

It is my conviction that racism cannot be eliminated unless reification in a commodity-centered society is dissolved. As Harry Chang acutely noted, reification lends the illusion of naturalness to social/racial categories of identification. Reification converts social relations into objects or things so that instead of social relations determining the world of commodities, it becomes the opposite: "The reification of racial categories into 'skin color,' etc. is an integral part of the racial logic, and a careful critique of it will show us, for instance, the historical specificity of racism. Simply put, racial categories are social distinctions devised in such a way that their differential moment can be left to a 'superstitious' conception of nature" (1985, 38). This "superstition" rests on the inescapable division between manual and intellectual labor that underwrites the power of abstract reason, a taxonomic reason integral to commodity production (Sohn-Rethel 1978).

Beyond the "false consciousness" of ordinary citizens is the transparent machinery and habitus of institutional racism discussed in chapters 1 and 2. George Lipsitz exposes how the civil rights rhetoric of liberal reformers has sanctioned racist practices by denying the salience of race. He analyzes in sharp detail the subtle workings of white supremacy in his valuable work, *The Possessive Investment in Whiteness:* "Racism in the United States sometimes proceeds through direct, referential, and overt practices of exclusion. But it manifests itself more often through indirect, inferential, and covert policies that use the denial of overt racist intent to escape responsibility for racialized consequences" (1998, 216–17). This is the reason why a critique of bourgeois ideology is needed to elucidate the "racialized and gendered class identities and ways of life," as well as "the self-understanding of workers creating and consenting to whiteness as a culture and political economy of domination" (Williams 1995, 307). Only a dialectical materialist method finessed in the Marxist tradition can adequately unravel the "mysteries" of racist ideology and its embodiment in the sophisticated practices and institutions of the racial polity. Theories of globalization, techno-multiculturalism, and postcolonial deconstruction can only repair and prettify temporarily the rotting fabric of this racial polity.

Corporate globalization runs rampant, exacerbating the world-systemic contradictions between the dispossessed majority and the minority transnational bourgeoisie (Sklair 1991). Because of the chronic crises afflicting the United States and its NATO allies (including Japan), it is not likely that pax Americana or its surrogate reincarnation can be revived and sustained. Samir Amin considers the hegemonistic strategy of the North led by the United States as "the main enemy of social progress, democracy and peace" today (2000, 16). What is more important to reflect on, in the middle of the ongoing crisis of finance capital with its huge arsenal of nuclear weapons, is "how conflicts [among the nation-states and regional blocs] and social struggles [for emancipation] will be articulated. . . . Will social struggles be subordinated, enframed by conflicts and therefore mastered by dominant powers, even instrumentalized to the benefit of these powers? Or will social struggles, on the contrary, conquer their autonomy and force the major powers to conform to their exigencies?" (Amin 2000, 17). With finance capital gearing for total victory or defeat, the alternatives for the twenty-first century stand out clearly: Socialism or barbarism? Given the disreputable record of "actually existing socialism," it is necessary to substitute the term "communism" defined by Marx as "the real movement which abolishes the present state of affairs," as the true alternative (Guattari and Negri 1990, 165).

Within the belly of the racial polity, the challenge of combatants like Mumia Abu-Jamal, Leonard Peltier, and other political prisoners actualizes the synergy of the "real movement" that Marx invoked. Their struggles create the vibrant places where the seeds of the future are germinating. Postmodern perspectivism has to be replaced by a sense of worldly totality; instead of promiscuous mass tourism, we should attend to our stakes in the places of that world as a result of our care and involvement. As Agnes Heller reminds us, "One 'has a world' only if one can change it, not only for oneself, but also for the denizens of the world" (1999, 189). Mindful of the long and sustainable tradition of popular insurgency by people of color against the onslaught of white supremacy and barbaric accumulation, it might be appropriate to repeat the old adage that, aside from a critique of discursive weapons, we need organized collective action to transform the material conditions and the institutions comprising the productive/reproductive relations of society.

We need a mass insurgency to renew our lives and resurrect buried hopes and dreams. There is a general agreement in this desideratum. In his eloquent manifesto *White Man, Listen!* Richard Wright addressed the enemy: "Look at us and know us and you will know yourselves, for *we* are you, looking back at *you* from the dark mirror of our lives!" (1957, 106). In our protracted resistance, we might derive inspiration

23

from Wright, as well as from Chief Joseph's eloquent response to the genocidal and ethnocidal practices of the U.S. government in the wake of the Nez Perce War of 1879, his plea that all peoples should be treated equally, or the well-known *testimonio* of Chief Seattle on the need to value our natural surroundings and reaffirm our connection with the earth. Their examples survive as symbols of change and shibboleths of secular redemption from the hammer-blows of combined racial/class oppression (Berkhofer 1978). However, we need to learn from the travails of the American Indian Movement a lesson of extreme significance expressed by one of its leaders: "Without an intellectual base we cannot build strength or consensus in the Indian community or achieve the capacity to critically assess ideas and people so as to determine what to do next" (Smith and Warrior 1996, 276). Indeed, the recent scandal caused by the publication of Patrick Tierney's *Darkness in El Dorado: How Scientists and Journalists Devastated the Amazon* offers proof that subalterns can and will speak even through the voices of others under the sign of hope and solidarity. Given my existential position as part of the Filipino diaspora, it seems appropriate to recall what the novelist John Berger once said: "Hope is an act of faith and has to be sustained by other concrete actions. . . . This will lead to collaborations which deny discontinuity. The act of resistance means not only refusing to accept the absurdity of the world-picture offered us, but denouncing it. And when hell is denounced from within, it ceases to be hell" (1999, 4). In our century of homelessness, migration, exile, and diaspora (to paraphrase Berger), when all of us have been uprooted from our home, whether it's the village or some other country and continent, an ancestral habitat long gone, or home now distant in time, the only defense against solitude and individual helplessness is the solidarity of all. This is a time-honored internationalist ideal to which, I hope, this book can serve as a finely tested agitprop emblem.

CHAPTER **1**

"Can We Get Along?"

Racial Politics and Institutional Racism

From the moment this continent was colonized, racism has been fundamental to this country's functioning on every level. To this day, racism is
systematically institutionalized in every aspect of the United States' political, economic, and social life. — Barbara Smith, *The Truth That Never
Hurts*

For many people, goodness is expressed . . . by wearing golden crosses
around their necks, while ignoring the burning crosses of racism. . . . They
do not confront the evils of oppression, the evils of poverty, of exploitation, or political repression. They think of themselves as moral, but never
examine the inequities and the injustices of this world, nor do they condemn the inhumane system that perpetuates those injustices, trampling on
the lives of so many people in the process. — Assata Shakur, *statement
honoring Marilyn Buck, political prisoner in California*

"Can we get along?" The pathos of Rodney King's televised comment
while the fires were raging in Los Angeles in May 1992 underscores the
centrality of racial conflict in the constitution of a stratified and class-
hierarchized social order such as the present United States of America.
At the outset I need to recapitulate here the cardinal premise of this work
by recalling Charles Mills's thesis of the United States as a racial polity.
There is nothing new in this assertion, but its utterance in times of crisis
is bound to scandalize the "gatekeepers" of the "American Way of
Life." Euro-American "common culture" is unthinkable without its

victims and their putative uncommoness. Absent in the philosophical discourse of the mainstream contemporary philosophers (Rawls, Walzer, Rorty) is the idea that the massive racial exclusions in the U.S. social contract that founded the nation-state — expropriation of aboriginal lands from the Native Americans, African slavery, conquest of Mexican territory and peoples, massacre of Chinese workers, internment of Japanese Americans, and so on — all testify to the foundational significance of racial antagonism between the European settlers and people of color. This racial divide constitutes "a form of stratification built into the structure of U.S. society" as a *Herrenvolk* democracy (Mills 1999, 25; van den Berghe 1978). It organizes the division of labor and allocation of property, together with the unequal distribution of material resources on which differential power relations depend. Racism, not individual prejudice or ethnic discrimination, underpins the social and political network of hierarchical institutions in the whole society.

White supremacy legitimizes sociopolitical inequality. It is, for Mills, "the ideological correlate of a fundamental organizing principle of the modern Euro-implanted social order," the mythical social contract that governs the "construction of the self, civic identity, significant sociopolitical actors, systemic structural privilege and subordination, racial economic exploitation, or state protection" (1999, 27). White supremacy legitimizes the differential entitlements, the system of advantage and disadvantage, the "wages of whiteness" (Roediger 1991; Lipsitz 1998). Mills elaborates, "The liberal-democratic *Rechstaat* of an ideal Lockean or Kantian liberalism, acting to protect the property and rights of its abstract citizens, functions here as the racial state, acting to protect differential white entitlement" (1999, 30). This social ontology is of course built on a pseudobiological fiction; nonetheless, the racializing of interests and group identity endows the fiction with verisimilitude. Critical race theory has reinforced Mills's proposition, with Richard Delgado claiming that "racism is normal, not aberrant, in American society" (1995, xiv). Patricia Williams concurs with her observation that "Blacks and women are the objects of a constitutional omission that has been incorporated into a theory of rationality. . . . It is the fixed, reiterated prophesy of the Founding Fathers" (1995, 121).

This thesis of the United States as a racial polity is certainly a heretical riposte to the prevailing consensual doxa of the United States as a democratic, egalitarian polity. It is anathema to liberal experts on "race matters" from Oscar Handlin to Thomas Sowell. Reviewing Oliver Cox's formidable treatise *Race, Class and Caste*, Handlin denounced its Marxist framework and explained race prejudice as an outgrowth of beliefs and "innermost emotions" (1957, 53). Sowell for his part censured those who used "ideologically defined vocabulary" because "mere tendentious words" obscured the empirical issues (1994, 155). In the discourse of neoliberal apologists, ethnicity absorbed race into a paradigm that dissolved the "racial divide" into psychological attitudes and ill-informed behavior amenable to educational therapy (see chapter 4). In 1967 Ronald Segal still could write about "mounting guerilla warfare of race" based on fear. Thirty years later, a college textbook on ethnic groups concluded that while "cultural pluralism" has not completely prevailed, "white racism has lessened" (Dinnerstein, Nicols, and Reimer 1996, 343). Cognizant of the ongoing debate on whether the use of the term *race* aids in promoting racism or not, Lucius Outlaw Jr. reminds us that for the last twenty years, "race has been the primary vehicle for conceptualizing and organizing precisely around group differences with the demand that social justice be applied to *groups* and that justice be measured by *results*, not just by opportunities" (1990, 60)—this hard precept of institutional racism, won by the civil rights movement, still encounters resistance, as witness Will Kymlicka's uphill battle to prove that normative liberalism can acknowledge national/ collective identities and that "group-specific rights can promote equality between minority and majority" (1997, 246). The only problem is that without a thoroughgoing overhaul of the social division of labor and legally sanctioned property relations sedimented in state and civil society, any claim to achieving genuine equality will remain a hypocritical formality. That is, in fact, what official multiculturalism today has succeeded in doing without knowing it.

Recent events, however, have revised the terms of group identity and differentiation. Now the conflict is to be conceived no longer between black and white as before, no longer construed in fact as racial. What preoccupies the ruling bloc (the monopoly elite and their representatives) is the task of displacing flagrant class conflicts and subsuming them into a new hegemonic, reactionary project, one that recuperates an old model of the United States as a nation of assimilated immigrants geared for what some observers (Harvey 1989) have called a "disorganized," more flexible mode of twenty-first century global capitalism. Still underpinned by the ethos, if not logic, of white supremacy, the racial polity has been reconfigured on the basis of posited cultural differences and ethnic particularisms (Mills 1999; Bonilla-Silva 1999).

What animates the refurbished agenda of resurgent racism at the beginning of the millennium is nothing new: it recycles a nostalgic invocation of the "good old days" of consensual peace and togetherness. A typical Establishment opinion instanced by Tom Morgenthau in *Newsweek* (18 May 1992) dusts off from the obscurantist archive a fin de siècle culinary relic:

> The devastated hopes of L.A.'s Korean-immigrant community, meanwhile, are a powerful reminder that the nation is rapidly moving toward a multiethnic future in which Asians, Hispanics, Caribbean islanders and many other immigrant groups compose a diverse and changing social mosaic that cannot be described by the old vocabulary of race relations in America. The race crisis of the 1960s has been subsumed by the tensions and opportunities of the new melting pot: the terms "black" and "white" no longer depict the American social reality. . . . Like it or not, we Americans are a hyphenated, intermarrying and increasingly blended people — and we are likely to become both more diverse, and more nearly like each other, as time goes by.

A meliorist gradualism is invoked here to bless the mixing and domestication of the multitudes for a program to resurrect a mythical homogenizing, if not homogeneous, polity. Morgenthau proposes the classic fundamentalist solution: "We now believe government must teach the values of work, thrift, marriage and personal responsibility to millions of resisting subjects . . . and the new gospel of family values and personal responsibility" is needed to revive the myth of the American "dream of success." Politics is once again mystified by the aesthetic aura of American exceptionalism, that is, the final resolution of class antagonisms that plagued the ethnic homelands of the old world.

New Frontier Assimilationism

Ever since the days of Hector St. John Crevecoeur and Alexis de Tocqueville, the quest for defining the essence of "the American" has been motivated by the "specter" of Europe's class-ridden social formations. Today, despite the demise of Soviet-style communism, the same specter compels the elite to resuscitate an ideal or trope of the American nation as united, democratic, egalitarian, harmonious. Conflated with this strategy of recuperation is a rhetoric of *divide et impera* — divide and rule — that draws its power not only from traditional nativism and ethnocentrism but also from an artificial notion of authentic Americanness. This contrived authenticity is equated with individual liberty and worldly success via diligent work and self-reliant discipline. The paradigm of laissez-faire democracy pivots around personal liberty that guarantees social equilibrium and functional integration. In the Cold War sixties, Seymour M. Lipset (1960, 1963) theorized the uniquely American ethos as centered in the norms of equalitarianism (equal opportunity) and achievement ("ethic of hard work"). National identity and consensus are therefore concretely realized through the effects of inequality and difference, just as consumerism is thought to expunge the incommensurable heterogeneity between North and South in globalized capitalism.

In the last twenty years, especially during the Reagan-Bush administrations, the profound disparity of wealth and power between the elite and the working people has seriously destabilized the national consensus. Just to cite a telltale index: real wages of the majority of Americans in the period 1970–1990 fell by a total of about 19 percent, a decline only exceeded in the nineties (Chasin 1998). To insure the preservation of hierarchy and undisturbed accumulation of capital, it became necessary to rearticulate markers of cultural plurality along the axis of equivalence, dissolving alterity into the sameness of a singular American mold. Despite or because of this monolithic model, a plausible mode of diversity, however, has to be preserved. A populist strategy of displacing class contradictions by foregrounding ethnic antagonisms is deployed by media publicists and religious propagandists of "white popular wisdom." One example of this is the work of Charles Murray of the conservative American Enterprise Institute who writes in *Newsweek* (11 May 1992, 50): "When blacks say they've suffered years of neglect, a lot of whites are looking at pictures on TV of black looters taking things from stores as a disconsolate Asian sits by and watches his life's work go down the drain. They're saying, "How is it that this Asian guy, who we've not done one damn thing for in terms of social programs, how come he doesn't deserve our sympathy instead of the looters?" Unless blacks come to grips with that reaction, we're never going to get anywhere." Unfortunately, Murray's white spectators may not be really sympathetic to the Korean merchants — are they really perceived as struggling and suffering persons? — whose long immigrant history of discrimination and ostracism cannot be divorced from the anticommunist crusade of the Korean War of the fifties, U.S. neocolonial domination of South Korea, and the U.S. public's attitude toward Asians in general (see chapter 3). This attitude has been colored by World War II, anti-Chinese propaganda, and the defeat of the United States in Vietnam. The war against Japan that culminated in the first use of nuclear bombs also led to the incarceration of 110,000 Japanese Americans during World War II. In 1982, a Chinese American, Vincent Chin, was killed by two Detroit autoworkers who were virtually exonerated by the courts despite public outcry. The victim was mistaken for a Japanese in the context of a nationwide campaign of scapegoating Japan's economic success as the chief cause of unemployment in the United States.

What is the lesson here? The complex history of U.S. imperialism is flattened by the media tactic of valorizing the "instant knowledge" afforded by simplified TV spectacles. What the media has done in the case of the Los Angeles revolt is to displace the anger (triggered by the verdict of police acquittal in the Rodney King trial) of the African American and Latino communities toward police brutality and decades of neglect and exploitation by zooming in on the plight of Korean storeowners and the Latasha Harlins incident (a fifteen-year-old girl was shot by Korean grocer Du Soon Ja, for which she was fined $500 and some community service). Is it Koreans or African Americans who constitute a social "disease" that needs to be quarantined? The racializing phantasm of segregation revolves around an implied American identity grasped only when stigmata of Otherness (once biological but now sociological and cultural) are shifted in accord with conservative and national-chauvinist political agendas.

Racism in the United States has metamorphosed, with new forms sublimating old elements in response to altered modalities of labor exploitation and status stratification. Here is Albert Memmi's definition of racism: racism is "a generalizing definition and valuation of biological differences, whether real or imaginary, to the advantage of the one defining and deploying them, and to the detriment of the one subjected to that act of definition, to the end of justifying (social or physical) hostility and assault" (2000, 184). This abstract definition needs to be fleshed out in varying concrete situations. Robert Miles has urged that the interpolation of racialization and racism needs to be historically contextualized and framed by the "analysis of the general political process of nation-state formation and reproduction and its interrelation with the process of capitalist development" (1989, 130).

Consequently, we need to anatomize the "physiognomy" of U.S. racism with a historical-materialist organon in order to combat it effectively. In addition to keeping track of the historical context, the cultural subtext, and the ideological pretext — terms suggested by Michael Dyson (1997), we need the transformationist approach propounded by Manning Marable. Marable insists that class — the basic power structure and ownership patterns — is central to the theoretical and programmatic critique of the U.S. racial polity: the diversity of ethnicities in the urban United States today "should help us to recognize the basic common dynamics of class undergirding the economic and social environment of struggle for everyone" (1995, 85; see also Goldfield 1997). The historical-materialist approach of Miles and Marable is, however, a minority trend in a predominantly neoconservative academy.

Another obstacle to comprehending adequately the nature of U.S. racism is the surface complexity of "civil society" that hides its racializing dynamic. Sociological wisdom fails to comprehend the constitution of a racial polity by the "combined forces of atheism, determinism, individualism, democracy and egalitarianism" (Guillaumin 1995). The creation of inferiorized Others by the seeming diktat of nature now legitimates the bourgeoisie's conquest of power. Bourgeois civil society harbors a fatal flaw, according to sociologist Jeffrey Alexander; liberty is defined in a discourse that legitimates friends and delegitimates enemies: "The discourse of repression is inherent in the discourse of liberty" (1992, 299). Adhering to the classic civil society/state bifurcation, Ronald Jacobs concludes his analysis of the Rodney King episode by defining the discourse of U.S. civil society as comprised of "contestatory and tragic discourses" (those protesting racial violence by the police) competing for interpretive authority with a utopian discourse of inclusion, "idealized and romantic sources" that resemble the "cosmopolitan" pluralism of Randolph Bourne (1998, 152). The racial discourse of civil society, then, will always be ambivalent, torn by irresolvable antinomies, paralyzed in schizophrenic fragmentation.

Why is this interethnic conflict in the Los Angeles "riot" seized by the media and academic intellectuals as equally if not more important than the contradictions between the ethnic communities and the state/corporate monopoly of power, between subaltern people of color and the Euro-American majority?

Postmodern thinkers on the "left" spectrum fail to comprehend the new dynamics of racism now reconfigured in the project of reconstituting the "essence" of the American "nation." Obviously the term *nation* needs to be problematized in the context of the interventionist state, the microtechnologies of ideological control, and the changing nature of labor diasporas, especially after the free-trade agreements between the United States, Mexico, and Canada. The demise of the welfare state and the emergence of WTO-oriented finance capitalism after the end of the Cold War requires a new cognitive mapping of geopolitical realignments. While I agree with Howard Winant (1990) that racial conflict in the United States functions as "the axis of political and cultural mobilization" in a deregulated polity, this axis is not linked to the problems of finance capital. Thus racism becomes a free-floating ideology unanchored to any pattern of historical circumstances. Moreover, his argument that in postmodern times there is no "fundamental ordering principle or hegemonic racial logic" that would articulate the existing political/cultural projects is a dogmatic non sequitur. If anything, it strikes one as a testimony to the failure of pragmatic or instrumental reason to grasp the laws of social motion and sociopolitical struggles in the United States.

It is now axiomatic that the doctrine of racialization/racism acquires determinate efficacy in concrete historical conjunctures. In contrast to the fashionable view that racial meanings and identities have become "decentered," I suggest that we engage ourselves with a critique of the process of centering, namely, the hegemonic process itself. In this process of asserting class rule via political coalition (Gramsci's "historic bloc"), the subjectivity or subject-position of "the American" and the "American nation" is constituted and reproduced in discourses, representations, and practices of everyday life in what Henri Lefebvre calls a "bureaucratic society of controlled consumption" (1971, 68). To enhance control, individualism is promoted through ethnic diversification. As a first step, I have challenged the absolutism of the ethnicity paradigm in my book *Racial Formations/Critical Transformations* as the dominant epistemic framework in analyzing racial and ethnic relations. Postmodernist theorizing, however, has reinforced capital's reification of social agency by eliminating history and any explanatory narrative of exploitation that would elucidate the mediation of ideological/cultural categories, in particular the mode of racialization, in the process of systemic reproduction. An urgent desideratum is to reground our inquiry in a dialectic of subjective and objective forces where collective intervention can be plotted on the basis of past experience and untapped potential.

Specter of Class Racism

Class consciousness has now been preempted by chauvinist moral panic in the midst of triumphalist neoconservatism. The dreamworld of mass utopia (of either socialist or capitalist genealogy) has dissolved into irretrievable catastrophe (Buck-Morss 2000). What is imperative for the oppressed working masses, especially the internally colonized people of color in the United States, is a radical critique of U.S. nationalism as the enabling ideology of racialized class domination (Giroux 1995; San Juan 1999b). White supremacist practices inform the functional core of this ideology. Given the historical specificity of U.S. capitalism, class struggle cannot be theorized adequately outside the conjunctures of the racial formation in which it acquires valency. I suggest that Etienne Balibar's thesis of the reciprocal determination of racism and nationalism (see his essay "Racism and Nationalism": Balibar and Wallerstein

33

1991) can provide initial guidelines in understanding the dynamics of U.S. racism as a historically mutable articulation of social relations of production and reproduction.

Signifiers of "culture" and ethnic difference are today replacing biology (although past racist formations are continuously revived) or, more precisely, supplementing sociobiology in sustaining the racializing order. They converge in affirming a "common culture" of the status quo that, in retrospect, is a euphemism for Eurocentric supremacy. A unifying pluralist culture in the United States is an invented imaginary whose resonance in recent academic debate ranges from the neoconservative project of Bloom and Bennett to the "cultural literacy" of E. D. Hirsch (Smith 1992) and the fluid, plural "national identity" of feminists like Alice Kessler-Harris. The cry for a common variegated milieu in effect drowns the voices of people of color — Native Americans, Blacks, Latinos, Asians — resisting such liberal incorporation into the hegemonic compromise known as "the American nation."

We are then confronted with the phenomenon of cultural or theoretical racism. In his inquiry into the discursive logic of racism and nationalism, Balibar discerns in theoretical racism the basic intellectual operation of classification and establishment of hierarchies (compare Goldberg 1993). This naturalizes the social and historical, that is, projects social and historical differences "into the realm of an imaginary nature." Human nature and natural differences are given "movement" by the symbolic category of genealogy and the legitimacy of filiation, already a principle of exclusion/inclusion, premised on certain anthropological or cultural universals, in particular the difference between humanity and animality. Balibar notes that "the systematic 'bestialization' of individuals and racialized human groups . . . is thus the means specific to theoretical racism for conceptualizing human historicity." When culture and other social codes replace race as a signifier for difference, concepts of *heritage*, *ancestry*, and *roots* lead toward a notion of a human ideal (the quest for the superior man, the pure type, and so on) and thus an aestheticization of social relations (see also Lopez 1998). Racism and nationalism join together when they invoke "a vitalized metaphor of certain sexualized values: energy, decisiveness, initiative and generally all the virile representations of domination or, conversely, passivity, sensuality, femininity, or again, solidarity, esprit de corps and generally all the representations of the 'organic' unity of society along the lines of an endogamous 'family'" (58). In sports events, classroom programs, mass media, and citizenship rituals of various ideological state apparatuses and mechanisms of civil society, we witness with obsessive iteration the sexual and aesthetic cathexis of Americanizing symbols transcending class through the celebratory rhetoric of pluralist American democracy (I elaborate on this in the next chapter). Cultural studies today, together with the corporate informational-cultural industry (Schiller 1989), help streamline this rhetoric into received "common sense."

In the practice of mass political mobilization in the United States, the project of hegemonic recuperation reconfirms the usefulness of class-defined racialization. Class politics operates through ethnic/racial codes of alterity and equivalence. Gender and sexuality are harnessed to complicate the problem and defuse any concentration on labor exploitation. Whenever a call is made by Establishment ideologues and public intellectuals to unite, purify, or strengthen the nation, to cleanse its tarnished integrity, and to halt the "decay of moral fiber" in order to reaffirm the nation's spiritual greatness and secular leadership of the world, in the same breath a call is made to control, expel, or eliminate those who do not belong, the exogeneous or impure, the foreign with their stigmata of inferiority and exteriority defined either by somatic features (vulgar racism) or coded cultural/sociological qualities. A metaphysics of prophylactic essentialism supervenes.

To be sure, origins need not predetermine destinations, although sometimes they anticipate the direction of movement. One can say that it is not by chance that the birth of the United States was accompanied by the systematic genocide of the indigenous peoples and aboriginal inhabitants of the continent: "For its part, the American 'revolutionary nation' built its orginal ideals on a double repression: that of the extermination of the Amerindian 'natives' and that of the difference between free 'White' men and 'Black' slaves. The linguistic community inherited from the Anglo-Saxon 'mother country' did not pose a problem — at least apparently — until Hispanic immigration conferred upon it the significance of class symbol and racial feature" (Balibar and Wallenstein 1991, 104). This foundational concordance of national identity and social formation is rehearsed in many synoptic historical accounts, among them Gabriel Kolko's *Main Currents in Modern American History* (1976), Howard Zinn's *A People's History of the United States* (1980), Manning Marable's *How Capitalism Underdeveloped Black America* (1983), and Peter Carroll and David Noble's *The Free and the Unfree* (1988). The manifold repressions coinciding with the emergence of national identity witness also the rise of the state and its apparatus of violence. In analyzing the linkage between race and nation, we need to avoid collapsing the distinction between the concept of the *nation-state* and of *nationalism*. Whence originates the will to exclude, to dominate? According to Anthony Giddens, "What makes the 'nation' integral to the nation-state . . . is not the existence of sentiments of nationalism but the unification of an administrative apparatus over precisely defined territorial boundaries in a complex of other nation-states" (1987, 172). That is why the rise of nation-states coincided with wars and the establishment of the military bureaucratic machine. In this construal, the state refers to the political institution with centralized authority and monopoly of coercive agencies coeval with the rise of global capitalism, while nationalism denotes the self-identification of peoples based on the perceived commonality of symbols, beliefs, traditions, and so on.

In addition, we need to guard against confusing historical periods and categories. Imagining the nation unified on the basis of secular citizenship and self-representation, as Benedict Anderson (1991) has shown, was only possible when print capitalism arose in conjunction with the expansive state. But that in turn was possible when the trading bourgeoisie developed the means of communication under pressure of competition and hegemonic exigencies. Moreover, the dissemination of the Bible in Europe in different vernaculars did not translate into a monopoly of violence by the national churches. It is obvious that the sense of national belonging, whether based on clan or tribal customs, language, religion, and so on, certainly has a historical origin and localizing motivation different from the emergence of the capitalist state as an agency to rally the populace to serve the needs of the commercial class and the goal of accumulation.

In U.S. history, the state evolved from the articulation of class, race, and nationality around the axis of white supremacy. One may hazard the speculation that the mass appeal of black nationalism (as signified by the enduring relevance of Malcolm X) and the seductive panacea of

Afrocentrism may have checked the excesses of state violence (Gold-field 1991) and the persistent marginalization of African Americans. However, the recent election of George W. Bush augurs a bleak prospect for resolving the "problem of the color-line." For one thing, it has dissolved the racial question underscored by the Los Angeles urban revolt into the politics of white suburbia. We should also take note of the official celebrations of Columbus (following the U.S./Western victory over a rising Islamic/Arab power, Iraq) and the unmitigated utilization in films and journalism of the historic subjugation of Native Americans now allegorized as a heroic epic of the sacrifices made by Western civilizers, all symptoms of the dialectics of racism and nationalism (Parenti 1989) that distinguish the symbolic construction of American global power and its claim to uniqueness in world history.

The recent NATO/U.S. victory over Yugoslavia is exemplary of the race/nation dialectic. It is ultimately designed to exorcise the ghosts of imperial defeats in Vietnam, Somalia, Afghanistan, and possibly Colombia, and also vindicate national honor. The quasi-religious appeal of a fabled, symbolic American nation neutralizes class, ethnic, and gender differences in the service of a messianic telos. When persons in the United States are interpellated as free, sovereign individuals par-ticipating in the heritage and destiny of the American nation, in this same process inequalities of class, race, and gender are sublimated into the corpus of a compensating, subsumptive identity and its aura of humanitarian power and privilege. This is the charismatic power of a quasi-utopian "common culture."

It now becomes understandable why one woman from the Ojibway nation in Canada told me recently that everywhere she went her U.S. audience could empathize with her as a victim of sexism or male su-premacy, but could not understand the racism and national oppression that she was subjected to. I replied that for them to be able to approach such a possibility, they have to question their identity as "Americans," an identity founded on the conquest and domination of Others/people of color (within and outside the continental United States) whose presence is both needed and negated at the same time (Spears 1999). Others (subordinate, inferior) are needed to identify the matrix of the imperial white Self. Such a task of problematizing and interrogating a totalizing American identity, an idealized constellation of inclusions and exclusions, has not even been faced by U.S. socialists who claim to be in the vanguard of world proletarian revolution. There are of course a few exceptions (chauvinists are rampant in feminist and left-wing vanguardists), but they prove the rule. In general, one can say that both revolutionaries of Marxist vintage and left-wing liberals ignore the problem of nationalism by the pretext that U.S. imperialism is either declining or no longer meaningful during the protracted crisis of a "disorganized," post-Fordist global economy. But are we already condemned to suffer the "pleasures" of a postcapitalist and postrevolutionary epoch?

The fact is that U.S. imperialism in its globalized stage is trying to revitalize itself by pursuing the hegemonic project of world hegemony via coded racial interpellations. Neofascism is one sign of this revitalization. The phenomenal rise of David Duke in Louisiana and his appeal to a great number of Americans should portend the vicissitudes of U.S. racial politics and popular movements in the next millennium. Carl Freedman (1992) describes the postmodern fascism of Duke as one that tapped the hidden but vast "reservoir of white hatred for blacks" — not only hatred but paranoid fear. While it is true that Duke demagogically mobilized the class resentment, frustrations, and fears of many unemployed, poor, and middle-class whites as well as of small entrepreneurs, he also deployed the racially coded references to "drug dealers on welfare" used by the Right and the core values of American liberalism signaled by the rhetoric of "fair deal," "equal opportunity," "level playing field," and so on. Racism can thus refunction the "principles" of liberal democracy insofar as they sanction the preservation of unequal power and property relations. In addition, the metaphysics of the exceptionalist American experiment in democracy serves to postpone the legitimacy crisis of the system.

What Duke and any number of rightist groups do is operate within the *problematique* or frame of reference of American nationalism as a libertarian communal project. One of its key documents may be glossed here: Arthur Schlesinger Sr.'s "What Then Is the American, This New Man?" In this text we have a celebration of the diligence, sobriety, and individualism of the pioneering farmers, the gospel of work, optimism, the "traditional spirit of self-reliance and free competition" that inaugurated the founding of the Republic, the idealism of making money, and "the profound conviction that nothing in the world is beyond its power to accomplish." This pervasive liberal ethos has falsified Marx's theory, according to Schlesinger: "Thanks to equality of opportunity with plenty for all, the class struggle in America has consisted in the struggle to climb out of one class into a higher one" (1985, 25). In this search for what Balibar calls "fictive ethnicity" to define the American nation, a search formalized (to allude to an egregious example) in the anthropological field devoted to culture and national character/personality formation, we see a characteristic gesture of classification and construction of hierarchy. Qualities found in the artisanal and "booty" stages of capitalism are dehistoricized and depoliticized, then infiltrated into predatory imperialist ideology. Paternalist racism is sublated within its competitive version (Bowser 1995). What emerges in effect is a judgmental culturalism that ascribes rights and positions as though they were natural or providentially decreed by occult forces. Solidarity through participation in the forging of a singular national destiny compensates for anomie, economic deprivations, and individual powerlessness. Even Herbert Gans, one of the first "connoisseurs" of symbolic ethnicity, is forced to admit that "ethnic prejudice and institutional ethnism" still infect the "top of the societal hierarchies" and "as long as the European immigration into America continues, people will still be perceived, classified and ranked at least in part by ethnic origin" (1996, 153). Within the framework of racial nationalism, immigration thus sanctions nativism and its logic of belonging and exclusion.

The Wages of Pluralism

By substituting ethnicity for race, the dominant ideology expunged class. In the sixties and seventies, the institutionalization of the ethnicity paradigm functioned inter alia as a strategy to defuse racial tensions by shifting class contradictions to that between the blacks and the relatively deprived white majority who tended to favor religious fundamentalism, authoritarian family patterns, and patriotism. White workers afflicted by alienating labor wanted to be different, too. Irving Louis Horowitz argues that the affirmation of ethnicity valorized race, sex, and property in order to surmount "the vacuity and vapidity of postindustrial capitalist life" and the breakdown of achievement orientation. In opposition to the welfare model of entitlement allegedly used by blacks and the educational model of empowerment used by Jews, Horowitz points out that ethnicity emphasized the renewal of ascribed values whose locus is the *Gemeinschaft*, or precapitalist community: "a pristine era in American life, before the melting-pot ideology boiled out the impurities of the immigrant generation with a weird mixture of external pressure and internalized guilt" (1977, 74). In this pursuit of authenticity, one apprehends the prophylactic drive of nationalized racism to classify, purge, and rank qualities in order to unify a discordant mass with a fiction or trope of oneness.

It is now generally acknowledged that the practice of internationalism dating back to the League of Nations and its privileging of the right of nations to self-determination has enhanced and exacerbated nationalist impulses everywhere. This trend is bound to ramify and aggravate interethnic confrontations such as the ongoing wars in the former Yugoslavia, Turkey, Ruwanda, Sri Lanka, Burma, Indonesia, the Philippines, and elsewhere (Geertz 1993). Extrapolating from the contemporary scene of racial polarization in the United States, one can surmise that the politics of racism for a future characterized by trade wars between nation-states and politico-economic blocs will be harnessing the potency of national belonging, of national self-definition of mission and tradition, and, as a supplement, the ideology of regional (for example, the European Community; Japan's new "coprosperity sphere") destiny and mission in the "New World Order." In the United States, militant nativism and populism (Higham 1971) will be reinvigorated in the exchange of symbolic capital and its multifarious replications.

Mediated by liberals like Glazer and Moynihan in the sixties, the intervention of the discourse of ethnicity in articulating the relation between class and race will be renewed in the late-modern version of pluralism: institutional multiculturalism (for illustrations, see I. Reed 1998). But its real function is integrally ideological: it sublates or displaces class and racial antagonisms to their marginal place in the task of interpellating individuals as "Americans." Multicultural nationalism — the ethos of racial diversity and heterogeneity — will be geared to the project of constructing citizens as participants in the assertion of American power and American uniqueness vis-à-vis rivals like Germany, Japan, and of course threats by "rogue" Others like Libya, Iran, Cuba, and Afghanistan.

Recent electoral politics has been portentously silent on immigration and the accelerated flight of U.S. capital to the peripheries. The dispute over reproductive rights may have overshadowed that over affirmative action, but the racialized terrain of contestation and its issues are there for all to see in the easily decipherable references to urban crime, drugs, and welfare. The unending supply of cheap labor power through immigration, illegal importation of labor, and influx of refugees feeds the drive for national identification via ethnicity. Colin Greer points out the linkage between immigration and the political use of ethnicity:

> Key in this framework is the continuing stream of immigration which has remained a basic ingredient in society. It is at once an aspect of active ethnic self-definition and a focus of the struggle between capital and labor in the context of which ethnic ideology derives. Ethnicity, then, can be seen as a central characteristic of American identity which is most clearly observed in relationship with, not by any means simply as a successor to, immigration. [The importance of ethnic identity] must be sought in its mediating role between two distinct functions in U.S. life. In effect, two basic, semi-autonomous realms are merged in the ethnic idiom: on the one hand, the belief in the do-it-yourself marketplace of immigrant achievement continues to justify an immigrant stream; on the other, the reality of government involvement in the lives of most Americans and their reliance on government is both hidden and justified through the identification with immigrant forebears. (1984, 131)

Here we encounter the immigrant myth of success, the mediation of state policies and programs, and the genealogical impulse to transcend class interests and recreate (for the new immigrants) a new American identity even while "native identity is constantly recreated."

It is almost a hallowed truism to say that the United States is "a nation of immigrants," with the obvious exception of the Native American nations. This received doxa has been consecrated by Establishment scholars, among them Oscar Handlin (whose classic work, *Immigration as a Factor in American History*, informs numerous dissertations), Glazer, Moynihan, Bernard Weisberger (whose article, "A Nation of Immigrants," appears in every issue of the *Annual Editions of Race and Ethnic Relations*), and countless others. Handlin's *Race and Nationality in American Life* (1957) published at the height of the Cold War reiterates the central role of immigration in the constitution of the American self-aggrandizing ethos. Indeed, as Kenan Malik recently observed with reference to Europe, "immigration has become a cipher, a means through which deeper social concerns are revealed" (1996, 183).

One key insight needs to be stressed: political pluralism based on immigrant success and self-reliance, the constitutive ingredients of public ethnicity, actually serves corporate business and the consumerist ethos. It now becomes clear how "the inclusionary power of ethnic identification as a national self-characterization" allows the reactionary pundit Murray (1984) to speculate on the sympathy of white viewers for victimized Korean proprietors even as the dominant proponents of law and order spontaneously release their fear/contempt on the blacks and Latinos more victimized by corporate and government policies than the Korean middlemen of the internal colonies. Immigration thus serves the mandate for reconstituting a distinct American national identity as a guarantee for the maintenance of law and order, the unimpeded accumulation of surplus-value, and the reproduction of racialized subject-positions in the bureaucratized global market.

New post-Cold War realignments compel us to return to a historical-materialist analysis of political economy and its overdeterminations in order to grasp the new racial politics of transnationality and multiculturalism (Bruin 1996). Obviously I am not advocating a vulgar Marxist (a.k.a. economistic or mechanical deterministic) approach in understanding race/ethnic relations. What may prove revitalizing for the post–1965 generation is a creative return to the "basics," perhaps a nuanced counterfundamentalism that Richard Appelbaum reformulates in these terms: "Capitalism has always reinforced class divisions with divisions based on race, ethnicity, gender, and other forms of ascription. In any system based to a large degree on the exploitation of one group of people by another, such distinctions provide a useful basis for justifying inequality. Not only does this foster a 'divide-and-conquer' ideology among those who otherwise might find common cause, but it also helps to foster a standard of exploitation based on what is accorded the least common denominator — whichever group finds itself at the bottom of the economic heap" (1996, 313). Together with Appelbaum's elucidation of global capitalism's flexibility instanced by the subcontracting modes of manipulating the commodity chains, we can learn from Edna Bonacich's analysis (1996) of how the Los Angeles garment industry deploys multiculturalism to cut production costs and increase surplus value. Certain recent developments, particularly the emergence of U.S. Asian neoconservatives (described by Omatsu [1994]) and the tension between Korean Americans and black communities, direct our focus to the fierce class war waged by the U.S. corporate elite against both the U.S. working masses and their international rivals (Japan, Germany). Meanwhile, the value produced by unpaid labor continues to be expropriated from thousands of Asian and Latino women in the sweatshops of the metropolis and "third-world" borderlands called "free-trade zones." I would like to mention here the presence of eight million Filipino "contract workers" engaged in domestic and low-paid or demeaning work in the Middle East, Hong Kong, Singapore, Japan, and many European countries.

In the light of these reconfigurations, we need not an ethnic politics for moderating the private expropriation of the social surplus but a counterhegemonic strategy that articulates the imperatives of ethnicity, gender, sexuality, place, and so on — the major coordinates of cultural identity — with class-based resistance and other oppositional trends charted within the political economy of racist exploitation and oppression. Such a united-front politics can only be viable within a larger framework of a wide-ranging program targeting the material foundation of iniquitous power and reification in the commodity logic of unequal exchange.

Revisiting Institutional Racism

Any inquiry into the problematique of multiculturalism and identity cannot proceed instructively without grasping what I consider the most useful concept of social theory forged in the civil rights struggles: institutional racism. A review of this concept and its usages might help offset the excesses of postmodernist constructionism bereft of historical grounding. In the entry on "Institutional Racism" in the *Dictionary of Race and Ethnic Relations* (Cashmore 1988), British sociologist Michael Banton criticizes the term as problematic in lumping together cultural assumptions, motives, institutions, attitudes, and beliefs about racial superiority that need to be distinguished and analyzed separately for the sake of social policy and remedial action. Introduced in 1967 by Stokely Carmichael and Charles Hamilton who questioned the persistence of racial disadvantage in the middle of liberal reforms, the term is meant to designate a phenomenon that "relies on the active and pervasive operation of anti-black attitudes and practices," in particular the racist attitude of white superiority that permeates the whole society "on both the individual and institutional level, covertly and overtly" (1968, 5). Outcomes, not intentions, are the measure of reformist success.

Various thinkers since then have refined the theoretical substance of the concept. Their aim was to distinguish it from "racism" as prejudice or belief-system in the form of deterministic theories based on biology or psychology, ideas that entailed practices of racial discrimination. Racism as an ideology can be described for the present context as "the deterministic ascription of real or supposed negative characteristics to a particular group" (Banton and Miles, 1988) whose social significance implies differential treatment (sometimes known as "racialism") or differential exclusion in the realm of politics, economy, and other areas of public life.

David Mason (1982) surveyed the usage family of "institutional racism" and found three versions of varying analytic worth. The first version, known as the conspiracy or instrumentalist type, is predicated on prejudice, or the concealed interest of the state or a hegemonic class, as the motive behind discriminatory policies; hence, if no evidence of prejudice or vested interest can be found, institutional racism doesn't exist. The second kind, labeled "structuralist Marxist," locates institutional racism "neither in the purposes nor the articulations of interested groups and their agents but in the consequences of state policies." For example, the superexploitation of migratory labor in Britain and their racialist segregation in housing, jobs, education, and other areas, result from system constraints tied to the structure of the capitalist economy at a certain stage of historical development, not from the ascertainable interests of officials or corporate managers. Because institutional racism is dictated by the imperatives of the capitalist mode of production, this argument is judged inadequate since it does not have much to say about purposive human agency, much less the unintended consequences of the state's role in stabilizing a conflict-ridden social order.

The last version of institutional racism is tied to "colonialism" and focuses on the conditions under which groups are incorporated into the "host society." While Robert Blauner (1972) argues that the entry of blacks as slaves affected their long-term allocation to social roles and their claim to rights and political power, John Rex (1970) posits the formerly colonized status of migrants to the United Kingdom as a causal factor in their relative disadvantage. The colonial (slave) experience is thus a system of structured inequality not derivative from beliefs or attitudes alone. For Blauner, "institutions either exclude or restrict the participation of racial groups by procedures that have become conventional, part of the bureaucratic system of rules and regulations. Thus there is little need for prejudice as a motivating force" (1972, 10). What is at issue then in elucidating the analytic value of the concept is the ratio of structure to agency, of object to subject, which it defines, a calibration crucial for a politics or ethics committed to changing power relations.

There is no escaping the subject-object dialectic of political economy. Institutional racism is now conceived as an effect of structural determinants of a social formation instead of being the product of actions of groups or individuals formulating and implementing policies that benefit particular groups or classes. Whether racist ideology functioning as policy initiator or rationale plays a role or not depends on the given historical conjuncture. Thus, even in the absence of racist policies or psychological racism among those who govern, one can explain the disadvantage suffered by racialized groups to be the effects of institutional networks of power. What seems to be lacking in such accounts is the linkage between the structural characteristics of a social formation and the actions by which subjects (interpellated by various state and civil-society apparatuses) produce and reproduce their positions/modalities of social existence. What exactly is the connection between this level of abstraction and the social or national imaginary that people mobilize to interpret their worlds and represent themselves to others? What is the precise interplay between social structures and individual performances, between material conditions and the complex sphere of subjectivity (or subject-position, in the poststructuralist idiom), in the field of "race relations"? A theoretical response to these questions may be found in Pierre Bourdieu's idea of habitus (more on this later), or Anthony Giddens's (1984) theory of structuration.

Controversy persists over the theoretical viability of "institutional racism." In *Race and Ethnicity* (1986), Rex points to the institutional orientation of "unconscious racism" embedded in commonsense reasoning. In a society like the United States with a long history of colonial and imperial wars, what passes for the commonsense knowledge of average citizens is pervaded with racist and paternalist assumptions, as demonstrated for example by the research of David Wellman (1977), or by recent media commentaries on the Los Angeles "riots." As for racial disadvantage, Rex seems to think that the central institutions involved in producing it are the free-market system and the formal bureaucratic processes of a competitive liberal society that can be corrected with the infusion of a universalist morality sponsored by the government. If so, Rex has not advanced that much from Myrdal's notion of racism as a distinctly schizophrenic moral dilemma amenable to remedy through gradualist social engineering.

The "cultural turn" in the last three decades has rediscovered the value of ideology-critique. In *Racism* (1989), Robert Miles envisages two sets of circumstances in which the operations of institutional racism can be perceived: one where exclusionary practices arise from or embody a racist discourse although they are no longer explicitly justified by it, and one where the explicitly racist element in the discourse is absent but another (say, cultural) discourse substitutes for it. In the latter case, the exclusionary mode of conduct may be said to have institutionalized the discourse, for instance, the British government's strategy of withdrawing from its former colonial subjects the right of entry because they cause social problems. Practices of selective coding and of inscribing subtexts into legislation criminalizing immigrants illustrate that institutional racism may be captured in the history of discourse, not in the consequences of actions.

A semantic and hermeneutic problem emerges here. Whether the locus is discourse or disciplinary regimes (in Foucault's sense), it appears clear that the complex of themes and notions encapsulated by the term *institutional racism* enlarges its compass too exorbitantly, forfeiting any rigorous delineation of historically specific practices, processes, and events. In another attempt to salvage the term, Jenny Williams seeks to develop an empirical model that would, among others, clarify (1) the differentiation of institutional operations into material and ideological elements — ideas cannot be conflated into objective social forms or practices; (2) other ideologies with racial consequences; (3) the resistance of the oppressed as an important influence on institutions; (4) the relations of various institutions that may suggest that racial inequality is not just the result of specific institutional operations; (5) the historical development of forms of inequality crystallized in institutions; and (6) "historical ideologies sedimented into existing understandings and racialized common sense" (1985, 334). Williams poses the key question: "If institutional racism is defined by its consequences, i.e., the presence of racial inequalities, does the existence of any form of racial inequality imply the existence of institutional racism?" Her answer is negative because available empirical research has not been able to settle on what is a legitimate comparative measure of racial inequality. She insists that we keep an open mind on the still untheorized "relationship between racist intent, racial expression in practices, and racial effect, i.e., forms of inequality" (1985, 339).

Notwithstanding this salutary advice, a skeptical note may be interpolated here. Could it be that we have arrived at an aporia or impasse on this issue so that this statement from *Newsweek* (18 May 1992) on the Los Angeles protests can now pass for pedestrian wisdom mock-mirroring our theoretical dilemma?

> We have no real choice but to try to disentangle this infinitely sensitive, infinitely complicated subject — to separate, as best we can, the residual problems of race and ethnicity from the problems of crime, poverty and despair that so frustrate public policy and public discourse. That racism and race friction still exist is undeniable. But neither can any longer be taken as a legitimizing rationale for violence, crime or the endemic problems of the urban poor. Those problems — all of them — are the result partly of the increasing concentration of poverty in the nation's cities and partly of an accelerating breakdown in the value structure that made America the least class-ridden and most optimistic society in the world.

If racism no longer accounts for crime and poverty, is the breakdown of "value structure" removed from the practices of institutional racism? Lest we be driven to invoke the well-known functionalist axioms of system-maintenance dependent on value consensus and blame the victims for failure to adapt, adjust, or assimilate, I would like to highlight the contribution of Philomena Essed's research, in particular *Understanding Everyday Racism* (1991), as a heuristic commentary to the working of institutional racism.

One of the problems in deploying the term *institutional racism* is the fraught interplay between the power of ideology and the multiple functions of ruling apparatuses that are targeted for pragmatic rearrangement, that is, legislative repackaging. Essed attempts to join micro- and macro-approaches to racism viewed as "a system of structural inequalities and a historical process, both created and recreated through routine practices" (1991, 39). System as regularized social practices between individuals and groups cannot be comprehended without a knowledge of the macro-structures of racial inequality characterizing the whole. In other words, institutional racism is concretely actualized in specific practices of agents that "activate existing structural racial inequality in the system."

Refiguring Everyday Life

The crucial concept of *everyday life* attendant to the reflexivity of modern urban existence mediates institutions and experience. Quotidian temporality provides the site for mediating structure and agency, mode of production and ideology, subject (consciousness) and object (life-world). Life in the everyday world may be conceived as a matrix of multiple social relations present in and reproduced by everyday practices, relations manifesting the pressures of lived categories such as race, gender, class, ethnicity, and so on.

Racism is embodied in the routine practices (cognitive, behavioral) of everyday life, activating power relations that prestructure the situation of individual subjects. Everyday racism then is a complex of heterogeneous practices mediated through gender, class, and other relations in which the dynamics of ethnic and racial domination appear insofar as differences in positions of power are racially or ethnically identified. Integrating culture and structure, everyday racism is, for Essed, a conflict-maintaining process that uses strategies of marginalizing, problematizing, and containing groups (people of color) whose labor power and subordinate status sustain the hegemony of the dominant Eurocentric power bloc.

48

Essed holds that "race" is a fundamental organizing principle of the social relations of the United States, the Netherlands, and many other societies. This concurs with my initial thesis of the United States as a racial polity. Essed defines everyday racism as "a process in which (a) socialized racist notions are integrated into meanings that make practices immediately definable and manageable, (b) practices with racist implications become in themselves familiar and repetitive, and (c) underlying racial and ethnic relations are actualized and reinforced through these routine or familiar practices in everyday situations" (1991, 52). In synthesizing knowledge with actions, meanings, and situations, the concept of everyday racism underwrites the rehabilitation of "institutional racism" as an event or process where the mechanisms of hegemonic rule can be discerned, diagnosed, and challenged. How indeed can we transform institutions and the ensemble of "rationalized" practices and discourses that constitute them? It is to the task of illuminating the gendered subject's (Surinamese women in Holland, African American women in the United States) craft of resistance to institutional racism that Essed makes her substantive contribution.

Given the current debate on the preferential option for multiculturalism vis-à-vis the neoconservative defense of a legacy of a "common culture," Essed's targeting of culturalized racism deserves closer attention. The concept of everyday racism is in fact addressed to those proponents of liberal tolerance who deny the existence of racist practices, let alone institutional racism. Essed contends that the valorization of cultural differences, which are then hierarchically ordered to privilege the dominant Eurocentric normative standard, turns out to be one ubiquitous symptom of everyday racism. The process of ethnization, the provision of "ethnic niches" that occasion active or passive tolerance (applied multiculturalism), objectifies and marginalizes people of color and thus controls them within the repressive milieu of a pluralist order. Here is one response of the tolerated subject that Essed quotes:

You've got to start by explaining how you are different. Where you're from and so on, and if you don't eat pork, then it's usually settled for you, oh, yes, so you are a Muslim and then comes an entire volume of what they all know about Muslims and so on and so on, you know. So, it always reverts to your being different. It's always negative, it's never nice. I think however positive they do it, it still has something negative, of not recognizing or seeing another as an equal. So, as far as that goes, for me, it is always negative [It is interesting to note that this woman is a Christian who happens to be on a special diet]. (1991, 211)

Essed provides us with a massive catalog of instances of everyday racism, from actions of overt intimidation to indifference; from malicious verbal insults to surveillance, petty harassment, patronizing gestures, casual jokes, and other techniques of containment and subordination. These instances are codified as "scenarios of racism" (SRs): for example, school test SR, meeting SR, dating a white man SR, searching for a room SR, and so on. She intends to expose the denial of racism (prejudice as an idea or attitude) as an ideological ruse justifying the normalcy of white supremacy. She seeks to uncover the microinteractional scenarios of everyday mundane life as the site where the racism of the cultural pluralist ethos is enacted. Her richly textured ethnography renders dramatically concrete for us the anatomy of the reproduction of racism in the scripts of everyday situations.

What seems to me problematic despite the convincing examples is Essed's implicit acceptance of a modified structuralist version of institutional racism. While subscribing to the view that racism is always historically specific, Essed upholds the functionality of racism as a regulatory force in the labor market. No doubt this is a factor, but does it exhaust all explanatory possibilities? While racism involves conflict over norms and values, as well as over definitions of the social world, what is fundamentally at stake is control over material and nonmaterial resources, the disposition of which is crucial for determining life-chances and the quality of everyday existence for millions. Essed underscores this insight: "Whether racism is racially or culturally expressed, the basic struggle is for power and control of society's resources. In both countries [United States, Netherlands] Black women are repeatedly and systematically frustrated in their pursuit of fair access to resources" (1991, 292).

By arguing that racism is "systematically integrated into meanings and routine practices by which social relations are reproduced," Essed directs our attention not to specific agents but to the "very fabric of the social system." What should be changed then is the logic of power relations, both superstructure and infrastructure. Everyday racism based on the experiences and understanding of black women affords a knowledge that can be used to combat cultural racism and interrogate the legitimacy of the existing balance of power. Essed constructs a dialectical perspective that foregrounds the interaction between the structuring activity of actors and their structured subjectivity, a view that resolves the classic empiricist antinomy between structure and subjectivity, system and event, in the "social praxis" (Rossi 1983, 318) of black women. While she is rightly critical of the Dutch government's displacement of opposition to racist marginalization into a program of trying to preserve ethnic identity (reducing culture to personality features), she does not provide a historical account of how cultural pluralism, or Dutch "common sense," has evolved as a key element in the ideological apparatus for reproducing ethnic labor segmentation; or how the racist mechanisms of marginalization, problematization, and containment are orchestrated (albeit in contradictory fashion) with other liberal democratic institutions of civil society and the welfare state.

A caveat may be registered here. While everyday racism, in Essed's inventory of social "games," indeed demonstrates the subtle covert working of institutional racism, we know that any society grasped as a dynamic totality results from the complex articulation of various levels of determination (political, ideological, economic) in which categories of race, gender, nationality, and so on overdetermine each other relative to the mode and level of production relations. In any social formation, ethnic and racial differences may be conceptualized as operative in a set of economic, political, and ideological antagonisms that saturate everyday life, particularly the realm of "common sense." In describing the "common sense" of Dutch or U.S. society as a more or less static unitary essence instead of a fissured or unstable constellation of negotiated compromises, Essed may have invented a closure that thwarts popular intervention. In short, how do we attempt to interrogate and dismantle this "common sense"?

More crucial is the absence in Essed's research of a framework calculating the alignment of the various political forces in each society contesting for hegemony (moral-intellectual leadership of a historic bloc or alliance), forces whose partisanship can be registered in their position toward laws on immigration, education, housing, employment, and other public spheres insofar as these affect the everyday life of people of color. What is required then is not more empirical data but further theoretical sharpening and testing of the conceptual tools that will articulate the various levels of each complexly structured social formation for the purpose of estimating the weight or pressure of racial and ethnic differences in the dynamics of their historical development.

One can argue that the practical everyday consciousness at work in everyday racism lacks coherence, just as daily experience impresses us as "disjointed and episodic," fragmentary and contradictory. A product and part of history, this "common sense" is, as Stuart Hall emphasizes, the terrain of conceptions and categories on which the practical consciousness of the masses of the people is actually formed, the field where more developed philosophies and ideologies contend for mastery, "the ground which new conceptions of the world must take into account, contest and transform, if they are to shape the conceptions of the world of the masses and in that way become historically effective" (1986, 20). If so, then there is room for transformative intervention, for devising tactics and strategies for collective action.

It is exactly this precarious terrain of everyday life that complicates the critique of institutional racism and its manifestations in speech codes, behavior, and so on. One can ask: Is there a habitus of institutional racism? By habitus, Bourdieu means "the conditionings associated with a particular class of conditions of existence that produce habitus, systems of durable, transposable dispositions, structured structures predisposed to function as structuring structures, that is, as principles which generate and organize practices and representations that can be objectively adapted to their outcomes without presupposing a conscious aiming at ends or an express mastery of the operations necessary in order to attain them" (1999, 108). One of the most poignant and lucid exemplifications of the racialized habitus of subalterns may be found in Richard Wright's lecture "The Psychological Reactions of Oppressed People" in *White Man, Listen!* (1957). Daily practices of surveillance have been internalized by subjugated natives so that external rules are no longer needed; the colonial subject inhabits Fanon's Manichean milieu where institutions condition the sensibility of subjects while the subjects' psychology matches the structures of civil society and the state. Reflection on habitus leads us next to Gramsci's central concept of hegemony (Buci-Glucksman 1982).

We may follow Hall in stressing the importance of Gramsci's precept that the cultural arena in the struggle for radical democratic transformation is decisive: "Every philosophical current leaves behind a sediment of 'common sense'; this is the document of its historical effectiveness. Common sense is not rigid and immobile but is continually transforming itself, enriching itself with scientific ideas and with philosophical opinions which have entered ordinary life. Common sense creates the folklore of the future" (1986, 326). But surely it remains for organic intellectuals and other partisans of political struggle to draw up the inventory of "common sense" and mobilize it for emancipatory ends. Culture is not just the historically grounded corpus of practices, representations, languages, and customs of a specific society, but it is also in a more decisive way the contradictory forms of "common sense" subtending everyday life. By extension, the subject enacting everyday racist practice is not a unified but rather a contradictory subject, a social construction, just as its victims are. The whole racial polity should then be mapped as a battleground for ideological and political combat.

From Barricades to Trenches

Let us return to our point of departure in the contemporary racial polity: "Can't we get along?" Rodney King's somewhat precarious enunciation of a plea for civility during the height of the Los Angeles uprising has provoked among concerned citizens an earnest attempt to put out the fires in the wake of the virtual militarization of the city. Given their commercializing disposition to seize the event for postmodern spectacles delivering instant gratification with plenitude of meaning, the mass media as usual projected the notion, now a received doxa, that interethnic conflict lies at the heart of this worst urban riot in U.S. history. Those "Others" are just unruly, untutored, and therefore unfit for civil treatment.

Even assuming that this conflict forms part of the total picture, what deeper motives and needs are served by the journalistic method of highlighting the differences among victims? One can offer a quick answer: it is part of the divide-and-rule strategy of the elite. It serves to displace the primary contradiction between the dominant ruling bloc and oppressed workers into that between fractions of the oppressed, thus sustaining and reinforcing the status quo. Yet many people won't agree because the hegemonic consensus gravitates around the limited scope of individual freedom, conformity to the laws on property, and peace to conduct business as usual. The ideology of consumerist freedom and property ownership hides the precarious, unstable, but nevertheless effective subjugation of the majority.

Now any research into so-called interethnic conflict can only obfuscate if not elide the complexity of this layered plot of urban history when the focus of explanatory analysis is directed on the problem of cultural misunderstanding, failure of communication, and the need for more education about minorities. Because the ethnicity paradigm prevalent in ethnic studies (see chapter 5) research mainly addresses the problem of group identity or identification as functional to social integration and stabilization of consensus, most academic inquiries tend to focus on the cultural dimensions of intergroup relations (orientations, values, goals of actors) and thus place the burden of their plight on the victims themselves. Questions erupt here: Is the phenomenon of ethnic difference reducible to cultural diversity? How does a cultural group claim to be distinctive and valuable? Can the expression of cultural uniqueness be tolerated if it refuses to obey the decorum of civic nationalism? Does the notion of citizenship resolve material inequalities or social injustices? If ethnicity is not primordial but is rather a strategic choice, will reforms of the liberal state get rid of institutional racism and prevent racially motivated violence? With the demise of the welfare state and the dominance of unregulated market competition, will ethnicity still function as a regulative principle of redistribution? Can a politics/ethics of recognition survive the juggernaut of possessive individualism under the aegis of white supremacy?

Phenomenology and empiricism for their part seek to foreground subjectivity but at the expense of giving functional positivism a blank check to underwrite everything. While these studies might claim to combat ethnocentrism and racist prejudice, their view that ethnicity — the group's self-representation — depends on ascription from both sides of the group boundary in question crucially ignores the matter of group categorization — from both sides of the boundary, and from the all-encompassing political regime. We never hear of police terror and state coercion in such studies in spite of their attention to agency and consciousness, although there are allusions to statistics about jobs, institutional discrimination, and so on.

I would concur with critics of this mode of ethnic absolutism by proposing that we engage with the "absolute centrality of power relationships" (Jenkins 1986) instead of, say, psychoanalyzing folkways, in order to elucidate the causes of racial conflict and violence. When, for example, the Asian American doxa of the "model minority" is imposed by the media and reactionary bureaucrats to lay the groundwork for gutting legislation on equal employment opportunity, curtailing social services, and justifying the "deindustrialization" of the whole economy, then we are confronted with a process of group categorization in the sense that the implication to be drawn is that African Americans, Latinos, and other deprived citizens should forsake welfare and conform to the sanctified if obsolete standards of meritocratic utilitarianism. After all, it's the nature of the impoverished "underclass," not the socioeconomic policies, institutions, and programs of the governing power elite that should be held accountable.

The phenomenon of interethnic behavior as transactional and situationally defined needs to be inscribed in the complex historical dynamics of a racial polity such as the United States. In this historical contextualization, we begin to understand how status, privilege, and power mediated through race as a synecdoche of class are subject to permanent political contestation (Baron 1985). Here the state, economy, and mass political mobilization at various historical conjunctures are key topics to be addressed. We need to go beyond celebrating ethnic identities, quaint customs, and picturesque ceremonies. Stephen Steinberg (1981) cautions us that the ideal of ethnic pluralism, of putative multicultural democracy, may be used to legitimate existing class divisions and apologize for the systemic inequalities that enable it. In other words, we need to go beyond the pleasures of identity politics and historicize the cultural symbols that construct identities and self-representations.

The fires raging in the aftermath of the Rodney King verdict may have darkened rather than illuminated minds cherishing the vision of a Rainbow Coalition becoming a reality, a foretaste of the coming of a genuinely participatory democracy eulogized by New Deal liberals. What has escaped many commentators is the emancipatory subtext of the urban rebellion, its fundamental thrust as a revolutionary-democratic insurrection against police fascism and state repression, a clamor for justice by the African American, Latino, and Asian communities that connects with the grievances of millions of citizens transcending ethnic and racial differences. One can interpret the riot as a spontaneous, politically motivated insurrection with roots in the civil rights struggles, fortuitously converging with what Mike Davis calls "the first postmodern bread riot, in fact a multiethnic rising of the poor of the city" (1992, 743).

Hard lessons could have been learned from understanding the causes of the urban rebellion in the sixties, but that obviously didn't happen. President Clinton's Initiative on Race is to be welcomed in calling attention to the endemic hardcore problem of racialized inequality. The commission's banal, if not moralistic, finding, however, seems to demonstrate that it may be a strategy of containment rather than critique. Even mainstream media call it therapy. Structural inequality and institutional discrimination, the substantive issues raised in the sixties, have not been fully addressed. Articulated with race, the analysis of the persistence of poverty should—to quote Adolph Reed Jr.—examine "its sources in the operations of the American political and economic system" (1999, 196), a step often avoided for reasons we all know. That historical materialist wisdom, however, continues to be submerged, constantly side-tracked, or silenced. No doubt, a racializing consensus still pervades the commonsensical procedures of our society—from the categories of the Census to the neoconservative attack on Affirmative Action and other achievements of the civil rights struggles. Racial thinking has acquired new life in the sphere of foreign policy whenever officials rearticulate the binary opposition beween us (heirs of Western civilization) and "them" (uncouth fundamentalists, rogue states, terrorists of all kinds). The common life or national identity springs from the rubble of differences stigmatized, ostracized, or erased.

Racism today has been institutionalized to the point of banal normality. From this angle, we can appreciate Alex Callinicos's admonition of considering racism not simply as a set of beliefs or ideas but something organically tied to "systematic inequalities in power and life chances stemming from an exploitive social structure" (1993, 11). Nevertheless, to subsume race completely into class is to violate dialectical method and the decorum of historical materialism. C. L. R. James's warning is strategic here: "The race question is subsidiary to the class question in politics, and to think of imperialism in terms of race is diastrous. But to neglect the racial factor as merely incidental is an error only less grave than to make it fundamental" (Marable 1995, 87). Mediated through racial and ethnic antagonisms, the corpse of capitalist hegemony reincarnates itself through its past bodily disguises and its metamorphosis. The sharpening of class conflicts articulated through race, sexuality, gender, nationality, and religion has revived a ruling elite project of reconstituting a pluralist nation that refunctions traditional ideas of individualism and "American exceptionalism." It goes by the name of globalization and transcultural/transmigrant exchanges in the disjunctures of the free market glorified by postcolonial rhetoric and post-al publicity.

Amid the shifting alignments of nation-states and regional alliances, the U.S. nation-state persists as a sovereign agent manipulating the technology of diplomacy and violence. American national identity, however, has always been a political/ideological effect of a managed or administered consensus tied to hierarchical discrimination based on iniquitous property relations and status asymmetry. In this reckoning, a common cultural identity is rendered untenable by the logic of capital (in its financial speculative form) in reproducing class divisions marked by cultural or ethnic differences. This contradiction precipitates endless crisis in the system. Faced by the irresolvable economic devaluation of surplus-value and its accompanying legitimacy crisis, U.S. global capital revitalizes racist practices and institutions through the ideology of differential culturalism utilizing ethnic diversity, immigration, and interventions against the counterhegemonic resistance of people in the "internal colonies" and the dependent nation-states of the South. What then is the prospect of a democratic-socialist transformation in the wake of resurgent populist nationalism in the U.S. political arena? Why is the U.S.-sponsored WTO humanitarianism with a populist rhetoric and neo-fascist agenda the public countenance of a more virulent form of exclusion and inferiorization? I venture a provisional answer that will be explored and inflected in various ways in the succeeding chapters.

Mapping the future as an imperialist clash between the three spheres of global power — United States, Europe and Japan, we see the need to rebuild consensus for war and other interventions. Crucial to this is the consolidation of the "internal colonies," the pacification of the people of color (who will be demographically substantial in the next five decades) that can only be secured by interpellating them as "Americans," people participating in the American global mission of safeguarding individual freedom for all humanity, of promising for everyone material affluence and self-gratification through unlimited consumption (San Juan 1998a). Sublimating the traditional notions of "the white man's burden" and the *mission civilizatrice* of the Europeans, the American nation's global role is no longer to defend the free world from the "Evil Empire" of Soviet communism and its satellites. It is now (as it once was, in another modality) to guarantee the "universal liberty of mankind" (Lincoln's words), to be "the guardians at the gate" of progress, and in so doing offer the promise of personal fulfillment as it once did to the Pilgrims from an oppressive Europe (E. Ahmad 1980) or barbaric fundamentalists like Iran and Afghanistan. In the context of a future marked by sharpening rivalry between the three spheres of power centered on Japan, the European bloc, and the United States, the corporate elite's reassertion of a patriotic consensus in one guise or another, answering the question of "who is the authentic American?" and redefining the global destiny of America, will be the hegemonic project of a racial politics centered on market rationality, civil privatism, cutthroat individualism, and other business ideals now christened as traditional American values deployed by the state to interpellate subjects for citizenhood.

Ideological struggle demands urgent attention in our overdetermined and disaggregated global scenario of the next two or three decades. In his suggestive essay "Toward a Socialist Theory of Racism," Cornel West (1990) correctly emphasizes the need for Marxists to pay attention to cultural practices — the vindictive return of the repressed superstructures! — that engender subjectivity or autonomous agency beyond those circumscribed by the axiomatics of industrial production. He proposes investigating the genealogy of racist ideology, the institutional mechanisms that sustain white-supremacist discourse, and the structural configurations of class exploitation and political repression. In spite of his will to formulate a comprehensive critique, West is strangely silent on the articulation of racism with American nationalism (more on this in chapter 2). His analysis privileges the black-white confrontation in U.S. history. American nationalism is, I daresay, the secret of racism's universal appeal and its protean durability, serving as the new "opium of the masses."

Race constitutes the wily mask of the nationalist gospel in the United States. It conceals the predatory system of class relations by inventing "buffer" races, criminalizing people of color, and exacerbating a retrograde politics of identity. I pursue the gendered and sexualized construction of the national-racial ethos in the next chapter. As Amiri Baraka memorably puts it, "Racist national oppression . . . is the fundamental philosophy of the American social system, reflecting its imperialist economic base"; and white supremacy serves as "the philosophical justification for the exploitation and oppression of most of the world's peoples" (1998, 392). It is time for progressives to examine the hegemonic discourse of the U.S. racial polity, and with it the parallel aesthetic essentializing of American national purpose and "self-evident" national character. For I think it is here that racist ideas and practices are formed, refined, elaborated, and reproduced daily as doxa and consensus, making the fires in Los Angeles but one of those T V spectacles and events that are continuously recycled and sanitized, packaged for academic forums and polite conversations, thus attempting to manage peacefully the endemic crisis and making tomorrow safe for "business as usual."

CHAPTER 2

Performing Race

Articulations of Gender, Sexuality, and Nationalism

The present female liberation movement must be viewed within the context of international social revolution and within the context of the long struggle by women for nominal legal rights. — Roxanne Dunbar-Ortiz, *Female Liberation as the Basis for Social Revolution*

Where cultural representations do not reach out beyond themselves, there is the danger that they will function as surrogates for activism. . . . I always go back to Marx's eleventh Feuerbach. This is because . . . it brings me joy: "Philosophers have interpreted the world in various ways. The point, however, is to change it." — Angela Davis, *The Angela Davis Reader*

One of the slogans of the initial phase of the women's liberation movement in the United States condemned sexism — male supremacy — as one of the major causes of racism. In what way are sexuality, racial inferiorization of people of color, and imperialism woven together in late capitalism? At the height of the social ferment in the sixties, the African American scholar Calvin Hernton argued that "the sexualization of racism in the United States is a unique phenomenon in the history of mankind; it is an anomaly of the first order" (1965, 6). After surveying in detail the vicissicitudes of the sexual transactions across the black/white divide, especially the castelike prohibitions and myths of miscegenation surrounding white-skinned and dark-skinned bodies, Hernton concludes, "The racism of sex in the United States is but another aspect of the unequal political and economic relations that exist between the races in the American democracy" (1965, 179). Women of color may even be conceived as constituting "a different kind of racial formation," according to Angela Davis, although the violence inflicted against them — "rape as a weapon of political terror" (1998, 145) — conjoined with familial servitude and social inferiority, testifies more sharply to the sedimented structures of class and national oppression embedded in both state and civil society.

It is difficult to deny that the racial polity pivots around the sexualized-gendered division of labor. After more than twenty-five years of civil-rights agitation and liberal reforms, Hernton returns to his theme and reflects that "the unwritten taboo" against racial intermingling still prevails, that "the sexualization of racism [in the United States] is a fait accompli" (1965, xiii). Hernton is actually pursuing an insight common to many commentators but pointedly stated by the novelist James Weldon Johnson: "Through it all I discerned one clear and certain truth: in the core of the heart of the American race problem the sex factor is rooted, rooted so deeply that it is not always recognized when it shows at the surface" (quoted in Hernton 1965, xxi).

Instead of simply recapitulating these testimonies of pansexualized racism rampant in the racial polity, I would like to explore here the articulations between sexuality and nationalism. What demands scrutiny is more precisely how the categories of patriarchy and ethnonationalism contour the parameters of discourse about citizen identities. How the idea of the nation is sexualized and how sex is nationalized are topics that may yield clues as to how racial conflicts are circumscribed within the force field of national self-identification. It is revealing but not enigmatic how a canonical treatise on the emergence of the U.S. nation-state such as Seymour Martin Lipset's *The First New Nation* is silent on the factor of sexuality in the nationalist discourse. Nonetheless, that muteness is disturbed somewhat by a single passing reference to the "ascriptive-elitist-particularistic-diffuse values" of the American South, "a major source of instability in the American polity" (1963, 214). In other words, the virtues of plantation patriarchy in the South fed off the bodies of enslaved African women. The fact is that the project of early American cultural nationalism was "tripped up by the racial difference it had repressed" (Lott 1995, 91) and severely limited in its originality by importing wholesale the normative male supremacy of Enlightenment political theory (Rousseau, Locke, Montesquieu).

Sexuality, unlike racial judgment, is of course not a pure self-evident category. It manifests its semantic and ethical potency in the field of racial and gendered politics. In his authoritative studies, Roger Bastide has acutely analyzed the psychodynamics of race, sexuality, and patriarchal nationalism in the relations between Europeans and people of color. He underscored the paradoxes and ambiguities surrounding sexual miscegenation as a form of racial/nationalist combat:

> For in the lovemaking of partners of different colour, in the courting which went before, in those privileged instants which seem to destroy race and rediscover the unity of the human species, we find this paradox: the insinuation of racialism in its most savage, most withering forms. In these bodies finding each other, fusing, there are two races at each other's throats. . . . In conclusion, that contrary to a widely held opinion, closer relationships between the colours, whether in marriage or in simple sexual pleasure, are not a sign of absence of prejudice: the Dusky Venus hides the debasement of the black woman as a prostitute; and the Black Apollo is seeking revenge on the white man. It is not so much that love breaks down barriers and unites human beings as that racial ideologies extend their conflicts even in love's embraces. (1972, 188, 197)

In the layering and sedimentation of beliefs about sexual freedom and national belonging in the United States, one will detect ambiguities and disjunctions analogous to those between sexuality and freedom delineated by Bastide, as well as the persistence of racist ideology. After noting how leading writers (Thoreau, Whitman, Melville) in the nineteenth century all embraced "Manifest Destiny" in their effort to assert a distinctive masculine, white American identity, Larzer Ziff comments on the often unacknowledged intertwining of sexual and racial issues: "Abolitionists recognized that the abstract principle of love for one's fellows that fueled their cause also implied greater sexual freedom; at the same time, one of their favorite images was that of the South as a great brothel" (1981, 170). Such ironies and paradoxes can only be untangled by a materialist analysis of how commodity exchange has de-eroticized the body even as it affords subjects the illusion of indulging the pleasure-principle and instinctual drives through techniques of repressive de-sublimation (Marcuse 1968a).

Purification Trauma

Why such an analysis is blocked may be clarified by the reaction to a recent event. The bombing of the Federal Building in Oklahoma City 19 April 1995 was at first attributed to Muslim terrorists by CNN and other media. But as soon as suspects were arrested who turned out to be white men from Middle America, "freedom-loving" right-wingers (according to *Newsweek*, 1 May 1995), the opportunity to galvanize a nationalist consensus by way of a fixed external enemy uniting the country disappeared. This threat, however, was diagnosed as "sickness somewhere within the American family," editorialized *Newsweek*. "Right-wing groups are much harder to stereotype. . . . They look like mainstream Americans (white, male, rural, blue collar) and their self-proclaimed patriotism masks their sometimes treasonous intent" (Alter 1995, 55).

Staunchly convinced of the sacred constitutional right to bear arms so as to protect their liberties against an intrusive state, numerous "right-wing" militias and paramilitary groups across the continental United States claim to derive their raison d'etre from such founding texts as the Declaration of Independence, *Letters from an American Farmer* by Michel-Guillaume de Crevecoeur, *Democracy in America* by Alexis de Tocqueville, and others: the nation equals rugged white male individuals confronting the dangerous frontier, the "new man" apprenticed to the soil, battling savages and others with strange languages and religions to protect their freedom and private property (land, women, children). This foundational ideal, as noted earlier, originally springs from a double repression: the genocide of the American Indians and the dehumanization of the African slaves. From Frederick Turner's thesis of the Western frontier to President Kennedy's "New Frontier," such discourses do not directly manipulate consciousness but rather act through the mediation of institutions and relays of collective practices and sedimented habitus.

The discourse of American nationalism uses icons and fragments from the archive of public memory and anticipation, deploying scenes not just imagined but lived, witnessed, and recorded to construct the nation, "people like us." Nation thus signifies a community or (better yet) communion of individuals who share "our way of life," what always returns, more precisely our own way of organizing our common enjoyment. Conversely the "Other" becomes those who steal our enjoyment, or that surplus of our own enjoyment that we find unbearable and cannot acknowledge except by projecting it onto the Other via fantasy, hence the fear, loathing, and secret desire for the Other (Salecl 1994, 212). The discourse of the national imaginary (the nation as trope or constellation of figures) necessarily bears an essentializing telos, one that can alter or mutate according to the pressures of changing historical circumstances.

A brief historical excurses on the character of the nation-state is appropriate here. It may be useful to recall the metaphysics of the origin of the nation elaborated in Ernest Renan's 1882 lecture "What Is a Nation?" This may be considered one of the originary loci of nationalism conceived as a primitivist revolt against the centralized authority of modernizing industrial states. While Renan emphasized a community founded on acts of sacrifice and their memorialization, this focus does not abolish the fact that the rise of the merchant bourgeoisie marked the start of the entrenchment of national boundaries first drawn in the age of monarchical absolutism. The establishment of the market coincided with the introduction of taxation, customs, tariffs, and so on, underlined by the assertion of linguistic distinctions among the inhabitants of Europe. Michael Polanyi's thesis of *The Great Transformation* (1957) urges us to attend to the complexities in the evolution of the nation-state in the world system of commodity exchange. We also need to attend to Ernest Gellner's (1983) argument that cultural and linguistic homogeneity has served from the outset as a functional imperative for states administering a commodity-centered economy and its class-determining division of social labor.

Postcolonial critics subscribe to a poststructuralist hermeneutic of nationalism as a primordial destabilizing force devoid of rationality. In my view, this error is due to separating the ideological phenomenon of nationalism from the institutional fact of the state. While the formation of the nation-state in the centuries of profound social upheavals did not follow an undisturbed linear trajectory — we have only to remember the untypical origins of the German and Italian nation-states, not to speak of the national formations of Greece, Turkey, and the colonized peoples; and the formation of the U.S. nation-state on the dual economy of free and unfree labor—that is not enough reason to ascribe an intrinsic instability and belligerency to the nation as such. States may rise and fall, as the absolute monarchs and dynasties did, but sentiments and practices constituting the nation follow another rhythm or temporality not easily dissolved into the vicissitudes of the modern expansive state. Nor does this mean that nations, whether in the North or the South, exert a stabilizing and conservative influence on social movements working for radical changes in the distribution of power and resources. We need to distinguish the specific alignment of core and periphery nations at various historical moments in the development of capitalism.

We have coalesced at this point the formalistic definition of the nation as a historic construct with the nation as a protagonist in the narrative of capitalist development in its colonial/imperial phase. What role this protagonist has played and will play is now the topic of controversy. It is not enough to simply ascribe to the trading or commercial class the shaping of a new political form, the nation, to replace city states, leagues, municipal kingdoms, and oligarchic republics. In the United States, the plantation aristocrats and their descendants have contributed immensely to the shaping of the racial polity both before and after the Civil War. Why such "imagined communities" should serve as a more efficacious political instrument for the hegemonic bloc of property owners is the question.

One approach to this question is to apply dialectical analysis to the anatomy of the nation sketched thus far. Historians have described the crafting of state power for the new bourgeois nations in Enlightenment philosophy. Earlier Jean Bodin and Hugo Grotius theorized the sovereignty of the nation as the pivot of centralized authority and coercive power (Bowle 1947). The French Revolution posited the "people," the universal rights of man, as the foundation of legitimacy for the state; the people as nation, a historical act of constituting the polity, gradually acquires libidinal investment enough to inspire movements of anticolonial liberation across national boundaries. Its influence on the U.S. Constitution as well as on personalities like Sun Yat-Sen, Jose Rizal, and other "third-world" radical democrats has given the principle of popular sovereignty a "transnational" if not universal status (on Filipino nationalism, see San Juan 2000a). Within the system of nation-states, for Marxists, "recognition of national rights is an essential condition for international solidarity" (Löwy 1998, 59) in the worldwide fight for socialism and communism.

Now this universal principle of people's rights is generally considered to be the basis of state power for the modern nation, "the empowerment, through this bureaucracy, of the interests of the state conceived as an abstraction rather than as a personal fiefdom" (Ashcroft et al. 1998, 153). A serious mistake occurs when the nation and its legitimating principle of popular sovereignty becomes confused with the state bureaucracy construed either as an organ transcending the interest of any single class, or as the "executive committee" of the bourgeoisie. A mechanical, not dialectical, method underlies this failure to connect the ideology, politics, and economics of the bourgeois revolution. This quasi-Hegelian interpretation posits the popular will of the post-Renaissance nation-states as the motor of world expansion, of nineteenth-century colonialism. Instead of the substance of the "civilizing mission" being informed by the gospel of universal human rights, according to postcolonial orthodoxy, it is the ideology of national glory tied to "the unifying signifiers of language and race" that now impels the colonial enterprise.

So nationalism — the need to superimpose the unifying myths of the imperial nation-state — is generated not only by the bourgeois agenda of controlling and regulating the space of its market but also by the imperative of seizing markets and resources outside territories and peoples and in the process extending its political-ideological influence. Nationalism is then interpreted by postcolonial theorists as equivalent to colonialism; the nation is an instrument of imperialist aggrandizement, so that if newly liberated former colonies employ nationalist discourse and principles, they will only be replicating the European model whose myths, sentiments, and traditions justified the violent suppression of "internal heterogeneities and differences." The decolonizing nation is thus an oxymoron, a rhetorical if not actual impossibility. Again, this repeats the error of confusing core and periphery formations.

There is no single definitive conceptualization of the nation separate from the historically specific articulation of elements by the dominant social bloc in the struggle for hegemony. Culture, language, race, sexuality, territory, religion, local experience, economic association — none of these can be made essential ingredients of the nation apart from the antagonisms of classes and social groups. Objective factors are raw materials combined to fashion a national identity. As Gunter Minnerup reminds us, "The qualitative step that elevates regional, linguistic, cultural, racial, religious, economic and other identities to the level of 'the national' is their *politicization*, the desire to make them the basis of self-government" (1984, 118). The U.S. Constitution and the historical circumstances surrounding the founding of an independent nation-state attest to the politicization of race and implicitly of gender in the articulation of the national identity. The U.S. national imaginary is indivisible with the encounter of Europeans and indigenous peoples, slaves from Africa, Spanish settlers in the "New World, Asian laborers, as well as with refugees from the Cold War and other international conflicts involving the United States as a world power. In this encounter, what defines *patria*, or home, for the victorious conquerors is their own self-validating attributes of gender, kinship or parentage, skin color, and other inexorable "natural"or naturalizing markers demarcating them from the subjugated and subordinated peoples.

Contagion of the Nationalist Imaginary

In the standard archive, the U.S. national identity is usually defined as commitment to a corpus of beliefs comprised of the abstract ideals of liberty, equality, and republicanism (government on the basis of consent) (Gleason 1980, 31–32). Not through homogeneity by common descent, religion, or language (although the "English only" movement has valorized language as an essentializing quality) but by interpellation of subjects through texts/discourses is the national subject or citizen constructed, according to the *Harvard Encyclopedia of American Ethnic Groups*. In addition to this ideological underpinning, U.S. national identity is distinctive in its affirmation of its newness — a new order without precedent has been inaugurated in the "New World" — and its orientation toward the future. The new beginning was not just a "glorious heritage" but also "a sacred trust." These elements make up the "symbolic order" of U.S. nationalism, which is elaborated in a whole archive of practices and disciplinary regimes.

In 1964, Arthur Schlesinger Sr. traced elements of the national character to the settler's "adventurous" and "rebellious" stance that fostered individualism, the acquisitive spirit, work ethic, and the peculiar idealism of making money. With the growth of urban industrial society, Schlesinger believes that to preserve "the traditional spirit of self-reliance and free competition" (29), fundamental principles of the national ethos, citizens placed their duties to government above their private interests, as reflected in the widespread support for the New Deal during the Depression. This liberal "New Deal" version of U.S. nationalism whose resonance can be found in versions of communitarianism and fantasies of a "common culture" has roots in a Hegelian conception of the state as the embodiment of ethical reason. The ideas of American educators like William Mcdougall and Josiah Royce lurk behind John Foster Dulles's insistence that the United States represented the highest morality during the Cold War (Davis 1978, 35). With the state enforcing an exclusivist, purified concept of the nation, one can understand the anti-immigrant hysteria of the Palmer Raids (1919–1921) and the incarceration of more than 110,000 Japanese Americans during World War II. In those conjunctures, "law becomes reified as an end of human conduct" and "fascism in America" becomes "the form of law without its content" (Aronowitz 1970, 16).

In the nineties, however, the ideology of Keynesian liberal democracy seems to have lost the positive cathexis it once enjoyed. Richard Pfeffer provides a lucid exposition of liberalism as the ideological underpinning of American nationalism:

> The ideology and mythology of American society, which apply in variations to its central institutions where men and women work, are liberal. Liberal ideology is founded on individualism, competition, private ownership of the means of production, formal economic and political freedoms, procedural due process, constitutional rights, legal equality of opportunity, and formal democracy. . . . In its mythology American liberalism asserts that these ideals are being practiced in our society and that that practice in fact contributes to social and individual well-being. The reality is quite different from ideology and myth. Within the context of capitalism, which necessarily has nurtured liberalism, liberal concepts today serve to legitimate a social system that, despite some positive aspects, is on the whole quite destructive to social and individual well-being and poorly serves the majority of its members. This reality, like the ideology and mythology, exists in variations throughout

the society, but it is most easily comprehended in such institutions as factories. There, liberalism is daily exposed as a thinly veiled class dictatorship, which, often in subtle ways, dominates all areas of life in the United States. (1979, 215–16)

The decline of the U.S. economy and the sharp conflicts over the welfare state and its future — marked by signs of social decay, intense racist violence, violence of the right-to-life movement against pro-choice doctors and health workers (Eisenstein 1994), the debate over Affirmative Action, pornography, "undocumented aliens," and so on — have undermined the classic U.S. civil religion, especially the state as the embodiment of the nation. Versions of globalization theory as well as eclectic feminism have also cast a cloud on expressions of banal nationalism, although of course they do not interrogate the racial syndrome of citizenship and how the state's ideological apparatus constructs men and women differently.

In the 1820s and 1830s, a primordial American nationalism pervaded the country. The state articulated the ideals enshrined in the Declaration of Independence, the Constitution, the Bill of Rights, the belief in the singular redemptive mission of the United States vis-à-vis the corruption and decadence of Europe. Anglo-Saxon nativism asserted white supremacy over the lesser breeds — from the time of the 1838 "trail of tears" to the 1882 Chinese Exclusion Act and the 1924 Immigration Act based on the national origins quota system. Later on, from the gospel of "Manifest Destiny" (Horsman 1981) justifying its acquisition of colonies during the Spanish-American War (the Philippines, Puerto Rico, Cuba, Guam, Hawaii), to the role of guardian/defender of the "free world" against the "Evil Empire" of Soviet Communism and its satellites, the state incorporated essential ingredients in U.S. civil theology (Pease 1993). National unity founded on racial/sexist hierarchy unfolded in a narrative inherently Oedipal, naturalizing, and imperialist. This self-ascribed providential role that sustained pax Americana after World War II began to self-destruct with the rancorous divisions over military interventions in Indo-China, Iran, Grenada, El Salvador, and Nicaragua. Only with the ascendance of Reagan-style neoconservatism, the entrenchment of the "national security state," the collapse of state-bureaucratic "communism," and the victory in the Persian Gulf War was U.S. civil religion able to recover. This seems to reinforce Joe Feagin's thesis that nativism — the "one-way assimilation to an Anglo-Protestant core culture" — remains "the norm and reality for new immigrants" (1997, 352).

Despite the rightist resurgence, the postmodern fragmentation of the "body politic" continues to challenge the unitary state, as I noted at the outset. With such challenges to gendered and racialized statism as the ethnic revival, the various regionalisms, the resurgence of religious fundamentalism, and the intellectual predilection for historicist and even sectarian versions of multiculturalism, can we predict a withering away of the United States as a "nation-state" endowed with as much libidinal investment as during the time when the colonies revolted against the British monarchy?

In 1971, the international monetary system based on the identification of the dollar with gold ended. In the globalized milieu, it seems that the concepts/referents of state and nation have begun to blur, dissolving into cultural artifacts and expressions. For Etienne Balibar, "every social community reproduced by the functioning of institutions is imaginary" (Balibar and Wallerstein 1991, 93). Consequently, the national imaginary really engenders and reproduces the people (peoplehood), not the state. State sovereignty as territorial control needs to be distinguished from the nation as quasi-familial ideal of purity, eroticized habitat, fetishized scenarios of identification — in short, the national imaginary. Except for the only viable secessionary threat at present — that is, the Hawai'i sovereignty movement, a trend that may not decisively affect the hemispheric geopolitical integrity of the state — the centralizing state still commands effective hegemony. The mode in which U.S. nationalism manifests itself as a quasi-religious impulse follows a traditional pattern: a passionate, organic attachment to family, locality (Gemeinschaft), and other modes of group belonging such as voluntary associations like the armed militias of white males feeling beleaguered by what they consider anti-American forces that have taken over the state in order to confiscate their guns and deprive them of religious freedom (betokened by the suppression of the Branch Davidian cult at Waco, Texas, in 1993).

Anthropology views kinship and nationality as structured in analogous terms, although "loyalty to and love for one's country is the most generalized expression of diffuse, enduring solidarity" (Schneider 1977, 68). While kinship valorizes the particularistic, biogenetic criterion of solidarity, nationality for its part privileges the commitment to a code of conduct, a system of symbols, and affective meanings that comprise a culture. At this point, we begin to understand how the nation as artifact or style of inventing subjectivity shares affinities with the practices of representation associated with religion, kinship, and gender system. Unlike the competing logics of scientism or the transnational corporate firm, both nation and sexuality are not so much "imagined communities" (in Benedict Anderson's terminology) as "volatile sites for condensing and displacing ecstasies and terrors of political life" (Parker et al. 1992, 13).

Like racism, nationalism invariably assumes diverse masks and performs assorted functions. Of the Janus-faced character of nationalism, Anthony Smith notes its divisive and integrative, modernist and traditionalist aspects. This polyvocality derives from its origin in the articulation of the "messianic assimilationism" of the intelligentsia who cherish "the vision of fraternity among equals" with "the ethnicity solution" of reforming and elitist-minded revivalists who accentuate "cultural differentia so necessary to the *renovation* of the community and the restoration of dignity through secession" (1971, 256). In the context of the United States, "secession" translates into exclusion or expulsion of "aliens" and "strangers" deemed not belonging to the white Euro-American kind.

I adduce here one instructive specimen of textualizing U.S. nationalism as an oxymoron, a mode of sublimating assimilationism and renovation. In his standard reference work *America as a Civilization* (1987), Max Lerner defined the U.S. nation's social myth as inherent in the universal "psychic hunger to belong" (904) centered on the central U.S. historical achievement of an "open society." Lerner celebrates the "practical messianism" of the American character that informs its "Big Empire internationalism" (893). While boosting the future of American entrepreneurialism, Lerner looks backward to a vanished utopia of rural family harmony. Reflecting on the sexual/cultural revolutions in the sixties and seventies, Lerner laments the radical transformations of the family polity: "Cohabitation, early out-of-wedlock childbearing, postponed marriages, single-parent households, resort to outside child-care services, shifting partners — these were not the building materials for enduring family structures" (987). Believing that the patriarchal family is the "cultural envelope for selfhood and relationships," Lerner bewails the reduction of human sexuality to a matter of "life-style taste and choice" in a "more hedonic [*sic*] society, less restrained by its Puritan origins and traditions." In the struggles over the nature of family life, religion, morality, and the home, the resulting backlash to this anarchic and permissive milieu revolves around abortion (between the "right-to-life" and the "pro-choice" forces) and pornography.

With eros brought into the political arena, sexual, religious, and family passions now converge into a traumatic if delayed shock of recognition. The AIDS epidemic, Lerner continues his commentary, "threw a cordon of fear and danger around the sexual act, for heterosexuals as well as homosexuals. For what had been a hedonic society it undercut the celebration of Freud's 'pleasure principle' which had once conquered the United States more completely than any other culture of the West. It played havoc with both the 'modernization' and the 'Americanization' of sex" (1987, 989–90). However, the AIDS menace may have been neutralized in such films as *Ghosts* where safe sex and the stability of the heterosexual order are achieved through a skillful montage of fantasy, superficiality, and mystical experience. Eugene Victor Wolfenstein's remarks accentuate the role of the national imaginary: "National or political identity is far more totalizing. Although it does not go so far as to constitute the spirit of a people in an Hegelian sense, through group psychology it often approximates to the Hegelian word made flesh. It may be that the spirit of the nation is a fantasy, but that doesn't mean it isn't real" (1993, 284). What such cultural texts elicit is the conversion of the "unhappy consciousness" of the petit bourgeois spectator into the self-deluding "good conscience" of the average law-abiding citizen (McRobbie 1992).

Lerner's mainstream reaction has been proved alarmist and premature. In 1968, the pop sociologist Vance Packard noted that despite the challenge of humanistic liberalism, radicalism, and the "fun morality" espoused by Albert Ellis and the "sexual anarchy" of the French Rene Guyon and the British A. S. Neill, American society still subscribed to the codes of bourgeois morality and feminine respectability, to middle-class norms of sexual behavior and care of the body (for European analogues, see Mosse 1985). Even in the transitional mood of the sixties, U.S. civil religion still pivoted around "traditional repressive asceticism" centered on marriage and procreative sex, supplemented with "enlightened asceticism" in which self-mastery and self-control — emblems of Puritan virility and of "high culture" — are learned by disciplining the sexual urges. Meanwhile, "fun morality" shared with "alternative lifestyles" promising immediate self-fulfillment the status of highly sought-after commodities in the mass market — countercultural modes of acculturation to the normative ethos of late capitalism.

In 1970, in his widely read *The Pursuit of Loneliness*, Philip Slater comments, "Even the 'sexual revolution' has been contaminated by male preoccupations with competition and achievement" (101). Critiquing Dr. Spock's child-rearing precepts as responsible for feminine domesticity, Slater ascribes to this "maternal overload" the production of men "who are vain, warlike, boastful, competitive, sadistic, and skittish toward women" (73). Because of their "fear of losing self-control, of becoming dependent on women, of weakness," these maternally privileged men "often huddle together in male gangs" exemplified today by the all-male militias that vehemently attack the state. If this is true, then these armed nationalists owe American mothers a singular debt: the defeat of the Oedipal complex and of state-worship.

Narcissistic Impasse

About a decade after Slater's book, Christopher Lasch denounced the dominant "culture of narcissism" and its therapeutic claims by nostalgically evoking the old progressivist slogan of "Americanization" around the turn of the century. The "sexual revolution" and feminism have undermined the work ethic and helped usher a "new paternalism," Lasch argues. "Americanism" identified with Progressivism is, however, equivalent to beliefs and values of industrial civilization such as "a belief in order, rationality, and science; a respect for production, efficiency, power, discipline, and above all work; the need for planning, organization, and even bureaucracy and the state . . . ; an intense interest in mass culture or the culture of the masses; stress on cooperation, participation, the importance of the well-being of the community; a vision of Progress, especially under science" (Lasch 1979, 83). This metanarrative of modernization has now been bracketed by "third-world" revolutionary struggles and disrupted by feminists and other subaltern victims of Eurocentric instrumentalism. Historical "Americanism" may, however, be opposed to the "Americanization" that Lasch has in mind, for he yearns for a "new order" — certainly not an androgynous utopia — to resuscitate the energies and inspiration of the past, for example, loving memories of the exemplary morality of the American farmer (as extolled, for example, by Michael Chevalier in the 1830s). It appears then that Americans have lost their virile, pristine virtues; hence narcissism is diagnosed by Lasch as the real enemy of the nation.

Unfortunately Lasch's critique is misleading because it confuses the diverse phases of historical development. It misses the point that we no longer inhabit the stage of early laissez-faire, competitive capitalism. In that period after primitive accumulation when exchange-value becomes generalized, the anal personality of the mercantile bourgeoisie becomes confirmed in the separation of sexuality from love and work resulting from repression in the name of performance, competition, and maximization of profits. These processes also underwrite the script of the national creed centered on liberty, equality, and representative government — the juridical-political forms surrounding private property and commodity exchange as the content. In time, the changes in the mode of production generate qualitative transformations of social relations and mutations in the texture of everyday life. In the early thirties, Antonio Gramsci already predicted the clash between the anal character and the petty-bourgeois motivation underlying the bohemian avant-garde reaction against the factory system: "It seems clear that the new industrialism wants monogamy: it wants the man as worker not to squander his nervous energies in the disorderly and stimulating pursuit of occasional sexual satisfaction. . . . The exaltation of passion cannot be reconciled with the timed movements of productive motions connected with the most perfected automatism" (1971, 304–5). Reification based on the disciplined and regulated bodies of workers (exchanged for their labor-power) negates sex as, in Wilhelm Reich's terms, "a material want" (quoted in Ollman 1979, 167).

Sexual pleasure is tabooed for the sake of monogamous heterosexual intercourse. Thus, in Locke's philosophy, the primacy of the male-dominated family, the space in which women's sexuality and the use-value of her reproductive labor are controlled is designed to insure the preservation of private property and its transfer to definitely ascertainable heirs (L. Clark 1979, 36–37). With the rise of monopoly capitalism, however, the obsessional anal character is required not only to produce (in particular, weapons of mass destruction consumed by states) but also to consume; this syndrome of compulsive consumption enables the reproduction of capitalist relations. Sexuality is released/sublimated to serve the reproduction process. Reimut Reiche points out that the rigid functionalism of early capitalism, as evidenced in its fostering of thrift and the postponement of gratification, has given way to controlled desublimation (1971, 46–47). This linkage of sexuality (the pleasure principle) and the national economy immanent in the performance principle of the market, a nexus of forces insuring the stability/legitimacy of the nation-state, is theorized by Herbert Marcuse:

> Without ceasing to be an instrument of labor, the body is allowed to exhibit its sexual features in the everyday work world and in work relations. . . . This socialization is not contradictory but complementary to the de-erotization of the environment. Sex is integrated into work and public relations and is thus made more susceptible to (controlled) satisfaction. . . . The range of socially persmissible and desirable satisfaction is greatly enlarged, but through this satisfaction, the Pleasure Principle is reduced — deprived of the claims which are irreconcilable with the established society. Pleasure, thus adjusted, generates submission. (1968b, 70–72)

From this perspective, the "narcissism" of the sixties as well as the philistine evangelicalism of the eighties and nineties appear as structural features of the consolidating hegemony of consumer capitalism and its possibilities of discharging aggression. Civilization's discontents are then rendered starkly visible in the contradictory impulses condensed in postmodern cultural phenomena such as the cult of the singer Madonna.

Patriotic Gore

There was a time in U.S. history when the figure of the nation was made to coincide with the virile, military warrior and its critique of effete, decadent business civilization. In the 1890s, public personalities such as Theodore Roosevelt, Henry Cabot Lodge, and Brook Adams upheld a republican moralism associated with putative Anglo-Saxon qualities of courage that rejected vulgar moneymaking and late-Victorian complacency. A perception of the nation's fall into decadence stirred messianic vigilance.

Fearful of impotence and anxious about the sterile and stagnant milieu of fin de siècle United States, former general and also former president Benjamin Harrison called for universal military training in 1894 — a few years before the Spanish-American War and the conquest of overseas colonies — because "a free, erect, graceful carriage of the body is an acquisition and a delight. It has a value in commerce, as well as war" (Lears 1981, 116). The disciplined male body, endowed with the classic bourgeois virtues of order, efficiency, and productivity, becomes an instrument to rejuvenate the heroic will, infuse reality into anomic existence, and restore authenticity and wholeness to the fractured ego. Anglo-Saxonist nationalism channeled libidinal resources to accomplishing a project of elite class regeneration: "The acquisition of empire reinforced the self-confidence, the economic power, and the cultural authority of a bourgeoisie which felt threatened by internal decay and lower-class discontent. . . . And the stage was being set for the full-scale militarism of the later twentieth century: the interests of the dominant class were being redefined as an ever-expansive 'national interest,' global and virtually limitless" (Lears 1981, 117).

We move to the era of Vietnam, Contra-Gate, and the Gulf War, especially the rediscovery of the "boy eternal" via the public spectacle of techno-muscular male bodies, "narcissistic and homoerotic" (Boose 1993, 588). What is at stake in all the contemporary culture wars and partisan debate on the "Contract with America" is American masculinity, the synecdoche of national honor, which was allegedly humiliated in Vietnam and Iran but eventually vindicated in the Gulf War.

The dogma of Anglo-Saxon supremacy, of course, dates back to the rise of English nationalism in the sixteenth and seventeenth centuries during the rivalry with Spain and other absolute monarchies. In the next two centuries, this myth became conflated with republicanism, democracy, Protestantism, laissez-faire capitalism, progress, and empire. It served as the fountainhead of "Manifest Destiny," the doctrine of white supremacy and of American warriors as the "chosen people" destined to rule and civilize "others" (Smedley 1993, 191). Amy Kaplan (2000) has documented how the theatricalized spectacle of white masculinity in the novels of the 1890s anticipated the performative male hero redeemed by female spectators as he "romanced" the "New Empire" of the twentieth century. In its historical and fictive genealogy, the diacritic of American national identity exhibits both racialized and sexualized dimensions.

Only after World War I was the hubris of the "civilizing mission" displaced by the Anglo-Saxon ethnocentrism that flared up during the 1870s and, with Wilsonian propaganda, equated "America" with "democracy." While there may not be any single national narrative or collectively sanctioned trope for the U.S. nation, whether that of the pioneering "American Adam" roaming the virgin frontier or the "pastoral myth" of the solitary, self-reliant cowboy, the valorization of canonical authors like Emerson and Hawthorne since the study of American literature became institutionalized suggests the power of a masculinist white supremacy embedded in the heart of the program to construct an American civilization as the "free world's" bulwark against communism (Shumway 1994, 124–26). The anticommunist crusade inflected the messianic charge to build "the City on the Hill" and redeem the fallen wilderness — a site now occupied by "internal colonies" of people of color in revolt against colonizing settlers and intrusive self-righteous missionaries.

The U.S. national imaginary underwent sexual polarization right from the beginning. While Miss Liberty (with torch and book, as Kafka conjured her in the novel *Amerika*), an early icon of the new nation, gained immense popularity for countless immigrants fleeing the feudal-authoritarian milieu of Europe, it was the male Uncle Sam that after the Civil War became the quasi-official personification of the nation-state. Uncle Sam incarnated not the government but the state conceived as "a great overarching, nonideological abstraction, the 'we-ness' of a complex, centralized, deracinated modern society" (Zelinsky 1988, 26). Uncle Sam shared the connotations of fatherly wisdom, masculine maturity, and independence associated with George Washington, Abraham Lincoln, Andrew Jackson, Buffalo Bill, and other folk heroes. All imagery of motherhood and feminine activism has been purged from the pantheon of national heroes, even though (as in third-world nationalist movements) women may still be regarded as "bearer of the community's memory and children" (Enloe 1989, 55).

Gendered interrogation of U.S. national identity dates back to the "Second Great Awakening" (1795–1835), the religious revival in which women assumed status as performers of "good works" and personal witness. Women became activists also in the abolitionist movement and in labor organizing in the New England textile mills in the 1830s. Patriarchy was questioned in 1848 at Seneca Falls, where the first Women's Rights Convention was held, and then challenged in 1851 by Sojourner Truth's indignant cry of "Ain't I a woman?" and later by Emma Goldman and Mother Jones in the early decades of the twentieth century. Three strands (movements divided into the white middle class, working-class women, and black women) converged in the civil rights struggles of the sixties. In 1968 we witness hundreds of women in the antiwar movement marching to the Arlington National Cemetery to stage "The Burial of Traditional Womanhood" (Zinn 1980, 497). But the U.S. nuclear family continues to be governed by white males as a castelike body. To sustain capitalism, the social construction of gender is imperative; patriarchal authority is needed to regulate the reproductive labor of women and the property relation embodied in the family and marital relationship. It is also required to inculcate "the ethos of possessive individualism" and the norm of competitive performance indispensable for reproducing the hierarchical relations of production and reproduction (Edwards et al. 1972, 354–55). The nation under white patriarchy guarantees the reproduction of the "American Dream of Success" and its efficacy in fulfilling each individual's longing for transcendence (material success is one form) that is renewed by immigration and the notion of ethnic/cultural pluralism as distinctive of the "American Way of Life."

Chauvinist Feminism

In spite of the resistance to the gains made by the women's liberation movement in the last four decades, Americanization is undeterred in deploying symbols of white women's "liberation" to project the liberal capaciousness of the state. Such symbols are, of course, incorporated in a co-optive or recuperative way and harnessed to promote the interests of transnational corporations (Sklar 1995). Meanwhile, women continue not only to mark and reproduce ethnic/racial boundaries but also to define citizenship by their roles in the family and in other state ideological apparatuses.

Recent developments point to the new modes of sexualizing national identity. In her comments on "The American Woman Soldier" in *The Morning After* (1993), the feminist scholar Cynthia Enloe reminds us that in the constitution of the American self, the image of the "professionalized, militarized woman patriot" after the Gulf War has become pivotal to the goal of unfixing the masculinized hubris of the American military and of rallying disaffected but not ideologically antagonistic women to support the state. This may also be interpreted as one way of resolving the crisis of masculinity in the forties and fifties when the traditional organization of the family gave women enormous power over the lives of children, resulting in "momism" and the mother-induced immaturity of males (Epstein 1995, 250). With the traditional family based on the male wage in eclipse, the ascendance of homosexuality as a major social force, and the questioning of gender roles, it seems that the image of the woman-soldier/patriot can be commodified without too much threat to the patriarchal regime.

Why was this sectarian, exclusivist construction of the feminine accepted by the public and even by some liberal feminists? The gendered stake of the Gulf War inheres not so much in the claim of liberating helpless Kuwait and curbing the evil Saddam Hussein as in certain assumptions about normative values that Enloe lucidly spells out: "Many Americans appear to view war as the institution where more than in any other, (a) the state and the nation converge, and (b) that convergence is suffused with both organized violence and selfless sacrifice. Violent sacrifice under state discipline in the name of the nation — this seems to get very close to what many Americans still today, at the dawn of the post-Cold War era, understand to be the essential criterion for first-class citizenship" (1993, 202). In this context, Fredric Jameson's insights in his meditation on the country's situation during and after the Gulf War are relevant: "To be anti-American from our view is not a matter of healthy national independence, but rather of evil: think of those things you would have to be 'the enemy' of — democracy, freedom, elections, etc. . . . the narrative is thus fairly written in advance, and its moral is not morality but autarchy and self-determination. . . . Perhaps some new alternative Utopian vision, politically more adequate and acceptable than either nationalism or fundamentalism, may now slowly begin to emerge" (1991, 146).

One explanation for this consensus on gendered and racialized patriotism lies in the persistence of the divide between civil society and state as the legitimating framework of liberal feminism. Carole Pateman has demonstrated how the division of the public (male) from the private (female) realm anchors sexual difference and engenders the patriarchal division of labor "not only in the conjugal home between the (house)wife and her husband, but in the workplace of civil society" (1988, 135). As long as this hiatus between the domestic sphere and the civil arena continues, national identity will remain sexualized as well as racialized, given the inverse modeling or analogizing of the bourgeois sexual contract (marriage, prostitution) on the relations between African slaves and Euro-American slave owners. The nation thus endures as a patriarchal white supremacist sovereign parasitic on the multiplication of heterogeneous forms of racial and sexual differences according to varying needs, limitations, and possibilities.

We might backtrack a little bit and contextualize the recent vicissitudes of masculinized nationalism. It used to be the consensus that the gendered politics of the Cold War coincided with the rise of the "national security state," the militarization of third-world societies at the behest of Washington, and the demonology of the communist threat. Not only women but everyone had been conditioned to feel the need to be protected by the gigantic weapons buildup and by sons and husbands in uniform. Wives of soldiers as well as mothers were trained to accept extra duties of household maintenance to safeguard the country from the enemies of democracy and freedom. Enloe clarifies the linkage of sexuality, gender, and doctrinaire anticommunism during the last three decades:

> The Cold War was a thicket of gendered relationships that had to be either reshaped or entrenched. Often those gendered politics of national security were played out under the glow of public celebration or the harsh light of public scrutiny. Usually they occurred within ordinary households. Women tried to figure out whether being a good mother meant waving a tearful though proud goodbye to a son going off to do his military service or hiding him from the army's recruiters. Men tried to suppress fears of emasculation when denied public roles in their country's political life or else took a manly pride in being allowed into the inner sanctum of their state's national security bureaucracy. Government officials devised occasionally uneasy relationships with church officials so that they could collaborate in the entrenchment of patriarchal family values. American girls dressed their Barbies in the latest doll fashion, an Air Force dress uniform, while their Yugoslav cousins stifled yearnings for degenerate Barbies of their own. (1993, 18)

The vindication of male honor springs from women's gaze nourished in the private or domestic realm where women exercise the role of custodians of the icons of solidarity, moral community, lineage, and so on. Thus whatever individual adjustments are made, the erotic investment in the romance of the nation's global supremacy and its redemptive mission remains integral to the sense of belonging and the uninterrupted reproduction of class warfare in a civil society held together by the imperial state.

Paradigm Retrieval

We have noted so far how the intersection of race, nationality, and gender presents a complex symbiotic if not synergistic totality. Nationalism and sexuality, categories from seemingly incompatible spheres of quotidian existence, appear to be intimate bedfellows rather than strangers in our understanding of the shaping of modernity. In his provocative research, George Mosse pointed out the historically defined relationship between nationalism and respectability, the latter referring to "decent and correct" manners as well as the proper attitude to sexuality. In Europe, specifically, the ideal of manliness — strength of body and mind — served as the foundation for the self-definition of bourgeois society and the national ideology; it symbolized the nation's "spiritual and material vitality . . . invoked to safeguard the existing order against the perils of modernity" that threatened blurring the distinction between the normal and the abnormal (1985, 23). Women, by contrast, functioned as the vehicle of the national mystique, standing for "immutability rather than progress, providing the backdrop against which men determined the fate of nations." Our concern here is whether this paradigm applies also to the origin and development of U.S. nationalism, its genealogy and metamorphosis, particularly in the context of debates on the centrality of race in the U.S. social formation. It will become evident that in the constellation of U.S. civil religion — concerns and scenarios of public memory and desire that enable the production of the abstract entity we call *nation* — problems of oppression based on sexuality and gender cannot be grasped fully without its complicity with racism and class exploitation.

In the national imaginary at the heart of the majoritarian consensus, the telos of American identity inheres in the paradox of anticipating the future by recycling the past. This mystique of innovation and abstraction, valorized as "creative destruction," relies on a methodological individualism parasitic on technology and the competitive ravaging of the environment. It has so far depended on the articulation of a masculinist/ patriarchal model of agency rooted inter alia in the historical myths of "newness," the exceptional future-oriented destiny of the United States, the challenge of the Western virginal frontier, and military supremacy. Such myths are framed within the ethos of a predatory individualism that has been expressed in various semantic modalities and contexts: nativism, Anglo-Saxon racial supremacy, "Manifest Destiny," defender of the "free world" against the "Evil Empire" (Soviet Union, China), and lately neosocial Darwinism shrouded with a pseudonuminous aura. Patricia Williams distills the ineluctable aporia of national self-aggrandizement evinced in "the fraternal bliss of romanticized racism, in which professions of liberty and inseparable union could simultaneously signify and even reinforce an 'American' national identity premised on deep social division" (1998, 258).

In neoliberal discourse, nationalism is sometimes differentiated from patriotism, the latter alluding to the glorification of a unique American heritage and destiny. Some examples may be illuminating here. Michael Kammen points to the motivation behind Tom Wesselmann's series of paintings called *Great American Nude* (1957–1965) and Larry Rivers's deliberate juxtaposition of the nude and the American flag. Of Wesselmann's painting, Kammen is excited about the pictorial representation of nudes — "available, wanton, and commercial" — since they epitomize a "nostalgic patriotism" free of "aggressive nationalism." Here is Kammen's commentary:

> Wesselmann's *Great American Nude #4* incorporates familiar icons — Gilbert Stuart's portrait of Washington, early American wallpaper, the flag and the pineapple (customary symbol of hospitality) — as a means of insisting upon the Americanness of this nude. . . . The nude is very pink and presents herself quite wantonly to George Washington's seemingly indifferent gaze. His coolness oddly offsets her provocative eroticism, but the rationale involves more than mere balance. The vulnerable woman, presented so explicitly as a sex object, dominates the foreground and therefore the present. George Washington and his early American accessories are all located in the background, and hence in the past. If the painting seeks to be American, it is also explicitly a statement about change over time and cultural discontinuity. (1991, 649)

One does not need acute deconstructive ingenuity to see here the instrumentalization of the white female body, however liberated, to accentuate presentism in the most literal sense. But the effect is ironic: the sense of the contemporary is parasitic on the perception of the past. All the details reinforce the American nation as the identifying framework for apprehending the nude, whose synecdochic value depends precisely on a metonymic chain of meanings. Thus, instead of patriotism eclipsing nationalism, nationalism of a narrowly selective ethnicity predominates. The social physiognomy of the American nation, its architectonics and cartography, arises from class struggle here as everywhere else. Background displaces foreground in a semiotic turn that Kammen fails to notice, thus restoring the status of the great white father, this time looking much more insouciantly patriarchal.

In the present neoconservative dispensation, anticommunist civil religion has been displaced by coded signifiers like "family values," restoration of motherhood, "the right to life," civic responsibility, and so on, all counterpointed by a revanchist nativism hostile to the alleged perversions ascribed to aliens, immigrants, and people of color in general. American self-identification thus stages a spectacle of consensus in which sexuality and difference are used to sublimate issues of class and race in order to project an "American" essence that establishes a ratio of equivalence among the white population and a logic of dominance over "Others," mostly people of color, in a world system of transnational rivalry for recognition, wealth, and power. While this nationalism may be, like others in history, a "transcendental illusion" claiming to have direct access to "the Thing," as Slavoj Žižek (1993) contends, there may be contained in it undamaged elements of the "utopian narratives of possible but failed alternative histories" that question its self-evident coherence and render it vulnerable to the antagonisms that sustain it, the play of contradictions that serves as its ultimate condition of possibility.

In the wake of the "Contract with America" and its variants, we enter a period where U.S. civil religion and its fate is played out in the plot of exacerbated class war and its systemic ramifications. But this war, as the polemical exchanges in the public sphere demonstrate, is disguised as a return to primordial American values of hard work, individual liberty (right to bear arms), refusal of "Big Government" intrusion into private lives, and so on. Racializing schemes (for example, meritocracy) are deployed to pit one group against another. Attacking basic constitutional and civil rights especially of the disadvantaged through the abolition of Affirmative Action in employment and education, the neoconservative regime seeks a restoration of a version of the "Victorian Age" in this era of disaggregated global capitalism: restoration of the death penalty, subjugation of women (cut off from Aid to Families with Dependent Children), child labor, immigrant servitude, oppression of lesbians and gays, destruction of labor unions, the unrelenting attack on the environment and the arts. Vowing to cut billions of tax dollars for social services and give more money to the Pentagon, as well as handouts and tax breaks to military profiteers and corporations, the "compassionate conservativism" of the free marketeers aims to destroy the fabric of social services and civil rights for people of color gained in the last sixty years of "welfare state" reforms.

The turn to the right far in excess of the banalities of the old "Moral

Majority," a turn that might conceivably herald an authoritarian, neofascist governance, has been signaled more egregiously by the return of a rehabilitated Social Darwinism. We see this in books such as Charles Murray and Richard Herrnstein's *The Bell Curve*, Robert Wright's *The Moral Animal*, and the prodigious writings of Huntington, D'Souza, and others. It might be useful to recall that Woodrow Wilson, who urged the principle and right of self-determination on all nations, believed that Social Darwinist laws governed international relations. This is the framework that explains Harry Truman's apology that "the Open Door policy is not imperialism, it is free trade" (Jones 1970, 236). Today the legitimation of social decay evidenced in homelessness, criminality, drug addiction, rampant impoverishment of African Americans and other people of color, and so on, invokes genetics as well as a theory of natural selection (adapted from the positivist sociology of Herbert Spencer) as unquestioned axioms of explanation (Cowley 1995; Teitelbaum 1976, 8–11). Even antiporn feminism and chastity education resort to this revival of biological determinism repudiated long ago. It informs the "difference" feminism that upholds family values and "right to life," a modern version of the Victorian ideology of separate spheres (Tanenbaum 1995).

Annunciation

Nationalism thrives on the naturalization of the sexual/racial division of labor. This entails the bifurcation of public and private domains, the relegation of women to the private domestic sphere, and their confinement there despite reforms and accomodations at moments of social emergency and global crisis. Examining the linkage between women and the nation-state, Floya Anthias and Nira Yuval-Davis demonstrate how women play decisive roles in the reproduction of national, ethnic, and racial categories, as well as state practices involving citizenship, immigration, and so on. Not only are women reproducers of members of ethnic collectivities and transmitters of their cultures; they also reproduce the boundaries of ethnic/national groups. Women perform centrally "as signifiers of ethnic/national differences — as a focus and symbol in ideological discourses used in the construction, reproduction and transformation of ethnic/national categories" (1994, 313).

It may not be inappropriate to speculate here that U.S. "civilization" today finds in the legendary "expenditures" of superstar Madonna Ciccone the erotic representation of Social Darwinism as the dominant national ethos. Her casual utterances are registered with aphoristic resonance, for example: "Power is a great aphrodisiac, and I'm a very powerful person," "It's a great feeling to be powerful . . . I think that's just the quest of every human being: power," "I'm tough, ambitious, and I know exactly what I want. If that makes me a bitch, okay" (Andersen 1991, vi, 54, 336).

Analogous to the resolution of contraries in "melting-pot" assimilative discourse, Madonna now reconciles the thematic oppositions in popular culture: in the classical Western film (morally pure individualist rooted in nature versus evil savages or degraded urban intruders), in the detective story, horror movies, science fiction films, and social melodrama (Cawelti 1976). Her biographer says that "millions pray at the altar of Madonna, Our Lady of Perpetual Promotion," "the smartest businesswoman in America" according to *Forbes* magazine (Andersen 1991, 375–79). This "Material Girl" has now totally replaced the brainless and docile Marilyn Monroe, the Playboy Ideal, with her own artifices of idiosyncratic parody and scandalizing pastiche (for example, "Like a Virgin," "Like a Prayer"). With her ambiguously nuanced and polyvalent performances, Madonna represents the nation as unfixed, unstable, and protean, thus allowing the dialectic of unity and difference to operate and grip the fantasies of millions. From the perspective of our topic, the Madonna phenomenon is a genuinely sexualized-nationalized simulacrum that nevertheless gestures to a referent, an old friend of ours: commodity-fetishism.

In *Truth or Dare*, angered by the Canadian censorship of "sacrilegious acts" in her Blond Ambition tour, Madonna waves the flag and boasts that in the United States she enjoyed unequalled freedom of expression, making her the most effective messenger of American "exceptionalism." National chauvinism and universal commodification cohabit together in Madonna's intuitive mapping of the world. Mixing messages of "safe sex" and promiscuity, Madonna is credited too with the exercise of "gender-free sex," blurring the male/female boundaries by flirting with bisexuality, multiple partners, cross-dressing, sadomasochism, and other permutations of forms of sexuality in her immensely popular MTV performances.

Arguing for a negotiated, oppositional semiotics, John Fiske discovers in Madonna's figure a politics of resistance: Madonna's image is "not a model meaning for young girls in patriarchy, but a site of semiotic struggle between the forces of patriarchal control and feminine resistance, of capitalism and the subordinate" (1993, 160). Madonna's exaltation of sexual-physical pleasure has nothing to do with men: "In choosing the navel upon which to center it, she is choosing a part of the female body that patriarchy has not conventionally sexualized for the benefit of the male" (1993, 162). Such speculations seem to tax credibility and confound any attempt at discriminating between different categories of power, between levels of analytic conceptualization, between individualist resistance and substantive political transformation of historically specific conditions for large embattled collectivities. Notwithstanding the threats posed by this style of cultural studies (discussed below in chapter 6), the status quo remains unchanged.

Postmodernist nationalism has arrived. Baudrillard reinscribes Madonna's postmodern stylistic register — waning of affect, loss of depth and critical distance, heterogeneity, absence of difference — in the new erotic culture he finds in the United States. This culture is distinguished by the questioning of sexual difference, of one's sexual identity amid the mixing of genders and genres. We encounter in Madonna's performance the search for a gender model or generic formula precipitated by the dissolution of the meaning/value of seduction, difference, sexuality itself, which is in the process of being replaced by a model/ideal of performance and of the genetic fulfillment of one's own desires: "After a triumphalist phase, the assertion of female sexuality has become as fragile as that of male sexuality. . . . The outer signs of masculinity are tending towards zero, but so are the signs of femininity. . . . No longer explosive figures of sex and pleasure, those new idols [including Madonna] pose for everyone the question of the play of difference and their own lack of definition" (1998, 46–47). Indeed, Madonna is the climax of the itinerary of U.S. nationalism from the self-love of a people with a divinely ordained mission — how far we have traveled from Miss Liberty and Washington and Lincoln to a transnational, cosmic gospel:

the American Dream of Success as the will-to-global power, the nation finally dissolving into the mirage of an all-encompassing, evangelical, charismatic exchange-value. Disavowing any sublimation in a futurist frontier or deterritorialized New World, this apotheosis occurs by the diktat of the World Bank and the International Monetary Fund.

Notwithstanding the success of middle-class feminism and its tokenized representatives, gender subordination along racialized class lines flourishes and intensifies. With the neoconservative evisceration of civil rights, we enter a period of uneven retrenchment and reaction. My conviction is that the links among racism, national identity, and gender inequality cannot be ruptured unless we reinstate cardinal principles that not only analyze the overdetermined social conditions today but also alter them in a democratic-socialist direction. I have in mind not the postmodernist doctrines of the incommensurability of differences, nomadic subject-positions, performative and border-crossing selves, ludic hybridity, parodic cyborgs, and so on, but rather the cautionary proposals (especially those addressing the private/public binarism) offered by Frigga Haug for a socialist women's politics. Where the "pre-understanding" axiom of class-struggle had been reduced before to one element of identity, as in neoliberal social-movement formulas of "intersection of gender, race and class," or flattened to classism in nomadic subject positions, cyborgs, or parodic impersonations, all of which easily slide into national citizenship discourse, Haug concentrates on the foundational support of reification and commodity-exchange, the public/private dichotomy:

> Everything that passes for the personal, the private sphere, is so inextricably interwoven with power that it functions as the breeding ground for the maintenance of existing social and political structures. The separation of different spheres, of politics and private life is itself a manipulation of power, and its consequences, including the very existence of professional politicians, constitute a division of labour which makes it impossible even technically for us to make a natural transition from the private realm into public life. The abolition of hegemony is a programme which must extend down to the smallest details of private life, only then is it possible to wage a radical, committed campaign on a mass basis and to transform our own conditions of life. (1992, 172–73)

This revision of materialist standpoint philosophy can frame future discussions of how to engage the classic antinomies of agency and structure, theory and praxis, in politically constructive and feasible ways.

Draconian Impersonations

The power of hegemonic nationalist discourse is often traced to its effective manipulation of the shibboleths of democracy and freedom. Around the world, Hollywood films, McDonalds, and other typical artifacts and idioms of U.S. popular culture proclaim themselves as universal and cosmopolitan, as inclusive as the World Showcase in Disney World. These global flaggings of U.S. nationalism project banal "Americanness" in sports, music, commodities, and so on, as semantic signs of goodness, reason, individual liberty, and progress (Billig 1995). By contrast, U.S. national pride, the claim of being No. 1 — both the Establishment variety and its inflections by the Aryan Nation and other right-wing militia groups — stems from its promise not just to satisfy the intense craving for knowledge about the ties between bodies and minds, but more crucially to assure and guarantee the security and order of the system in which they have profound libidinal and symbolic investments. That is the system of white supremacy whose boundaries are marked by class, racial, sexual, and gender markers of identity and belonging. The stakes for the majority of poor working whites are the illusion of being in control and the assurance of enjoying virility and purity. In *Race and the Education of Desire*, Ann Laura Stoler remarks how the U.S. civil rights movement resituated "racism as inherent to the inclusionary myths and exclusionary practices of democracy and freedom" (1995, 24).

Immigration enshrines the illusion of liberty and rational control underlying white patriarchal racism. Based on the historical record, immigration has always subserved the needs of the economy for the control of the labor supply at any given time. But as any process is overdetermined by contradictory factors, the immigrant paradigm operates in response to the ideological and political imperatives of the corporate elite. Quotas are shuffled and reassigned periodically according to electoral opportunism and ethnocentric calculation. As I noted in my previous book *Beyond Postcolonial Theory* (1998a), the manipulation of immigration laws and procedures has perennially contributed to a revitalization of the racial polity. Of pivotal importance to the renewal of the racism syndrome are themes of laissez-faire competition, individual immigrant success, and neo-Social Darwinism that are integral to the construction of an American national identity founded on white supremacy (Mills 1999). In sum, the fabled trope of the "melting pot" gave way to a Manichean Cold War psychosis — "It became necessary to destroy the town [Ben Tre, Vietnam) to save it," according to the U.S. military (Loewen 1995, 241) — followed by a paranoiac "clash of civilizations" amid celebrations of a multicultural America.

Multiculturalism in the realm of civil society has been proposed as a substitute for obsolete "melting-pot" assimilationism (discussed below in chapters 4 and 5). Corollary to this is the highly touted concept of civic or republican nationalism. Conceived as a framework for harmonizing ethnic differences, this genre of white supremacy is bound to reproduce the racialization of identity and the processes of stigmatization and marginalization witnessed in the genocide-ridden formation of the U.S. racial polity. Others who are constituted as different, inferior, or subordinate are then stipulated to be the law-determined subjects of the republic; these Others are excluded or exteriorized in order to establish the boundaries of the nation-state. In the process, a fictive ethnicity of the civic nation as its primordial guarantee emerges to validate its legitimacy and naturalness. Fictive or symbolic ethnicity becomes the warrant for the racializing criterion of descent. "Ethnic status emerges," George Fredrickson explains, "when a group of people with a real or fictive common ancestry assert their dominance over those who are believed to be of a different and inferior ancestry. . . . The essential element is the belief, however justified or rationalized, in the critical importance of differing lines of descent and the use of that belief to establish or validate social inequality" (2000, 84–85).

What becomes clear after further analysis of the theory of civic nationalism qualified by cultural pluralism is its constitutive assumption of race as a valid premise. In these constitutive strands of the national identity and ethos, the necessary element is racial stratification, the sociopolitical construction of racial hierarchy. In this context, all questions of citizenship and individual liberties ultimately hinge on the understanding of "race" and its protean ideological guises, together with their deployment in various political and ideological practices of the state and civil society. Although chattel slavery was abolished, "wage slavery" is still with us. As George Jackson sums up in his brilliant treatise *Blood in My Eye*, "Racism is a fundamental characteristic of monopoly capital" (1972, 157). I am not denying progress on the civil rights front and other Keynesian reforms. However, as the legal scholar Lani Guinier argues, race continues to be an organizing principle of the nation-state. She holds that "majority rule is not a reliable instrument of democracy in a racially divided society. . . . In a racially divided society, majority rule may be perceived as majority tyranny" (1995, 207). Race, then, is required for identity construction while an unacknowledged class war intensifies (Gran 1993; Johnston 1999).

Even if race as idea becomes problematic, racism as social practice endures. While vestiges of pseudoscientific racism still exist, the political use of race as a biological or anthropological concept is no longer tenable. Ever since I came to this country in 1960, people have always asked me without hesitation: "Where are you from? Where do you come from?" Spatial origin acts here as a stand-in for descent, heredity, or some kind of naturalized provenance. On second thought, the pattern of questioning may be diagnosed as a symptom of the need to affirm a measure of common value or sense of sharing/belonging (via acts of exclusion) as the majority of ordinary citizens struggle to find their bearings in the late-modern milieu of alienation and reification. Identity politics has been resurrected, transmogrified, and overlaid with multiculturalist aura and postcolonial mystique.

The twentieth century began with a reassertion of an imperial teleology as realized in the spectacle of U.S. military forces seizing or policing territories in Asia, the Pacific, and the Caribbean inhabited by peoples with their own singular cultures, economies, and histories. State-funded experts claim that the rewards of modernization compensated for their loss of sovereignty. The Spanish-American War inaugurated the United States assuming full-fledged imperial status, a global power that after World War II would displace its old European contenders and impose a pax Americana (through the Bretton Woods Agreement, U.N. multilateral agencies, and so on) of the free market on the ruins of fascist Germany and Japan. In the ensuing Cold War, this peace also rested on a neo- (not post)colonial discourse in which the United States legitimized its mastery of the "free world" in the crusade against communist despotism. But, as "third-world" critics such as Frantz Fanon, Che Guevara, Walter Rodney, and others have argued, this hegemony over nation-states (especially among formerly colonized and now neocolonized countries) is always already predicated on the continuation of the European narrative and vision of world domination, on white supremacy. This applies equally to the North American "internal colonies."

W. E. B. Du Bois questioned the presumed universality of American nationalism when he wrote in 1945, in an essay entitled "Human Rights for all Minorities," that black people in the United States were "a nation without a polity, nationals without citizenship." Liberal academics today condemn any talk about national autonomy, collective rights, or empowerment of communities, as inimical to the unity and stability of the country. The "national question" involving people of color in the United States, which may be the key to unlocking the race enigma, remains unanswered by all participants in the culture wars, by deconstructionists, cynical fence-sitters, and law-and-order folks alike.

Meanwhile, the theater of global ideological conflict now has been refurbished. Racism moves to center stage in a recasting of the Cold War as, to borrow Samuel Huntington's words, a "clash of civilizations." From this we can infer the future as the worldwide installation of apartheid, permanent segregation of North and South, bantustans and metropolis coexisting in uneasy equilibrium. We need not prophesy the advent of this coming "war" under the hegemonic oversight of transnational corporate business. It may already be here. It is no secret that we all live in one world where the World Bank and the International Monetary Fund occupy pride of place in the pantheon. We are confronted everyday in the media with scenes of ethnic cleansing, earlier in Bosnia and Kosovo, now Sierra Leone and Indonesia, all over what was formerly the Soviet Union, in Afghanistan, and in Latin America where the indigenous populations remain subjugated and marginalized. Racial antagonisms smolder in various parts of the world, including the metropolitan centers (Los Angeles, London, Paris, Berlin) and their comprador satellites.

Lacking any countervailing movement to enlarge civil to human rights for all, citizens or not, racism in the United States will continue to be intractable and irrepressible. It will in fact be reinforced (witness the burgeoning corporate industry of prison management) as long as reification, the despotism of commodity-exchange, guarantees class antagonisms and the administered fragmentation of social life. Social alienation underwrites racial apartheid. The imperial nation-state will guarantee its normalizing efficacy not for its own sake but in order to reinforce the sovereignty of capital. Contrary to globalization theorists, the nation-state and its will to homogeneity will survive, subsisting on the logic of racial, sexual, and cultural taxonomies required to maintain the asymmetrical distribution of social wealth and power. In brief, any theory of liberal nationalism ostracizes the ideals of equality and redistributive justice. I also hold that recognition of others as different but equal within the nation-state requires the moral and structural prerequisite of global equality, something inconceivable if not anathema in the globalized "free market" (Lichtenberg 1999).

Given the bloody encounters between Europeans and people of color in the North American landscape sketched earlier, the racialization of the American national identity will unfold in novel ways. However, it will recuperate the past so long as citizenship and individual rights are needed to legitimate private property. American nationalist discourse has historically been centered on defining citizenship based on graduated inclusions and contingent exclusions, a biopolitical management of social life that has used the hierarchization of moralities, competencies, codes of conduct, and other norms to regulate gendered and racialized bodies. One need only recall how the sexuality of slaves before the Civil War were racialized according to jurisprudential guidelines: slaves were considered property of the owner while their children belonged to others in the "free market" of circulating goods (including unfree labor). The normative and disciplinary mechanisms to quarantine Asian and Mexican labor also demonstrate a similar intentionality and effect. Racism as a scavenger or promiscuous discourse may indeed be diagnosed as "a very insistent desire for knowledge" (Balibar 1995, 200) about the connections between individual bodily appearance and the moral/intellectual dispositions of groups. Such a desire, however, begets invidious and murderous results only when institutional mechanisms (legal codes on citizenship rights and immigration, customs, religious practices, and hygienic rules) enable these bodies to perform for the governance of capital accumulation and its libidinal instrumentality. Such performativity, dramatizing the U.S. civil religion of white supremacy, proceeds undeterred today despite skirmishes with anarchist guerilla resistance and self-serving ludic trangressions.

CHAPTER 3

Allegories of Asian American Experience

Frantz Fanon said, "Each generation must, out of its relative obscurity, discover its mission, fulfill it or betray it." I think today part of the mission would be to fight against racism and polarization, learn from each other's struggle, but also understand national liberation struggles.
— Yuri Kochiyama, "With Justice in Her Heart"

One of the important lessons I learned through this involvement is the need to think dialectically, i.e., to recognize that in the course of any serious struggle new contradictions inevitably emerge, confronting us with new and more challenging contradictions and the need to create new visions.
— Grace Lee Boggs, *Living for Change*

Classic American nationalism finds its crucible in the ordeals of Asians whose pilgrimage to the "Gold Mountain" and its other incarnations defy Baedekers and guidebooks. Both space and time are scrambled in these Asian passages. The catastrophic fall of the region's financial market following the disintegration of Thailand and South Korea as the miracle NICs (Newly Industrializing Countries) or Asian "tigers" cannot but alter the parameters of theory and representation that engender and reproduce the image/knowledge of Asians inhabiting the North American continent. In a review of recent developments, Evelyn Hu-DeHart (1999) described the dual schematization of Asian positioning in the public sphere: either role models like Gary Locke, governor of Washington, and Bill Lann Lee, assistant attorney general; or John Huang and other Asians (like indicted physicist Wen Ho Lee) under suspicion or on trial for violations of the law. So far the epistemology of Ethnic Studies concerning Asian Americans or U.S. Asians (to use my alternative rubric) is circumscribed by the "model-minority" myth and the perennial "Yellow Peril" stereotype. Assimilationist ideology of late has been refurbished by a neoliberal policy of multiculturalism, affording us a schizoid if pragmatic optic to handle this racializing dilemma.

Mocking all hermeneutics of suspicion, the enigmatic superminority image of Asian Americans persists. Lest we be overwhelmed by all the predictions of impending absorption of U.S. Asians into the larger body politic, I offer as a kind of reality check this concluding observation of the U.S. Commission on Civil Rights in their 1992 report:

> The root causes of bigotry and violence against Asian Americans are complex. Racial prejudice; misplaced anger caused by wars or economic competition with Asian countries; resentment of the real or perceived success of Asian Americans; and a lack of understanding of the histories, customs, and religions of Asian Americans all play a role in triggering incidents of bigotry and violence. The media have contributed to prejudice by promoting stereotypes of Asian Americans, especially the model minority stereotype; by sometimes highlighting the criminal activities of Asian gangs; and by failing to provide the indepth and balanced coverage that would help the public to understand the diverse Asian American population. Furthermore, the media give little attention to hate crimes against Asian Americans, thereby hindering the formation of a national sense of outrage about bigotry and violence against Asian Americans, a critical ingredient for social change. (1992, 191)

That report has been updated and reinforced by the *1998 Audit of Violence Against Asian Pacific Americans* (1999) scrupulously prepared by the National Asian Pacific American Legal Consortium. It highlights the cases of Filipino American Joseph Ileto killed by an Aryan Nation follower, Japanese American Naoki Kamijima shot dead in Chicago, and Korean student Woon Joon Yoon slain by a fundamentalist white-supremacist group member, among myriad incidents. Are we faced with the old enigma, the "changing same"? In a revealing analysis of Judge Karlin's sentencing colloquy in the 1992 trial of Du Soon Ja (accused killer of Latasha Harlins) that inter alia sparked the Los Angeles "riots," Neil Gotanda (1995) found that old stereotypes are alive and well, fruitfully cohabiting with the new "model-minority" doxa. Amid the thoroughgoing reconfiguration of the planet's political/ economic map, why this persistence of a racializing syndrome targeting Asians?

Duplicitous Metaphysics

Let us review the demographic scene. By the year 2020, the population labeled "Asian Americans" in this country will number 20.2 million. The Asian Pacific American population increased from 1.5 million in 1970 to 8.8 million in 1994, with Filipinos becoming the largest component (more than 2 million, up from 1,406,770 in the 1990 Census Report [Gonzales 1993, 181]). In the year 2000, Asians and Pacific Islanders will total 12.1 million, about 4 percent of the total population. In California, the projection is that the number of Asians will grow from 2.9 million to 8.5 million in 2020. In the context of the manifold interethnic conflicts amid large-scale social crises, this increase is bound to complicate the multiplication of differences enough to confound taxonomists and the high priests of a normative "common culture."

Given the heterogeneity of the histories, stratification, and cultural composition of the post–1965 immigrants and refugees, all talk of Asian panethnicity should now be abandoned as jejune if not harmful speculation. Not so long ago, Roger Daniels (1993) stated the obvious: "The conglomerate image of Asian Americans is an illusion." This is more true today. No longer sharing the common pre–World War II experience of being victimized by exclusion acts, antimiscegenation laws, and other stratagems of racialization, Vietnamese, Kampucheans, and Hmongs have now diverged from the once dominant pattern of settlement, occupation, education, family structure, and other modes of ethnic profiling. After 1965, one can no longer postulate a homogeneous "Asian American" bloc without reservations. Fragmentation now characterizes this bloc even as new forms of racism totalize the incompatible subject-positions of each nationality. To use current jargon, the bureaucratic category "Asian American" (not even including "Pacific Islander") has been decentered by systemic contingencies. The putatively homogeneous inhabitants of the Asiatic "Barred Zone" (ascribed by the immigration laws of 1917 and 1924; see Reimers 1992) have been deconstructed beyond repair to the point where today, among postmodernist scholars, a cult of multiple and indeterminate subject-positions is flourishing — the Asian in the United States as a cyborg or borderland denizen genealogically akin to Aihwa Ong's (1999) parachute cosmopolitans.

We are still wrestling with the dangers of the ethnicity paradigm in which an essentializing use of culture, not race, predetermines class and status (Glazer and Moynihan 1975). A global imaginary is used to glamorize this outworn paradigm. As Werner Sollors (1986) puts it, ethnicity is not a matter of descent or lineage but "of the importance that individuals ascribe to it." Voluntarist nominalism begets notions of hybridity, "in-betweeness," ambivalence, and their kindred reifications. In effect, form (or social construction) determines content (political consequence). Numerous scholars (for example, Takaki 1987; San Juan 1992; Okihiro 1994) have already repudiated the fallacy of subsuming the diverse experiences of subjugation of people of color under the ethnic immigrant model that privileges the teleology of Eurocentric assimilation in defining the U.S. nation-state (see Janiewski 1995; Balibar and Wallerstein 1991). But obviously the lessons have not been learned. Or else the specter of "American exceptionalism" has a way of being resuscitated, especially in periods of economic crisis and neoconservative resurgence.

Panethnicity is one specimen of the ideological recuperation of what I would call the *Myrdal complex* (the presumed schizoid nature of U.S. democracy preaching equality but institutionalizing discrimination) that plagues all formalist, mechanical thinking, including its empiricist and pragmatic variants. The more profound motivation for pan-Asianism is the historically determinate racism of white supremacy toward Asians. As Sucheng Chan noted perspicuously: "In their relationship to the host society, well-to-do merchants and poor servants, landowning farmers and propertyless farm workers, exploitative labor contractors and exploited laborers alike were considered inferior to all Euro-Americans, regardless of the internal ethnic and socio-economic divisions among the latter" (1991, 187). Instead of valorizing ethnicity or cultural difference per se, we need to concentrate on what Robert Miles (1989) calls the "racialization" process, its ideological and institutional articulations.

The distinctive experiences of racialization undergone by various

groups is the key to working out a genuinely popular-democratic counterhegemonic strategy. An example might be instructive. Distinct from
other Asians, the Filipinos experienced the full impact of U.S. colonization as "wards" of the government's Bureau of Indian Affairs (San Juan
1998b). The violent subjugation of the Philippines and its revolutionary
republic after the brief Spanish-American War (at the cost of at least
eight thousand U.S. soldiers and about a million natives — the blank
space in most history textbooks) gives us the background to the sub-
alternized and disintegrated nature of the Filipino community here (now
the largest of the Asian American category). When queried why the
American conduct of the war has been flagrantly ruthless, Senator Albert Beveridge of Indiana replied, "Senators must remember that we are
not dealing with Americans or Europeans. We are dealing with Orientals" (San Juan 1996b, 3). Such an "Orientalist" remark has often been
repeated from then on up to World War II (against the Japanese), the
Korean War, and the unconscionable interventions in Indo-China.

It should now be obvious that the ethnicity of Asian Americans
cannot be understood apart from the historical trajectories, the workings
of the state, and the contingencies of political economy (R. Chang 1995).
We need to comprehend the effects of the racializing dynamics of global
politics and the resonance of modernization/developmentalist ideology
in the colonizing maneuvers of the U.S. government around the world.
Because international rivalries of nation-states (despite post–Cold War
compromises) affect ethnic/racial boundaries and their realignments in
the United States, I would also urge a comparative approach in examining the racializing of ethnic relations across classes and genders, among
European immigrants and their descendants and the dominated peoples
of color, in relation to power disparities and conflicts.

We must remember that the incorporation of Asians and Pacific Islanders occurred in times of fierce class wars (articulated through race)
from the start through the Civil War, the subjugation of the American Indian nations and the Mexican inhabitants of the occupied southwestern
region, up to the imperialist encroachments into Latin America, Hawai'i,
and the Philippines. Ideology and jurisprudence followed the logic of
capital expansion and colonial administration. State power and ideological apparatuses of civil society functioned within this wider framework to determine the shifting value of ethnic properties (or whatever

salient cultural attribute is defined as "ethnic" at a given conjuncture) within the dynamics of fundamental and subsumed class contradictions.

What this implies then is that in rehearsing the narratives of victimization of Asians in the United States, a task that seems to have labeled us as experts in the putative science of "victimology," we need to beware of the temptations of liberal patronage. I think it is not enough to simply add that we possess a rich archive of resistance and rebellion. There may be something suspect in claiming that the Chinese or Japanese movement, in seizing the guarantee of equal protection under the Constitution's Fourteenth Amendment to redress grievances, blazed the trail for the civil rights movement — a global phenomenon that embraced national liberation struggles in Asia, Africa, and Latin America — or in celebrating the fact that Japanese and Filipinos spearheaded strikes and militant union organizing in Hawai'i and California from the beginning of this century up to the founding of the United Farm Workers of America. Such occasions (too numerous to inventory here) demonstrate how resistance to capital overcomes the pernicious effects of ethnic separatism, identity politics, and segregation due to "divide-and-conquer" tactics and blandishments.

Bootstraps Unravelled

Recent scholarship on the ideological construction of "whiteness" in U.S. history should illuminate also the invention of the "Asian American" as a monolithic, standardizing index of classification. It is clear that the diverse cohorts classified by official bureaucracy as "Asian American" manifest more discordant features than affinities and commonalities. The argument that they share similar values (for example, Confucian ethics), ascribed somatic characteristics, and kindred interests in politics, education, social services, and so on, cannot be justified by the historical experiences of the peoples involved, especially those who came after World War II. This does not mean that "U.S. Asians" (to use this amalgamating rubric) did not and do not now engage in coalitions and alliances to support certain causes or cooperate for mutual benefit; examples are numerous. In fact, the insistence on pan-Asianism can only obscure if not obfuscate the patent problems of underemployment and unequal reward ("glass ceiling"), occupational segregation, underrepresentation, and class polarization. One need only cite the high rates of poverty among Asian refugees: 26 percent for Vietnamese, 35 percent for Laotians, 43 percent for Cambodians, and 64 percent for the Hmongs (Kitano and Daniels 1998, 179). All studies also show that most Filipinos today find themselves condemned to the secondary labor market — low-wage jobs in the private sector — in spite of higher educational attainment (Cabezas and Kawaguchi 1989; for a general survey, see Ong 1994a).

Errors of ethnic absolutism still muddle the landscape. A recent textbook *Asian Americans* (1995) edited by Pyong Gap Min, for example, has no hesitation predicting that Asians will be easily assimilated in time. While admitting the perception that language barriers still exist and the old stereotypes of disloyal or enemy aliens still affect mainstream perception, Min relies on three factors alleged to promote rapid assimilation: (1) the presence of well-assimilated native-born Asian Americans will neutralize the image of the "stranger"; (2) multiculturalism or cultural pluralism will promote the toleration of "subcultural differences"; and (3) the economic and political power of Asian nation-states will create a positive image in general. These reasons can be cancelled by a few arguments whose suasive force has still not been properly registered.

The last reason cited is quickly countered by what I call the *Vincent Chin syndrome*: political demagoguery in times of economic crisis can shift the target of scapegoating onto the Japanese, the Korean, or any Asian who can reactivate the sedimented persona of the wily, inscrutable, shifty-eyed foreigner among us. The second reason is fallacious since "cultural pluralism" has been around since the attenuation of the Anglo-Saxon supremacy/nativist movement; multiculturalism is now, in fact, the enshrined co-optative formula for peacefully managing differences among the subalterns (San Juan 1998a). And finally, the process of acculturation of second- or third-generation U.S. Asians has been qualified (by Min himself) as valid only for the narrowly cultural, not the social, dimension. In fact, the sociological indicators lead to this seemingly paradoxical conclusion: "Although the vast majority of second-generation Asian Americans will lose their native language and cultural tradition, they are likely to maintain a strong ethnic identity and to interact mainly with coethnics" (Min 1995, 279). Acculturation, then, heightens ethnic difference and even fosters separatism — an ironic result.

At this point, some conscientious readers might already be ruminating about "model minority," the contemporary version of the "yellow peril" that used to haunt white supremacist America. One recent textbook complacently declares that "the history of Asian Americans combines the immigrant's quest for the American dream and the racial minority's confrontation with discriminating laws and attitudes" (Dudley 1997, 14). The scandal of the "model minority," despite being exposed and refuted by numerous critiques that begin to replicate each other, exhibits a curious buoyancy and seems to enact the "return of the living dead" in some comic, late-night T V melodrama.

Initiated by pundits of the mass media, this myth was canonized by President Reagan in 1984 and then echoed by *Newsweek*, C B S, and current textbooks. Reagan praised Asians for their high median family incomes ostensibly due to their "hard work" and idiosyncratic "values" that are allowed to flourish within "our political system" of free enterprise and self-help utilitarianism. Some Japanese Americans and Asian Indians have "outwhited the whites," so to speak. Space here forbids me from reiterating the massive fallacies of such ascription, fallacies belied by facts about the spatial distribution of Asians, number of workers per family, the "glass ceiling" for Asian mobility, labor-market segmentation resulting in bipolar status, and so on. Discrepancies exist between effort and achievement, between achievement and reward, enough to expose the disingenuous and indubitably tendentious manipulation of selected data. Deborah Woo comments, "By focusing on the achievements of one minority in relation to another, our attention is diverted from larger institutional and historical factors which influence a group's success. Each ethnic group has a different history, and a simplistic method of modeling which assumes the experience of all immigrants as the same ignores the sociostructural context in which a certain kind of achievement occurred" (1989, 186–87). This critique is, however, double-edged. Such highlighting of differences, while useful in questioning the claims of hegemonic standards of representation, fails to attack the nerve-center of capital itself, its substantive kernel that insidiously — like the proverbial trickster of indigenous folklore — thrives in the reproduction of novel hybridity, aporias, and deceitful mimicries fashioned under its aegis.

Again we need to contextualize and ground such propositions in current realities. Between the white supremacist world and the subalterns of color, a "buffer" zone exists to stabilize an always reconfigured hegemony. This new stereotype of America's "preferred minority" must of course be placed within the intense class warfare of the eighties that established the groundwork for today's "Contract with America" intent on abolishing the welfare state. This raging class war coincides with the decline of U.S. hegemony in the international economy (given its trade imbalance and its change from a creditor to debtor nation), the rise of what some scholars call the "underclass," the precipitous deterioration of the white middle class, and other symptoms of social decay. In a deindustrializing milieu where poverty, homelessness, and alienation have worsened, this myth is meant to breathe new life into the consensual ideology of individual success, "habits of the heart," or "common sense" received from the tutelage of the Puritan "errand into the wilderness."

What needs emphasis, I submit, are the uses to which this "model-minority myth" has been deployed. First, it reinforces the homogenizing mechanisms of the state and the disciplinary institutions that reduce diverse individuals into one classified, sanitized, uniform "minority." Second, it obscures the presence of disadvantaged Asians and blocks any help for finding employment, learning English, and so on. Third, it serves the "divide-and-rule" scheme of the system by pitting one racialized group against another. If Asians can achieve the American "Dream of Success" by dint of internalizing a work ethic, why can't poor blacks and whites on welfare? It is crucial to keep in mind that the sweatshops in the garment and computer industries, as well as the service sectors, are inhabited more and more by a predominantly multiethnic workforce, thus requiring a more sophisticated policing technique.

Ethnicity and racializing technologies of governance converge here. Ironically, the paradox of absolutizing certain elements of ethnic identity appears when Asians are conceived as both passive and aggressive, complacent and competitive, family centered and individualistic. Pride in their heritage, family solidarity, fragments of Confucian morality, and so on are used to explain both upward and downward mobility, sporadic recognition and endemic disadvantage, appreciation and resentment. Meanwhile, as I have noted earlier, incidents of hate crimes, bigotry, denial of equal opportunity, and violence against Asians have proliferated in the last decades. This culminated in the spectacular fires of 1992 in Los Angeles after the first verdict in the Rodney King trial. Aside from deaths and injuries suffered by individuals, 2,700 Korean businesses — California's new middlemen minority — were destroyed by what is regarded as the first multiethnic rebellion in the United States, a rebellion against police brutality, economic deprivation, and, from a totalizing perspective, the terrors of a regime of postmodern flexible accumulation.

Notwithstanding massive empirical evidence, versions of the "melting-pot" theory are recycled to homogenize variegated multitudes and flatten out material disparities. A monograph of the Population Reference Bureau on Asian Americans, *America's Fastest Growing Minority Group* by William O'Hare and Judy Felt, acknowledges disparities but lumps its subjects indiscriminately: "While Asian Americans have slightly higher average family incomes than non-Hispanic whites, they also have much higher poverty rates" (O'Hare and Felt 1991, 15). Many other studies have arrived at the conclusion that the economic success story of U.S. Asians is undermined by two facts: their reward is not commensurate with their educational attainment, and they have higher poverty rates than non-Hispanic whites (Woo 1989). The myth of the "model minority" persists in obscuring these facts. Because of this, U.S. Asians are collectively perceived as a threat by other minority groups, especially blacks in New York, Washington, D.C., and Los Angeles; and whites who fear the competitive power of Pacific Rim countries. Asian Americans are thus caught between two antithetical pressures: "On one hand, Asian Americans are lauded as a 'model minority' that is fulfilling the American dream and confirming the image of America as a 'melting pot.' On the other hand, they seem hampered by invisible barriers — a so-called glass ceiling — that keep them from climbing to the top rungs of power" (O'Hare and Felt 1991, 15). What is clearly reconfiguring this dilemma is the contradiction between ideology — the imaginary mode of connecting subjects to reality — and the limits of a racialized political economy, the constraints of transnational, globalized, late capitalism.

A strategy of pacification is being mounted to contain dissidence and disruption from unruly sectors of the U.S. Asian populace as rivalry among regional powers accelerates and the debt crisis deepens. One indication is the multiculturalist approach deployed by Stanley Karnow and Nancy Yoshihara in which the "model-minority myth" and a naive Orientalism find renewed life. We are told that "despite their dissimilarities, Asian Americans share common characteristics. Whether their backgrounds are Confucian, Buddhist, Hindi, Muslim, Christian or animist, they tend to adhere to the concept of filial piety, and see achievement as a way to honor their families" (Karnow and Yoshihara 1992, 6). Asian Americans in general subscribe to the classic American virtues of hard work, discipline, and postponed gratification. Strangely enough, these virtues are also labeled Confucian. Because of their obsession with education and social status, Asian Americans are considered the new Horatio Algers, "America's trophy population." The sum of these pundits' wisdom is encapsulated in the discovery that "apart from Japanese Americans, most Asian Americans are immigrants. Many though not all come from countries with despotic and corrupt regimes, and are either unacquainted with the democratic process or distrust government" (Karnow and Yoshihara 1992, 7).

I contend that the duplicitous metaphysics I alluded to earlier is here exhibited without any scruples at all. Note that the fissure between the patronizing endorsement of the "model-minority" archetype and the factual errors compounded with a self-righteous paternalism betrayed by the second quotation, is not as wide as it seems. For both are symptomatic of the doctrine that Asian immigrants, like all aliens, should be measured against a white supremacist standard, a measure that precisely guarantees the hegemony of capital's "civilizing mission" that is now being challenged by its unruly subalterns in core and periphery. I think that U.S. Asian scholarship, despite the avant-garde triumphalist voice of its postmodernist faction, has not been able to grapple successfully with this old but persistent and even revitalized episteme. This failure vitiates all conversation about revising invidious immigrant or national paradigms since the ghosts of the past, unless we settle accounts with it, will forever continue to haunt us in our future peregrinations and sabotage all attempts at liberation.

In/Quest of Chinese America

We can examine a more provocative scenario and its literary figuration by turning to the beleaguered plight of the Chinese as the salient actor in the Asian American theater of misrecognition. In his reassessment of the balance-sheet surrounding the Asian/American binary, David Palumbo-Liu surveys the "uneven, complex, and multiple imbrications" of Asians in the racial polity. He concludes that on the face of "Manifest Destiny" and the "racial frontier" that has defined American exceptionalism, the coupling of "Asian/American" marks both inclusion and exclusion. Sutured to the racializing order, this juxtaposition implies "a dynamic, unsettled and inclusive movement" (1999, 3). In what way has this dynamic movement been articulated? What contradictions has the dialectic of expression and imitation, symbolism and mimesis, in Chinese American literary practice succeeded in resolving, or sublating to a more nuanced, determinate plane?

Caught in the unflagging "culture wars" of the United States, any inquiry into the status of a region of creative expression as Asian American, more specifically here Chinese American, writing is fraught with all the old issues over the relation of art to the political and social formation it inhabits. For the dominant consensus, literature occupies a transcendent space free from prior moral or ideological commitments; hence readers can enjoy Amy Tan and Maxine Hong Kingston on the same level as they would Gertrude Stein or Katherine Anne Porter. Since the sixties, however, the consensus has allowed for the reconfiguration of "minority" writing in the new category of multicultural literature of the United States, assigning them "equal and separate" positions. This gesture of tolerance is both compromising and complicitous.

One may ask: Is Amy Tan's *The Joy Luck Club*, inserted into the diversity curriculum, now to be celebrated as an integral part of American literature? That question is more contentious if trivial than the one of whether Maxine Hong Kingston, now canonized as a major American writer, is perfectly assimilated so as to erase the ethnic patina and render her safe for general, not just elite, consumption. Has the original

"Chinese" aura produced by reviews of her novels been subsumed into the hegemony of pluralist America to make her representative? Clearly the question of nationality, of identifying with a nation or citizenship granted by the nation-state, becomes crucial when we (I from the Philippine perspective, my colleagues from Hong Kong or Taiwan from another) view a concrete literary formation in the context of specific times, places, subject-positions, and so on.

Before I shift the focus from the general to the particular, I want to remind you that the antagonism between the aestheticist and the socially committed stance persists among the *litterateurs* of Asian America. Consider, for example, the opinions expressed by Garrett Hongo (1998) on Cynthia Kadohata and Pulitzer-winner Robert Olen Butler. Hongo chides Asian Americans for being "immature" because they are "so unused to seeing cultural representations" of themselves that they criticize Kadohata for not mentioning the internment camps in her novel *The Floating World*. Hongo praises Butler for creating "commonality" in his stories of Vietnamese refugees, for his "humanistic politics" and "powerful artistry." Hongo then blames the confusion of "general thought in American culture (as enacted by media and the ephemeral communal mind) [which] tends to oversimplify complex social and artistic issues, with the habitual comminglings and false oppositions of matters of art with matters of social justice. The problem, ultimately, has to do with confusing and, finally, conflating the two realms" (55). Although Hongo evinces awareness of the dangers of "minstrelsy by the white culture ventriloquizing the ethnic experience and colonizing the mind of the Other for the purpose of reinforcing cultural dominance" (53–54), he is curiously naive in accepting the contrived separation between art and society, humanism and racism, that generated in the first place the confusions from which he himself suffers. The symptoms of extreme alienation, anomie, and paranoia that characterize everyday life in late-capitalist society cannot be fully comprehended without grasping the larger history of the sociopolitical formation of the United States as a complex overdetermined totality of social relations. One striking symptom of fragmentation alluded to before is racism. I submit that the underlying cause of the "culture wars" between a white-supremacist order and the subordinated peoples of color cannot be grasped and resolved adequately without transforming the material socioeconomic conditions that make them possible. What is imperative is a critical review of the racial/class hierarchy that constitutes the social order of the United States, its historical construction as a hegemonic structuration of classes, races, nationalities, genders, and locations, together with the manifold contradictions that define the parameters for change.

On the question of where Chinese Americans are positioned in the historical development of the racial polity, and where its cultural modalities can be inscribed, a succinct response can be sampled in a recent essay by Ling Chi Wang. Wang is critical of two paradigms: the assimilationist one based on the melting-pot myth that subsists on the ideology of white supremacy, and the loyalty paradigm. The latter involves the emphasis on preserving a Chinese cultural identity that entails some kind of political/economic loyalty of "overseas Chinese," the "sole obsession" of both government policies and scholarly inquiries by both governments in Taiwan and mainland China. Wang rightly criticizes both paradigms deployed in scholarly studies of Chinese in the United States as simplistic, biased, and totally inadequate. Aside from assuming Chinese America to be homogeneous and monolithic, the two frameworks "exclude the perspectives, interests, rights, and well being of the Chinese American community."

Abstracting from the empirical record, Wang points to three crucial factors that define the Chinese diaspora in the United States: "(1) the resistance against racial oppression and extraterritorial domination; (2) the impact of U.S.-China relations on the formation and development of Chinese America; and (3) the segmentation and conflict within the community by class, gender, and nativity over time and the sentiment, perspective, and voice of each segment" (1995, 158). By a simple inversion, Wang proposes an alternative paradigm that would reconceptualize assimilation and loyalty, substituting for assimilation the concept of racial exclusion or oppression, and for loyalty to the homeland the notion of extraterritorial domination. These two trends — racial exclusion and extraterritorial domination — then "converge and interact in the Chinese American community, establishing a permanent structure of dual domination and creating its own internal dynamics and unique institutions" (1995, 159). After reviewing the historical vicissitudes of these two trends, Wang concludes that "liberation from the structure of dual domination is therefore the goal for the emergence of a new Chinese America in the multiracial democracy of the U.S. envisioned by the Chinese Americans involved in the civil rights movement of the late 1960s and early 1970s" (1995, 165).

The invocation of a "multiracial democracy" without altering property/power relations is a fatuous reflex. Notwithstanding this reservation, I think Wang has usefully summarized the political genealogy of Chinese America—the ideological foundation of exclusion in contract labor, the presumed nonassimilability of the Chinese, the reactionary local institutions and practices that permitted the intervention from the governments in Taiwan and mainland China, and lately the transnational movements of information, capital, and people in global capitalism. What is starkly missing is any analysis of how precisely the ideological and cultural apparatuses of the hegemonic order—no radical change is suggested for this—continue to reproduce the assimilationist paradigm as well as reinforce the loyalty compulsion. In fact, Wang notes the influence of the cultures and lifestyles of China, Taiwan, and Hong Kong on the already segmented Chinese American community.

A rhythm of challenge and response syncopates the heteroglossia of this community. Confined to ghettoes by the Chinese Exclusion Act of 1882, a flagrant symptom of the hegemony of finance capital at the turn of the nineteenth century, the Chinese American community was forced to resort to the nostalgic reaffirmation of traditional life-forms. This exhibited itself in the dualism of influence between the secret "tongs" and the "benevolent associations," reflecting the class warfare in mainland China. Attempts in the ideological field to break out of this confinement failed until the civil rights struggles of the sixties. Artists like Maxine Hong Kingston and Frank Chin have cultivated in their varying ways the popular-democratic strain in the tradition, while Fae Ng and Amy Tan, among others, continue to appeal to residual ethnocentrism and its promise of reconciliation. Those attempts sought to establish continuity amid discontinuity, valuing permanences over ruptures. But in the emerging regime of postmodernist multiculturalism, they (except Chin) have proved vulnerable to co-optation and canonical assimilation.

No doubt times have changed. Chinese Americans are praised by archconservative Linda Chavez (1998) as super-performers in climbing the ladder of social mobility, serving as protowhites placed between African Americans and the Euro-American majority. Peter Gran describes the "buffer race" strategy for preserving the status quo: "The state through its immigration policy inserted one or more groups, the buffers, into society between black and whites to conflict with the interests of both, thereby deflecting the focus on race off the black-white issue, diffusing it into what is now called multiculturalism" (1996, 347). This obviously complicates the race/class/gender dialectic. The mutations in social relations of reproduction that accompany the change from finance capitalism at the turn of the century to the Depression, the Cold War, and the new globalization schemes of monopoly capital are elided by a narrow focus on bureaucratic adjustments. The absence of a dialectical construal between the logic of capital and the hegemonic process vitiates the critique of assimilationism and intervention from outside through local agencies. Taking account of transnational border crossings and fluid "ethnoscapes" will not challenge capital's monopoly of power over the processes of immigration, job discrimination, residential segregation, and other institutional mechanisms of the regulatory state.

Empiricism vitiates any simple tabulation of factors surrounding racism and extraterritorial intervention. Starkly absent from Wang's summary is the change of the older stereotypes of Fu Manchu or "heathen Chinee" as evil incarnate to the model-minority exemplar in tandem with the rise of neoconservative Asian American "middlemen" as key players in the political scene. Social analysts have registered this dramatic transformation of the Asian American "yellow horde" into overachievers, an intermediate category or "racial buffer" between whites and a burgeoning "underclass." Add to this the phenomenon of what Peter Kwong calls the "new Chinatown" whose underground economy of "internal colonialism" outside the mainstream U.S. economy and labor market escapes Wang's dual paradigm and its alternative. We should factor in the conjuncture of the fin de siècle petit-bourgeois anarchism and the neoliberal agenda for universalizing "free trade" and privatization everywhere. Glenn Omatsu (1994) has chronicled the emergence of Asian neoconservatives in California, dismantling the panethnic racialization of the sixties by underscoring the resurgent class antagonisms in a moribund racial order.

In retrospect, it is perfectly conceivable to believe that freedom from the dual tyranny of racial exclusion and extraterritorial domination can take the form of a pluralist/multicultural ethos and an ethnocentric politics of identity. Despite their challenge to orthodoxy, both Tan's oeuvre (from *The Joy Luck Club* to *The Thousand Secret Senses*) as well as the more sophisticated artifices of David Hwang, Fae Mae Ng, Shawn Wong, Wing Tek Lum, Marilyn Chin, and others can and have been appropriated for disempowering their agents and entrenching a "separate but equal" prophylactic compromise. Kingston herself is now a sacred icon of Establishment feminism. Civil rights demands for some have been fulfilled by the fetishism of hybridity and heterogeneity, making the hyphen the erotic marker of a privileged difference. If the margin has moved to the center, or has been accomodated to the core by a strategy of co-optation and displacement, racism is preserved and strengthened in its political-economic functionality and ideological effects. Eulogizing boutique multiculturalism above the political economy of maintaining consensus, postmodernist thought runs rampant in the service of an overused metaphysics of the free market and individual fulfillment via consumerism (San Juan, 1998a; 1999c).

Outflanking the Beast

One way of exploring how to seize the "weak link" in the racial polity is to pursue a historical-materialist critique of the contradictions that underlie the U.S. racial order. I want to use Frank Chin's writings as allegories of Chinese American historical specificity. In "Revisiting an 'Internal Colony': U.S. Asian Cultural Formations and the Metamorphosis of Ethnic Discourse," a chapter in my book *Beyond Postcolonial Theory*, I alluded to Chin's attempt to dismantle the bipolarizing logic of the hyphenated sensibility found in Jade Snow Wong and other pre–World War II writers, and project instead a heroic myth of the Chinese workers who built the railroads, excavated tunnels, cleared the wilderness of Hawai'i, and made enormous sacrifices to fashion the infrastructure for industrial capitalist America. Place-based politics is grounded here on a nuanced labor theory of value. One can argue that Chin's art has been able to neutralize the humanist reconstitution of the self with a "postmodern pastiche that may be an astute maneuver to undermine commodity fetishism" (San Juan 1998a, 189). *Commodity-fetishism* is my shorthand term for the whole regime of alienation, more exactly reification (as defined by Lukacs and Goldmann), that distinguishes everyday life in a society centered on exchange-value, on the operations of the market. Reification manifests itself as racial oppression, exclusion, marginalization, and subordination of peoples marked as Others/ aliens to constitute a majoritarian identity, articulated with class, sexuality, gender, and nationality.

Reification in the cultural field today expresses itself as the valorization of difference to compensate for the damages inflicted by a predatory Eurocentric universalism. What David Harvey calls the "Leibnizian conceit" (1996, 69), in which a monadic subjectivity internalizes the world and its totality of relations, was displayed earlier in Hongo's bifurcation of aesthetics and politics as two separate realms. This conceit also legitimizes the idea of the artist as demiurgic force so prevalent in postmodernist apologetics. Chin suceeds in destroying the Leibnizian conceit by emphasizing historical specificity and the sociopolitical constitution of the mode of literary production. Deploying a distancing slyness reminiscent of Brecht (see Jameson 1998), Chin refunctions his own life history as a means of carrying out a painstaking demystification of the ideology and politics of assimilation.

In a contribution to Studs Terkel's volume *Race*, Chin (1992) explores the embeddedness of the Chinese habitus in everyday life and its indivisibility from the vicissitudes of the class/race/nationality parameters of subordination. He states that from his childhood he has been "trying to find out exactly what" he is, an American of Chinese descent. I should like to emphasize that this is not a quest for an essential attribute of "Chineseness" but a cognitive mapping of the terrain of a deeply racialized formation. Sucheng Chan (1991), King-kok Cheung (1990), and others condemn Chin's "machismo" and his alleged claim to be the only "authentic" Asian American writer. There is some basis for this, but it does not properly appreciate Chin's larger implied project of a disarticulation of the hegemonic order and reinterpellation of the erased and subjugated subject.

Unlike Asian postmodernists, Chin strives for a synthesizing appraisal of the social totality. His mode of calculating how the "ethnic" negotiates the American scene offers a critique of liberal pluralism and its corollary metaphysics of ethnic absolutism: "Oakland is the Tower of Babel. All these languages. And nobody even speaks English like everybody else. I've come to believe that monotheism encourages racism, whoever practices it. There is only one God and everyone else is an infidel, a pagan, or a goy. The Chinese look on all behavior as tactics and strategy. It's like war. You have to know the terrain. You don't destroy the terrain, you deal with it. We get along, not because we share a belief in God or Original Sin or a social contract, but because we make little deals and alliances with each other" (1992, 310). Chin points out that because he was raised by white folks during World War II, he was saved from ideas of Chinese inferiority, of parents having proprietary rights over children, from the seductions of yellow minstrelsy. The powerful influence of the black radical movement in the sixties — dramatized in satiric and elegiac ways in *The Chickencoop Chinaman and The Year of the Dragon* — is mediated in the typifying *gestus* of the Chinatown Red Guards who command Chin to "Identify with China!" The California Maoists beat him up and accuse him of being a "cultural nationalist." As a teacher, Chin was attacking stereotypes, racism in its overt forms, a racism that reduced Chinese Americans to "an enclave, like Americans working for Aramco in Saudi Arabia. Chinatown may be a stronghold of Chinese culture, but we're Chinese Americans" (312). He denounces the practices that have converted the Chinese Americans into "a race of Helen Kellers, mute, blind and deaf," the perfect minority worshipping Pearl Buck and embracing Charlie Chan, "an image of racist love," as "a strategy for white acceptance" (313).

Chin takes account of how social peace via individual/group competition is preserved by the inculcation of prejudice throughout the population. He recalls how David Hilliard of the Black Panthers got up in Portsmouth Square and said, "You Chinese are the Uncle Toms of the colored peoples" (314). Chin finds this apt, but Chinese youth imitating black populism is not the solution. Nor is the temporary strategic ruse of using English "as a matter of necessity" in a white man's world, which he observes among the Indo-Chinese immigrants whom he describes as "the unredeemed Chinese Chinese" (314).

A kind of peasant cunning retooling the "weapons of the weak" characterizes Chin's bravado, his predilection for exhibitionist belligerence. This has earned him sharp rebukes from self-avowed gatekeepers of Asian American culture and their philistine allies. Chin's method is not a matter of deconstructing texts but rather of a retrieval of a submerged tradition: the practical materialism of the Chinese plebeian grassroots, the proletariat in city and countryside (Needham 1975). To interrogate self-contempt as a tactic of survival and legitimize a Chinese American sensibility in his works, Chin is often quoted as adopting a heroic martial posture and outlook based on his application of Sun Tzu's *Art of War* and the autochthonous tradition embodied in the classic texts of *Three Kingdoms*, *The Water Margin*, and *Monkey's Journey to the West*. Some commentators also impute to Chin the role of reconstructing the Chinese tradition in the way of Caliban and Kwan Kung (Leiwei Li 1991). But Chin is not interested in postcolonial mimicry or a recovery of a primordial Chinese American tradition. In his essay "Our Life Is War," Chin argues that "what is of supreme importance in war is to attack the enemy's strategy" (28), hence the importance of surveying the terrain or context of the struggle, analyzing the contradictory trends immanent in the forces engaged, and seizing the "weak link" to resolve the contradictions by stages and enable a release of human potential for future projects of liberation.

Facing Inscrutabilities

To do justice to the power of Chin's contestatory art will require an extended treatise. Suffice it here to illustrate Chin's dialectical mode of problematizing with reference to his latest work, *Gunga Din Highway* (1994). The novel is an elaborate neopicaresque staging of a pretext for satirizing highbrow and mass culture, rehearsing the familiar repertoire of racist cliches, stereotypes, icons, and folkloric doxa of the white majority. It is organized around the conflict of generations, specifically between Longman Kwan, the father of Ulysses, who aspires to be the first Chinese to play Charlie Chan, after having had a career of playing Chan's Number Four Son and as "the Chinaman who dies." Ulysses, the third son of a father produced by incest, revolts against the patriarch who urges him to take on "the image of the perfect Chinese American to lead the yellows to build the road to acceptance towards assimilation" (13). Which road will the prodigal son take?

The parodic form leads to an inversion, if not an abortion, of a young artist's development found in the traditional education novel. Ulysses and his friends, Diego Chang and Benedict Han, are instructed by their Chinese schoolteacher to "master all the knowledge of heaven and earth . . . so as to see the difference between the real and the fake." They outwit their teacher. They anticipate the precept that good judgment springs from a hermeneutics of suspicion. The last chapter of the novel renders the success of Ulysses in refusing the legacy/inheritance of Charlie Chan, a synecdoche for the Americanization of the Chinese, even though at the end he accepts being a figurehead for the extended family. The father's prestige is vindicated as he is described in a fictional movie, *Anna May Wong*, an airplane movie with an all-Chinese bomber crew, in which the father departs from the Chan syndrome/Gunga Din Road and enjoys a symbolic resurrection and rehabilitation.

The lesson seems to be that the past is always redeemed at the moment of crisis, the instant of danger, when we seize the opportunities for transformative action. "Life is war. . . . Let the good times roll!" Diego Chang intones. If life is war, a combat for an ampler life, then Ulysses wins it when he refuses all the conventional expectations of the dominant society. Contrary to modernist decorum, *Anna May Wong* and its takeoff sequence splices the father's death with the joyous drive toward birth, a delivery and deliverance at the same time. The trope of flight, passage, and transition unfixes the dual reflex of assimilation/loyalty and affirms the emancipatory thrust of the narrative.

Still, we cannot evade the thematic burden of identity, whether filial, collective, private, decentered, or intertextual. What are the conditions of its possibility? And is this task of identification meaningful for a novel that with its critical edge undermines the quest for origins, essences, authenticity, destinies, transcendent, and/or primordial forms? Chin pokes fun at the notion of a singular isolated tradition: "If Charlie Chan uses first-person pronouns, does not walk in the fetal position, is not played by a white man, and looks and acts like a real Chinese, he's not Charlie Chan anymore" (355). This suggests that identification is always dialogic (in Bakhtin's sense), or better yet, heteroglossic and intertextual.

The form of *Gunga Din Highway*, at first glance, seeks to reconcile the disintegration of the traditional world with the artist's desire for wholeness of understanding. The attempt executed partly through mimesis of Joyce and Homer only heightens the contradictions and, at best, instigates us to react to the crisis of the old order. Broadly surveyed, the four parts of the novel unfold the history of the Chinese in the

United States in the adventures of Ulysses Kwan, the descendant of the god of fighters and writers, and variants of his character. Before "Home" can be reached, the protagonists have to experience a protracted agon from "Creation" to "The World" and "The Underworld."

One can discern a chronological progression in the novel's design. It proceeds from the mother lode country of California in World War II to San Francisco coffeeshops in the fifties, passing through a Seattle rock-flamenco-blues festival and the activities of radical groups in the sixties to off-Broadway and the orientalist version of Pandora's box in the seventies, to middle age in the eighties, and finally to the disclosure of family secrets in the nineties. In Chin's genealogy, the hero is basically the antihero, a subversion of identity politics by a carnivalesque meta-narrative and collage of episodes without much logical causality. The rationale is provided by his reading of Chinese mythology: "The world, the giant, and the Mother of Humanity create a world where every hero is an orphan, a failed scholar, an outlaw, an outcast, an exile on the road of life through danger, ignorance, deception, and enlightenment" (vii). The education of Ulysses attains a climactic point in his encounter with the Horse, their Chinese teacher, at a historic juncture when the United States is fighting a war in Korea while the French have just suffered an unprecedented defeat at Dien Bien Phu in colonial Indo-China. The Horse's teaching sketches the secular, open-ended triangulation of Ulysses' emergent identity:

> "I can teach you to read and write Chinese," the Horse said, "but you will never be Chinese. And by now you should all know no matter how well you speak English and how many of the great books of western civilization you memorize, you will never be *bokgwai*, white European Americans. The Chinese kick you around for not being Chinese. And the whites kick you around for not being American. Obviously you are neither white nor Chinese, but you tell me what does that mean? What is it? You are the stone monkey come to life. To learn the difference between stone idea and living flesh and blood, you must learn everything Chinese and American there is to know, you must master all the knowledge of heaven and earth, become The Sage equal to The Emperor of Heaven so as to see the difference between the real and the fake, the knowledge of what being neither Chinese nor *bokgwai* means." (93)

In Chin's aesthetics, a strong modernist conception of the artist's singularity coexists with a profound sense of art's ethical responsibility. The artist bridges incompatible domains of value and interest. This is translated in the novel when Ulysses and his friends respond, "The Horse made us feel special. Unlike anyone else in the world, we were neither Chinese nor American. All things were possible. No guilt. We were pure self-invention," something like Milton's Satan in *Paradise Lost*: "self-begat." Lest this theory of self-invention, eloquently invoked also at the beginning of *The Chickencoop Chinaman*, induce us to ascribe to Chin an ethnic refurbishing of Neoplatonic individualism, with a touch of the Emersonian cult of novelty, I want to stress the circumstantial density that limits the affirmation of independent agency that Chin's characters embody in their comic resilience and vitality. I don't see any warrant here for the mystique of the Flaubertian artist-deity. The discourse of *Gunga Din Highway* can only lend itself to a full-blown nihilistic interpretation, if the weight of history and the sociopolitical determinants that afford "objective correlatives" or, in Raymond Williams's term, "structures of feeling" are willfully ignored.

Judging from the meager reviews, this historicizing aspect of Chin's fiction has been neglected in favor of its colorful rhetoric and somewhat exhibitionist idiosyncracies. For example, the *New York Times* (Ricci 1995) reviewer focuses on Chin's fascination with Hollywood stereotypes and the penchant of superimposing on life a cinematic pattern that makes "The Movie About Me" the foil to the real world. The "Me," however, is a defensive mimicry of the hegemonic individualist liberal ethos. Public anxiety with Chin's alleged humorous if "deadly cynicism" and canny ironic tone that distance the characters from the reader may indicate a certain resistance to the critique of media and mass culture in the novel, a critique that the publishing industry would be loathe to endorse. Another reviewer calls attention to the "frenetic, irreverent and episodic father-and-son saga that encompasses some five decades of American clichés, moviemaking and image bashing. . . . Chin sets Ulysses' serendipitous adventures within a comic book-style cultural survey that mocks everything American, from movies to music, drugs, politics, the media, pornography, and racism" (Seaman 1994, 111). Reviewer Robert Murray Davis (1995) speculates that the reader is expected to have seen every movie from *M* to *Wild in the Streets* and

Night of the Living Dead, as well as some invented ones like *Charlie Chan in Winnemucca* and *Anna May Wong* to get a full appreciation of Chin's demystification of their aura. But the reference to these numerous artifacts of mass culture need not detract from the writer's purpose of carrying out a general demystification of appearances, especially when such appearances provide pleasure and catharsis that prevent the acquisition of knowledge required for unmasking the legitimacy of what the racial polity upholds as normal, natural, and reasonable.

Chin's programmatic satire aims to interrogate the ideology of reification, in particular the reification of ethnicized gender and sexual practices. In the third section, "The Underworld," Chin recounts an incident he reported in the aforementioned interview with Studs Terkel. This deals with the time when he was challenged by the Chinatown Red Guards as he led his students reciting "Ching Chong Chinaman." Ulysses explains the rationale: "Satire is where you make fun of how *they* think and what *they* say in order to make *them* look stupid" (1994, 257). This satiric motivation acquires a Rabelaisian accent in the summary of Benedict Mo's *Fu Manchu Plays Flamenco*; the play, according to Ulysses, aims to create not a hybrid artifact symbolically overcoming exclusion and antimiscegenation laws, but "a Chinese-American culture that kicks white racism in the balls with a shit-eating grin" (1994, 261). The play functions as the antithesis to the Charlie Chan archetype. But what is the play really about? Here is a partial summary:

> In the play, Fu Manchu tells the white captive to give up the secret to Kool-Aid or he will let his beautiful nympho daughter give him the dreaded torture of a thousand excruciating fucks and exotic sucks. But the white man defends the secret to Kool-Aid, and Fu's luscious daughter wheels the captive off to her silk-sheeted torture chamber. When the director sees Ulysses offstage watching, still in character, he tries putting Fu Manchu back onstage, reciting classical Japanese haiku of Issa and Basho, breathlessly watching his daughter torture the white man by seduction. Then Ulysses gets the idea to have Fu play the guitar in rhythm to his daughter's hips while badmouthing the white captive's sexual organs, skills, and style in Spanish, English, and three dialects of Chinese. . . .
>
> So who knows and who cares whose idea it is for Fu Manchu to end his flamenco in the torture chamber by ripping open his robe and showing

his body in a bra, panties, garter belt, and black net stockings, licking his lips as he makes a move on the white man, while Fu's daughter straps on an eight-inch dildo? The captive American screams the secret formula, not only for Kool-Aid but for Bisquick and Crisco, too. (1994, 258)

The critic Sau-Ling Wong (1992) has commented on the preoccupation of American-born Chinese writers with the effects of the gendering of ethnicity — the reflex of effeminizing the Asian men and ultra-feminizing Asian women — while recent immigrant writers are more concerned with the ethnicizing of gender. The quotation above shows Chin's hyperbolic displacement of stereotypes by the manipulation of a sign system immanent in commodity aesthetics (Haug 1986). Chin's strategy of deploying various perspectives — not only Ulysses but also his sworn blood brothers Diego Chang and Benedict Mo — is designed to counter any single narrative authority, even though his voice with its mocking insinuations and insouciance seems to predominate. Ego-building, as qualified above, is not the agenda but the collective response to white racism.

I want to emphasize here that Chin's carnivalesque stance linked to the subversive impulse of comedy effectively counters any psychologizing of racism and liberal ideology. The satiric and comic framework neutralizes the psychoanalytic obsession over the enigma formulated by Suzanne Yang: "What is the opposite of an Asian woman?" We confront again the problematic of Orientalism — the objectification of the exoticized Other — that inheres in the valorization of difference as such. Yang analyzes the enigma of racist love as the "scopic constitution of racial identity mediated through an imaginary representation of the desire of the Other" (1998, 140). This Lacanian formula of ethnicity as a syndrome of ignorance, love, and hatred coalesced together, leads to an answer to the question of representation: the remainder (of what?) imagined as lost in the Other produces an aporia, which is the terrain of curiosity, desire, racism. *Gunga Din Highway* exposes this aporia as an illusion generated by the contradictions in real life. Racial categorizing, one telling symptom of lived contradictions, results from the spontaneous reproduction of bourgeois social relations mediated by money, commercial transactions, and the pervasiveness of commodity fetishism in media and all cultural practices. In the everyday transactions of warring racialized classes, the legitimacy of the system can thrive on the continued reproduction of differences normalized in a system of dependency: the Other lacks what I (the white master) as owner of the means of production/reproduction have, and I know it. In short, the role of the actor Charlie Chan, born from this system of dependency and representation, can never be played by a Chinese.

The conclusion of the novel returns us to George Stevens's film *Gunga Din*, after whom this highway of negotiation of "subject-positions," as the fashionable idiom has it, is named. Ulysses confidently asserts that "this is not The Movie About Me"; his father is patently absent in it. It is "nothing but the real old movie." Aside from indexing the circumstantial conjunctures of the individual episodes, variants of a talk-story addressed to a select audience (mainly aficionados of Asian American literature), the Hollywood productions referenced throughout exemplify the ideological apparatus of racialization that, once internalized, produce symptoms of the Gunga Din complex. But what I want to call attention to is not this accumulation of period references and artifacts that gives us a sense of how the racial subordination of the Chinese and other Asians has been maintained. Rather, I want to stress that it is from the subtle undercutting of the postmodernist styles of pastiche, collage, discordant rhetorical registers, and so on, counterpointed to a narrative scaffolding derived from Chinese and Western mythology and modernist practices, that Chin fabricates this peculiar form of literary "installation" meant to dereify the commodification and the alienation ravaging the ethnic communities. Heterogeneity of novelistic form is thus meant to lay bare, expose, or defamiliarize the real contradictions taken for granted in the commercial routine of everyday life.

Reflexive Inscriptions

For Chin, the project of dereification began in the sixties, notably with the plays *The Chickencoop Chinaman* and *The Year of the Dragon*: clichés, stereotypes, and the doxa of white supremacy were dismantled by techniques of allegory, reverse ventriloquism, theatrical distancing, and so on. From the somewhat mannerist, self-conscious Faulknerian rhetoric of "The Chinatown Kid" and other stories in his collection *The*

Chinaman Pacific and Frisco R.R. Co., Chin switches to the flat reportorial idiom of Donald Duk in which the whole saga of thousands of Chinese workers building the transpacific railroad is spliced with the artifice of sustaining a communal ethos in Chinatown (indigenized ghetto/reservation and locus of pacification) through the shared dreams of parents and children. Chin repeats his injunction via the Father's declaration to his son: "History is war, not sport! . . . You gotta keep the history yourself or lose it forever, boy. That's the mandate of heaven." A sense of long duration in historiography is evoked at the end of *Donald Duk* as the 108 toy airplanes explode in flight: ". . . and Donald Duk remembers dreams, the 108 horsemen galloping across the cloud over the ten miles of track just layed by the 1,200 Chinese and eight Irishmen. And very quickly they are all gone. Not a sound. Not a flash. All 108 stick-and-paper model airplanes gone. "Anybody hungry?" Dad asks. . . . Like everything else, it begins and ends with *Kingdoms rise and fall. Nations come and go*, and food" (1991, 173). Food, of course, functions here as a marker of an oppositional cultural politics, as in much Asian American fiction (Waller 1995), but surely this whole culinary knowledge/praxis cannot be dissociated from the nexus of gender, sexuality, class, and other patterns of socialization. The transitory, cyclical, and permanent coexist in the myth-making impulse of the novelist, but what endures is the totality of history in which the Chinese in America, stratified by class, gender, and sexuality, continues as a racialized collectivity embroiled in a protracted, ferocious class war.

Ultimately, Chin's strategy of calculating social relations harbors a utopian element. His vision of the place of the Chinese in an evolving multicultural U.S. society inheres in transfiguring the idea of process — in this case, the topos of the road/physical route institutionalized by Jack Kerouac, Robert Frost, Robert Penn Warren, Paul Bowles, and others — into a matter of geopolitical strategizing (life/history is articulated as antagonism of forces). What is at stake is not a heroic masculinist dispensation but the recognition of Chinese creativity and the communal virtues of discipline and cooperation. In the essay "Rashomon Road: On the Tao to San Diego" (1997), Chin continues his attack on Betty Lee Sung and others who preach from "the pulpit of acceptance, absorption, and assimilation," who persist in "ornamenting white fantasy" and denying the place of the Chinese as producers and contributors to an evolving American civilization. In a gesture of "militant particularism" (Harvey 1996), Chin inscribes Chinese American history in the recursive texts/memory of concrete locales and sites, hyphenating ethnic places in the geopolitical arena:

> The history of the Chinese in California is written in miles of old mining roads, and the railroad. . . . The road was going to be an adventure with father and son discovering the deserts, valleys, mountains, volcanoes, birds, cities, friends. . . . Asian American writers born and raised in America without feeling split between two incompatible cultures . . . the Asian American identity crisis didn't exist for us. We knew Chinese or Japanese culture and knew white American culture, and knew we were not both, nor were we the best of the East and the best of the West. We knew we were neither. Being neither did not mean we contemptuously ridiculed and stereotyped every culture we were not. . . . For us, the adventure in Asian American writing was not just in the writing but in the study, the discovery, the history. . . . (1997, 290)

In an ongoing research project, I inquire into Chin's strategy of a cognitive remapping of the U.S. racial formation, its uneven-and-combined development, to ascertain the "weak link" where popular-democratic forces can attack. For the moment, I want to conclude by commenting on Chin's response to a recent event. On October 15, 2000 Professor Murray Davis, president of the Western Literature Association, recommended to his organization that Chin be given the Distinguished Lifetime Achievement Award in its year 2000 meeting. Davis's colleagues objected on various grounds: Chin was abrasive, a misogynist, and also a homophobe; in short he was unacceptable. Davis threatened to resign; eventually, a compromise was reached and Chin was invited to speak/read at the 2000 WLA Conference.

Informed about the entire situation, Chin wrote Russell Leong, editor of *Amerasia Journal* and dismissed the event as a "kangaroo court." Chin compared the proceeding to the way the Asian American Studies Association treated Lois Ann Yamanaka when the Filipinos objected to her receiving a prize from the association. Chin concludes that without considering the literary merits of Yamanaka's novel, "Yamanaka became the asteroid that killed the dinosaurs." Having warmed up by denouncing the Filipino Caucus as a bunch of ignoramuses, Chin now launches into a tirade against specific and vaguely generalized enemies, the specific ones being those "feminists" on the executive board of the association who "had heard about my rotten personality, not anything of mine they'd read." Chin unleashes his offensive ruse:

> I wonder how many Asian American writers have heard of the Western Literature Association? I wonder how many will mount up their mighty superior minds and demand they give me the association lifetime achievement award? No, I don't. And there's no need to wonder at how many Asian American writers will write the association saying, they have no business telling the Association what to do with its lifetime achievement award, except never to stick them with it. There's only one like that. And I'm it. And they're not giving me their award. They're giving me a kangaroo court instead. And the incoming president of the association is mad. The association magazine won't publish his account and protest of what happened in Sacramento. Perhaps you will.

A character in *Gunga Din Highway*, Diego Chang, intones: "Life is war. . . . Let the good times roll!" Chin's agonistic strategy is basically satiric in intent. We can discern Chin's satiric stance in the letter to Leong, a satiric motive explained by Ulysses in the novel: "Satire is where you make fun of how *they* think and what *they* say in order to make *them* look stupid" (1994, 257). Satire tames indeterminacy by a dialogic ruse in which the Other deploys mimicry not to create an interstitial or liminal "third space," but precisely to fill that gap by fixing the absurd on the basis of comparison and contrast. An inventory of subject positions (including self-criticism) such as that adumbrated in Bakhtin's dialogics (1981), inscribed in historical time-space grids, precedes the calculation of tactics and strategies in ethnic critical transformative agendas. This is not a matter of memorializing trauma, nor a plea for ludic forgetfulness that would "enable the imagining of hybrid — and even pleasurable — spatial, racial, and cross-class convergences" (Lee 1999, 254) complicit in perpetuating stark asymmetries of power in the transnational marketplace. I am sure Chin would assent to Grace Lee Boggs's exhortation to apply on our practice the injunction of Amilcar Cabral: "Our experience has shown us that in the general framework of daily struggle this battle against ourselves, this struggle against our

own weaknesses — no matter what difficulties the enemy may create —
is the most difficult of all, whether for the present or for the future of our
people" (Boggs 1998, 154).

Self-Fashioning the Undecidable

Writing and living, for Chin, are matters of strategy concerned with
relations, transitions, and passages from one position to another. Strategy is involved with establishing connections, linkages, and modalities
of change from one situation to another. Structured between cultures/
histories — China/America, the Chinese American artist confronts the
additional predicament of mediating differences brought about by the
whole racialized history of the United States: genocide of the American
Indians, slavery and segregation of African Americans, colonization of
Mexicans, Puerto Ricans, Filipinos, Hawai'ians, and so on. Asians as a
"buffer race," the "model minority" disengaged from the state apparatus of institutional racism — this condition is one way the in-between
predicament is resolved, but ironically it reproduces the lower classes of
the group as inassimilable or permanent aliens. In "Back Talk," Chin
urged that the strategy of resistance must replace the psychology of
laying low, the habitual exercise of "forestalling the Great Deportation"
for those who have accepted the status of sojourners (1976, 557). Lacking "an articulated, organic sense of our identity" and plagued by a
suicidal "dual personality" produced by America's racist love, Asians
need to reflect on their history, on their positions and locations in the
American landscape. Although Chin insists that Asian culture is martial
and migratory, not migrant, he is unable to escape the nexus of America
as the road, depot, marketplace, and its tropological construction as a
moving terrain for immigrants. By indigenizing this trope, Chin safeguards himself from being instrumentalized by a conservative cultural
nationalism such as that of Singapore, for example, which recuperated
David Henry Hwang's *M. Butterfly* to serve reactionary authoritarian-
capitalist ends (Lye 1995).

Given this materialization of history for Chin, American culture is
not a fixed but a pidgin or bastard culture; like the language it is "a
pidgin marketplace culture" (1997, 295). Anything has value so long as
it can be exchanged (the sensuous particulars reduced to quantitative

abstraction), so long as it enters into market circulation. If this is so, then what awaits the new immigrants from Taiwan, Hong Kong, and China who conceive of the U.S. racial polity not as a temporary place to work in but as a new home with great economic opportunities (Takaki 1989)? Why are these new immigrants still perceived as the perpetual foreigners, countless potential Vincent Chins indistinguishable from the aggressive "oriental" competitor, the Japanese (Chasin 1998)? In fact, we now have a situation where the new rich Chinese immigrants from Hong Kong, whom Aihwa Ong calls "transnational cosmopolitans," have rearticulated the resonance of extraterritorial domination with their familial biopolitics and parachute kids, a force strong enough to supposedly challenge the "American class ethos of moral liberalism" (1999, 284).

Frank Chin's career and substantial accomplishment is certainly an exception to the model-minority catastrophe, a subversion of the "transnational" cyborgs hailed by Ong. His revolt against U.S. internal colonialism followed an apprenticeship to "black nationalism" in which he learned how to deploy a versatile strategy of satire, self-irony, and complex artifices of defamiliarization. In his fiction, however, Chin modulated his modernist strategy from "affective imitation" to an active and "intellective" (to use Spinoza's terms) remapping of the U.S. racial polity. Unlike postcolonial syncretism and decentering, Chin's art explores the determinate causality of illusions, simulacra, and media-generated representations of Asian Americans in general not only to promote demystification but also to articulate a collective social agency allied to a counterhegemonic social bloc. Chin elaborates a "technique of internal sabotage" that, while vitiated by a tendentious aestheticism reminiscent of the modernist avant-garde, nonetheless initiates a reclaiming of the alienated communitarian power immanent in the rational-analytic praxis of beleaguered lives. Chin's essentially comic vision approximates Lenin's belief that revolutionary action demands attacking the "weak link" that lies between the anarchist politics of identity and the liberal consensus of global capitalism. This "weak link" may be located in the persistent denigration or discounting of Asian American productivity and its determinate historical causality.

We can now rehearse the dangerous questions that Chin has tried to narrativize: Is racist love now eliminated by this new phenomenon of performative, not normative or even "accidental" Asians: "cultural citizenship as subjectification and cultural performance" (A. Ong 1999, 286)? Or are those now gifted with unearned symbolic capital still compelled to traverse *Gunga Din Highway* filled with supermalls, reproducing an exchangeable use-value (a quintessential Chineseness, whatever that is) in the service of global capitalism? (I respond to these questions in the next chapter.) These are questions that Chin has attempted to answer and that Chinese as well as other Asian writers will have to respond to in the next millenium for the sake of much more worthy ideals.

The emergence of China as an Asian Pacific power has transvalued decisively the political economy of the Chinese community in the United States in the last two decades of the twentieth century. At the crossroad of the *Gunga Din Highway*, Sinic "civilization," in Samuel Huntington's futurist eschatology, may replace the Islamic as the formidable antagonist of Eurocentric hegemony. With respect to the Asian/Pacific Rim countries whose destinies now seem more closely tied to the vicissitudes of the U.S. market, the reconfiguring of capital's strategy in dealing with this area requires more careful analysis of the flow of migrant labor, capital investments, media manipulation, tourism, and so on. There are several million Filipinos (chiefly women) employed as domestics and low-skilled workers in Hong Kong, Singapore, Japan, Taiwan, Korea, and Malaysia (Boti and Smith 1997; see my afterword). Their exploitation is worsened by the racializing process of inferiorization imposed by the Asian nation-states, the Asian "tigers," competing for their share in the global accumulation of surplus value (profit). In this milieu, the Western press then reconfigures the Asian as neo-Social Darwinist denizen of booty capitalism in the "New World Order." All speculations about citizenship as accessible through the "neutral" and ethical state, or through civil society and the realm of culture, are now rendered void and inutile.

In a study of immigration in the nineties, Paul Ong, Edna Bonacich, and Lucie Cheng conclude that "racial inequality is one of the fundamental social injustices accentuated by restructuring" (1994, 23). Racialized class polarization distinguishes the new epoch of globalized accumulation. While Anglos continue to dominate the top tier, African Americans the bottom tier, and Latino migrants the source of below-minimum-wage labor, Asian immigrants occupy a wide spectrum of roles, from managers, professionals, and entrepreneurs to low-wage workers in light manufacturing and service industries. Within the Asian group, however, class polarization goes on, with Filipinos, Vietnamese, Cambodians, and Laotians suffering twice the proverty rate of the dominant society. Paul Ong and John Liu assert that anti-Asian racism is alive at the threshold of the new millennium: "Asians have not escaped the reemergence of overt racial discrimination in the U.S." (1994, 66).

All these recent developments inevitably resonate in the worldwide image of the Asian — its foreignness, malleability, affinities with the West, and so on — that in turn determines a complex of contradictory and variable attitudes toward U.S.-domiciled Asians. Such attitudes can be read from the drift of the following questions: Is Japan always going to be portrayed as the scapegoat for the loss of U.S. jobs? Is China obdurately refusing to conform to Western standards in upholding human rights and opening the country to the seductions of market individualism? When will Tibet be liberated from Chinese rule? Are the Indonesians as "uncivilized" as the East Timorese? What about "mail-order brides" from the Philippines and Thailand as possible carriers of AIDS virus? Are the Singaporeans that barbaric? How is the Hawai'i sovereignty movement going to affect the majoritarian perception of the "natives"? And despite the end of history in this post–Cold War milieu, will the North Koreans continue to be the paragons of communist barbarism? Are they hopelessly atavistic and irredeemable? All these questions converge for the Euro-American majority in one problematic crux: What can we expect from the enigmatic Asians in our midst?

My inventory of the social field is necessarily incomplete. In effect, given the demographic and sociopolitical rearticulation of the U.S. Asian collectivities, we have not even begun to address what Nancy Fraser (1995) calls the "redistribution-recognition dilemma," that is, how political-economic justice and cultural justice can be realized together by the thorough institutional restructuring of property relations instead of refurbishing liberal nostrums so popular among people of color, especially Asian Americans in the academy. How do we build coalitions with other communities and interests to promote not juridical equality that we supposedly enjoy but substantive social justice? In short, the challenge of transformative critique still needs to be taken up as we confront the disintegration of pan-Asian metaphysics and neo-liberal discourse amid the post–Cold War realignments of geopolitical power blocs in this new millenium where the corporate elites of various nation-states have begun to capitalize more and more on the profitability of ethnic and racial differences.

A Postscript from the Pacific Rim

"It's good you got out of Taipei soon enough!" my friend Esther Pacheco, director of the Ateneo de Manila University Press in Quezon City, Philippines, e-mailed me a few days after Taiwan was rocked by an earthquake in late September 1999. Taiwan, the Republic of China, was my destination for two trips during that summer to participate in conferences at the Academia Sinica and at Tamkang University, Tamshui, Taipei. Perhaps I was luckier when I skipped a trip to Istanbul, Turkey, a few months earlier. The international conference to which I was invited bore the uncanny title, "Global Flows/Local Fissures: Urban Antagonisms Revisited," sponsored by the World Academy for Local Government and Democracy in Istanbul. Tremors of the arrest of the Kurdish revolutionary leader Abdullah Ocalan — think of how many million Kurds have been struggling all these years for national self-determination! — are still reverberating in that region not so far from Chechnya and Palestine.

Yet the return to Pullman, Washington, was not exactly a retreat to the halcyon days of the fifties: the news of the racially motivated shooting in California, in which "only" a lone Filipino American postman was killed, greeted me together with follow-ups of the trial of the killers of James Byrd Jr. in Jasper, Texas. Meanwhile the tumultuous scenario in Kosovo was quickly being overshadowed by the carnage in East Timor, this time by a "third-world" military, the Indonesian army, supported for so long by successive administrations in Washington since the anticommunist bloodbath of 1965. No one is scandalized these days by atrocities broadcast in the media. Postmodernists such as Baudrillard can assure you that those are simulacras and, besides, those "Others" are the terrorists, not us.

The various "Others" I met in Taiwan were mostly academics, but I was able to converse with Wen-hsiung Peter Huang, the chairperson of the Taiwan Association for Human Rights; Father Edwin Corros, pastor of St. Christopher's Roman Catholic Church in the heart of Taipei; Prof. Ping-hui Liao (National Tsing Hua University); and Dr. Yu-cheng Lee and Dr. Wen-ching Ho (fellows of the Academia Sinica). Many colleagues queried me about the racial and ethnic situation in the United States. Both were curious about Department of Comparative American Cultures (CAC) at Washington State University where I served as the department chair (1998–2001). In what way is it different from an ordinary Ethnic Studies department?

In response I explained that aside from performing the usual functions of an "Ethnic Studies" department with a broad outreach to the public, we are also trying to do comparative studies linking different communities and cultures by situating them in the history of a racial formation like the United States. Our aim is to understand why racism and ethnic discrimination persists in a liberal "democratic" society like the United States. We are also moving beyond the group-specific approach, away from narrow and essentialist nationalisms, toward a comparatist and diasporic orientation. Accordingly we hope to focus our inquiry into the underlying social processes and constellation of power-relations common to groups, facilitating collaboration across disciplines and thus enhancing teaching/learning competencies.

In this new "cultural studies" outlook, CAC is breaking new ground. Our curriculum would deepen and enrich the Ethnic Studies field with the exploration of wide-ranging themes and problematics. We would be engaged in teaching and research into immigration, slavery, colonial conquest, capitalism, postcoloniality and identity, sovereignty struggles, and globalization in its cultural, economic, and technological contexts. We would be studying group formation in a global setting. In this way we would be equipped to articulate general principles that shape ethnic and race relations across boundaries of gender, class, sexuality, location, and so on. These are new trends generated as a response to the pressures of rapidly changing realities around the world. An ambitious scheme of reconfiguration, to be sure, but challenging and self-renewing — not exactly a way of "living dangerously."

"Well, are you facing difficulties and opposition?" my Taiwanese comrades asked. Yes, of course. Annual budget crunches. Proprietary outlook over academic turfs. Posturing. Traditional ethnocentrism. Survivals of identity politics everywhere. Eurocentric chauvinism in neo-liberal guise. Careerism. And of course the "iron law of bureaucracy." As the old saying goes, "There's nothing more vicious and more petty than academic squabbling." Overall, consumerism in jobs, enrollments, grants, and even the quest for a fabled "excellence" (see Readings 1996). But enough of this shoptalk. What I can say about the plight of our academic counterparts in Taiwan is nothing new; they share the good fortune but also the tribulations of the whole society. Perhaps they are enjoying the undisclosed perks of neomandarins. One thing is sure: they know how to entertain royally their poor brothers and sisters from North America and Europe.

Taiwan, the Republic of China, this "young tiger" once a pariah (their enemy calls it a "renegade province") of the developing world, has now become a model of industrial success for aspiring formerly colonized societies. Literacy is at nearly 100 percent; 80 percent of families own their homes. Real per capita income is way above other underdeveloped regions: more than $5,000 in 1989, exceeding that of mainland China by a factor of 12 (McCord 1996). Having been a student of "Mao Tsetung Thought" not too long ago, I was of course the most skeptical about what Chiang Kai-shek had wrought on this island where native "Formosans" — the ruling party now is of Taiwanese origin and orientation — have struggled against and survived the successive brutalities of the Europeans, the Japanese, and the Kuomintang warlords. Because of peculiar historical conditions, Taiwan has achieved a quasi miracle, thanks to its Western capitalist patrons.

Compared to derelict Manila and other "third-world" urban sprawls, Taipei is a modern dynamic metropolis powered by an export-driven technological renaissance. It could not have occurred without a drastic and thorough land reform, coupled with abundant U.S. aid especially during the Korean War and the Vietnam War. Notwithstanding this "great leap forward," and the recent move away from one-party dictatorship and international isolation, Taiwan is afflicted with huge problems. You have ethnic, generational, and class tensions among the few thousand aboriginals deprived and marginalized, less than 2 million original KMT followers, and the Taiwanese majority who have acquired stature and agency since Chiang Kai-shek's demise. Among the 21.8 million population, you find thousands of young highly educated and skilled men and women departing daily for North America, Australia, and Europe in search of wealth and distinction. A few trickle back for nostalgic and other personal reasons, or become the parachute trans-migrants of Aihwa Ong.

Because of the lack of necessary labor-power, hundreds of thousands of Filipinos (115,000 Overseas Contract Workers, to be exact, most of whom are domestics or modern indentured servants), Indonesians, Viet-namese, Thais, and other nationalities, enter Taiwan as low-paid con-tract workers without adequate civil-rights protection against abusive employers and criminal elements both within and outside the govern-ment. An ironic situation? A Leibnizian conceit? Exploitation and op-pression are inflicted on other people of color by the Taiwanese as a hegemonic nation-state — by the oligarchic elite, to be sure; a situation not reckoned by sophisticated postcolonial theory or "transnational" cultural studies, the latter of which is thriving as exhibited by an active Cultural Studies Association (see Chen 1996).

Before I left, I was told that celebrity philosopher Richard Rorty recently visited the island to spread the gospel of the new ethnocen-tric pragmatism. Thanks for the hospitality, Ping-hui, Yu-cheng, Wen-ching, and other colleagues. For all their newly acquired prosperity, the threat of mainland invasion (the "one-nation two states" formula of Lee infuriated the state-capitalists of Beijing) and a nativist independence movement will continue to make life for the Taiwanese exciting, un-predictable, and precarious. But isn't that normal and expected in the global marketplace? Which brought me back to the academy to face another year of weathering the cutbacks and reinforcing the trenches, very remote indeed from the agenda of storming the Winter Palace of bigotry and white supremacy that have reared their ugly heads again at the threshold of this new prophetic millennium.

CHAPTER 4

Ethnicity and the Political Economy of Difference

When I look back now from this high hill of my old age, I can still see the
butchered women and children lying heaped and scattered all along the
crooked gulch as plain as when I saw them with eyes still young. And I can
see that something else died there in the bloody mud, and was buried in the
blizzard. A people's dream died there. . . . [T]he nation's hoop is broken
and scattered. There is no center any longer, and the sacred tree is dead.
— Black Elk of the Oglala Sioux, *Black Elk Speaks*

The materialist doctrine that men are products of circumstances and upbringing, and that therefore changed men are products of other circumstances and changed upbringing, forgets that it is men that change circumstances and that the educator himself needs educating.
— Karl Marx, "Theses on Feuerbach"

With the persistence of the neoconservative tide and the accelerated
rollback of civil rights gains and initiatives throughout the country, it
might be superfluous, if not an otiose imposition, to rehearse once more
the predicament of Ethnic Studies in the U.S. academy today. What can
be more droll or dismaying even for besieged scholars and beleaguered
community activists? It might be the "changing same," as Amiri Baraka puts it. But history never repeats itself exactly in the same manner — at least because we intervene through collective praxis, memory,
reinscriptions, and other transformative ways. And often the past, the
repressed, has a way of returning without consulting us in order to make
us aware that history is what hurts. The cases of Mumia Abu-Jamal,
Leonard Peltier, Assata Shakur, not to speak of Wen Ho Lee, and who
knows how many undiscovered cases of enslaved migrant workers in

Los Angeles, New York, Miami, and the new global cities — all these remain "hurts" left for us to discover. They are not Baudrillard's simulacras or counterfactual simulations regurgitated by cyborgs. George Lipsitz (1998) has cogently warned us of the "ruinous pathology of whiteness" that continues to sustain the "absence of mutuality," responsibility and justice in our society, while David Harvey (2000) reminds us how Marx long ago taught us that the constructions of race and ethnicity are implicated in the ongoing circulation process of variable capital — labor power as commodity now racialized in the global marketplace.

With the changed global/local conditions, a reassessment of our critical tools and paradigms is needed. The conversation on the situation of Ethnic Studies today is always an act of historicizing, a process of articulation in the moments of passage from one crisis to another. Every interruption of "business as usual," no matter how minor, opens up the space for strategic interventions. Crisis implies not just danger but also the break for seizing opportunities to intervene in refashioning our life-world.

The discourse on race and ethnicity — both dynamic sociopolitical constructs — remains as politically charged as before. Less insistent now is the debate over terminologies: "race" vis-à-vis racial formation, race versus ethnicity. The predicament I address may lie in the forgetting of origins and concomitantly in the loss of purpose. Our new brochure at Washington State University's Department of Comparative American Cultures foregrounds our beginning in the midseventies with the setting up of individual programs and their gradual if conflicted coalescence: Chicano Studies, Black Studies, Native American Studies, Asian American Studies. Aside from the tasks of improving ethnic representation in body counts of students and faculty, one of the tasks CAC has tried to address is that of "investigating and criticizing the traditional ways of understanding U.S. society and history that deny the centrality of 'race' and ethnicity to the American experience." The department has to reinvent itself anew every year amid budget cutbacks, downsizing, and retrenchment. In the last two decades, the field of Ethnic Studies as a whole has found itself placed on trial and besieged by its enemies, with foes often masquerading as friends. Paradoxes and antinomies afflict our horizon of thought, making a retreat for self-reflection, regrouping, and renewal necessary. What follows are remarks needed to situate ourselves historically, to project ourselves as sharing the plight of Others, in order to make what we do analytically comprehensible and thus open to reconstitution and renewal.

Paradox Unbound

In 1995 Evelyn Hu-DeHart wrote a wake-up piece for *The Chronicle of Higher Education* entitled "The Undermining of Ethnic Studies." She reflected on the paradoxical situation of Ethnic Studies as an academic discipline — paradoxical because it is both widely endorsed and universally ignored, long-established but still marginalized (Butler 1991). Why this coexistence of being both blessed and maligned at the same time? It may be that the paradoxical condition of the field — simultaneously promoted and undermined — may be a symptom of the crisis of pluralist transnational capitalism, more specifically a crisis of political legitimation (San Juan 1995). That is, the co-optive maneuvers to contain this emergent discipline reflect the systemic contradictions of the social and global formation we inhabit. The latest attempt to neutralize this challenge to received ideology is by way of postcolonial nostrums of hybridity, ludic body politics, and chic populism ascribed to diasporic intellectuals in first-world academies and their neoliberal "fellow-travelers."

All departments of Ethnic Studies, to be sure, have experienced the anxieties of in-betweenness and contingency, "trips" of indeterminacy. Their survival is nothing short of a miracle. Except that this miracle, seen in historical perspective, involves secular agents: the ordinary and daily acts of resistance by people of color against ostracism and various forms of oppression. I have in mind the mobilization of popular energies against discrimination and racist violence throughout U.S. history — a dialectic of forces that have constituted the polity from its founding. The birth of Ethnic Studies in the fury of emergencies, in the fires of urban rebellions and national liberation struggles inscribed within living memory, has marked its character and destiny for better or worse, perhaps to a degree that explains the risks and the stakes in this peculiar "form of life" (to use Wittgenstein's term).

All the bad ways of "using" or, more precisely, manipulating Ethnic Studies described by Hu-DeHart persist, including the way its singular virtue—as an "integral part of multicultural education" (Banks 1991)—is harnessed to conceal existing inequalities. Could there be a more instructive specimen of bourgeois hegemonic strategy in action? This shows that the field (I hesitate to call it "discipline" because my colleagues, including myself, are products of various disciplinary formations) is susceptible to being utilized by forces inimical to its emancipatory vocation. One might retort: So what else is new? Neither area studies, minority studies, panethnic multicultural studies, nor an adjunct of American Studies of Cold War provenance, a species of Ethnic Studies has in practice become a means to an end: to promote a version of cultural diversity required by Equal Opportunity and Affirmative Action laws. Now that this requirement—part of the "fire insurance program"—is gone, a substitute rationale has appeared: multiculturalism. This ties in with student service demands, altered demographics, and the multiethnic marketing niches of globalization.

We are witnessing today a fateful turn of events in the politics of local/global cultures as we enter the first half of the twenty-first century. Although its viability and provocativeness still draws sustenance from the historicity of its advent, the plight of Ethnic Studies also depends on the conjuncture of circumstances. It depends chiefly on the sense of responsibility of "organic" intellectuals to their communities. Everyone recognizes that this discipline would not have been possible without the radical democratic engagements of women, youth, people of color in "internal colonies" and overseas dependencies—in projects to achieve cultural autonomy, sovereignty rights, and self-determination. One might say that our field is concerned with the theorizing of such variegated praxis (for historical background, see Steinberg 1995; San Juan 1992; Brecher et al. 1993).

With the neoconservative counterrevolution of the eighties, such conditions of possibility may have been extinguished, hence the ambivalent and even amphibious mapping of this field. Hu-DeHart is sorely pressed to argue for its scholarly legitimacy and respectability, thus she tries to reinvent its reformist "contract" with society by invoking the somewhat triumphalist claim that Ethnic Studies is here to stay because "it is an integral part of multicultural education." I do not mean to ascribe a naive optimism to Hu-DeHart; her view is partly substantiated by demographics and the revitalized opposition to the neoconservativism of the last two decades. Ethnic Studies will stay so long as its practitioners adhere chiefly to the power/knowledge regime of the "role model" and regard this subject-position as the pedagogical transcoding of the chameleonic politics of identity (otherwise known as "border," hybrid, and cyborg lifestyles). The routine slogan for these role models goes like this: "Look, marvel at our inimitable crafts, performances, apparel, idioms — we contribute to making America a colorful salad bowl of differences!" Angela Davis rightly objects to this co-optative management of diversity for corporate profit making, incapable of challenging the gender, class, and race hierarchies that structure the major institutions: "A multiculturalism that does not acknowledge the political character of culture will not . . . lead toward the dismantling of racist, sexist, homophobic, economically exploitative institutions" (1996, 47).

Meanwhile, I want to provoke here an exploratory reflection on these themes of telos and commitment in this time of cynical reaction by posing the following questions: If multicultural education (for some, the "cult of literacy") has displaced the centrality of mass social movements, does this signify that we have again been subtly recolonized? Has the "power elite" (to use C. Wright Mills's old-fashioned term) succeeded in obscuring fundamental inequalities (class, gender, nation) by shifting the attention to cultural differences, lifestyles, and the quest for authentic selves? Has ethnic pluralism erased racism? Is the generic brand of Ethnic Studies and its discourse of diversity not culpable of problematizing Others of its own invention? Is it now simply used to manage and harmonize differences by refurbishing the trope of the "melting pot"? Has it been retooled to perform what Marcuse once called "repressive desublimation"? Or is it deployed as prophylaxis to service the aspirations of the comprador intelligentsia of the subalterns and ultimately pacify the populace?

Historicizing the Lexicon

Before surveying this particular terrain of American ethnic relations, a necessary detour in semantic genealogy may help elucidate the uses to which *ethnic* and *ethnicity* have been deployed, since usage spells the real significance and value of language in praxis. Etymologically derived from Latin *ethnicus* and the Greek ἐθνικός, pertaining to a group of animals or humans. The early Christians inherited from the Jews a split terminology. In the Greek version ἔθνος are the non-Jewish people, but in Paul's Letter to the Romans, ἐθνικός is translated sometimes as "heathens" or "gentiles" even though the reference is to Christianized pagans. Y. V. Brombley (1974) distinguishes *ethnikos* as the "historically established community of people" and *ethnos* as a network of communities akin to the Russian *narod* or *natsionalnost*, the German *das Volk*, and the French *peuple*.

According to Raymond Williams (1983), the word in English usage since mid-fourteenth century denotes "heathen" (from old English *haethen*), hence pagan or Gentile. In the nineteenth century, *ethnic* is superseded by *racial*. In 1961, *ethnic* in the United States is considered "a polite term for Jews, Italians and other lesser breeds." The terms *ethnology* (theories of cultural development) and *ethnography* (descriptive studies of customs), subbranches of anthropology, date from the 1830s and 1840s. In the middle of the twentieth century, ethnic suggests "folk" or "native" with reference to food, dress, music; or else it applies to a contemporary style of fashion in commercial advertisements.

In Marx's *Ethnological Notebooks* (circa 1857–1858; Krader 1972), the emerging discourse on relations of production eclipses the interest in other differences that traverse the class structure. Using Henry Lewis Morgan's hypothesis that the family in its consanguineal form is not separated from society, Marx posits the "gens" as "the first organized form of society" (Krader 1972, 63). The gens as the primordial ethnic form, the oldest form of social existence, represents the totally classless stage where property is communal and equality prevails; this gentile constitution — as Engels, building on Marx's *Notebooks*, later develops in *The Origin of the Family, Private Property and the State* (1884) — is broken up by the beginning of monogamy, the nuclear family, exploitation based on private property and the emergence of the state. Engels points out how the ethnic (kinship or blood ties) eventually metamorphoses into the economic and political (including gender) roles defined by private property. In *The Communist Manifesto* (1848), Marx and Engels hoped that ethnic or "national" differences will be transcended by the thoroughgoing proletarianization of all societies, culminating in a solidary union of all workers confronting the single world bourgeoisie. What ensued was the opposite: the revolutionary potential of class formation was disarticulated along lines of ethnic differences gravitating around notions of national identity and interest.

In "On the Jewish Question" (1844), Marx located ethnic distinctions (such as religious belief) in civil society dominated by egoistic individualism, in the bourgeois world where rights of private, fragmentary interests competed against one another. In contrast, the right of citizens (*citoyen*) guaranteed by the state existed in an abstract, "spiritual" community that ignored cultural differences. For genuine human emancipation (species-being/*Gattungswesen*) to be realized, the political abstract citizen needs to coincide with the self-interested individual to discover the socialized powers that sublate cultural and other particularistic differences. In their writings on Ireland, Marx and Engels affirmed the ethnic distinctiveness of the Irish nation on the face of the English extirpation of their language and rich traditions, an organic complex of practices connected with the intimate attachment of the Irish peasantry to the land. Exhorting the English proletariat to support the Irish struggle for independence, Marx pronounced the axiom, "Any nation that oppresses another forges its own chains" (1972, 163). For the English working class, Marx wrote, "For them the national emancipation of Ireland is no question of abstract justice or humanitarian sentiment, but the first condition of their own social emancipation" (1972, 294). From this dialectic of nation/society, Lenin derived inspiration for his affirming the principle of the colonized peoples' right to self-determination, a right that includes the practice of national language, customary rituals, and other ethnic life-forms.

Among U.S. social scientists of the 1920s and 1930s, ethnicity replaced the biologically based racial paradigm of eugenics and Social Darwinist theories of cultural evolution prevalent in the late nineteenth century. "Ethnic group" instead of "race" became the category that defined group-formation process based on descent and culture (religion, language, customs, nationality, and political identification). Gunnar Myrdal's *An American Dilemma* (1944) valorized ethnicity in its analysis of the African American problem of nonassimilation and economic-political subordination, a move to legitimize procedural forms of individual liberty on which rests a liberal democracy sustained by class inequality and racial hierarchy.

The first serious Marxist critique of "ethnicity" is the handiwork of

Oliver C. Cox, an African American sociologist. He defines as ethnic "a people living competitively in relationship of superordination or subordination with respect to some other people or peoples within one state, country, or economic area" (1948, 317). Ethnic systems or regimes can be classified according to the following criteria: (1) degrees of cultural advancement (simple or complex); (2) type variation (Occidental, Oriental, and so on); (3) pattern of variation in language, religion, and so on; (4) physical distinguishability (racial or mixed blood, and so on). When ethnics belong to the same race, Cox explains, the relations involve nationality or minority-group problems; when physical characteristics become the basis of differentiation, we confront race relations or race problems.

Cox thus historicizes intergroup transactions. He expounds on the national ethnic communities as power groups whose actual or potential antagonisms depend on the actual history of their interrelationships; for example, between English and Irish, between Jews and Catholics in Spain, between Hindus and Muslims in India. Cox believes that although castes and estates comprise status systems of socially inferior and superior persons, political-class and ethnic relations do not constitute "ordered systems but rather antagonistic regimes" (1948, 318). Although ethnics may either oppose or try to assimilate with the prevailing status system, "in political-class action not only status groups but also ethnics may be split to take sides on the basis of their economic rather than their ethnic interests or status positions." Ethnic antagonism thus complicates political class conflict to the point that it assumes the phenomenal guise of "race war."

The other challenge to the neoconservative use of ethnicity theory has been launched by Michael Omi and Howard Winant. They criticize its divorce from "the concrete sociopolitical dynamics within which racial phenomena operate in the United States" (1986, 22). Based on a monolithic dependence on the European immigrant model, ethnicity theory cannot grasp the racially defined situations of people of color (blacks, Asian Americans, Chicanos, American Indians) and the profound racialization process that operates in U.S. state and civil society. Omi and Winant's concept of "racial formation" attempts to reinscribe ethnicity as one determinant within a complex ideological mode of interpellation inspired mainly by Foucault and poststructuralist thought (San Juan

1992). But their unintended reification of race prevents them from grasping the "interplay between the social relations of production and the racialization process" (Miles and Torres 1999, 33). Despite the wide-ranging attacks on this usage of ethnicity, the concept of racial formation remains as an alternative heuristic organon of social explanation.

Problematizing Ethnicity

The doctrinal ethnicity paradigm authored by Nathan Glazer and Daniel P. Moynihan and sanctified by the *Harvard Encyclopedia of American Ethnic Groups* offers a hypothesis of how groups assimilate or not, depending on the "different norms" they bring to bear "on common circumstances" in U.S. society. The allusion to "common circumstances" not only begs the question but denies the historical record. Ethnicity is made untenable by being limited to group-held beliefs or values. This has been challenged by economists such as Michael Reich, David Gordon, and Richard Edwards. Their labor segmentation theory approach emphasizes class differentiation of the labor market; racial inequality is structural, determined by the labor-control system and "divide-and-rule" policy of the capitalist state. Meanwhile, Edna Bonacich formulates a split labor market approach to show how ethnicity combines with class to differentiate labor price. Ethnicity functions only as a variable without much decisive force.

Within the boundaries of the U.S. nation-state, ethnicization of the workforce has proceeded along with occupational hierarchization. Immanuel Wallerstein locates the function of ethnicity or cultural differentiation within the capital-labor antinomy prevalent in a particular national territory. Since proletarianized household structures need to be socialized into particular sets of attitudes that legitimate the complex hierarchy of the labor market without the state violating the formal equality of all citizens, ethnicization or peoplehood (according to Wallerstein) "resolves one of the basic contradictions of historical capitalism — its simultaneous thrust for theoretical equality and practical inequality . . . by utilizing the mentalities of the world's working strata" (1991, 84). Ethnicity then functions as a basic Gemeinschaften formed within the world-historical *Gesellschaft*, the capitalist world economy. This renders futile the debate on citizenship acquired either through juridical entitlement (state) or cultural authentication (civil society) since both are dialectically coalesced in the totality of social relations.

Cognizant of the inadequacies of the ethnicity paradigm, other social analysts have experimented in refining it via supplements and modifications. Utilizing the historical background of colonialism, John Rex tries to refine Max Weber's notion of "status" by taking account of ethnicity and class to elucidate group conflict, exploitation, and domination. Rejecting the anthropological construal of ethnicity as "primordial attachment" and the situational interpretation of ethnicity as a matter of boundaries, Rex proposes to use the category of ethnicity (a quasi group defined by kinship, common residence, shared customs) with race, nationality, and class to analyze issues of oppression and exploitation between groups. Rex posits the existence of two ethnic modalities, the benign and the malign, the first referring to the anthropological theory of ethnic boundaries (after Frederick Barth) and the second to cases of exploitation and oppression evidenced in colonial and postcolonial societies. Rex envisages in industrialized formations "the emergence of independent class struggles mobilized around national, ethnic and race ideologies." His viewpoint claims to be more sophisticated than others: "The exploitation of clearly marked groups in a variety of different ways is integral to capitalism and that ethnic groups unite and act together because they have been subjected to distinct and differentiated types of exploitation" (1986, 407).

Rex's analysis accords with the view of the African National Congress and the South African Communist Party that in formerly apartheid South Africa, the racial structure divides the white and black class factions into antagonistic camps. This concept of *colonialism of a special type* has been challenged by Neville Alexander, who argues that the nationalism of the racially oppressed conceals a form of "color-caste" consciousness. Under the slogan of "One Azania, One Nation," Alexander contends that racial or ethnic groups should be abolished as revolutionaries undertake the chief political task of nation building and universalizing equal rights: "The nation has to be structured by and in the interests of the black working class . . . by changing the entire system. A non-racial capitalism is impossible in South Africa. The class struggle against racial oppression becomes one struggle under the general command of the black working class and its organizations. Class, colour and nation converge in the national liberation movement" (Alexander 1985, 53–54).

Meanwhile, immigration and the diasporic flows of populations after World War II have introduced variables without precedent. The influx of former colonial subjects into the United Kingdom and other European industrialized countries after 1945 has necessarily diversified the working class and further stratified the labor market. The ideal of class-for-itself, now mediated by noneconomic factors in which exploitation occurs in varied unorthodox forms, appears to diverge from the canonical notion of class-in-itself, given the need for popular alliances in which the agreed political objectives condense multiclass conjunctural demands and aspirations.

To confront this new situation, Robert Miles foregrounds ethnicity as a dimension of the political economy of migrant labor and stresses the central role of racist ideology in late capitalism. Ethnicity, like race, possesses no explanatory or analytical value. Ethnicity enters into the process of "racial categorization," the reification of concrete social relations into ideological categories (1989, 73–77). For Miles, class absorbs ethnicity in the social construction of "race," in "the reproduction of class relations . . . by economic, political and ideological processes" (Solomos 1986, 100). Miles thus privileges "social relations of production" as the necessary framework in which to examine ethnicity as well as the racialization process. Through the mediation of this more dialectically tuned sensorium or analytic register in which the race/class nexus is more concretely delineated we can now examine the predicament of the variegated multitude labeled "Asians" in the United States.

Situating Asians in the Empire

Where are the Asians located in the racial polity? As numerous scholars have argued in examining the complex racial politics of U.S. history, we can no longer continue to use the white/black sociological paradigm to understand how the racialization of Latinos, Native Americans, Asians/Pacific Islanders, and other groups in this country has operated to establish, reproduce, and maintain a precarious Euro-American hegemony (Guerrero 1996; Martinez 1996). For one, the 1992 Los Angeles multiethnic rebellion, labeled "riots" by the mass media, escapes this functionalist paradigm (Chang 1994; Roediger 1992). I propose the axiom of historical specificity and the methodological primacy of material social relations to guide us in apprehending how the value of ethnicity cannot be grasped fully without the overall framework of the political economy of race in U.S. history. Except for proponents of the "Bell Curve" and other reactionary sophistries, the term *race* has by scholarly consensus no scientific referent. It is a socially constructed term embedded in the structures of power and privilege in any social formation. Its signifying power comes from the articulation of a complex of cultural properties and processes with a mode of production centered on capital accumulation and its attendant ideological apparatuses to rationalize iniquitous property relations. This system depends primarily on material inequality in the appropriation and exploitation of land, labor power, and means of reproduction by a privileged minority of European origin or affiliation. The historical genealogy of the United States as a peculiar settler formation with internal colonies and subjugated subalterns is, I submit, the necessary framework within which one should chart the post–Cold War vicissitudes of late-capitalist Herrenvolk democracy (van den Berghe 1978; Janiewski 1995).

By the year 2000, roughly ten million people of Asian descent will be residing in U.S. territory. This is part of a demographic trend in which the racial minorities (always conceived as a problem to the dominant majority) are bound to become the majority in the next four or five decades — a frightening prospect for Euro-Americans who still cling to the assimilationist melting-pot of yore. Globalizing trends, however, are able to contain both homogenizing and heterogenizing impulses enough to modulate shocking upheavals in the social landscape.

By 2020, U.S. Asians will probably reach a total of about twenty million (O'Hare and Felt 1991; Demko 1992). But chances are that even with this phenomenal increase, Asian Americans (the official rubric homogenizes more than thirty distinct groups) in general will still "look alike" to the majority. Such a will to classify "them" versus "us" is not a natural disposition, but rather a crafted scapegoating response that has become normalized (for racializing mechanisms, see Lee 1995). It is the ressentiment felt by the casualties of economic devaluation and social dislocation: someone (who happens to look or behave differently, the "strangers" in our midst) ought to pay for the crisis we are in. I cite only

the most well-known example. In 1992, two unemployed white autoworkers in Detroit mistook a Chinese American, Vincent Chin, for a
Japanese and clubbed him to death. Chin's father was a World War II
veteran and his grandfather was one of the thousands of Chinese who
built the trancontinental railroads in the nineteenth century.

About one hundred years ago, the first federal law targeting a racially
denominated group, the Chinese Exclusion Act of 1882 (not repealed
until 1943), was passed after years in which the Chinese served as
sacrificial offerings — to lynchmobs (Chan 1991; Takaki 1989). (Note
that in 1858 California passed the first law barring Chinese and "Mon-
golians"). "Kill the foreigners to save our jobs! The Chinese must go!"
were the demands of unions in California before and after 1882. Samuel
Gompers, then president of the American Federation of Labor, is famous for his statement: "Every incoming coolie means the displacement of an American, and the lowering of the American standard of
living." What needs underscoring is something marginalized in the
textbooks: Ever since the 1790 Naturalization Law, which specified that
only free "white" immigrants would be eligible for naturalized citizenship, a racially exclusive and not simply ethnic pattern of development
became ascendant in the growth of the U.S. nation-state.

Just as landmark cases like *Dred Scott v. Sanford* (1857) and *Plessy v.
Ferguson* (1896) registered the ideological effects of racial struggles in
the past, so we find analogous developments today concerning Asians.
This racially exclusivist drive to discipline Asian bodies, inflamed by
economic crises and sharpening class antagonisms in the public sphere,
informed all the laws reinforcing the 1882 Exclusion Act, the 1907–
1908 Gentlemen's Agreement regulating the entry of Japanese and
Koreans, and finally the 1917 and 1924 legislation of the "barred zone"
prohibiting the entry of all Asians, including those in the Asian part of
Russia, Afghanistan, Iran, Arabia, and the Pacific and Southeast Asian
Islands not owned by the United States. The "Barred-Zone" law is a
unique milestone in the annals of territorial purification. Clearly, the
state was neither neutral nor paternalistic in the racialization of this
hemisphere. I need not recapitulate here the narratives of brutalization
of these Asian subjects, all of which have been plotted by the discursive
and disciplinary practices of an order geared to facilitate commodity
exchange and surplus-value accumulation (Higham 1971, Myers 1960).

Up to World War II, Asians were perceived as "perpetual foreigners" because of their physiognomy and therefore had to "stay in their place." They were considered "unassimilable," recalcitrant, intractable, because of either language, customs, religions, or political beliefs — in short, their appalling victimage and their refusal to submit (U.S. Commission of Civil Rights 1992). Ethnicity acquired meaning and import within the existing class hierarchy and the vicissitudes of its internal antagonisms. Ethnicity, in short, became racialized and more visibly inscribed in the class struggle. The historian Sucheng Chan sums up the effects of state ideological and coercive apparatuses that circumscribed the location of Asians in the racial order: "In their relationship to the host society, well-to-do merchants and poor servants, landowning farmers and propertyless farm workers, exploitative labor contractors and exploited laborers alike were considered inferior to all Euro-Americans, regardless of the internal ethnic and socio-economic divisions among the latter" (1991, 187). When 112,000 Japanese Americans were "relocated" to concentration camps in 1942, this surveillance and confinement of bodies climaxed almost a century of racial politics initiated with the methodical extermination of the American Indian nations, refined in the slave plantations of the South, and extended after the Mexican-American War of 1846–1848 to Mexicans and the indigenous inhabitants of Hawai'i, Puerto Rico, Cuba, and the Philippines.

Various historians have pointed out that we cannot understand the economic and geopolitical expansion of the U.S. nation-state without constantly keeping in mind the physical displacement of masses labeled "Others," and the political subjugation of dark-skinned peoples by a civilization founded on white supremacy (Wallerstein 1991; Miles 1989; Goldberg 1993). The notion of cultural pluralism is rooted in and complicit with the permanence of systemic inequality. In retrospect, the Enlightenment principles of equality and individual rights constituted the abstract logic that legitimized the commodification of human bodies (chattel slavery) and the predatory forays of the "free market." Eventually, white supremacy and ethnocentrism acquired pseudoscientific legitimacy with the rise of Social Darwinism and the tradition of racist thinking begun by Carl Linnaeus and elaborated by Robert Knox, Arthur de Gobineau, Francis Galton (founder of eugenics), Herbert Spencer, Houston Stewart Chamberlain, and their numerous American counterparts. When the majority of Asians entered U.S. territory after the Civil War and the pacification of the Native Americans in the West, they entered a space where their subjectivity was mediated, if not produced, by this interpellation of a racializing discourse in the service of class exploitation. The boundaries of domination over Asian and Hawai'ian bodies exceeded the geographical contours of the nation-state when the United States annexed Hawai'i, Puerto Rico, Cuba, and the Philippines as colonies by the turn of the century (San Juan 1996b). The Cold War interventions in Korea in the fifties and Vietnam in the sixties and seventies explain the influx of refugees, war brides, orphans, and the "brain drain" from those unsettled regions now targeted for global modernization by transnational corporations. (And, lest we forget, these transnational entrepreneurs are not reading Max Weber's theory of modernization but rather Sun Tzu's *Art of War* and other guerilla manuals from medieval Japan.) Has the margin then become the center, or has the center been revalidated by the marginalized?

It should now be obvious that the ethnicity of Asian Americans cannot be understood apart from this history, the workings of the racial state, and the contingencies of political economy. We need to comprehend the effects of the racializing dynamics of business politics and the resonance of modernization ideology in the colonizing maneuvers of the government around the world. Because international rivalries of nation-states (despite post–Cold War compromises) affect ethnic/racial boundaries and their realignments in the United States, I would also urge a comparative approach in examining the racializing of ethnic relations across classes and genders, among European immigrants with their descendants and the dominated peoples of color, in relation to power disparities and conflicts.

We must remember that the incorporation of Asians and Pacific Islanders occurred in times of fierce class wars (articulated through race) from the start through the Civil War, the subjugation of the American Indian nations and the Mexican inhabitants of the occupied southwestern region, up to the imperialist encroachments into Latin America, Hawai'i, and the Philippines. Ideology and jurisprudence followed the logic of capital expansion and colonial administration. State power and ideological apparatuses of civil society functioned within this wider framework to determine the shifting value of ethnic properties (or whatever salient cultural attribute is defined as "ethnic" at a given conjuncture) within the dynamics of fundamental and subsumed class contradictions.

[September 11 intrudes: The "Attack on America" proves a boon, not just a catastrophe. The power elite has reinforced its legitimacy, uniting the masses under a flag already frayed by aggressions, recession, and race war. Terrorism pays. It preempts any concern with racism or exploitation. But whose faces are identified as the enemies? Terror begets massive counter-terror — a crusade against barbaric Others thought to envy America for its liberty and democracy. But the outraged populace cannot distinguish between suspected followers of Osama bin Laden, the demonized "child" of the CIA, and ordinary citizens of South Asian or Arabic descent now targeted for ostracism, physical harassment, and killing. If justice, not revenge, is the goal, we need a rational critique of the conditions (U.S. imperial policies) that continue to mobilize the "weapons of the weak" against the only remaining superpower in a sharply polarized world (Johnson 2001).]

Ethnicism, the absolutizing or mystification of ethnicity, occludes racism and delegitimizes resistance to it. We need instead to avoid reifying cultural traits and show how such allegedly fixed and static attributes change under the pressure of circumstances and the transformative force of people's actions. What is imperative is to historicize the so-called ethnic predicament — the salience of cultural practices, customs, traditions, languages, and so on, in situations of uprooting, surveillance, alienation, exclusion, violence — by inscribing the racial marking of Asian bodies and their labor power in the unevenly synchronized but universalizing narratives of the growth, consolidation, and expansion of U.S. capital in the continent and around the world (Applebaum 1996; Ong, Bonacich, and Cheng, 1994).

In Search of a New Problematic

Taking into account the altered character of working-class struggles made more complicated by ethnic, gender, regional, and other contingencies, neo-Marxists have now formulated a new approach that focuses on the flexible, more genuinely dialectical articulation of "superstructures" and "base," of various modes of production that constitute a given social formation. Ethnicity is factored into class in a social totality "structured in dominance."

Influenced by Gramsci and Althusser, Stuart Hall and his followers — formerly centered around the Center for Contemporary Cultural Studies, University of Birmingham — reconstruct the Marxist problematic by allowing ethnicity and "race" to exert a relatively autonomous impact on class consciousness and class antagonisms in historically specific conjunctures. What is important is to analyze the concrete articulation between race, ethnicity, and class.

Within a milieu characterized by authoritarian statism and popular racism in Britain, Hall argues that the regime of late capitalism structures the labor force through differentiation by ethnic, gender, and national characteristics (1986, 24). Since identity is socially and discursively constructed, Hall sees a renewed contestation over the term *ethnicity* in the politics of representation. Ethnicity has been used before to disavow racist repression, but the term needs to be disarticulated by people of color from the liberal discourse of "multiculturalism" and transcoded into the overdetermined field of sociopolitical differences: "The term ethnicity acknowledges the place of history, language and culture in the construction of subjectivity and identity, as well as the fact that all discourse is placed, positioned, and situated and all knowledge is contextual" (1992a, 257). Hall (1992b) envisages the "return of ethnicity" as diasporic communities in Europe and elsewhere question the hegemonic nationalisms of the old nation-states and in the process generate hybrid, syncretic identities out of diverse ethnic properties. Ethnicity is thus reconceptualized as relatively autonomous within the overarching process of multiform struggles involving class, gender, race, nationalities, and so on in historically specific formations.

Since the late seventies and eighties, feminists from African American, Latino, Native American and Asian communities in the United Kingdom and the United States have registered their objections to the purely white middle-class feminism of the women's liberation movement of the sixties. Instead of organizing protests around reproductive rights or domestic work, feminists of color have articulated ethnicity and race with their mass actions centered on political prisoners, rape, and sexual harrassment in the workplace and "ghetto" neighborhoods, unemployment, and other issues cutting across gender and class lines. Ethnic exclusion and racial oppression, for feminists of color, intertwine and inflect class exploitation to the extent that racism determines the temper, nuance, and physiognomy of everyday life. Some have even rejected the label "feminist" as a cover for white supremacy, choosing to unite with their male comrades in liberating the whole community or nation from racialized subalternity.

The postmodern tendency toward space-time compression (Harvey 1989) has led some observers to postulate the ongoing globalized homogenization of cultures even as aspects of ethnicity/otherness become consumer objects for an international market. Because of unequal relations of power between the West (including Japan) and "the Rest," globalization remains basically the export of Western commodities, priorities, and values. At best an uneven process, globalization allows for a new articulation between the "global" (Western capitalist domination) and the "local," now subject to relativization. Ethnic and racial markers become "floating signifiers" with meanings dependent on who articulates them, for what purpose, under what circumstances of production and reception, in what place, and at what time.

After World War II, the unprecedented phenomenon of mass migration from the colonized periphery to the metropolitan centers has produced ethnic-minority enclaves in many Western nation-states — for example, Arabs and Africans in France and Belgium; Turks and North Africans in Germany; Caribbeans and people from India, Pakistan, Sri Lanka, and other Commonwealth African countries in the United Kingdom, and so on. In the United States, by the year 2000, California and major cities such as New York, Chicago, Miami, and so on will be preponderantly inhabited by people of color — Latinos, Asians, African Americans, and other new arrivals.

Although the term *multiculturalism* has been used by liberals to describe the coexistence of diverse cultures, it is best for analytical purposes to evaluate their political directionality. Claude Meillassoux, for example, has proposed the term "social corps" to incorporate nonclass features into "bodies serving the social classes" (1993, 3). One can specify two major effects of the pluralization of previously closed, unified national cultures in the framework of globalization and the mi-

grant influx: first, the resurgence of ethnic absolutism and a homogenizing concept of *tradition* in nationalist, local-centered movements
among the majority (Solomos and Back 1996); and, second, a strategic
return to a defensive ethnic identity among minority communities. A
creative alternative also exists. With the category "black," for example,
Afro-Caribbeans and Asians in the United Kingdom construct a coali-
tional political identity at the conjuncture of other cultural and social
differences. Ethnicity, in this case, becomes a positional articulation of
identity and difference, a problem of translation and negotiated self-
interpretation, precipitated in particular milieux exposed to the tranfor-
mative pressures of diversity and otherness brought about by the profound global crises of late-"transnational" capitalism.

Now liberals have proposed that we need multicultural education to
solve the contemporary crisis, one that would get rid of the basis of
institutional racism and any form of "ethnic cleansing" such as the
lynching and murder of targeted populations. Everyone knows that the
movement to revise the Eurocentric canon and curriculum in order to
allow the teaching/learning of our society's cultural and racial diversity
has been going on since the introduction of "third-world" and Ethnic
Studies in the sixties. But one may ask: Has the formula of adding and
subtracting texts, or even deconstructing the canonical discourses and
hegemonic practices, really succeeded in eliminating chauvinist stereotypes and covert discrimination, not to speak of institutional racism
and genocidal policies? Do we really need a pedagogical strategy of
commodifying cultural goods/knowledges that consorts well with de
facto apartheid in cities such as Los Angeles, Atlanta, Detroit, Chicago,
Miami, and others?

Like the nativists of old, present-day advocates of immigration reform as well as the sponsors of Proposition 187 in California contend
that multiculturalism is precisely the problem. They believe that the
"large influx of third-world people . . . could be potentially disruptive
of our whole Judeo-Christian heritage." Multiculturalism even of the
liberal variety is considered politically correct terrorism. It allegedly
undermines high academic standards. Above all, like feminism, multiculturalism is suspected of threatening Western civilization and its legacy of free enterprise, rationality, free speech, and so on.

Stunned by the large immigrant flow from Latin America and Asia,

Senator Alan Simpson of Wyoming warned of the danger to national security: "If language and cultural separatism rise above a certain level, the unity and political stability of the Nation will — in time — be seriously eroded. Pluralism within a united American nation has been our greatest strength. The unity comes from a common language and a core public culture of certain values, beliefs, and customs, which make us distinctly 'Americans.' " *Pluribus*, it seems, can be tolerated only by dispensation of the *Unum*. Diane Ravitch condemns ethnic particularisms (such as Afrocentrism) and insists on privileging "a common culture," precisely that culture which for all its claims to universality and objectivity sparked the protests and rebellions of the last four decades (Takaki 1994, 288). What Ravitch, Simpson, and others are actually prescribing is a return to the ideal of assimilation or integration couched in terms of diversity, a refurbished "melting-pot" notion of community that would by some magical gesture of wish-fulfillment abolish exploitation, gender and racial inequality, and injustice. The renewed call by assorted fundamentalists to rally behind the flag — a nationalism coded in terms of fighting for freedom, democracy, human rights, and so on — is presented as a substitute for the comfort of ethnic belonging, but I think this can only restore the paranoia of alienation and the scapegoating of the last half century. It is also problematic to simply claim that we all benefit or suffer equally unless we see the mutual dependence of victimizer and victimized — the proverbial moralizing, cosmopolitan nostrum of tolerance and love for one another pronounced at the conclusion of this weekend's sermon.

Back to the Future

Given this background of systemic contradictions, the production of knowledge in Ethnic Studies reflects the tensions of colliding lines of sociopolitical forces in national and world history. It is not a scandalous gesture to observe that the contentious and contestatory situation of the field — to echo my initial assertion — mirrors the systemic contradictions of globalized, late capitalism headquartered in the metropolitan centers of North America, Japan, and Europe. Now with the increase of postmodernist and ludic academics, together with the flourishing of the postcolonialist industry, Ethnic Studies has acquired a new orientation more adapted to the imperatives of globalization. Globalization is, simply put, the "formalization of neoliberal ideology" (Lazarus 1998–1999, 95). It is the triumphalist rhetoric of the centralized free market, privatization, deregulation, a return to an administered technocratic Taylorism. Of course, it's not just rhetoric but actual practices that generate concrete, substantive effects. This is not the occasion to delve deeper into this topic. Suffice it to ask: What are its implications for our work? The university itself has become a conduit if not apparatus for transnational business schemes such as the emphasis on "brand" marketing, distance learning, and other flexible transactions lauded as cosmopolitan humanism and transcultural excellence.

Let me take first the issue of official multiculturalism as the new rationale for the academic interest in ethnic, as well as gender and sexual, differences. Slavoj Žižek, the Slovenian philosopher, calls multiculturalism "the cultural logic of multinational capitalism" (1997, 28). Like any cultural turn, this has elicited its antithesis in the form of what is called "the new racism" in which cultural differences become reified, fixed, immutable (Hoogvelt 1997). In spite of this multiculturalist syndrome, William Greider and others refer to a "prefascist situation" here and in Europe where populist politics exacerbates ethnic suspicions and hostilities (Martin and Schumann 1997). Others have referred to this way of conceiving Ethnic Studies as "a peaceful management of differences," a way of doing identity politics without tears (San Juan 1998a) — so long as "difference" and civil-society identity function as covers for foundational inequality. Has the vogue of identity politics ever questioned private property or the surplus value created by unpaid labor?

The politics of difference within the global political economy complicates the analysis of ethnic processes. In the light of the historical conflicts surrounding the emergence of Ethnic Studies, Ramon Gutierrez emphasizes certain "methodological principles" of the field derived from the intensive study of the histories, languages, and cultures of America's racial and ethnic groups in and among themselves. Aside from the situated and partial nature of all knowledge claims, Gutierrez assumes a postmodernist stance in upholding the principle that "culture was not a unified system of shared meanings, but a system of multivocal symbols, the meanings of which were frequently contested, becoming a complex product of competition and negotiation between various social groups" (1994, 163). Although I would agree that the focus of our discipline is comparative and relational — we explore commonalities and divergences in the experiences of racial and ethnic groups domestically and worldwide — this does not imply a thoroughgoing relativism or nominalism that would reduce history to a matter of equally suspect perspectives or personal points of view. Such would be the ethnicist "insider's" approach. In analyzing the historical dynamics of race in the United States positioned in global and comparative grids, we are precisely grounding interpretations and judgments based on a consensus of historians that is open to falsifiability. Otherwise, the "culture wars" based on identity politics would not only rule out dialogue but also all rational communicative action.

Gutierrez extols the University of California at San Diego's program in its replacement of the vertical model of single ethnic-based programs with "a horizontal model that focused on common trends and experiences among social groups," that is, a comparative-culture approach. Boundaries of disciplines supposedly erode when processes of ethnogenesis, the construction of borderland identities, and hybridization are examined, as Johnella Butler (1991) earlier surmised. But frankly I haven't witnessed this change. Now, can the refinement of Ethnic Studies as comparative cultural studies, including research into diasporas, immigration, transcultural, or border-crossing phenomena, insure us against subordination? Can a repackaging of Ethnic Studies as transcultural or transmigrant studies do the trick of producing knowledge useful for an oppositional, not to say emancipatory, project true to its original plebeian grassroots inspiration? Do we abandon these narratives and make do with local stories and pragmatic tactics espoused by de Certeau and Lyotard? The sacred doctrine of "American exceptionalism" is supposedly challenged, but American Studies internationalized simply resuscitates the canonical texts, this time read in the ludic postmodernist and postcolonial way. Addition of the excluded others in the canon without structural change doesn't alter the hegemony of "possessive whiteness," just as the multiplication of difference — "recognition politics," as Nancy Fraser (1997) formulates it — does not translate into achieved equality or fairness in the redistribution of social wealth.

A replay of the culture wars, focusing on issues of American exceptionalism and identity politics, occurred recently in the *Chronicle of Higher Education*. Sean Wilentz (1996), Professor of History at Princeton University, bewailed the celebration of fragmentation and difference ascribed to provincial scholars in Ethnic Studies. He called for their incorporation into orthodox American Studies with a cosmopolitan dressing. Wilentz celebrates in turn American culture's "cosmopolitan roots and global impact." American Studies will concentrate not just on a multicultural society but on "multicultural individuals" integrated together in a new all-encompassing commonality. Cosmopolitan individualism supplements multiculturalism to glamorize the way things are and to vindicate American ascendancy. To which some Ethnic Studies stalwarts, among them Jesse Vasquez and Otis Scott, responded by denouncing Wilentz's imperial and elitist presumptuousness.

Remapping Transitions

Clearly, we need to reassess the fundamentals of our intellectual project. Manning Marable (2000) summed up the case for a renewal, if not a revitalization, of the field by calling attention to the way international power relations has reconfigured racialized ethnicities in the light of capital's attempt to shore up declining profit margins. Marable appropriately reviews the separate genealogies of the categories of "race" and "ethnicity" against the background of the political economy of the United States from the period of slavery to the epoch of immigration in the nineteenth and twentieth centuries. Marable rehearses the debate between Ronald Takaki, now ranked among the multiculturalists who champion the cause of racialized ethnicities, and Nathan Glazer, who (together with Daniel Patrick Moynihan) represents the "cultural universalists," a rubric that I think doesn't capture their drive for reimposing a diehard white-supremacist world outlook. Exponents of the latter view, from Wilentz to Werner Sollors and postethnics like Richard Rorty and David Hollinger, have shifted the discourse of racism and inequality to citizenship and the politics of recognition (see Perea 1998). Ultimately, Marable believes that the ordeal of the practitioners of Ethnic Studies pivots around negotiating the binary opposites or "twin problems," in his words, of "cultural amalgamation" and "racial essentialism" (also known as "cultural nationalism"). Lost in this rather dualistic schematization is the dialectics of the global and local, of the logic and rhetoric of the power/knowledge combinatory, as delineated by Arif Dirlik (2000), Arnold Krupat (1998), and others.

Whatever the vicissitudes of his problematization of the field, Marable has sharply diagnosed the urgency of revaluation, of synchronizing theory and practice. He feels that we, experts in the critical study of racialized ethnicities, should gear up to the challenge of analyzing the new globalized reality of capital mobilizing racial and ethnic categories for its aggrandizement. The problem of the color-line has assumed a metamorphosis, the knowledge of which requires a recasting of speculative, analytic instruments: "A new racial formation is evolving rapidly in the United States, with a new configuration of racialized ethnicity, class, and gender stratification and divisions. . . . Traditional white racism . . . is being [replaced] by a qualitatively new color line of spiraling class inequality and extreme income stratifications, mediated or filtered through old discourses and cultural patterns more closely coded by physical appearance, legal and racial classification, and language" (2000, B7). Hence we need to revise and renew the critical optic of our evolving discipline if we want to confront such realities in the United States, not to speak of such facts of the political economy of globalization as, for example, the horrendous exploitation of eight million Filipino migrant workers (most of whom are female domestics) in the Middle East, Europe, Asia, and North America (Aguilar 2000).

Aside from the multiple diasporas occurring around the planet, the intensity of ethnic and racialized conflicts after the end of the Cold War has signaled the onset of a new stage of the historical "long period" we are living in. Works like Evelyn Hu-Dehart's *Across the Pacific: Asian Americans and Globalization*, Hans-Peter Martin and Harald Schumann's *The Global Trap*, Mike Featherstone's *Global Culture*, David Harvey's *Spaces of Hope*, and others have decentered the influential paradigm of a flexible "racial order" that proponents of racial-formation theory believe still prevails. Racialization has assumed new forms and functions in a techno-mediated accumulation process. A world-systems analysis needs to be supplemented by what Peter Gran calls a "Gramscian analytic of hegemony" in which race and racism operate as crucial variables, combining both culturalist and political-

RACISM AND CULTURAL STUDIES

economy approaches in ascertaining the new logistics of racism in late capitalism.

We still inhabit a regime of more intense commodification, not a postcapitalist or postliberal ecosystem. What has happened is, I think, a more profound radical disaggregation of the nation-state system and a reconstitution of world hegemony that have encouraged the postmodernist assertion of the end of the Enlightenment metanarrative, among others. Race and ethnicity thus have to be reconceived in the light of a universal "dereferentialization" and the collapse of the old capitalist logic — which argues for a return to the methods of Marx and Lenin as applied to the new flexible, cyborglike, even performative imperialism.

A response to the postmodernist argument may clarify my position here. In his brief for inventing a new community of dissensus and singularities in the wake of the end of the nation-state and its ideals of autonomy and of citizenship, Bill Readings contends in his book *The University in Ruins*, that we should abandon the old notions of identity, consensus, and so on. Although I disagree with his rather premature thesis of the end of the nation-state and the pragmatic cult of Otherness, Thought (with a capital T), and singularities, Readings can provoke and perhaps infuriate those not already convinced. His thesis presupposes a historicist reading of structural mutations:

> It is the desire for subjective autonomy that has led North Americans, for example, to want to forget their obligations to the acts of genocide on which their society is founded, to ignore debts to Native American and other peoples that contemporary individuals did not personally contract, but for which I would nonetheless argue they are *responsible* (and not only insofar as they benefit indirectly from the historical legacy of those acts). In short, the social bond is not the property of an autonomous subject, since it exceeds subjective consciousness and even individual histories of action. The nature of my obligations to the history of the place in which I live, and my exact positioning in relation to that history, are not things I can decide upon or things that can be calculated exhaustively. No tax of "x percent" on the incomes of white Americans could ever, for example, make full reparation for the history of racism in the United States (how much is a lynching "worth"?) Nor would it put an end to the guilt of racism by acknowledging it, or even solve the question of what exactly constitutes "whiteness." (1996, 186)

156

Despite his adherence to a ludic postality — posthistorical, postcultural, postnational, and so on — and a neopragmatism that refuses alibis, Readings can only offer a hope that thinking together within the ruins of the university may construct the community of singularities, the ersatz utopia, that will be the only alternative. How that goal can be achieved by a gestural negation of the capitalist logic of accounting and exchangeability that legitimizes the university as a transnational corporate machine in our era, remains to be seen. Despite gestures of resistance, the task of revolutionary transformation is shirked.

Maneuvering into Positions

Meanwhile, we toil in the shadow of the university's ruins, far from the aura of Plato's cave or the Socratic forum. Former fellow-travelers have resigned themselves to "cultivating their garden," acquiescing to the still pervasive hold of utilitarian individualism, the neoliberal ideology of the market, that justifies the operations of the World Bank/International Monetary Fund and the WTO. Education in the United States remains racialized in open and covert ways (Bonacich 2000). Following his style of ambidextrous signifying, Henry Louis Gates Jr. has made his peace with the Establishment in a mimic compromise. He believes that we cannot escape the complicity of self and other, the antinomies of center and periphery "where the center constructs the margin as a privileged locale, [where] you assume authority by representing yourself as marginal, and, conversely, you discredit others by representing them as central" (1992, 298). The threat to alterity is not assimilation or dissolution, Gates pontificates, but its preservation by the center, homogenizing the other as simply other. Since you cannot escape this complicity, you might as well accept Harvard's offer to make W. E. B. Du Bois respectable, if not the model of inclusiveness and extroversion. Hence literary culture proves its worth once again in its ideological service to the nation-state (Shumway 1994) that, in this post-Kosovo period, has experienced a fitful revival despite claims that it is not ethnic but civic nationalism of republican vintage that we find in the United States.

Well before the end of the millennium of pax Americana, we are asked to resurrect a convivial or consensual society committed to egalitarian principles. With the presumed end of ideology and of history as well, the system in crisis does not need to establish its legitimacy. There is no alternative — TINA, to cite an old Thatcherism. Culturalism sanctions the equality of cultures, of relativism and nominalism also premised on a hierarchical division of social labor. But contradictions persist, as well as the manifestations of good old "institutional racism." Samir Amin observes that with the triumph of the "free market," "this neoliberal utopianism [of global capital] . . . is forced to cohabit with its opposite: ethnic communalism, the spread of irrationality, religious cultism, the rising tide of violence, and all sorts of fanaticism" (1998, 119). Within the corporatized academy, the cry for accountability reverberates. Richard Ohmann considers this imperative of accountability — accountable to the elite, not to the disempowered citizenry — the project of the right to contain social movements dating back to the sixties, and for global capital to recompose itself internationally. A kind of burlesque parody of the corporatized university may be found in the acts of the intelligentsia who update Myrdal's schizoid metaphors and perform as gadfly publicists funded by corporate money in order to urge the humanities to "restore the public rigor of the metanarratives" (Miyoshi 2000, 49).

Are the fields of pedagogy and ethics the new frontier to be conquered? It would be useful to conduct a massive assault on the academic bureaucracy responsible for the commodification of education, but this would be ill conceived. It is a mistake of taking the part for the whole. Although embedded in concrete institutions and agencies, marketizing forces are systemic and structural, enabling individual and collective agencies to exercise their efficacies and instrumentalities everywhere. The ratio of commodification here is the theory and practice of multiculturalism. What can a department or program of Ethnic Studies offer as a means of resistance when it has become transformed into an instrument to camouflage, if not directly advance, the interest of universal commodification?

Permit me to hazard some proposals. One strategy is the frontal assault by polemic and mass mobilization of students and faculty to expose institutional racism. The other is the Gramscian "war of position" favored by "armchair guerillas" engaged in ideology-critique, deconstruction of discursive racism, and counterhegemonic programs to dissolve boundaries and other sociopolitical constructs. Culture in its various guises (performance, popular practices, transmigrancies, and so on) becomes the key topic, if not the site of ideological and political battles. If culture is a relational site of group antagonisms — culture is what enables the thought of the Other in the form of belief, of stereotypes, and so on — then the ideal object of inquiry is cultural production and practice. (Here the works of Erving Goffman in *Stigma* as well as George M. Fredrickson's comparative histories of racism are extremely relevant.) Our field would then engage the study of group relations and the dichotomous processes they enact, processes that symbolically replay versions of Gramscian hegemony and historic blocs. Ethnic struggles can be clarified by the investigation of class formation and the political economy of cultural process and habitus. It might be useful to learn something from Fredric Jameson's project of recasting the agenda of Cultural Studies as an inquiry into the dialectics of class and group in action:

> Whatever group or identity investment may be at work in envy, its libidinal opposite always tends to transcend the dynamics of the group relationship in the direction of that of class proper. . . . In general, ethnic conflict cannot be solved or resolved; it can only be sublimated into a struggle of a different kind that *can* be resolved. Class struggle, which has as its aim and outcome not the triumph of one class over another but the abolition of the very category of class, offers the prototype of one such sublimation. . . . "American democracy" has seemed able to preempt class dynamics and to offer a unique solution to the matter of group dynamics. . . . We therefore need to take into account the possibility that the various politics of difference — the differences inherent in the various politics of "group identity" — have been made possible only by the tendential leveling of social identity generated by consumer society; and to entertain the hypothesis that a cultural politics of difference becomes feasible only when the great and forbidding categories of classical Otherness have been substantially weakened by "modernization" (so that current neoethnicities may be distinct from the classical kind as neoracism is from classical racism). (1995, 275–76)

Jameson's insight into the submerged problematic of Cultural Studies suggests a need to reorient the field of Ethnic Studies within the parameters of the hitherto ostracized matter of social totalities — the dreaded "totality" exorcised by Lyotard cannot be evaded — and more importantly within the arena of antagonisms of all kinds (not just the Weberian conflict of tradition and rationality) underpinned by class relations of production and social reproduction in history. This will also center stage the issues of "internal colonialism" and neocolonialism underlying contemporary diasporas, transmigrations, and other current phenomena in the international division of labor.

Attempting an Inventory

Has progress in refining the theory and practice of Ethnic Studies been achieved? No doubt more people are aware, even appreciative, of cultural differences. But these new knowledges or information merely function as additions to the conventional furniture of suburban lifestyle. They do not alter the political and economic structures of the status quo. Although I generally agree with the historical and structural approach of a reconstructed Ethnic Studies, an inquiry into the dynamics of race and ethnicity in global and comparative contexts, including the dynamics of diaspora and immigration, I am skeptical whether this new retooling can give a pedagogically sharper analysis and critique of racism, ethnic conflict, nationalism in its various modalities, and exploitation in its late-capitalist disguise. Given the absorption of innovative schemes by a marketized logic of equivalence, no amount of multidisciplinarity and border crossing, I am afraid, can grasp the material processes that condition our epistemological apparatus, our frames of intelligibility, especially the nature of the contradictions inherent in the racial polity. Unless we factor in the dialectic of social institutions and collective agencies that constitute the history of social formations within the world-system of accumulation, and especially the need to transform the totality for the sake of saving lives and our environment, Ethnic Studies will continue to be a futile academic exercise. However, I am hopeful that the post–Battle of Seattle generation will cultivate a fresh revolutionary sensibility that will not fear the prospect of radical transformations and regenerative, even utopian, visions of the future.

After five years in an Ethnic Studies department and three years as chair of the Comparative American Cultures Department, what have I learned? (An autobiographical footnote: For more than twenty years I was a professor of English and American literature engaged in traditional formalist aesthetic criticism. In the early nineties when I joined the Department of Ethnic Studies at Bowling Green State University, my work shifted gradually from comparative literary inquiries to "third-world" cultural and ethnic studies, culminating in my 1992 book *Racial Formations/Critical Transformations*.) Nothing earthshaking. One thing, perhaps: people of color can victimize themselves by the successful exploitation of liberal guilt and by various compensatory rituals of self-affirmation. If we want to avoid being tokenized, exoticized, or used to sell multicultural commodities and legitimize the ideological rationale of the university, and by extension the neoliberal state, we need to begin a critique of institutions (among them the university) in their historical matrix and trajectory. We need to abandon again the methodological individualism of our distinct ethnicities and forge alliances against what is proclaimed the objective necessity of the privatized market, the forces of deregulated Taylorism and of a populist/elitist brand of Social Darwinism. We need solidarities and coalitions that will release humanity's and also nature's potential for overcoming the wreckage and destructive havoc inflicted by capital since Columbus started the genocide of the indigenous peoples whose contemporary struggles for land and sovereignty measure our advance toward planetary, ecosystemic emancipation.

Clearly we need to distance ourselves from complicity in neoliberal schemes of recuperation either by reforming citizenship standards, or indulging in an antistatist, anarchist culturalism. Pretending to resist assimilation, some of our colleagues have succumbed to enchanting varieties of philosophical idealism. Even a cursory study of T. H. Marshall (1950) on the paradox of democratic citizenship premised on class inequality could have saved us all those vacuous texts on citizenship within the U.S. nation-state, immigrant acts of representation, consent, and so on, that litter the archives of Asian American scholarship. In truth, the mutual recognition of rights to property and the formal equality of individual citizens are the key precondition for economic exploitation regulated and supervised by the liberal-democratic state (Jessop 1982). In short, representative democracy thrives on the spoils of wage-slavery.

It is therefore imperative that we attend to the political economy of differences inscribed in the material histories of interlocked groups, classes, sectors within a global arena of conflicting political forces. I would propose that instead of accenting cultural difference and its potential for bantustans, turf wars, liberal apartheid, and — even worse — "ethnic cleansing" in practice and discourse (a cliché that has portentous resonance for the field), we need to attend to the problem of power, the knowledge it produces and that legitimates it, the uses of such knowledge in disciplinary regimes, and its mutations in history. We need to examine not only the diverse cultures of ethnic groups vis-à-vis the dominant society, the solidarities and conflicts among them, but also how ethnicity itself is linked to and reproduces the market-centered competitive society we live in; how ethnic particularisms or selected cultural differences are mobilized not only to hide systemic contradictions but also to defuse the challenges and resistances integral to them. As Stephen Steinberg argues, no amount of glorifying ethnic myths and other cultural symbols of identity can hide or downplay the inequality of wealth, power, and privilege in our society that underpins the production of knowledge and the claims to objectivity and transcendent universalisms (Steinberg 1981). Such an insight into foundation should not be taken as dogma but a heuristic guide to counter essentializing of identities or utopianization of ethnicity. We cannot theorize the uneven terrain of contestation without a conceptualization of the totality of trends and tendencies. Neither privileging the global or the local, our approach should be dialectical and praxis oriented so as to take up the inaugural promise of Ethnic Studies: to open up a critical space for enunciation by those who have been silenced — Paolo Freire's speechless subalterns, or Frantz Fanon's *les damnes de la terre* — within the horizon of a vision of a just society accountable to all. The question is: Can we imagine a different and better future for all?

Such a consensus on common purpose should not foreclose disagreements or differences. What it safeguards in this period of nihilism or pragmatic relativism is the temptation of indulgence in playful self-irony, infinite ambiguity, or fluid polyvocality with the pretense that this is the most revolutionary stance against reaction and all forms of determinisms. In this time of so-called populist backlash, when the politicizing of citizens has been unleashed by the really "politically correct" officials and corporate philosophers, Gutierrez counsels us not to forsake the "grand narratives" even while appreciating the local and familiar: "At a moment when nationalism is reemerging powerfully among students in the United States as well as many other nations and states around the globe, it seems imperative that we see that glorification of local systems of knowledge which are rooted in racial, religious, and ethnic distinctions, as fundamentally tied to the globalization, commodification, and massification of social life" (1994, 165).

We need to investigate above all the reality of racism and the accompanying racial politics embedded in the everyday practices of business society, the interaction of racial ideologies with other categories (for example, gender, sexuality, locality, nationality, and so on) in order to cross the boundary between academic theory and practice in the real world. Unless we simply want to be used to manage peacefully the crisis of differences among the "natives" and reinforce the status quo ethos of liberal tolerance, "business as usual," then the practitioners of Ethnic Studies need to be self-critical of received ideas and be not just adversarial but oppositional in accord with its revolutionary beginnings, performing the role of, in James Baldwin's words, unrelenting "disturbers of the peace" (Baldwin 1988, 11). Finally I want to say something outrageous, not a proposal but a thought-experiment. We may need to phase out eventually, or sublate into some other form, the Ethnic Studies program and relocate the focus of our energies elsewhere, in teach-ins outside and inside the university, in various organizing movements. We then ought to disperse our faculties to the traditional departments that meanwhile have become entrenched bastions of "white supremacy," given the fact that Ethnic Studies has become the monopolistic agency of cultural diversification. And we may need to intervene directly in the "culture wars," in the controversies over the revamp of Cultural Studies and the reconfiguration of American Studies here and internationally. At any rate, I foresee Ethnic Studies as submitting to the unrelenting labor of the negative, settling accounts with the aborted promise of the civil rights struggles of the sixties, and launching forth into areas once the preserve of scholastic, quarantined regimes of reaction.

Otherwise, the alternative is paralysis and gradual extinction. We might resemble the three dead Chinese recently found inside a cargo container aboard a ship from Hong Kong by Seattle immigration officials (Zalin 2000, 4). Eighteen other immigrants survived the three-week ocean journey inside a 40-foot-long container, 12 feet high and

10 feet wide, customarily used for shipping electronic goods. There is a cautionary parable inscribed here. Do we need to redesign our academic Trojan horse to insinuate the tidings we carry, delivering our messages from the "belly of the beast" into the empire's heartland? Or do we need to invent new weapons that will harness the energies of the world proletariat, women and indigenous peoples, and all the pariahs and outcasts of the earth, in order to overcome the Leviathan of capital whose most seductive and impregnable masquerade is white supremacy, "the possessive investment of whiteness," the Moby Dick of Euro-American racism that has haunted the prehistory of the world as we have known it so far? May the prophecy of Black Elk be reversed, if not altogether redeemed, in our common struggle for a better life for all.

"Culture Wars" Revisited

There is no document of civilization which is not at the same time a document of barbarism. — Walter Benjamin, "Thesis on the Philosophy of History"

The old is dying and the new cannot be born; in this interregnum there arises a great diversity of morbid symptoms. — Antonio Gramsci, *Prison Notebook*

From the polyphonic voices of heterogeneity, let us turn to a monologue soliciting assent with somewhat disingenuous candor. The other day I received a mailing from the National Association of Scholars soliciting donation and membership with a cover letter describing the association's raison d'etre:

> A few years ago, some very disturbing trends in American higher education convinced me [writes the president and executive director, Stephen Balch] that the academy was on the verge of becoming an intellectual wasteland.
>
> Concepts like "political correctness" and "multiculturalism" (along with the latter's handmaiden, "diversity") had laid an iron grip on college and university campuses across America, threatening freedom of thought and expression, and destroying traditional measurements of academic achievement. Even worse, the rigorous curriculum I had known as an undergraduate was being increasingly diluted and trivialized.

On the fourth page of the letter, the president concludes a recitation of achievements with the news that "after years of domination by ideologues and zealots, there are now real indications that fresh winds are blowing through American higher education," as evidenced by the creation of "new" traditional curricula — the designing and promotion of "a new undergraduate course of study at the University of Wisconsin (Milwaukee) emphasizing the Great Books of Western civilization," and the formation of an "insurgent" organization such as the National Association of Scholars. In the parlance of Asian lore, this stratagem has been codified under the rubric: "Borrow a Corpse for the Soul's Return" (Von Senger 1991).

Lest some honest souls suspect that the culture wars have abated, brought into a lull, petered out, or simply gone away, read any periodical reporting on the fight, say, between pro-choice advocates and antiabortion militants. Just recently, an outcry from Idaho residents greeted former president Clinton's proclamation that a national monument should be built at the Minadoka Relocation Center where Japanese Americans were interned during World War II. The controversy rages on. I must confess that I am a bit surprised that the association has not computerized their list of enemies, as yet; otherwise, they would not send their invitation to one they might consider one of the "ideologues" of politically incorrect revisionism and nonconformity, something anathema to received orthodoxy.

For the last four decades I have been frankly an active protagonist in this struggle over collective ideals, projects, and goals. My article entitled "Problematizing Multiculturalism and the 'Common Culture' " was published in the journal MELUS in summer 1994 and was expanded into the last chapter of my 1995 book *Hegemony and Strategies of Transgression*. The contextual frame then was the impact of Newt Gingrich's "Contract with America" on welfare-state patronage of the arts and humanities (Isikoff 1995). Despite this deviation, perhaps I am still susceptible of performing last-minute penance and retraction. For in the aforementioned article I expressed reservations about the possible co-optive and pacifying effect of the one-size-fits-all brand of "multiculturalism" commodified by the academic marketplace. In his fiery book *Critical Pedagogy and Predatory Culture*, Peter McLaren discriminated between the spectrum of "multiculturalisms" — from conservative to liberal, left-liberal, and finally to his chosen kind, critical or resistance multiculturalism. Given my "boondocks" background, I tend to side with the resistance kind without the bonus of a postmodernist icing.

Before reflecting on the differences, and why multiculturalism itself has become a "buzzword" of contention if not opprobrium, allow me to review the theoretical backdrop to what is misleadingly labeled "culture wars." Wars of this kind have been going on since the monotheists battled the polytheists in ancient Egypt, and even before that — at least since the pivotal split between manual and mental labor. In the context of late modernity, however, it would be useful to invoke here Antonio Gramsci's ideas about ideological disputes functioning as synecdoche for social conflicts with incalculable resonance.

Gramsci postulated that hegemony (political and intellectual leadership) in most societies is realized through a combination of peaceful incremental reforms and violent confrontations. He distinguished between a war of maneuver in which the dominated masses confront head-on the central fortress of the state and a war of position in which the partisans occupy trenches found in civil society that surround and penetrate the coercive state apparatuses. Specific circumstances dictate which mode of struggle, or what combination of the two, is appropriate in order to win hegemony, that is, the consensual submission to power. Culture wars are emblematic: they signify engagements with ideological-moral positions that at some point will generate qualitative changes in the terms of engagement and thus alter the balance of power in favor of one social bloc against another. In modern industrial formations, the struggle is not just to occupy city hall, as it were, but also (from a radical, plebeian-democratic point of view) transform the relations of power, their bases and modality, on both material and symbolic levels.

In what way can culture be conceived as a site for such maneuver and positioning? How and why has culture been subsumed into the figure of war? And what are the prospects of a truce, a culture armistice or time out? A digression on semantics might be of some help.

From Genealogy to History

A semantic excavation may be useful here. Raymond Williams, in *Keywords*, instructively distinguishes three meanings of the word *culture*: culture understood as (1) a general process of intellectual, spiritual, and aesthetic development; (2) a particular way of life; and (3) works and practices of art and intelligence. The last two senses have survived, often distinguished between culture as "material production" and culture as "signifying or symbolic systems." On the surface, the conflict revolves around the latter in the form of what principles or ideas are embodied by canonical texts and which texts should be taught in the curriculum. But on closer examination, this conflict about texts implicates the former sense insofar as acts of signifying occur in specific historical settings and that texts cannot yield their full and proper meaning without assaying their socioeconomic habitats. This is not a case of which term should be accorded priority: being or consciousness (in the old jargon: base or superstructure). The debate in fact concerns the disputed relation between the two, their reciprocal or dialectical connections, their existing separation and fragmentation, in the epoch of global capitalism, in the determinate context of the U.S. racial polity.

Given the complex interanimation between the formerly compartmentalized spheres of economics, politics, and culture in late modernity, we need to confront the new reality of linkages, mixtures, displacements, and sublimations. The geopolitics of contestation embraces all aspects of society. Culture is not just one sphere separate from economics and politics; it now signifies the totality of social relations. Cultural clashes then occur in several arenas all at once: on the level of "utterances" (in Bakhtin's sense of interlocutory discourse) and interpretive/hermeneutic methods, on the level of their production, circulation, and consumption among specific communities, on the level of standards for evaluation and judgment, and so on. In any event, the complex terrain of discursive exchanges and practices can be mapped by observing how opposing points of view differ in their understanding of the relation between text and contexts, utterances and their socio-ethical matrices. In general, the recurrent contradiction (with hybrids and mutations across them) is that between an essentializing and hypostatizing stand versus a historicizing, realist/materialist one. What are the stakes in the clash between these two approaches, sensibilities, and *problematiques*?

A general historical accounting would help illuminate the field of combat. But for the moment I want to explore briefly the possible answers to this question, which of course involves a more fundamental inquiry into the role of educational institutions, media, and other power/knowledge constellations in reproducing social relations. Reviewing the impact of Cold War ideology on the humanities, Richard Ohmann (1997) gives us a succinct answer: education plays a decisive role within the hegemonic social process by helping reproduce inequality — differential access to cultural capital and networks of privilege — as a product of formal procedures that spell out the terms of differential opportunity and meritocratic competition. It might be instructive here to illustrate the range of "talking points" by juxtaposing two commentaries, one by Gerald Graff (1992) and the other by Russell Jacoby (1994a). After this I go on to examine Charles Taylor's theorizing of the politics of identity or recognition and then allude to some problems of critical multiculturalism with reference to Rigoberta Menchú's intervention in this colloquium among white males, dead and alive. Consider this a long prologue to an ongoing extraacademic conversation on the problem of difference, alterity, and the much-touted impossibility of subaltern speech.

It might be appropriate to begin with things usually taken for granted, or with facts that some claim have already evaporated into the postmodern space of simulacra and the hyperreal. Since the late sixties, the crisis of the world system, more precisely of capital accumulation, has wrought deep, massive changes whose disturbing symptoms in group and personal lives we all experience daily. Ironically, this crisis has been celebrated throughout as the triumph of free enterprise, democracy and freedom, over Soviet communism and its totalitarian "Evil Empire." It is the Manichean allegory of the bourgeoisie's triumph over its own self-contradictory nature, yielding their gravediggers in the womb of the dying order.

One of the starkest symptoms of the crisis in our society is the increased gap between rich and poor. The number of people living below the poverty line grew from 24 million in 1977 to 35 million in 1986. As of 1992, the richest 1 percent in the United States controlled more than 60 percent of the national wealth (assets declared) while 90 percent of families have no net wealth (Chasin 1998; Perlo 1996). Such egregious concentration of wealth and power, entailed by unemployment due to deindustrialization and de-skilling, cutoff of social services, the deterioration of living conditions of the middle class (not to mention the homeless and those stigmatized as the "underclass"), and the decay of cities and environment, has led to what Michael Parenti (1994) calls

"Third Worldization of the United States." Its features include "an increasingly underemployed, lower-wage workforce; a small but growing moneyed class that pays almost no taxes; the privatization or elimination of human services; the elimination of public education for low-income people; the easing of restrictions against child labor; the exporting of industries and jobs to low-wage, free-trade countries; the breaking of labor unions; and the elimination of occupational safety and environmental controls and regulations" (Parenti 1994, 81; Mantsios 1995).

When we look at the condition of the racial minorities — African Americans, Native Americans, and Latinos — the situation appears bleak: black unemployment and infant mortality is more than twice that of whites, life expectancy seven years less; median per capita income is three-fifths that of whites (same with Latino-white ratio). One out of four black men between the ages of twenty and twenty-nine are either in jail, on probation, or on parole. The prison population, doubled since 1980, is mainly composed of people of color. The statistics for Native Americans are even worse: a higher proportion live in poverty than any other ethnic group (Bordewich 1996). When we conflate the demographics of race/ethnicity into this process of stratification (chapter 2 surveyed the interweaving of race, gender, sexuality, and nationalism), the background for class and ethnic antagonisms manifesting itself in the accentuation of differences in tastes, values, beliefs, and ethos implicated in the series of events called "culture wars," will be more or less complete.

By the year 2050, according to census extrapolations, the population of the United States will be comprised mainly of people of color: Latinos, African Americans, Asian/Pacific Islanders, American Indians, and other diasporic settlers. This would mean that the global majority of people of color in the continents of Africa, Asia/Oceania, and Latin America would become predominant in a nation-state that since World War II has epitomized Western hegemony over the planet. In the event that the former numerical minority becomes the majority, would the existing power relations and social divisions today be fundamentally changed? How would this affect the production, circulation, and allocation of material wealth and symbolic capital? So far, though, the status quo of asymmetrical power relations remains unchanged. In fact, the civil rights gains of the fifties and sixties — in particular, Affirmative

Action that benefited chiefly white middle-class women — are being rolled back, slandered, gutted, and erased from memory.

Despite these changing demographics and attendant dislocations, or mainly because of them, we have witnessed a backlash. Holly Sklar observes that to the institutional discrimination of people of color (patronizingly called "minorities") is added insult:

> It's common for people of color to get none of the credit when they succeed — portrayed as undeserving beneficiaries of affirmative action and "reverse discrimination" — and all of the blame when they fail. A study of the views of fifteen-to-twenty-four-year-olds found that 49 percent of whites believe that it is more likely that "qualified whites lose out on scholarships, jobs, and promotions because minorities get special preferences" than "qualified minorities are denied scholarships, jobs, and promotions because of racial prejudice. Only 34 percent believed that minorities are more likely to lose out." . . . One revealing epitome of this backlash is a Republican presidential candidate's ultimatum to the national convention: "There is a religious war going on in this country. It is a cultural war." In the audience, delegates waved signs with the slogan "Gay Rights Never," among others. Apropos of the Los Angeles multi-ethnic rebellion after the acquittal of the police who beat up Rodney King, Pat Buchanan remarked: "I met the troopers of the 18th Cavalry, who had come to save the city. . . . And as those boys took back the streets of [that city], block by block, my friends, we must take back our cities and take back our culture and take back our country." (1995, 127–28)

Translated into academic idiom, we get the best-sellers of this genre: from Allan Bloom's *The Closing of the American Mind* and William Bennett's "To Reclaim a Legacy" to the potboilers of Dinesh D'Souza, Diane Ravitch, Lynne Cheney, Roger Kimball, and others.

Meanwhile, the venerable Arthur Schlesinger Jr. bewails the cult of ethnicity and group self-esteem. He complains that because of glorifying pluribus and not unum, "the melting pot yields to the Tower of Babel," that is, incoherence and chaos. His stratagem is a version of the search for scapegoats summed up in the Chinese aphorism: "Let the Plum Tree Wither in Place of the Peach." Schlesinger advocates a return to a singular, unitary American canon founded on a postulated commonality of experience (the Puritan errand into the wilderness, the frontier/pioneer myth of taming a virgin land, and other tropes privileging the position of the white patriarch) with its undeniable European provenance. Instead of what he deems cultural and linguistic apartheid, Schlesinger insists on reaffirming a homogeneous "American tradition," the American heritage embodied, for example, two centuries ago by Hector St. John de Crevecoeur who envisioned "individuals of all nations" melted into "a new race of man" in America (1994, 295). With qualifications, this paradigmatic racializing individualism still informs the possessive/acquisitive variant practised today in either neo-Social Darwinist or utilitarian-populist guises.

Heritage always imposes a principle of division and discrimination. In response to this thesis of a "common culture," a particular ethos become hegemonic, Ronald Takaki argues that national unity or identity cannot exist in a society where "rights and nationality have not been extended to all groups." Indeed, the worsening inequalities and institutional racism I just reviewed belie the presence of a "common culture" of democracy, human rights, and social justice (1994, 299). Unlike Schlesinger, Takaki believes that attacking Eurocentrism is not enough; one needs to interrogate "the material basis of racial inequality," the structural ground enunciating differences as asymmetry and hierarchy of power — in short, the unequal property relations predicated on the dispossession of the working masses' means of livelihood.

Point Counterpoint

Let us compare at this juncture the ethicopolitical stances of two protagonists in this skirmish, Gerald Graff and Russell Jacoby, to illustrate the field of power and its disposition of symbolic capital.

Formerly based at the University of Chicago, Graff is one of the most articulate humanists today who translates his ideas into action as a leader of the Teachers for a Democratic Culture. His book *Beyond the Culture Wars* elaborates on his single vision encapsulated by the slogan "teach the conflicts." Graff is aware of the economic and political changes to which I have alluded. Unlike either camp, he believes that the raging debates attest to a healthy burgeoning milieu fertile with new transvaluations of reality. We need controversies and conflicts of ideas to help us adjust to the changing world. The problem, however, is that constructive dialogue is absent, blocked by the disjunction of the curriculum, by "the evasive compromise represented by the pluralist cafeteria counter curriculum, which leaves it up to students to connect what their teachers do not" (1992, 12). So Graff preaches the need for an integrated curriculum where conflicting positions are displayed and related, for collaborative teaching. He believes that both liberal pluralist and conservative solutions to the disarray in higher education are useless because they do not afford a common learning experience.

In his concluding chapter, Graff elaborates on the theme of "the principle of making conflict the basis of community," a principle operationalized in experiments in curricular integration strategies, team teaching, clusters of thematic courses, and so on. Graff believes that the partial successes attained so far can integrate humanistic culture, research, and business technology that one finds in the major universities. Graff does not say anything about corporate-funded research, about entrepreneurial techniques applied to education, about the business and market orientation of many schools. Instead Graff assumes that the context for all the experiments he recommends is "the dynamics of modern academic professionalism and American democracy" (1992, 195) — the latter entity, as well as its connection with the former, is never problematized in the text. In effect, for Graff, pedagogical disagreements and theoretical differences can be exploited as (to use his mentor Leo Marx's words) "a source of interest, vitality, and direction."

We arrive at a quick-fix solution. The disagreement between a feminist and a neoconservative New Critic, between a neofascist deconstructionist and an Afrocentric activist, if properly packaged according to the tried-and-true formula of peacefully managing differences, can get rid of academic doldrums, relativism, and mass-produced mindless fantasies. Graff is concerned, then, with the form or shape of these debates, not the substantive issues. You can teach Joseph Conrad's *Heart of Darkness* and Chinua Achebe's critique of it or any of his novels, and still have your martini, Mozart, and a good night's sleep.

It appears that the limits of Graff's liberal-pluralist panacea for the systemic crisis inheres in his penchant for gimmicky technocratic solutions. His pragmatism is quite naive in its claim of successfully reconciling extremes. His realism may gesture to the structural causes of the crisis, but that is merely a sop to the radical mob. Essentially he doesn't see anything profoundly wrong in the system. What is needed is retooling, readjusting, tinkering with the machine since it has performed well in the past and with some streamlining should perform better in the future. His faith in the academy is diametrically opposed to Bill Readings. "It is only by such peaceful coexistence that the university could have achieved the improbable feat of becoming modern society's chief patron of cultural innovation without ceasing to stand for staunchly traditional values" (1992, 7). Such faith in the recuperative power of the university to resolve the conflict by teaching it, I am afraid, begs so many questions. This stratagem succeeds in displacing the relative sequence of cause and effect, a ruse distilled in the Asian folk maxim: "Clamor in the East, Attack in the West."

Let us turn now to Jacoby's *Dogmatic Wisdom* (1994a). One of its attractive virtues is its witty and sometimes flippant satire on the foibles of both neoconservative and left-wing intellectuals. The criticism of academic self-serving delusions is well taken. It is founded on a grasp of the antinomies and paradoxes of liberal society sustained by an oxymoronic logic of exploiting "unfree" labor in the free market. In a world afflicted with alienation, where commodification runs rampant and the laws of the market dictate lifestyles and life chances, how can educational practices and institutions not reflect and reproduce such a world? In short, the market gets the culture it deserves. Where symbolic goods compete, you find cultural battles. Jacoby writes, "Yet these conservative critics barely breathe of the real force corroding liberal education: an illiberal society. They sputter about tenured radicals and stay mute about an instrumental society. An unbridled desire for practical knowledge and good money recasts higher education, as it has for decades, even centuries" (1994a, 8). I am sympathetic with the tenor of this exposé. But one may ask: Is Jacoby a vulgar materialist, one of those economic determinists supposedly made obsolete by the fall of the Berlin Wall and the victory of the World Bank?

Jacoby faults Graff for concentrating on elite universities, not on local public education. Because Graff shares the ethos of managerial technocrats, he practices what Jacoby calls "academic boosterism," functioning less as a critic than a "cheerleader of professional life." Graff loves the academization of literature and the sophisticated jargon of conferences, so that (according to Jacoby) he succumbs to tautologies and banalities: "We should teach students to talk, think, and write as we do. Why? Because this is what we do" as professionals and adults who are serious about power, money, and jobs. While this simplification may be unfair to Graff, there is a big grain of truth in it. Jacoby dismisses Graff's response to the policing of "political correctness" thus: "Graff prescribes hustling conferences of upscale professors fleeing their campuses as the cure, not the disease. He confuses networking with teaching, back-scratching with scholarship, jargon with thinking. The scramble for self-advancement, not the crackle of thought, heats up the atmosphere at professional conferences" (1994a, 188).

With this tone and register, Jacoby is in the respectable company of satirists like Mark Twain, H. L. Mencken, Philip Wylie, and Kurt Vonnegut. His polemic should be framed and judged according to that genre. His own prescription for the crisis is, however, anticlimactic and cautiously understated. It bears a populist, homegrown appeal like a Zen aphorism: "A thousand studies and ten thousand reports and what is necessary is nothing fancy: decent classrooms, good libraries, devoted teachers, small classes, committed students, low tuition. If these were in place, hostilities over schooling, curriculum, affirmative action, racism, and free speech would shrink; pools of acrimony would drain away" (1994a, 194). Such an easy way out of this mess, and fools that we are have not taken thought and lifted our imported bootstraps.

Whatever their claims to honesty and open-mindedness, both Graff and Jacoby have easily avoided the crucial questions that need to be posed concerning the production of knowledge, its power and effects, who controls it and for what purpose. Henry Giroux formulates them in this way: "Whose authority is secured through the form and content of specific canons? What does it mean to organize the curricula in ways that decenter its authority and power relations? What social relations have come into play to give university teachers and students control over the conditions for producing knowledge?" (1996b, 190). In short, how are the imperatives for standard and excellence valorized by those defending a supposedly battered "Western civilization" espousing the cause of freedom and representative democracy? To contend that criteria of complexity and depth needed to judge great literature should transcend the boundaries of race, gender, sexuality, class, or place of national origin (see Fox-Genovese 1995) is to foreclose the horizon of critical inquiry and succumb to vacuous subjective metaphysics.

Autobiographical Digression

Before addressing the thesis of Charles Taylor's now classic touchstone in this debate, "The Politics of Recognition," I want to interject a short autobiographical note. About thirty years ago, when I began graduate work in English and American literature at Harvard University in September 1960, Fidel Castro had just marched victoriously into Havana, Cuba. Several African countries — Ghana, Kenya, and so on — gained their independence, student sit-ins in Nashville and the freedom rides in the south were just beginning. But so powerful was the neo- (not post)colonial education I had in the Philippines that such upheavals did not affect my rather scholastic concentration on Henry James, William Faulkner, Ernest Hemingway, and other canonical authors. New Criticism was then the opium of the Filipino intellectuals; and in tandem with my generation I pursued the routine of formalist inquiry, little knowing that the philosophical and ideological grounds of such thinking were being eroded by the worldly circumstances unfolding in the sixties, in particular by inter alia the escalation of the war in Vietnam, George Jackson and the Black Panther Party, the Cultural Revolution in China, the burning of major cities here when Martin Luther King Jr. was assassinated, Che Guevara, and the founding of the revolutionary New People's Army in the Philippines.

Who of us can truly foresee the unpredictable turns of our brief sojourn on earth? And so I am somewhat embarrassed to confess that it was not until the early seventies, when I was reading the most formidable Marxist philosopher Georg Lukács (I edited a collection of his essays in 1972) together with George Jackson's *Soledad Brother* while the campus of the University of Connecticut was slowly transformed into a battlefield between students and state troopers — it was only then (better late than never!), during the time of real wars (in cities of the center and the wilderness of the periphery) that challenged the hegemonic culture, that I was compelled, willy-nilly, by so many happenstance detours and fortuitous encounters, into educating myself about the realities of life in the twentieth century. Literature in the academy could no longer serve then as a refuge from the fury of struggles going on because my students themselves, and some colleagues, were caught in the fray. So I acquired (if I may put it) the rudiments of a historical-materialist consciousness.

Beginning with the seventies I tried to see the world in a way completely different from before, sensitive now to class, gender, sexuality, race, and nationality — to the complexities of ordinary lives in the "belly of the beast." My past life was under trial, my future under surveillance — up to now. I am now compelled to be accountable, to answer to the conscience of Others. Indeed I woke up to the age of desperado imperialism. While I studied Marx, Lenin, Lukács, Adorno, Gramsci, Mao, Che Guevara, Althusser, Rosa Luxemburg, and C. L. R. James in the eighties, it was only in the last six or seven years that I began to realize the overriding importance of the "race" (not ethnicity) question as a theoretical field of inquiry, even though earlier I had been teaching Malcolm X, Du Bois, Baraka, Frantz Fanon, Amilcar Cabral, and other revolutionary third-world thinkers and artists. In writing *Racial Formations/Critical Transformations* (1992), I began to wrestle with the complex interconnections and mutations of the race/class nexus while teaching non-Western cultures and comparative literature within the traditional disciplinary framework. My move to the field of Ethnic and Cultural Studies may indicate my commitment to the emergent field of comparative cultural studies, interdisciplinary and crosscultural, where problems of race and ethnic relations, articulated with class, gender, nationality, and the geopolitics of late or global capitalism, are considered key to understanding the "laws of motion" and possibilities of radical transformation of unevenly aligned societies around the world. Where possibilities for the war of maneuver are not feasible, then we focus our energies on the war of position as part of a larger strategy of an emancipatory and oppositional cultural politics. And it is in this crucible of the emancipatory imagination where my intervention should be inscribed.

The Stakes of the Wager

I now return to the problematic of class-conditioned racism that sutures these reflections on the linkages of class, race, gender, and nation in late modernity. Charles Taylor contends that behind the culture wars is the more fundamental conflict encapsulated by his term "politics of recognition." Proceeding historically, Taylor traces this politics to the modern concept of individual dignity, in an ecumenical and liberatory sense, at the heart of the Western heritage from the Enlightenment and the bourgeois revolution. Romanticism (Rousseau and Herder) contributed the ideal of authenticity, which replaced the aristocratic concept of honor: "Being true to myself means being true to my own originality, which is something only I can articulate and discover. In articulating it, I am also defining myself. I am realizing a potentiality that is properly my own" (Taylor 1994, 31). Because life is fundamentally relational or dialogical, this authentic identity is realized in the public sphere as the politics of equal and reciprocal recognition. The problem arises in the public sphere in our liberal construal: a politics of universalism privileges the equal dignity of all citizens, the equalization of rights and entitlements. This ignores the historical specificity of groups that have been denied reciprocity, in short, collectivities (women, racialized communities, indigenes) excluded, marginalized, discriminated, and oppressed across time and space. Are all cultures and their group embodiments equal?

Taylor, who is sympathetic to the dilemma of the French Canadians, believes that there is no universal standard yet that can be used to answer that question. In search of a compromise between the homogenizing demand for recognition of equal worth and the "self-immurement within ethnocentric standards," Taylor resorts to a hope in the encounter of incommensurable horizons of meanings and values peculiar to each culture. The presumption that all cultures are of equal value, Taylor concludes, requires of us "not peremptory and inauthentic judgments of equal value, but a willingness to be open to comparative cultural study of the kind that must displace our horizons in the resulting fusions. What it requires above all is an admission that we are very far away from that ultimate horizon from which the relative worth of different cultures might be evident" (1994, 73).

As though in response to Taylor's challenge, Robert Hughes's *Culture of Complaint* tries hard to approximate this requirement but falls short. This is not hard to grasp because, first, Hughes believes that he already can understand Others (he claims himself as belonging to that region of alterity) and, second, because of a showy dilettantism and eclecticism that trivialize culture's powerful normative political/ethical causalities and effects. Under the pretext of a capacious humanism, Hughes conceals his real intent of celebrating the "protean energies of capitalism" (1993, 81) — a stratagem called in the old adage, "Follow the Emperor and Cross the Sea."

Not counting the cynics, the protagonists of our present culture wars fall into two camps: the communitarians like Taylor who question the ethical neutrality of law in a liberal polity and who want the state to promote a specific conception of the good life, and liberals like Rawls, Dworkin, Rorty, and their ilk. Having posited that dichotomy, Habermas asks, "Does not the recognition of cultural forms of life and traditions that have been marginalized, whether in the context of a majority culture or in a Eurocentric global society, require guarantees of status and survival — in other words, some kind of collective rights that shatter the outmoded self-understanding of the democratic constitutional state, which is tailored to individual rights and in that sense is 'liberal'?" (1994, 109) Habermas believes that there is an internal connection between the individual rights of private persons and the public autonomy of citizens; if the system of rights is to be actualized democratically, then citizens' autonomy must be activated to take account of the social and cultural differences that contextualize such autonomy. The liberal theory of rights, the establishment of normative rules of behavior, is influenced by the society's political goals and thus expresses a particular cultural form of life, the self-understanding of a collectivity; that is, the ascriptive network of traditions, intersubjectively shared contexts of life and experience. This self-understanding of course changes when the social makeup of the population changes; historical circumstances alter the persons involved in the dialogue that shapes the discourse of identity. Such ethical-political decisions of a nation of citizens embody a conception of the good and a desired form of authenticity that necessarily exclude and discriminate over Others. What sparks culture wars, to follow Habermas's reasoning, "is not the ethical neutrality of the legal order but rather the fact that every legal community and every democratic process for actualizing basic rights is inevitably permeated by ethics" (1994, 125–26).

We need then to distinguish between ethics as private morality and ethics as civic responsibility to others without whom we cannot be fully human as social individuals. If we resituate the question of ethics in this terrain of "the battle of the books" (books, it is understood, are figures for assemblages and collectivities competing for allegedly scarce resources), the fundamental philosophical question may be better ascertained. It involves understanding both the failures of deconstructive essentialism that has underwritten postmodernist identity politics, and the pluralist multiculturalism illustrated by Graff, Jacoby, and others. Nancy Fraser contends that "both fail to connect a cultural politics of identity and difference to a social politics of justice and equality. Neither appreciates the crux of the connection: cultural differences can only be freely elaborated and democratically mediated on the basis of social equality" (1996, 207). It is, needless to say, a formidable challenge.

Menchú's Intervention

Let us subject these binaries of difference/justice and identity/equality to interrogation by the indigenous Others. Not too long ago, the schisms of cultures were settled by the customary bifurcation of East and West, now translated into North and South. The Spanish philosopher José Ortega y Gasset (1956), for example, distinguished Europe as the land of "clear and distinct ideas" from the Others stuck in a marshland of myths and taboos. The dialectic of Enlightenment prompts us to find a way out of this labyrinth of errors, from the syndrome of received prejudice and its corollary nexus of self-deception.

The plight of the fabled "speechless" subaltern pleads for attention. For this occasion, I want to use the Menchú controversy as a site for rehearsing the problem of how and whether the Other can be represented in the discourse of modernity, or its postmodern antithesis. It's not just a matter of liberal tolerance or latitude. Just consider, for example, how can we mediate the cultural differences between the now classic testimonio *Me llamo Rigoberta Menchú y así me nació la conciencia* of Nobel prize-winner Rigoberta Menchú, a Quiche Indian from Guatemala, and the canonical texts of Plato, Shakespeare, T. S. Eliot, and so on? How shift from the unique worldview of the Quiche people that refuses to recognize the separation of humans from nature, of the individual from the community, to the central premises of a liberal polity centered on possessive, exclusivist individualism?

Obviously I am not suggesting a stratagem of substitution, of "tossing out a brick to attract jade." We need to face the singularity of an antitext, one that questions, for example, the innocence of the Judeo-Christian tradition. Notwithstanding the recent theology of liberation utilized by Menchú, this tradition has legitimized the conquest of the continent and the genocide of its aboriginal peoples, and today sanctions their continued repression by an oligarchic government armed and supported by various U.S. administrations. In such confrontations, the usual asymmetry of civilization (the West) and barbarism (the Rest) is scrambled, reversed, or discombobulated. The center of gravity for now has shifted from Guatemala to Chiapas, Mexico, and the guerilla zones of Colombia.

What or where can we find the basis for a constructive dialogue in these strife-torn lands? Let me explore briefly the conflicts and speculate on the implications. Obviously, given its condition of production — the encounter in Paris between a Venezuelan anthropologist and an activist Indian — Menchú's text needs to be distinguished from the Western genre of autobiography, interview, or even conventional ethnographic discourse. Suffice it to mention a few facts to establish the parameters of exchange: by the time Menchú's book came out, a conservative estimate is that at least 100,000 indigenous peoples had been killed by the U.S.-supported government; at least 40,000 had disappeared, 450 villages destroyed, and 250,000 people turned into refugees because of "antiguerilla" campaigns against the native population together with labor, human rights, and church activists (Childs 1993). The origin of this horrendous situation can be traced to the colonial underdevelopment of the country as a "banana republic" where 98 percent of the land is owned by less than 150 people (counting each foreign corporation as a person). U.S. foreign investments dominate the country, with the United Fruit Company as the biggest landowner. When Guatemalans elected a democratic government headed by Jacobo Arbenz (1952–1954), Arbenz began to institute a mild land-reform program. This triggered a 1952 CIA report that "Communist influence . . . based on militant advocacy of social reforms and nationalistic policies" was dominant, leading to "the persecution of foreign economic interests, especially the United Fruit Company" (Chomsky 1986–1992, 47–48). President Eisenhower allowed the CIA to topple the Arbenz regime. The president of the United Fruit Company then happened to be Allen Dulles, CIA director; and Walter Bedell Smith, who directed the CIA before Dulles, became president of the United Fruit Company after Arbenz was overthrown. Included in the directorship of the company were Henry Cabot Lodge, U.S. ambassador to the United Nations, and John Cabot, assistant secretary of state for Inter-American Affairs; U.S. Secretary of State John Foster Dulles was legal adviser to the company (Greene 1970).

After the military coup, the Johnson and Kennedy administrations gave massive aid to the Guatemalan military that quickly transformed the country into the "killing fields" of the last four decades. Carter's "human-rights" administration did not change anything. During the period of Reagan's support of Rios Montt in the early 1980s, the genocidal slaughter of tens of thousands of Indians occurred, decimating entire regions. Julio Godoy, a Guatemalan journalist, returned from Europe in 1989 and contrasted the situation there with that in Central America. He found the East Europeans luckier because "while the Moscow-imposed government in Prague would degrade and humiliate reformers, the Washington-made government in Guatemala would kill them. It still does, in a virtual genocide that has taken more than 150,000 victims [in what Amnesty International calls] "a government program of political murder. . . . One is tempted to believe that some people in the White House worship Aztec gods — with the offering of Central American blood" (Chomsky 1986–1992, 50).

Text and discourse are never innocent of complicity with events. The current controversy over Menchú's truthfulness and her authority as an indigenous spokesperson brings into sharp relief the substantive issues of objectivity versus human interest, between rationality and partisan ideals. It serves as a timely reminder that the dispute over truth (now referred to as "truth-effect," after Foucault) and its representation is transnational in scope and perennial in nature. It evokes the memory of some durable controversies in the humanities and social science disciplines that have assumed new disguises since the heyday of the "two cultures" of C. P. Snow, or much earlier, the anarchy/culture polarity of Matthew Arnold. Should the tale be trusted over the presence of the teller, as D. H. Lawrence once advised? Or is it the case that if there is no teller, there is no worthwhile tale?

Obviously the question of knowledge of what is real, its legitimacy and relevance, occupies center stage. Much more than this, however, in the secular/technological milieu of late modernity, what concerns us is the usage to which such knowledge, whether of the natural world or of society, is put. What is the objective of truth-seeking? Who benefits? Who loses? Inflected in the realm of knowledge about culture and society, the problem of representing the world (events, personalities) looms large, distilled in such questions as: Who speaks now? For whom? For what purpose? One way of responding to such questions is by shrewd evasion. The pursuit of instrumental truth ironically dispenses with speaker, circumstance, and addressee. It displaces what Bakhtin calls the dialogic scene of communication. The truth-seeker interested in the content of the tale asks: Is Rigoberta Menchú telling the truth, that is, conveying accurately the objective facts about the torture of her family?

Anthropologist David Stoll, the author of *Rigoberta Menchú and the Story of all Poor Guatemalans* (1999), testifies that Menchú is lying. Seemingly adhering to a traditional positivist standard, Stoll argues that Menchú's testimonio "cannot be the eyewitness account it purports to be" because he compares it with the reports of his selected informants in Guatemala. No one, however, has checked the veracity of these informants. Are they more reliable? Under what criteria? Stoll contends that Mayans who did not side with the guerillas are more trustworthy, or at least their reports vitiate Menchú's credibility. Stoll accepts quite naively the other versions of what happened in Guatemala, and for him they are more authentic, if not more veridical. Those versions turn out to invalidate the truth-telling authority of Menchú's testimony.

Protagonists on either side do not stake their positions on details but on the theoretical framework that makes intelligible both Menchú's narrative and Stoll's interrogation. Literary critic John Beverley, for example, emphasizes the genre or discursive structure of Menchú's testimonio. He underscores Menchú's ideological agenda and her pragmatic aim of inducing solidarity. By contrast, Stoll, D'Souza, and other detractors try to counter Menchú's revolutionary agenda by their own politically correct demand for truth regardless of genre or stylistic form in which such truth is lodged. In a review of Stoll's book and Menchú's recent testimonio *I, Rigoberta Menchú: An Indian Woman in Guatemala*, Greg Grandin and Francisco Goldman (1999) cogently show the inconsistencies of Stoll's position. Both sides, it seems, do not quarrel over certain "givens" described in other accounts (see, for example, Eduardo Galeano's *Guatemala Occupied Country*). Consider also this report by sociologist John Brown Childs: "At least 100,000 indigenous peoples have been murdered by (U.S. supported) government forces; at least 40,000 have 'disappeared,' which is to say they have been murdered; 450 villages have been destroyed; and 250,000 people have been turned into refugees because of government 'anti-guerilla' campaigns aimed at the Mayan population" (1993, 20). Since Menchú is not expressing this "given," it seems acceptable tacitly or not to all parties.

Hermeneutic Agon

We are not rehearsing the ancient dictum about objective scientific truth in chronicles and annals that everyone takes for granted. Many members of the academic community are familiar, to one degree or another, with the antithetical modes of historiography and the attendant controversy elucidated sometime ago by E. H. Carr (*What Is History?*). There is a flourishing debate between those who espouse a naturalist or scientific point of view typified by historians like Marc Bloch, and those who advocate a hermeneutic or interpretive view upheld by R. G. Collingwood, Barraclough, and others. Carr himself tried to strike a compromise when he asserted that "the historian is engaged in a continuous process of moulding the facts to his interpretation and his interpretation to his facts," unable to assign primacy to one over the other. But, in the first place, what are the facts? Obviously one cannot search for the facts without some orientation or guideline framing the totality of social relations and circumstances where those "facts" are located and from what angle they are perceived. Otherwise, how can one distinguish a fact from a nonfact? What principle of intelligibility is being applied?

Postmodern thinkers influenced by poststructuralist trends (deconstruction, de Certeau, Butler) contend that objective truth in historical writing is impossible. History is not a body of incontrovertible, retrievable solid facts (in Mr. Gradgrind's sense) but a text open to various, disparate interpretations. Foucault's lesson for us is that historical accounts are problematic representations of life because they are constituted by heterogeneous cultural codes and complex social networks entailing shifting power differentials. Knowledge, in short, is always complicit with power. Ultimately, questions of truth reflect conflicting ideologies and political interests associated with unstable agencies. Reality is not a mere invention or fiction, but its meanings and significances are, to use the current phrase, "social constructions" that need to be contextualized and estimated for their historically contingent validity. Such constructions are open to critique and revision. From this perspective, both Menchú's and Stoll's texts are riddled with ambiguities and undecidables that cannot be resolved by mere arbitration over facts — such arbitration and facts are themselves texts or discourses that need to be accounted for, and so on. In the end, it's all a question of power and hegemony.

The excesses of postmodernist reductionism are now being acknowledged even by its defenders and practitioners. What discipline or method of inquiry can claim to be justified by a thoroughgoing skepticism and relativism? While I do not subscribe to an overvalorized notion of power, whether decentered or negotiated through an "infinite chain of signifiers," a power not embedded in concrete sociopolitical formations, I think the stress on historical grounding is salutary. This is perhaps a commonplace. But I mention it nevertheless to foreground the need to be more critical of the lethal sociopolitical effects of what is involved in historical representation of non-Western groups, collectivities, and peoples by intellectuals of the economically powerful North. Self-awareness of the limits of one's mode of knowing Others is now a precondition for any engagement with subjects that once were defined and constituted by ethnocentric, predatory worldviews and their coercive machinery. We need this preemptive caveat.

We confront here an enactment of the sly politics of Othering, not the now banal identity politics, when Stoll subjects Menchú to interrogation. When "first-world" producers of knowledge of indigenous peoples claim to offer the "truth" or the credible representation of people of color inhabiting "postcolonial" (read: neocolonial) regions and internal dependencies, shouldn't we stop and ask what is going on, who is speaking to whom and for what purpose? There are no pure languages of inquiry where traces of the intonation, words, idioms, and tones of the Others cannot be found. Pursuing Said's thesis on the West's "Orientalizing" drive, Zhang Longxi reminds us that the hermeneutic circle is not closed but open for self-reflexive alterations by "the things themselves." Further, demythologizing the myth of the Other proceeds from the act of contradistinguishing the real from the imaginary differences, arriving at what Gadamer calls "the fusion of horizons" (Zhang, 1988, 131). The subalterns can speak if there are listeners who can perform a prior act of self-distancing required to grasp the others as existentially distinct in their freedom, a step necessary to attain a more catholic view and traverse determinate boundaries of cultures, languages, and so on. In that way, the power and privilege of representation in historically engendered conflicts can be rendered reciprocal (Khare 1991).

Disenchantment becomes salutary here. It may be that anthropology and other social research programs today have abandoned their original mission of elucidating "the relations and structures of power in, through, and against which ordinary people have lived" (Roseberry 1996). A thoroughgoing nominalism and cynical relativism prevail among the experts and technocrats. One example of this genre that claims to ascribe agency to victims is Nicole Constable's (1997) studies of Filipino domestic help in Hong Kong in which millions of overseas contract workers are romanticized as (Edward) Saidian "exiles" endowed with contrapuntal visions! Causality and political judgment disappear in the thicket of ethnographic minutiae and entertaining anecdotes. Rare is the self-reflective inquirer who insists on the transparency of power relations and the need to demystify the enchanting aura of knowledge-production. One example is Ellen Gruenbaum's view on the controversy over clitoridectomy — and by extension over other cultural practices prejudged unacceptable by Western standards — in which she urges the study of health problems together with economic and political issues. Gruenbaum reminds us, "Cultural adaptation and maladaptation cannot be divorced from the question of differential effects of a practice or social institution on different categories of people in a society. . . . Whether a cultural practice is adaptive or maladaptive depends to a large extent on whose viewpoint is taken, where the political forces for and against it lie, and whose interests are served by change" (1996, 470). Likewise, we can ask of Derridean deconstruction, Foucauldian genealogy, and Lyotardean antitotalism: Whose interests do they ultimately serve? Are they part of the problem or part of the solution for millions of exploited and oppressed, including those oblivious of their plight, so long denied even a modicum of social justice and human dignity?

Mikhail Bakhtin once suggested that differences can be fully appreciated through a receptivity to the carnivalesque polyphony of utterances from situated subject-positions. Others are possibilities of ourselves mediated through complex social linkages. Although Alasdair McIntyre, Emmanuel Levinas, and recent communitarian thinkers have confronted the ethical and moral ramifications of the encounter with others, the corollary problem of producing historical knowledge of the Other has not been fully diagnosed. The Other cannot be known adequately if its voice is disrespected, impugned, or traduced. Linda Alcoff points out the foundational value of subaltern utterance: "Speaking constitutes a subject that challenges and subverts the opposition between the knowing agent and the object of knowledge, an opposition that is key in the reproduction of imperialist modes of discourse" (1991, 23). Indeed, the silence of the conquered speaks volumes — if there are listeners. I want to cite a recent case involving the relation between contemporary American scholarship and the production of knowledge about Philippine history that inflects the Menchú-Stoll controversy in terms of peoples speaking to, for, and against collective interests, memories, and goals.

"Benevolent Assimilation" by Force

The centenary celebrations of the 1896–1898 Philippine revolution against its former colonial power, Spain, had just ended when interest in Spain's successor, the United States, was sparked by the U.S. government's recent demand for virtually unlimited rights of military access to Philippine territory. With the loss of its military bases in 1992, the United States tried to regain, and reinforce in another form, its continuing hegemony over its former colonial subjects.

The Filipino revolutionary forces succeeded in defeating the Spaniards, but Spain's sovereignty over the country ended when the United States intervened in 1898. The Filipino-American War broke out in February 1898 and lasted for at least a decade. A lingering dispute exists regarding how many Filipinos actually died in this "first Vietnam."

Stanley Karnow, the lauded apologist of the U.S. "civilizing mission," cites 200,000 Filipinos; the Filipino historian Renato Constantino puts the number of casualties in Luzon Island alone at 600,000, a figure given by General Bell, one of the military planners of the "pacification" campaigns. Another scholar, Luzviminda Francisco, concludes that if we take into account the other campaigns in Batangas, Panay, Albay, and Mindanao, the total could easily be one million (1987, 19). Do we count the victims of "collateral damage," the euphemism for civilians killed although not involved in direct fighting? U.S. strategy in fighting a guerilla war then was to force all the natives into concentration camps in which many died of starvation, disease, and brutal treatment. What is the truth and who has it? Where are the reliable informants who can provide authentic narratives? Whom are we to believe?

In the Balangiga, Samar, incident of September 28, 1901, exactly forty-five American soldiers were killed by Filipino guerilla partisans. The Filipinos suffered 250 casualties during the attack and another twenty soon after. In retaliation, General Jacob Smith ordered the killing of all Filipinos above the age of ten; in a few months, the whole of Samar was reduced to a "howling wilderness." No exact figures of total Filipino deaths are given by Karnow and other American historians. Exactly what happened in the numerous cases of American military atrocities against Filipinos investigated by the U.S. Congress, is still a matter of contention up to now. But there is general agreement that the war was characterized by, in the words of Filipino historian Teodoro Agoncillo (1970), "extreme barbarity." Exactly how many died in the Samar campaign, or during the entire war, is again a matter of who is doing the counting, what are the criteria employed, and for what purpose. Historiographic methodology by itself cannot answer our demand for a sense of the whole, a cognitive mapping and assessment of the total situation.

Of more immediate relevance to the Menchú/Stoll nonexchange is the recent hullabaloo over the stature of the Filipino revolutionary hero, Andres Bonifacio (1863–1897). An American specialist in area studies, Glenn May, acquired instant notoriety when his book *Inventing a Hero: The Posthumous Re-creation of Andres Bonifacio* came out in 1992. May questioned the veracity of certain documents attributed to Bonifacio by Filipino intellectuals and political leaders. Without any actual examination of the documents in question, May, hedging with numerous "maybes" and "perhaps," accused Filipino historians — from Agoncillo to Reynaldo Ileto — of either forging documents or fraudulently assigning to Bonifacio certain texts responsible for his heroic aura and reputation.

The Filipino-American War is being fought again, this time in the ideological realm. Except for exhibiting the pedestrian rationale for the academic profession, this exercise in debunking an anticolonial hero easily lends itself to being construed as a cautionary tale. It can be interpreted as a more systematic attempt by a member of the superior group to discredit certain Filipino nationalist historians who are judged guilty of fraud and other underhanded practices unworthy of civilized thinkers. Ileto's defense tries to refute the prejudgment. He accuses May of privileging "colonial archives" over oral testimonies and of deploying the patron-client/tutelage paradigm that prejudices all of May's views of Filipinos. Ileto cannot tolerate May's thesis that the Philippine revolution was really a revolt of the elites, not of the masses. In short, May's version of the "truth" is unwarranted and untenable. In the context of the continuing subordination of the Philippines to the United States, May functions as an apologist of U.S. imperial policy, a role that has a venerable genealogy of scholars from the anthropologist Dean Worcester to academic bureaucrats like David Steinberg, Theodore Friend, and Peter Stanley. Their scholarly authority cannot be divorced from the continuing attempts of the U.S. government to impose its control, however indirect or covert, over Philippine political, cultural, and economic affairs. The recent Visiting Forces Agreement is one incontrovertible instance. One may suppose that joining this group of luminaries is enough compensation for May and other "disinterested" seekers of what passes for "received" truth.

As in the Menchú/Stoll confrontation, May's outright condemnation of at least four generations of Filipino scholars and intellectuals since formal independence in 1946 is revealing in many ways. The following heuristic questions may be offered for reflection: Should we still insist on the axiomatic dualism of objective truth and subjective interpretation in accounts of fraught events? Shouldn't we consider the exigencies of the dialogic communication: who are the parties involved? In what historical moments? Who are the victims and who the victimizers? In what arena or set of circumstances can a citizen of a dominant global power question the veracity of a citizen/subject of a subordinated country without this act being considered a recolonizing alibi and ruse? Can the investigation of individual facts or events in these dependent polities be considered legitimate as sources of "objective" knowledge without taking into account the hierarchical ordering of nation-state relations? What attitude should researchers from these powerful centers of learning adopt that will dispel the suspicion of "third-world" peoples that they are partisans of a neocolonizing program, if not unwitting instruments of their government? Obviously, the more immediate stakes in the ongoing "culture wars" are social policies and programs within the United States, with secondary implications in terms of foreign policy and academic priorities. Still, we cannot ignore how the attacks on testimonios like Menchú, or heroic figures of nation-states that claim to be sovereign and independent (including the public intellectuals of these nation-states), are both allegories of internal political antagonisms (class warfare) as well as the literal battlefields for recuperating the now tarnished glory of pax Americana of the Cold War era.

Contrary to some pundits of deconstruction, I believe the subaltern, whether Menchú or Agoncillo (now deceased), can perform the role of witnesses and "speak truth to power." Menchú can and has indeed struggled audaciously to represent herself and her people in times of emergency and crisis. For the indigenous peoples of Guatemala and other places, the purpose of speech is not just for universally accepted cultural reasons — affirming their identities and their right of self-determination — but, more crucially, for their physical survival. Such a capacity to speak entails responsibility, hence the need to respond to questions about "truth" and its worldly grounding.

For postmodernist nominalism, truth is anathema (Jameson 1992). Inquiry becomes self-reflexive. A warning by Walter Benjamin may be useful to clarify the notion of "truth" in lived situations where "facts" intermesh with feeling and conviction. In his famous "Theses on the Philosophy of History," Benjamin expressed reservations about orthodox historians like Leopold von Ranke whom Marx considered "a little root-grubber" who reduced history to "facile anecdote-mongering and the attribution of all great events to petty and mean causes" (1969, 255). Benjamin speculated that the "truth" of the past can be seized only as an image, as a memory "as it flashes up at a moment of danger" (255). I believe this moment of danger is always with us when, in a time of settling accounts in the name of justice, we see the Stolls and Mays suddenly come up with their credentials and entitlements in order to reassign the "upstart" subalterns to their proper place.

Under the Volcano

Another brief autobiographical footnote is needed to demonstrate how the local intersects with the global, resonating in the chief U.S. neo-colony in Southeast Asia. My wife and I visited the Philippines in 1991, when the volcano named Mount Pinatubo was exploding and scattering ash all over the region and eventually around the world, particularly on the U.S. military bases (Clark and Subic) as our plane from Detroit landed at the Manila International Airport (renamed after Senator Benigno Aquino, who was killed by the Marcos military right on the tarmac, in 1983). Inside the airport, the announcements in English and in Japanese took no notice of the fact that almost all the disembarking passengers were brown or dark-skinned natives who conversed in the vernacular tongues. Who cares anyway about Filipino domestics returning from Japan, Canada, or the United States?

Are we in a global Babel-like metropolis? Despite the "New World Order," the national language of close to 80 million Filipinos called "Filipino" — is it intelligible like MacArthur's "I Shall Return"? — did not exist for transnational carriers now named "Desert Storm I" and "Desert Storm II." In a talk at the University of the Philippines, I was asked by a student whether "Taglish" was a viable language. This clearly was a symptom of divisions and schisms across the body politic: divisions of class, gender, ethnic identity, and so on, which makes the emergence of a "Filipino" identity problematic — a legacy of four hundred years of colonial servitude to the Spaniards, North Americans, Japanese, and to their indigenous surrogates. Would the presence of Filipinos need a Mount Pinatubo to be acknowledged by the multicultural masters of the world?

Our first impression of metro Manila confirmed the "third-world" stereotype: swarms of people (the city counts almost 12 million residents, many of whom are refugees from the countryside) fighting for space in jeeps, malls, and cinemas amid poisonous exhaust and industrial pollution grown several times worse since our one-year sojourn after the February 1986 "People Power" uprising. Modernization via foreign investment, "free-trade zones," tourism, and so on, consorted with the refeudalization of society (a return to the days of the oligarchic warlords) to make daily life an ordeal for the average citizen. Neo-Social Darwinism in a dependent "free-market" system seemed to be the order of the day.

Appearances may deceive, but you have to live with them: garbage littered most streets dotted with gaping manholes. Beggars, petty criminals, and the homeless have proliferated. In one of the worst monsoon floods in July, we were stranded on Roxas Boulevard overnight. In Ermita, however, business in brothels and beer joints was booming, probably the only "social service" still available. Neither Marcos's New Society nor "Calamity Cory's" (yes, the epithet for then president Corazon Aquino was also borrowed like the yellow ribbon) dispensation had been able to render life for the masses a little bearable by the improvement of basic sanitation. News of victims of typhoid and dysentery caused by contamination of the city water supply had made necessary the boiling of drinking water. Meanwhile the Philippine General Hospital wards were overflowing, malnourishment continued to plague a majority of Filipino youth — more than half of the total population — and the threat of AIDS fostered by a tourist culture had become more real.

Because of soaring inflation due to the rise in oil prices and the unprecedented unemployment (the worst in twenty years), you now needed to carry wads of hundred-peso bills when you take a taxi, go to restaurants, or do any shopping. The peso had become worthless, thanks to IMF-World Bank structural conditionalities imposed on any dependent government begging for more credit. Everyone we met bewailed the subservience of the ruling elite to foreign corporations and the selfishness of U.S. diktat — the latter shown in the case of U.S. personnel from Clark Air Base refusing to take Filipino passengers as they fled in their cars.

It seemed then that nothing had changed since we visited in 1987, after the February insurrection. Aquino restored the power of the moribund oligarchy. Although the corrupt and subservient Estrada regime was overthrown by the January 2001 "People Power II" uprising, the return of traditional politicians from the camp of previous presidents (Aquino and Fidel Ramos) did not augur well for any genuine improvement of the economic and social welfare of 80 million Filipinos, especially as long as the World Bank/WTO and transnational corporations decide the policies of the oligarchic elements surrounding the new president, Gloria Macapagal Arroyo. But let me return to the end of our 1991 visit.

In the Philippines, culture wars have raged on under the long lingering shadow of the Cold War. Since the early nineties, newspaper columnists and church officials have continued to lead the chorus of Redbaiters, with military officers and Pentagon agents beating the war drums against the durable New People's Army and the Communist Party of the Philippines. Of course, during the Estrada regime, the Moro insurgents became the prime scapegoats for the failures in the economy and other catastrophes. Back then, the Moonies-backed CAUSA, the World Anti-Communist crusade, and General Singlaub's local "contras" were operating freely, with thousands of fundamentalist evangelists from the United States and Australia extracting money and support from movie actors, generals, businessmen, and ordinary citizens. Anticommunist fanaticism was alive and well in those tropical islands halfway between Hollywood and Baghdad. Meanwhile, in central Philippines and elsewhere, heavy fighting between government soldiers and the New People's Army (and in Mindanao, the Moro Islamic Liberation Front combatants) inflicted casualties on all sides. In Iloilo City, for example, a veteran from the underground talked of periodic clashes between guerillas and soldiers in many contested villages outside the city. None of this was reported in the media. Refugees not only from Mt. Pinatubo's eruption but from AFP atrocities (as in Marag Valley, Cagayan) were multiplying. This is why the government still banned the late Lino Brocka's powerful film *Oraproñobis*. In the arts, the most promising and original contribution to emancipatory culture was being made by such performers as ASIN, vibrant women artists, indigenous cultural activists, and lively underground journals while the Western-oriented Cultural Center of the Philippines stagnated in incestuous elite patronage.

Certain rituals of solidarity (too numerous to detail here) signaled prospects of significant change in the future. I recall recurrent questions posed to me by audiences at the University of the Philippines, Ateneo de Manila University, and elsewhere, questions that evoked scenarios of the past: the utility of Western theory for Philippine Studies, the role of diasporic intellectuals abroad, the crisis of "socialism" in Europe and elsewhere, the relevance of Western feminism, and so on. But in no instance was any awareness betrayed that the fundamental problem of racism and the neocolonizing ideology accompanying it is what lies at the root of the continuing economic and political underdevelopment of the nation. What did my colleagues learn, I wonder, from the lectures of such celebrities as Richard Rorty, Benedict Anderson, and other visitors?

Hordes of Filipino Overseas Contract Workers filled the airport lounges and corridors. Since Marcos's promotion of the "warm-body export" in the seventies, Filipinos/as have become servants/maids of the world (more on this in the afterword). While thousands of Filipinos trek to the Middle East, Europe, Hong Kong, and Japan to sell themselves as cheap labor to feed their families back home and service the country's foreign debt (much of it siphoned off by the Marcos dynasty and its successors), government apologists insist on how Filipino maids in the racist United Kingdom, Hong Kong, and elsewhere should be grateful for wages higher than those paid in the Middle East and elsewhere, so they shouldn't complain even if they're beaten up, fed leftovers, made to sleep in bathrooms, raped, or whatever. Didn't a certain senator much acclaimed in the United States say that the victims should enjoy it while being raped? Meanwhile our local intelligentsia floated the idea of "nationalist industrialization" through military coercion, and the moderates urged peace talks between the government and the insurgents. One self-proclaimed "socialist" who used to host a popular TV talkshow had just climbed the ecologist's bandwagon, mouthing the slogan of "sustainable development." Progressives cohabited with former Marcos (and later Aquino) sycophants. Only a few survivors of the McCarthy era and the abysmal days of martial law seemed to hold on steadfastly to the vision of an independent Philippines freed from the shackles of racial-imperialist domination, envisaging alternatives born from the unrelenting struggles of people of color throughout the planet.

Sporadic ash-fall graced our last few days in Manila as the talks on the base treaty ended — the Philippines Senate upheld the Filipino right of self-determination and finally terminated U.S. occupation dating back to the intervention of Admiral George Dewey's fleet in 1898. We visited the sisters at St. Theresa College who narrated tales of evacuated U.S. troops seeking refuge in some coastline barrios in Cebu, which immediately converted themselves into little Angeles and Olongapo cities, so miraculous was the effect of dollars circulating in the local economy. We heard President Aquino (who wanted to commodify Mt. Pinatubo's ash for the world market like holy fragments of the Berlin Wall) threatening to mobilize "people power" to prolong the imperial stranglehold — proof that the once charismatic widow was after all fit heir to her ignominious predecessors in office. The mythical "people power" had now been irreversibly prostituted to the tune of 60 million pesos paid to those attending rigged demonstrations. But Cory did not have even a million for the thousands of victims of Mt. Pinatubo, so as a nation we continue to depend on charity instead of transforming the economic and political structures of our society to equalize the distribution of wealth mainly produced by impoverished workers and peasants. Given the parasitic nature of the elite habituated to wasteful consumption, we cannot invest the surplus value of labor in industrializing the economy to satisfy the basic needs (food, shelter, medicine) of the majority and thus enhance the ordinary citizens' life chances and guarantee their dignity in a truly independent, self-sufficient nation.

So Mount Pinatubo then replaced the airport tarmac in the world's attention despite the hypocritical rituals of those who claim to have fought the Marcos dictatorship but who continue to enjoy petty privileges from their U.S. patrons. I remember how for many years we spent resources and energy in the Anti-Martial Law Coalition and the Friends of the Filipino People (these two unsung organizations did more than anyone else to neutralize Marcos's lobbying for more U.S. aid and help the victims of military brutality) to convince the inert Filipino community to protest Marcos's despotism — I recall my whole family distributing anti-Marcos leaflets around New York City's Port Authority in freezing weather. We fought without expecting awards, money, or gratitude from anyone; it was our nationalist commitment that sustained us. But who remembers the snow of yesteryears? Have Filipinos in the racial polity learned anything from reading Karnow's *In Our Image*, attending consulate rituals, and doing their yearly Balikbayan pilgrimages? A forgotten sage once said that history progresses through disasters, setbacks, defeats. The earthquakes, Mount Pinatubo, massacres in Escalante, Marag Valley, and other infamous horrors commited by the regimes that followed Marcos; typhoons, rapes of domestics in the Middle East, wholesale stealing of public money by the *trapos* (traditional politicians) and the feudal, comprador, bureaucrat-capitalist bloc — these may be providential if ambiguous signs for *Pilipinas*, homeland of migrants around the planet.

Our friends urged us to return for the May 1992 elections — an exciting free-for-all among so many antediluvian "presidentiables"! That event would later culminate, unfortunately, in the empowerment of the Estrada clique of gangsters, *jueteng* lords, paramilitary criminals, and their unconscionable retinue. We said we would return when all political prisoners have been freed, when the Aetas have found another mountain to inhabit — Mt. Pinatubo is, for them, the scourge of heaven against the injustice and oppression in a presumably Christian society; when the bases — Subic and other installations, not just Clark — have been fully recovered from the invaders, when the Moros have regained their occupied homeland. That is, when comprador bourgeois state power has been conquered by progressive nationalist forces in the name of the working masses. But when would that be? We might settle for a compromise. After the January 2001 insurrection — a thin wedge in a tight opening — we might be returning soon. I end with a quote from Carlos Bulosan, the great revolutionary proletarian writer, in a letter to his nephews a few years before he died in Seattle, Washington, at the height of Cold War McCarthyism of which he was one of the victims: "Never forget your people, your country, wherever you go. Your greatness lies in them. . . . Do not misuse your gift; apply it toward the safeguarding of our great heritage, the grandeur of our history, the realization of our great men's dream for a free and good Philippines. That is real genius; it is not selfish; it sacrifices itself for the good of the whole community. We Filipinos must be proud that we had the greatest genius in Jose Rizal, who sacrificed his life and happiness for the people" (1995, 33–34).

Historicizing Imperative

Reflections on homeland and identity are standard by-products of fragmentation and anomie in modern capitalist society. In our postmodern
milieu, the obsession with personal identity as an atomized entity has
erased the web of social relations on which it depends. Commodity-
fetishism and reification explain the dissolution of the historico-social
matrix of individuality. Reacting to the utilitarian individualism of the
metropolis, Nawal El Saadawi counters the eviscerated monadic ego of
bourgeois life by invoking the constitutive forces of her life-world: "For
me there is no identity without home, no identity without a land on
which I can stand, without a language, without the means to keep it alive
and help it to flourish and grow, without an organization and a pen
with which to struggle for freedom and justice and love and peace, for
women to know that they are human beings, for blacks to feel that all
the colours in the world are what make it glow" (1997, 126). Communication and reciprocal engagement between peoples can only be
possible on this premise of recognizing and appreciating this sociopolitical grounding of one's personal existence.

Neoliberal pragmatism refuses that grounding. Wedded to private
property, liberal thought is initially compromised as the legitimizing
ideology of capital accumulation. It inaugurates the "free"-market relation between the dominant (property owners) and the subordinate (dispossessed workers, slaves). We need to take cognizance of this asymmetrical setup. The historically determining categories in understanding
culture are domination and subordination, the dialectical process of
incorporation and resistance. Obviously, before there can be a real social
basis of equality as the prerequisite for multicultural exchange, we need
to understand the complex links and interdependencies between what
used to be called "center" and "periphery," between the dominant
hegemonic military-economic powers and nation-states and the subaltern societies, in the world-system.

And so, cultures as collective maps of meaning not only diverge but
also collide in complex societies. We often encounter the charge that the
present culture wars will persist because we do not share a "common
culture" made up of shared beliefs, patterns of behavior (mores, rituals),

and codes of interpretation that inform the "imagined community." Communalism is then presented as an alternative to the atomistic and competitive liberalism of "rights." The magic word *community* compensates for the lack of organic cohesion evinced in common institutions among groups with warring interests. The proposition of a need for a shared value system or dominant ideology to legitimate the social order originates from Talcott Parson's misreading of Durkheim's notion of "collective consciousness" (Featherstone 1991). In a polity (such as the United States) structured by a long history of divisions along class, gender, race, and nationality, the claim that there is a single moral consensus, "habits of the heart," or *communitas* can only be a claim for the ascendancy of a particular ruling group (Harvey 2000). And it is around the hegemonic leadership of the propertied "power elite" that hierarchy and stratification, along with the norms and rules that constitute canons and disciplinary regimes, become legitimized.

Liberal pluralism and its variants obfuscate this hegemonic process conducted, to use Gramsci's terminology, via wars of position and maneuver. Establishment pluralism exalts diversity, multiple identities, as "a condition of human existence rather than as the effect of an enunciation of difference that constitutes hierarchies and asymmetries of power" (Scott 1992, 14). From this pluralist perspective, group differences and discrete ethnic identities are examined in a static categorizing grid; that is to say, they are not examined relationally or dialectically as, in Joan Scott's words, "interconnected structures or systems created through repreated processes of the enunciation of difference" (1992, 17). Cultural pluralism then legitimates and reinforces the status quo.

Although there are numerous maps of meaning, one index or code has succeeded in affording intelligibility to all. Viewed from this angle, the code of a "common culture" interpellates individuals and articulates them in a serial gathering of monadic identities. Instead of a composite identity overdetermined by manifold lines of interests and affiliations, one acquires an identity defined by this "common culture." Implicit here is the constitutive role of the market, specifically the buying and selling of labor power as commodity, which guarantees and is predicated on individual rights. Thus, if the "common culture" of Bennett, Schlesinger, and Ravitch is affirmed by the status quo in education, workplace, family, and other institutional matrices of subjectivity, then there will be no room for encountering, much less recognizing, the integrity of Menchú's text — not to speak of the multiple cultural practices and artistic expressions of people of color within and outside the North American continent. In that case, culture wars, more exactly the conflicts of values/beliefs as products of group action and social constraints, will continue until the present hegemonic order is transformed and antagonisms are for the moment quelled. With the reactionary troops still on the rampage, an armistice or even a temporary truce seems remote for now.

In a recent report, "The Dissolution of General Education: 1914–1993," the same group I quoted at the outset, the National Association of Scholars, lamented the phenomenon of college graduates deficient in the basics of Western culture. Balch, its president, warned that the nation is "in danger of losing the common frame of reference that for many generations has sustained our liberal, democratic society" (Sanoff 1996, 58). This would not be a problematic diagnosis if a direct connection can be established between the nontraditional but now fashionable study of Madonna's MTV ads or rap music and its fostering of illiberal practices. In actuality, there is a "common frame of reference" thriving though with uncommon results. As the redoubtable Russell Jacoby remarks in unmasking "the myth of multiculturalism": "For better or worse only one culture thrives in the United States, the culture of business, work and consuming" (1994b, 122; see W. Haug 1986).

Still, this one dominant culture serves as the arena for intensifying ethnic, gender, and religious conflicts that pervade everyday life. Could there be a compromise between antagonistic positions, a middle ground of stalemate where the conversation on collective ends and purposes can be carried on with constructive effects? Pragmatic mediators in our buy-and-sell milieu are always ready to offer their services. For example, one attempt to negotiate between the extremes of populism and elitism in the conduct of comparative literary studies — the "extremes" are, to my mind, not at all opposed since they belong to the domain of liberal ideology — has been suggested by Elizabeth Fox-Genovese: "Social democratization occurs when we ensure the openness of our self-consciously difficult and demanding discipline to practitioners of all backgrounds" (1995, 142). This upper-class "democratization" is patently deceptive and self-serving. What it really conveys is that there is no need to critique and revise the discipline, its substance and form, everything's fine; just don't impose racial, gender, and ethnic requirements on those (how many? who? where and when?) admitted to this exclusive and highly policed profession in the precincts of the Western academy. Class in effect is enough to maintain the prevailing standards and buttress the Establishment.

Culture wars are therefore needed to preserve both the present economy of symbolic goods and its obverse, the exchange of commodities, underwritten by the bourgeois habitus (Bourdieu 1999). For some critics, this is an impasse that can be surmounted by the contrivance of "discrepant cosmopolitanism," or a worldly "denationalized internationalism" (Robbins 1993, 196) in cultural criticism that would transcend left or right positions, indeed be "an international competence or mode of citizenship" to which the Quiche Indians, New York intellectuals, Saddam Hussein, and anyone else can be submitted for analysis, interpretation, and judgment. Anxious not to be accused of partiality, the new cosmopolitanists are naively uncritical of their inhabiting an imperial vantage-point that, whether they know it or not, subtends their opinions. Self-reflexive critique of one's historical situatedness, a complicity in what has been done to those "others," can be dispensed with only at the expense of those lacking the cosmopolitan's privilege, her or his claim to high moral credentials, and security. Neither victims nor executioners, yes, but from what place and time do we claim to speak? For whom? To whom?

The metropolitan culture industry prospers unimpeded by critique. In our image-saturated public sphere, the debate on "common culture" proceeds without any kind of historical consciousness. A few decades ago, across the Atlantic, Raymond Williams worried this theme in criticizing the minority elite version of culture (putatively organic and common to all British citizens) purveyed by a long tradition of intellectuals from Edmund Burke to Thomas Carlyle, T. S. Eliot, and F. R. Leavis. Williams's ethicopolitical strategy was to shift the definition of culture from a class-based to a radically democratic conception based on solidarity and working-class institutions: culture as "the whole way of life of a people." He specifically wanted to emphasize "the idea of the common element of the culture — its community — as a way of criticizing that divided and fragmented culture" (1989c, 35) caused by property relations, by class, ethnic, and gender divisions.

Culture as civility may be ordinary but the modes of acquisition and distribution are not. In "The Idea of a Common Culture," Williams precisely underscored how, not only in Britain but also in many places, the creation of meanings and values that all ordinary people engage in, the community's process of self-realization, has been limited by the denial of education and political participation to various groups in society. Hence the possibility of a common culture — "the common determination of meanings by all the people" — cannot be realized without genuine democracy and equality of resources. This is not just another fashionable politics of identity, of representation. It concerns community rights, survival, and reproduction of unique forms of life. Instead of an individualistic and conformist culture of "uncommunity," Williams envisioned a democratic community where cultural practices engaged by every citizen draws from "a common human inheritance" and produces unique, original, new forms and values that can be shared by all.

The problem of a British "common culture" in the period that Williams surveyed is no worse or better than the contemporary situation in the multiethnic United States. What is common so far is the knowledge that class inequality has sharpened unprecedentedly in the eighties and nineties, and with it racist intolerance has become rampant and virulent with the rise of unemployment, religious bigotry, Proposition 187 in California, and the passage of a new immigration law targeting "undocumented aliens" and new immigrants. A revision of ethical and philosophical paradigms is needed (more on this in the succeeding chapters). Given the present political environment and the alignment of forces, I do not see how the symptomatic "culture wars" over the canon can be negotiated into permanent peace "in our time," and the dream of commonalty in enjoyment of cultural goods and experiences — not just sacrifices and privations — can be achieved for the majority. This is so unless the conditions and forces determining access to resources and participation in political decisions are radically changed. The recent explosive controversy over the way certain American anthropologists have "used" and exploited the Yanomamo Indians in South America attests to how remote we still are from the ideal of a "transnational America" that Randolph Bourne suggested in 1916.

Clearly, cultures are not autonomous from social structures and the historical contexts of institutions and practices. A decade ago, Herbert Schiller concluded that the fight is over. "Culture Inc." has resulted from the complete "envelopment of informational and cultural space by the transnational corporate system (1989, 5). About the same time, Stephen Greenblatt, an academic defender of truthful and therefore great art as a response to barbarism, expressed a self-incriminatory idea: "If we allow ourselves to think about the extent to which our magnificent cultural tradition — like that of every civilization we know of — is intertwined with cruelty, injustice, and pain, do we not, in fact, run the risk of 'deculturation'? Not if our culture includes a regard for truth" (1994, 290). Who is the referent of "our"? "Truth" in this usage enacts its question-begging message. Meanwhile, the market values and consumption ideals that Cornel West (1993) and other intellectuals of color bewail as inhumane and unjust continue to operate and to enforce the "melting pot" that, whether we like it or not, has now been globalized into a battlefield of prodigious contending voices and ideas across national, linguistic, and religious boundaries. Amid the "clash of civilizations," can the new prophetic "desire" of Cultural Studies protect us from the barbarism of the market and the profit-obsessed culture/ information industry?

CHAPTER 6

Questioning Contemporary Cultural Studies

Times would pass, old empires would fall and new ones take their place, the relations of countries and the relations of classes had to change, before I discovered that it is not the quality of goods and utility which matter, but movement; not where you are or what you have, but where you have come from, where you are going and the rate at which you are getting there.
— C. L. R. James, *Beyond A Boundary*

The Great Method is a practical doctrine of alliances and of the dissolution of alliances, of the exploitation of changes and the dependency on change, of the instigation of change and the changing of the instigators, the separation and emergence of unities, the unselfsufficiency of oppositions without each other, the unification of mutually exclusive oppositions. The Great Method makes it possible to recognize processes within things and to use them. It teaches us to ask questions which enable activity.
— Bertolt Brecht, *Book of Changes*

One survivor of the conflicts I just rehearsed is the discipline or field of inquiry called Cultural Studies (hereafter cs). Since the intervention of cs in the academy began with violating the conventional protocols, I start with a similar transgression by a preface of travel notes. In March 2000 my wife and I attended a convention of the National Association of Ethnic Studies in Orlando, Florida, where we encountered the tourist holiday crowd in full force. Among the attractions disseminated by hundreds of publicity paraphernalia is the Salvador Dali Museum located in St. Petersburg, Florida. The museum's brochure describes the place in six languages (German, Spanish, French, Portuguese, and Dutch); the English version reads:

> World-famous, the Salvador Dali Museum ranks as one of the top attractions in Florida receiving the highest rating by the Michelin Green Guide — the only such attraction on the west coast to be so honored. Daily tours of the museum's fascinating collection will educate, yet entertain you, about one of the 20th century's greatest artists — Salvador Dali. Bewildering double images and incredible paintings will surprise; sculptures, holograms and art glass will amaze; and early impressionist-style paintings and melting clocks will delight you. You are assured of finding something special. Be sure to include time for the Dali Museum in downtown St. Petersburg in your plans.

No doubt the museum has been competing with such popular favorites as Epcot Disney, Universal Studios, Sea World, Wonderworks, and a thousand other diversions — from ethnic restaurants, boutiques galore, art galleries, curio shops, and diverse simulations of Disney World iconography in numerous malls. We visited the museum for verification. The reality was not far from the media hype. Shopping at the museum, with surrealist-art mementos and assorted merchandise — zapping for pastiches and visual language games — summons to mind Michel de Certeau's tactics of makeshift creativity and historiographic place making (Poster 1997). Welcome to Dali-land!

Shift to another CS venue. Later in March, I participated in an international conference organized by the Faculty of Letters and Social Sciences at Chiba University, Tokyo, Japan. The theme of the conference was "Searching for the Paradigm of Pluralism: Cultural and Social Pluralism and Coexistence in South and Southeast Asia." Scholars from Thailand, the Philippines, India, Pakistan, and Sri Lanka came; the plenary lecture was given by a leading Japanese scholar, Professor Mitsuo Nakamura, who spoke about "Islam and Civil Society — Hope and Despair." My topic for the opening keynote address was "The Paradox of Multiculturalism: Ethnicity, Race, and Identity in the Philippines." Mindful of the Japanese Empire's goal of building a "Great East Asia CoProsperity Sphere" during World War II and the peculiar ethnic homogeneity in Japan, I remarked that the dialogue was a good start in exploring the transformative potential of "multiculturalism" that, initiated in the West as a theme, genre, policy, and disciplinary orientation, can be recontextualized in the Asian setting and merged with the larger research projects of intellectuals, government officials, and other protagonists in the public sphere.

There is some distance, of course, between these initiatives and CS. Disneyworld, Dali, and Japan are coeval in the frame of my diasporic experience. How do we connect both the Dali Museum and the Japanese interest in pluralism, and my position as a Filipino scholar based in the United States as constituent elements in the field of CS? Given the fact that the analytic and synthesizing practice called "cultural studies" has acquired a distinct temper at every case of "situational appropriation," one can call both the placing of the Salvador Dali Museum in the tourist-shopping cosmopolis and the multiculturalist conference in Chiba, Japan, as innovative points of departure for reflection on the plight of CS. As a comparative literature scholar from the Philippines and also a specialist in ethnic studies in the U.S. academy, I consider myself a conjunctural site for the encounter between various disciplines in the social sciences and humanities, between "third"- and "first"-world cultures, and between popular/plebeian layers of culture and the mainly Eurocentric discourse of the academy. Obviously I may be an exceptional case, analogous to the situation of Taipei, Taiwan — an emergent global city — that has become one venue for the exchange between Western CS and its local practitioners.

The trajectories of traveling ideas do not, of course, immediately translate into a neat geopolitical calculus. So in what way is this encounter productive of knowledge and pedagogical practice that can be used for undoing the hegemony of "transmigrant" capital? Can the critical apparatus of concepts, idiom, rhetoric, and style be imported or transplanted from Birmingham and Chapel Hill, USA, to Asian, African, and Latin American milieus without reinforcing postcolonial hegemonies? How do we negotiate, for example, the tensions between World Bank/International Monetary Fund imperialism and the subjects of CS as stratified heterogeneous movements?

Souvenirs of Overdetermination

In the postscript to the now orthodox textbook *Cultural Studies* (1992), Angela McRobbie celebrates the demise of Marxism — the reflectionist and mechanical kind she attributes to Fredric Jameson and David Harvey — as an influence on the field and its replacement by deconstruction. Although she notes with it the disappearance of the "organic intellectual" (in Gramsci's sense) and of any social class as the agency of emancipation, she claims nonetheless that the essays in the anthology demonstrate "a mode of study which is engaged and which seeks not the truth, but knowledge and understanding as a practical and material means of communicating with and helping to empower subordinate social groups and movements" (1992, 721). In what sense can this still inchoate and contested terrain called "cultural studies," distinguished for the most part by formalist analysis of texts and discourses, be an agent for emancipation, let alone revolutionary social transformation, of the plight of oppressed peoples around the world?

A brief background may provide an orientation to my critique of contemporary orthodox cultural studies. When the field was initially outlined in Britain by its first proponents — Richard Hoggart, Raymond Williams, and E. P. Thompson — it was originally intended to critique the elitist and antidemocratic methodologies and traditions attendant on the study of cultural expression. The immediate post–World War II milieu was characterized by the triumph of liberal democracy over fascism, the installation of the welfare state, and the beginning of the Cold War. Cultural criticism reflected the progressive impulses of that period. Instead of replicating the class divisions that separated the canonical works from the artifacts of mass culture, cs conceived of the whole of cultural production, including texts and all signifying or discursive practices, as its open-ended domain. Thus advertising, popular genres like thrillers and romances, films, music, fashions, and so on can be read (like literary texts) as communal or social events, and no longer as aesthetic icons removed from their contexts of production, circulation, and consumption.

Culture thus signifies not just beliefs and values but patterns of behavior and symbolic action. It is a layered complex of dispositions and

206

institutions that Bourdieu (1998) distills in the concept of habitus, embracing both objective structures and mentalities. By theorizing cultures as historically shaped "designs for living," whole ways of life, the early practitioners of CS engaged themselves with the critique not only of activities and artifacts in "civil society" and private lives but also with their ideological resonance and the political implications they have for the total social order. Put in a dialectical idiom, culture may be conceived as the mode in which the social relations of a group are structured and shaped; "but it is also the way those shapes are experienced, understood and interpreted" (Clark et al. 1976, 10). The pioneers of British CS crafted their practice as an intellectual-political engagement with the realities of power and inequality in late-modern capitalism.

After the founding of the Center for Contemporary Cultural Studies at the University of Birmingham in the seventies, the field underwent a tortuous growth in the aftermath of the ferment of the sixties youth revolt, the civil rights and antiwar struggles in the United States, the Chinese Cultural Revolution, and the revival of "humanist Marxism." It proceeded from the empiricism of its initiators to a structuralist phase, then to an Althusserian/Lacanian one, followed by a Gramscian moment, up to its dissolution in the deconstructive poststructuralism of Ernesto Laclau and Chantal Mouffe. Because the field was committed not only to institutional analysis but also to ideology critique, the classic problematic of the relation between subject and object, traditionally formulated as the relation between consciousness and society, reasserted itself as the opposition between culturalism and structuralism. One must recall that both Thompson and Williams reacted against a positivistic Marxism that insisted on the strict determination of thought and action by economic forces. Within a generally Marxist perspective, they shifted the emphasis to the experiences of everyday life as creative interventions of social groups in the making of history.

The first director of the center, Stuart Hall, although inspired by his socialist mentors, laid the groundwork for the questioning of culturalism and its empiricist predisposition. The adoption of a structuralist problematic derived from Althusser enriched the analysis of ideology as the prime cultural mediation whereby individuals were interpellated as subjects (in a process of misrecognition, as though they were free agents). The subject was thus theorized as a subject-position defined by historical coordinates and, with a Lacanian inflection, biographical circumstances. Empirical truth was displaced by meanings and inter-pretations within determinate contexts. The Cartesian self, also called the transcendental ego of science, was displaced by the concept of a subject-position produced as an effect of textuality, more precisely, of discursive practice. Instead of experience as the key category, represen-tation via the mass media and other technologies of disseminating infor-mation became the privileged locus of investigation.

Culture then began to be construed as the production of meanings and subjectivities within discourse and representation. Since the subject was an effect of signifying processes, it was then easy to move to concep-tualizing politics as a struggle over representation. Not only is the sub-ject an identity or position constituted by social and historical structures; it was also an actively experiencing subject, thanks to the paradigm lent by Gramsci. Although the Italian communist was construed through revisionist lenses, it was Gramsci's crucial interpretation of hegemony as the securing of consent by a historic bloc struggling for domination and moral-intellectual leadership that provided the means for reascrib-ing to the subject-position (constrained by Althusser's "Ideological State Apparatuses") some degree of agency. In the study of youth sub-cultures, for example, Dick Hebdige (1979) argued that working-class youth were not passive and unreflective consumers of American mass culture; rather, they transformed the meanings of what they consumed, rearranged images, styles, and vocabularies of American popular culture as forms of resistance to middle- and upper-class cultures. What was omitted was Gramsci's belief that the class-conscious leadership of the working-class, together with its cadre of organic intellectuals, would lead the hegemonic struggle of the toiling masses against the oppres-sion and exploitation of capital. Because of this drastic alteration of the paradigm, it might be instructive to review Williams's problematiz-ing of culture and its interpretation (more on Williams in chapter 8) to place in perspective later developments in the field which his oeuvre inaugurated.

Recognitive Mapping

By consensus Raymond Williams is considered the inventor of the field
of "cultural studies," at least in its British exemplification. His two
books, *Culture and Society* (1958) and *The Long Revolution* (1961),
followed by *Marxism and Literature* (1977) and *The Sociology of Culture* (1981), may be regarded as foundational documents enunciating
axioms, theorems, and hypotheses that need to be explored, qualified,
and further elaborated. A fully responsible cultural studies, he suggests
at the end of his 1982 summation, needs to be "analytically constructive
and constructively analytic" in dealing with "altered and alterable relations" in both cultural forms and social circumstances. I take it that if
there is any coordinating vision to this project, then it is the principle
that a historical, processual, and relational view of the social totality be
applied in order to achieve a democratic, socialist conception of culture.
The phrase *cultural materialism* has been often used to designate Williams's theory and practice of cultural analysis, his distinctive framework for critical analysis and interpretation.

In *The Long Revolution*, Williams sums up his observations on the
limits of the British culture-and-society tradition (examined earlier in
Culture and Society). With a synoptic stance, he describes "culture"
as the site where crucial questions about historical changes in industry, democracy, class, and art as response to these changes converged.
Against the traditional emphasis on ideas or ideals of perfection divorced from material social life, Williams defines culture as the pattern
of society as a whole, the differentiated totality and dynamics of social
practices. Culture is a constitutive social process, an expression of general human energy and praxis. This goes beyond the ethnographic, doc-
umentary definition of culture as "whole way of life" (1958, 325). Art
in this framework is no longer the privileged touchstone of the highest
values of civilization; it is only one special form of a general social
process in the exchange of meanings, the development of a common
"ordinary" culture. So literature and art, the artifacts of high culture, are
simply "part of the general process which creates conventions and institutions, through which the meanings that are valued by the community are shared and made active" (1961, 55). All social relations, in-

cluding the formal rules for symbolic exchange and their structural constraints, need to be investigated as actual practices and "forms of human energy" whose full range no given system of domination and subordination can totally exhaust.

In *The Sociology of Culture*, Williams rejects the idealist understanding of culture inherited from the bourgeois-artistocratic tradition and modifies the mechanical materialist version. He underscores the fact that cultural practice and production are not simply derived from a constituted social order, but rather are themselves constitutive. His new approach envisages culture as the signifying system "through which necessarily (though among other means) a social order is communicated, reproduced, experienced and explored" (1981, 13). Cognizant of the "culturalist" deviation, Williams posits as fundamental the axiom that meaning is always produced under determinate empirical and existential conditions. Language is "a socially shared and reciprocal activity, already embedded in active relationships, within which every move is an activation of what is already shared and reciprocal or may become so" (1977, 166). In a fully historical-materialist position, the use of signs — utterance or speaking as social practice — becomes "notations" for performance. Money, for example, like any sign, becomes a notation performed under certain historically limited conventions. The dichotomy between signifier and signified is thus displaced in Williams's thesis that language is not a sign system but "notations of actual productive relationships" (1977, 170). The term that covers the performance of notations in changing circumstances is *communication*, a network of practices that engenders "variable societies" comprised of the acts of communal affiliation or solidarities.

For Williams, then, signification concerns language in history, the chief theorem of a dialectical-materialist semiotics. Inspired by Bakhtin/ Voloshinov, Williams stresses the vocation of cultural studies as the analysis of the social and historical production of signifying systems, systems that are constituted and reconstituted modes of formation. Concretely particularized in *The Country and the City* — "the analysis of all forms of signification, including quite centrally writing, within the actual means and conditions of their production" (1984, 210), this approach is defined by Williams as "cultural materialism."

Williams's method of analyzing ideological/intellectual formations may be considered as his distinctive mode of tackling the classic problematic of the relation between the economic base and the superstructure. We confront once again the problem of articulating in a nonreductive way the complex articulation between consciousness and reality, the claims of immanence and signification, as registered in the social categories of thought and in the ongoing dialectic between knowledge and material power-relations. How do we grasp the connections between social existence and mentalities without the reduction of complex group/individual experiences to their spiritual essences or static social forms? Williams recommends this guiding axiom: cultural analysis begins with "the attempt to discover the nature of the organization which is the complex of these relationships." By studying "a general organization in a particular example," the cultural critic seeks to discover "patterns of a characteristic kind." By connecting the separate activities of art, trading, production, families, and politics, cultural inquiry seeks to grasp how interactions betwen practices and patterns are lived and experienced as a whole.

Williams's overall research project concerns the dialectic of form and content, of intentionality and the occasions of realization — that is, "all the active processes of learning, imagination, creation, performance." In his inquiry, the object of knowledge is no longer just the individual but also the communities of form, the collective subject realized in active processes of self-definition: "It is a way of seeing a group in and through individual differences: that specificity of individuals, and of their individual creations, which does not deny but is the necessary way of affirming their real social identities, in language, in conventions, in certain characteristic situations, experiences, interpretations, ideas" (1980, 28–29). Cultural criticism is concerned with grasping "the reality of the interpenetration, in a final sense the unity, of the most individual and the most social forms of actual life." To accomplish this, we must go beyond isolated texts/products to investigate "its real process — its most active and specific formation." We engage again the pursuit of determination in terms of the levels of institutions and formations articulated with material means of cultural production, actual cultural forms, and modes of reproduction.

How are the grammar and syntax of history woven into Williams's method? To capture the configuration of interests and activities that distinguishes a historical period and at the same time register the "actual living sense" of a community that makes communication possible, Williams deploys the term "structure of feeling": "We learn each element as a precipitate, but in the living experience of the time every element was in solution, an inseparable part of a complex whole" (1961, 47). In the practice of cultural historiography, Williams was engaged in tracing historical patterns, especially the actively lived and felt meanings and beliefs that mix with "justified experience" or systematic worldviews. In analyzing formations, Williams spelled out both the fixity of "structure" and the spontaneous flow of (for want of a better word) sensibilities. Instead of describing patterned wholes, Williams sought to apprehend "forming and formative processes, . . . practical consciousness of a present kind, in a living and interrelating continuity," through this conceptual device of a "structure of feeling" that captures accurately the dialectic of the social and the idiosyncratically private or personal. The subtext to this interpretive strategy is easily discernible: Williams opposes the assignment of ideas, meanings, and experience to the domain of the received notion of the superstructure that, being merely reflective of and determined by the economic base, has no autonomy or social effectivity of its own. Culture cannot be simply folded into the realm of ideology in the sense of "false consciousness" or Althusser's "imaginary relations."

One way to illustrate how "structure of feeling" functions as a mode of historical accounting of signification is to focus on Williams's series of essays on modernism in *The Politics of Modernism*. In one essay, Williams begins with a juxtaposition of two strands of events in a unique historic conjuncture. In Zurich in 1916, a cabaret of Dadaism was being performed in Number One, Spiegelgasse, while in Number Six of the same street lived a certain Herr Ulianov (Lenin). One of the founders of Dadaism, Hugo Ball, reminisced how Lenin must have heard the artist's music and tirades, their quixotic and "unpurposeful" counterplay to the Bolshevik "thorough settling of accounts." Williams remarks that within five years of Dada's launching, a revolutionary avant-garde theater appeared in the newly founded Soviet Union, Europe's periphery. Williams sums up by observing that the emergence of modernism from metropolitan experience marks the peculiar confluence of residual, dominant, and emergent cultural trends, often overlapping and contrapuntal, from both the metropoles and the patrolled borderlands of the empire.

The concept of "structure of feeling" as a heuristic instrument for elucidating the social history of forms also informs Williams's extended inquiries, in particular *The Country and the City*, as well as his chapters "The Social History of Dramatic Forms" and "Realism and the Contemporary Novel" in *The Long Revolution* and *Television: Technology and Cultural Form*. In this latter book, Williams stresses the desideratum that technology, its application and responses, can only be understood "within the determining limits and pressures" of particular historical periods in specific societies. Seen thus, television for him began to manifest its cultural form as a response to the specific crisis of industrial capitalist society, especially the conjunction of the social complex of the privatized home and mobility. The sequence or flow in television programming embodies, for Williams, both residual, dominant, and emergent trends in the history of communication.

Meanwhile, in *The Country and the City*, Williams charts the vicissitudes of tone and feeling toward the mutable and metamorphosing spaces of city and countryside. He warns us not to reify images or memories, to be sensitive to the immense actual variation in our ideas about lived spaces, and to register the confluence of persistence and change: "For we have really to look, in country and city alike, at the real social processes of alienation, separation, externality, abstraction . . . experiences of directness, connection, mutuality, sharing, which alone can define, in the end, what the real deformation may be" (1973, 298). Through his notion of "knowable communities," which links epistemological realism and utopian speculation, Williams qualifies "totality" as a mode of communication and transaction among diverse practices. His accent is on relations, not autonomy of spheres of activity. According to Alan O'Connor, "knowable community" describes "a strategy in discourse rather than immediate experience or an 'organic' community" (1989, 68). In other words, there is no such thing as an organic, seamless community where experience is not discontinuous, fragmentary, in need of a connecting intelligence or sensibility. The connections are fashioned by artistic works and by critical analysis. In the course of this historicized aesthetics of place, Williams reminds us again of the dialectic between social consciousness and needs. He underscores the imperative of openness to the changing objective world in which the critic is "always already" imbricated: "For what is knowable is not only a function of objects — of what is there to be known. It is also a function of subjects, of observers — of what is desired and what needs to be known" (1973, 165). And so the concept of determination operates in the sense of "limits and pressures," introducing levels of effectivity into what would otherwise be a monolith of "indissoluble practice" that is identical with sensuous, socially constituted praxis.

Williams returns to the issue of determination in a substantial essay, "Base and Superstructure in Marxist Cultural Theory," where he answers his critics' refutation of his organicist stand. Williams assents to the layered architectonics of any cultural conjuncture. He refines his notion of a manifold totality founded on social agency and the class organization of society: "The principles of this organization and structure can be seen as directly related to certain social intentions [connected to] the rule of a particular class" (1980, 36). This intentionality is given more precision by reappropriating Gramsci's theory of hegemony. Hegemony for Williams refers to our experienced or lived reality, the "whole body of practices and expectations; our assignments of energy, our ordinary understanding of the nature of man and his world," the "common sense" that legitimizes the existing social system of distribution and hierarchy of power. But no sociopolitical order can exhaust the full range of human practice, energy, and intention because "modes of domination select from and consequently exclude the full range of actual and possible human practice." Ultimately, then, determination is uneven and can only be formulated as a sense of limit and pressure, not control or strict causality, allowing for prefigurative and utopian experiments in mapping a redeemed future — something that evokes Ernst Bloch's teleology of critical phantasy and a practice of inheritance to welcome the "Not-Yet" (D. Howard 1977).

We can now gauge the distance CS has traveled from Williams's "cultural materialism." Conceived as a mediation of subject and object, the concept of "structure of feeling" has been reconfigured, if not discarded, by the postmodernist fetishizing of representation and its articulation of the decentered neoliberal subject. Not only is the dialectic of differentiating complex formations jettisoned for a microphysics of dispersed power and its local narratives, but also the polarity of subject/ object is construed as merely "an effect of the conditions of operation of the enunciative function," with knowledge itself being an effect of a generalized will to power. From Williams's cultural materialism, we move on to the time of "anarcho-Nietzscheanism" that denies in effect the possibility of objective knowledge and social emancipation (Callinicos 1982). CS's protean transmigrations and wayward metamorphosis may be tracked by the inventory of its various trends and tendencies.

Cunning of Conjunctures

The omnibus collection *Cultural Studies* (1992) edited by Lawrence Grossberg, Cary Nelson, and Paula Treichler has established a consensual doxa about the discipline. We can now appreciate CS as a superior form of bricolage, context dependent but anti/post/multidisciplinary, pragmatic, strategic, and self-reflective, with a tradition and lexicon that defy codification, affording no guarantees of validity or authoritativeness and stimulating endless self-reflexive interrogation. It is a contentious field crisscrossed by diverse positions and trajectories, putatively open-ended. What does bricolage mean? It encompasses textual analysis, semiotics, deconstruction, ethnography, interviews, phonemic analysis, psychoanalysis, rhizomatics, content analysis, survey research, and so on — a carnivalesque bazaar for any handyman!

The British CS expert Richard Johnson describes the three models of CS in terms of "production-based," "text-based," and "studies of lived cultures" (1996, 107). While claiming that there is no single narrative or definition of CS, Grossberg and his colleagues cite the double articulation of CS: cultural practice and production as the ground on which analysis takes place simultaneously with political critique and intervention. Investigating the historically grounded practices, representations, languages, and customs of specific formations, CS also studies "the contradictory forms of common sense" or commonplace understandings that presumably provide resources to fight the constraints of the social order. Grossberg and colleagues write, "It is nevertheless true that from the outset cultural studies' efforts to recover working-class culture and history and to synthesize progressive traditions in Western intellectual history had had both overt and implicit political aims" (5). But what are the concrete consequences and implications of terms such as *political critique*, *progressive*, and *intervention*?

The overt and implicit political aims turn out to coincide with language and sign systems. Poststructuralism has resurrected formalist idealism. From here on, the reduction of the ideological component of cultural production to discourse and knowledge-power (to borrow the Foucauldian term) and questions of representation has become routine. In 1992, Hall reaffirmed the primacy of discursive and textual processes over political economy: such processes are "not reflective but constitutive in the formation of the modern world: as constitutive as economic, political or social processes [which] do not operate outside of cultural and ideological conditions" (1992b, 13). It is one thing to say that economic and political processes "depend on meaning for their effects and have cultural or ideological conditions of existence"; it is another to conclude that textuality or representation, in tandem with economic and political forces and in isolation from them, construct the social and political system we inhabit. The subsumption of relations of power to relations of discourse or cultural practices returns us to a one-sided culturalism that Hall originally wanted to move away from, even though now a theory of discursive articulation is introduced to anticipate such critical objections of reductionism and of idealist formalism to what pretends to be an improvement over vulgar Marxism.

This crux was already prefigured in the entire trajectory of Williams's wrestling with mechanical materialism and also with Lucien Goldmann's sociology of culture. His attempt to resolve the disjunction between theory and practice resulted in the highly nuanced category of "structure of feeling" enunciated in many works, in particular *Marxism and Literature* and *Problems in Materialism and Culture*. But here I would like to address the latest reconstruction of the problematic of cultural studies that has been quite influential, namely, the theory and method of articulation of various levels of significations embodied in forms of cultural representation, a problematic first elaborated by Stuart Hall.

Hall tried to clarify his research orientation and agenda in a 1985 interview:

QUESTIONING CULTURAL STUDIES

> An articulation is thus the form of the connection that can make a unity of two different elements, under certain conditions. It is a linkage which is not necessary, determined, absolute and essential for all time. You have to ask, under what circumstances can a connection be forged or made? So the so-called "unity" of a discourse is really the articulation of different, distinct elements which can be rearticulated in different ways because they have no necessary "belongingness." The "unity" which matters is a linkage between that articulated discourse and the social forces with which it can, under certain historical conditions, but need not necessarily, be connected. Thus, a theory of articulation is both a way of understanding how ideological elements come, under certain conditions, to cohere together within a discourse, and a way of asking how they do or do not become articulated, at specific conjunctures, to certain political subjects. (Hall 1996b, 142–43)

This approach reformulates the Althusserian idea of interpellation. It seeks to disentangle the elements of any ideological complex from their class roots or association, endowing the new ensemble with a power to "discover its subject" and enable that subject to make intelligible its historical situation without "reducing those forms of intelligibility to their socio-economic or class location or social position" (Hall 1996b, 142). This implies that an ideology like Thatcherism, while anchored to Tory conservatism, entails a politics of positionality contrived by juxtaposing ordinary commonsense beliefs of the masses with a class-based worldview. Elucidating this hegemonic drive requires a theory of discursive articulation to reveal the principle whereby diverse elements have been organized to promote a neoliberal political platform.

Trajectory of Desire

How parts are assembled together rather than their substance or import commands priority. Translated into the grammar and syntax of CS, the theory of articulation becomes almost a methodological dogma. Hall states, "An articulation is thus the form of the connection that *can* make a unity of two different elements, under certain conditions. . . . The 'unity' which matters is a linkage between that articulated discourse [composed of elements without any necessary 'belongingness'] and the social forces with which it can, under certain historical conditions, but need not necessarily, be connected" (1996b, 141). Hall stresses the a priori contingency and adhoc transitoriness subtending the practice of articulation. One suspects that whoever commands enough political clout can alter the contingent to the necessary.

Indeterminacy unfolds its seeming opposite: opportunist realpolitik. Beginning as a reaction against determinism, the reduction of ideology to political economy, this theory of articulation betrays itself as a pragmatic epistemology of explaining social change as arbitrary, even gratuitous, susceptible to the dictates of who commands the most power. When Hall illustrates this cs modus operandi by using the Rastafarian movement as an inflection of disparate ideological elements along certain historical tendencies, he gestures to the need to take into account "the grain of historical formations." However, the move is aborted. What transpires is a return to the primary thesis that religion, like any ideological complex, operates like a language or discursive enunciation open to a wide range of experimental play. So ideology (if that is still a viable notion), which interpellates individuals into political agents, is not given necessarily in socioeconomic structure or in objective reality; in short, "the popular force of an organic ideology" is "the result of *an articulation*" (1996b, 145).

I rehearse part of the debate here in this question: Can all cultural practices then be reduced "upward" as discourse or language, and all subjectivities or subject positionalities be conceived as discursively constituted? Hall registers a limit to the theoretical reductionism of Laclau/Mouffe and its extension in psychoanalytic exercises. He instructs us to locate cultural/discursive practices "within the determining lines of force of material relations, and the expropriation of nature. . . . Material conditions are the necessary but not sufficient condition of all historical practice," but such conditions need to be thought of "in their determinate discursive form" (1996b, 147). This notion of practice approximates the materialist dialectic of object and subject conceived as an interactive process of being and becoming.

Hall is cognizant of the abuses of a theoretical bricolage influenced by realpolitik pragmatism, as found in some applications of Foucault and the deconstructionist archive. Unfortunately, such abuses are fostered by the inadequacy of articulation theory: it cannot comprehend the internal relation of parts within a dynamic whole since its level of abstraction refuses to grasp the internal impulses and potential within the elements being articulated, the unity and contradiction distinguishing them, as the force that shapes the way in which the whole galaxy of forces is configured. What is lacking is the dialectical unity of the continuous and discontinuous that generates dynamic coherence (Lefebvre 1968). Further, the internal transformation of each articulated moment — the categories of mediation within the totality (Meszaros 1972) — remains obscure, if not mystifying. While Hall acknowledges that Rastafarianism centers on the "determinations of economic life in Jamaican society," its status as a product of discursive articulation, as a unified force with a nonunitary collective subject, originates elsewhere. Rastafarianism is conceived as the unifying ideology that subsumes economic determinations and constitutes its bloc of social/political forces in a nonholistic way, through negotiations, compromises, and other realignments. But exactly how that ideology materialized remains mysterious.

Whatever our wishes may portend, the real world has proven itself more recalcitrant and intractable. CS pundits are discovering it everyday. As the sociologist Jorge Larrain has shown, the old Marxist concept of ideology would suffice to enable the critique of Thatcherism as a "return, with a vengeance, to the old and quintessential principles of bourgeois political ideology which had been progressively obscured by years of social democracy, welfare state and Keynesianism" (1995, 66), the old ideological values of a mythical "free market" — freedom and self-interest based on property. But this time, the conjuncture of the eighties does not replicate the Victorian conflation of Bentham and Mill. Hence the Thatcherite emphasis on authority, law and order, family and tradition; patriotism is invoked to hide the real origins of the capitalist crisis, a crisis whose symptoms are unemployment, poverty, racist discrimination, criminality, new forms of violence, national and regional divisions, intensified class conflicts, and so on. Such populist authoritarianism is neither arbitrary nor contingent. To counter its effects, we need the framework of the organic crisis of the capitalist system without which a method of articulation can only discover short-range opportunism and even a deceptive liberalism in Thatcher's agenda.

Viewed as a programmatic formation (in Williams's sense), Hall's

theory of articulation responds to a new historical-political development that resists elucidation by this semiotic maneuver. Hall addresses
not so much the novel features of bourgeois hegemonic rule as the need
to recognize the political economy of class interfaced with race, gender,
nationality, and other "new social" movements. Class is, to be sure,
not just another banal aspect of identity. For these movements to interact, it is necessary to understand what background totality would enable
them to dialogue and form alliances, to forge the "chain of equivalence" that Laclau and Mouffe believe is the catalyzing element for
radical democracy.

Poststructuralist fallacies prove damaging here. By valorizing the
moment of articulation and even reifying it, Hall tends to occlude the
larger epochal background that functions as the condition of possibility
for making sense of conjunctural particularities. To use Williams's terminology, the moment of "lived experience" overshadows again the
category of formation (residual, dominant, emergent), the structuring modality of "feeling" with which cultural analysis is preoccupied.
Fredric Jameson considers articulation or mediation (to use the philosophical term) as "the central theoretical problem" of Cultural Studies.
He views it as "a punctual and sometimes even ephemeral totalization
in which the planes of race, gender, class, ethnicity and sexuality inter-
sect to form an operative structure" (1995, 269). Although Hall states
that articulation names the unity of a discourse with social forces under
certain but not necessary conditions in history, he is careful to point out
that the result is an "articulated combination" and not just a "random
association" — "that there will be structured relation between its parts,
i.e., relations of dominance and subordination" (1992, 325).

What concerns me here is the way such a theory of articulation has
been deployed in contemporary CS. The problem may be a replay of the
anxieties over the reimposition of class reductionism or economism as a
reaction to identity biopolitics and the anarchism of local narratives.
Earlier I alluded to the recurrent concern of CS practitioners that in foregrounding social history and political economy, the matter of agency
will be sacrificed. One scholar, for example, contends that women's
consumption of Hollywood cinema, or any object of cultural exchange
for that matter, does not simply illustrate "the power of hegemonic
forces in the definition of women's role as consumer"; rather, con-

sumption "is a site of negotiated meanings, of resistance and of appropriation as well as of subjection and exploitation" (quoted in Strinati 1995, 218). Taking passive consumption as an autonomous activity, populist-oriented CS ignores the aestheticization of commodity production itself (Wood 1996), mistakenly attributing to the form of value (exchange) instead of the real value (use) the source of pleasure and agency (Sohn-Rethel 1978). Meanwhile, the division of manual and mental labor born of commodity-exchange and bourgeois property relations continues to hide the historicity of images, codes, artifacts, and habitus — culture remains naturalized, opaque, and instrumentalized.

Can we renew the radical inspiration of CS? Stuart Hall constantly reminds us of the core problematic of CS at its foundational moment: culture (meaning, symbolic forms, signifying practices, discourses) situated in the context of mutable social relations and the organization of power. The analysis of semiotic and discursive practices — the linkages between language/literature and political economy/mode of production — includes with it the examination of the position of collective subjects in history, generating a critique of those practices and positions. Hall comments on a later development: "A formal deconstructionism which isn't asking questions about the insertion of symbolic processes into societal contexts and their imbrication with power is not interested in the cultural studies problematic" (1996a, 390). Cultural Studies then is distinguished by its disclosure of how cultural practices are enmeshed in networks of power. But is it enough to insist as a desideratum of legitimacy for this new approach the linkage of discourse, society, and power? What does "power" signify here? How is it related to political economy and the complex dynamics of social relations? Isn't this by itself a formula, a game of empty abstractions, since there is no investigation of purpose, agenda, or historical direction? Isn't this a rehashing of the rudimentary empiricist demand that ideas be framed in social and political contexts?

All commentators agree that a version of Marxist reductionism, otherwise known as *economism*, triggered the revolt against the left. What happened in the reaction to a caricatured "actually existing" Marxism? Despite claims that the rebels were reinstating agency and freedom to the subject, a swing to atavistic ideology and obscurantist reaction occurred. I believe the correction offered, namely, the overemphasis on a formalist methodology conflated with organicist (Leavis) or nihilistic assumptions (poststructuralism), resulted in the unwitting co-optation of CS. It was never radical enough to destroy the logic of capital and the ideology of quantifying concrete-use values into abstract equivalents (the cash nexus), the law of laissez-faire exchange that governs the market. Eventually CS has become an Establishment organon, or an academic "ideological state apparatus" preventing even the old style of *Kulturkritik* to function. Terry Eagleton calls our attention to the crippling flaw in both Kulturkritik and modern-day culturalism in their lack of interest in "the state apparatus of violence and coercion" (2000, 43).

Vulnerabilities

One of the most astute diagnoses of this decay is by Francis Mulhern. In utilizing Gramsci's complex notion of hegemony to ascribe more freedom to the subject, postmodernist CS overexaggerated the possibility of liberation over the established fact of domination. Both subordination and resistance are found in popular culture, the impulses of resistance embedded in relations of domination and imperatives of commodification. Rejecting totality, according to Mulhern, CS has ignored elite cultural forms and elevated popular/mass culture as intrinsically subversive of the exploitative mode of production, thus overlooking "the overwhelming historical realities of inequality and subordination" that condition both (1995, 34). In privileging commodified recreation and subsistence activity found in marketed "lifestyles," Mulhern argues that the "spontaneous bent of cultural studies is actually *conformist* — at its worst, the theoretical self-consciousness of satellite television and shopping malls" (1995, 35).

Pierre Bourdieu has already argued convincingly that culture legitimates social inequality, with consumption fulfilling the function of legitimating social differences. Taste itself is a profoundly ideological discourse, a marker of class (Thompson 1984). Enforced by schools and other institutions, a "cultural arbitrary" inflicts symbolic violence by inculcating a habitus of misrecognition: cultural hierarchies appear rational and so justify economic and political domination (Bourdieu 1993). No doubt we need an adequate theory of cultural politics. If the culture of everyday life is politicized and all difference regarded as immediately emancipatory, then Mulhern contends, this dissolves the "possibility of culture as a field of political struggle." Why? Because politics is a deliberative and injunctive practice that seeks to determine the character of social relations while culture, whose major function is to produce meanings, does not have for its chief purpose the determination of social relations by deliberation, injunction, and coercion. The two realms should not be collapsed or conflated. Political judgment and cultural judgment are distinct and do not coincide, as Gramsci taught us.

Mulhern concludes that orthodox CS treats all differences as absolute, whereas politics aims for united fronts and tactical alliances in pursuit of specific ends. By eliding that distinction, dissolving politics into culture, CS abandons the search for political solidarities and freezes "the particularisms of cultural difference," of varying cultural practices as political in themselves. Mulhern perceives CS as bankrupt in accepting without criticism the bondage of the masses to consumer capitalism — the ironical end-result of their will to resist all determinisms: "There is no space, and in fact no need, for struggle if all popular culture, abstracted from "high" culture and from the historical realities of inequality and domination, is already active and critical, if television and shopping are already teachers of subversion" (1995, 40). One needs to discriminate between culture as universal value and culture as specific life-forms. This has also been sharply formulated by Neil Larsen in his critique of the populist brand of CS advocated by John Fiske. Fiske simply reads off the popular as "immediacy," as the "everyday," while the "aesthetic" is quarantined in idealized transcendence — "the antinomial ideology of modernism itself, but here with its normative polarities reversed" (Larsen 1996, 91).

Apart from the historical misfortunes of the radical left in Britain (where the Birmingham experiment in CS was first launched), the poststructuralist "exorbitation" of language and semiotics contributed to what I would call a *metaphysical turn* in CS. Socioeconomic determinants shaped its immanent vicissitudes. The evolution from cultural empiricism to Althusserian structuralism ended in a neutralist, if not counterrevolutionary, revision of Gramsci (Bocock 1986). The concept of ideology was purged and hegemony replaced ideology-critique. Entirely overlooking the distinction between class-in-itself and class-for-itself already found in Marx's *Eighteenth Brumaire* and other works, Laclau interpreted the Gramscian concept of hegemony hinging on working-class moral/intellectual leadership as equivalent to the "historic bloc." This bloc constructs political subjects (working class, women, environmentalists, and so on) by the figure of equivalence — in short, politics as "articulation." A heterogeneous bloc serves as the stage for performative, disingenuous "free play."

Immanence displaces transcendence by tergiversation. While Laclau and Mouffe (in their joint work, *Hegemony and Socialist Strategy*) grant that the collective will of such a bloc is forged by organic intellectuals, a will expressed in the politics of compromise uniting the bloc, they argue further that there is not just one hegemonic center in society but many. A field of "articulation" is posited in which society is no longer a totality sutured together, but rather an open field; "the openness of the social as the constitutive ground or 'negative essence' of the existing, and the diverse 'social orders' as precarious and ultimately failed attempts to domesticate the field of differences" (1985, 95–96). Rejecting the notions of "mode of production," "social formation," "overdetermination," and the like, Laclau and Mouffe claim that all social reality is constructed by articulatory practices that establish identities of elements through relation. Thus, "all identity is relational. . . . There is no essence, no structure, which underlies the signifier, social identity is symbolic and relational, not fixed independently of any articulation," although temporary nodal points in the symbolic field for fixing meanings are conceded (1985, 113). But what rationale or purpose lies behind articulation? Unaffected by the elements it articulates, what is the direction of articulatory practice? I submit that the motivations and ends of this research program, however, are not obscure: they are geared to legitimizing the indeterminacies of post-Keynesian "market" fluctuations, privatization of socially produced knowledge, and the sublimation of irreconcilable contradictions in every society wracked by the profound crisis of the capitalist world-system.

Carnivalesque Closure

The imperative of contingency and indeterminacy becomes almost fetishized in the work of Lawrence Grossberg, a disciple of Hall and editor of the chief institutional organ of cs. In surveying current theories of identity, Grossberg refuses what he calls the logics of modernity founded on difference, individuality, and temporality. He proposes an alternative logic of otherness, production and spatiality for a theory of human agency and historical change. Agency, for Grossberg, is defined by "the articulations of subject positions and identities into specific places and spaces . . . on socially constructed territories" (1996, 102). Constructionism thickens with the entailment of conventions.

Mystifications based on nominalist relativism pile up amid triumphalist cs rhetoric. Grossberg upholds a notion of singularity underlying a community envisioned by the Italian philosopher Giorgio Agamben. It is somewhat of a puzzle that Grossberg endorses Agamben's view that the 1989 Tiananmen Square demonstration in China instances the singularity of belonging without identity; ultimately, the place, the exteriority of locale, constitutes the singular community. What is egregiously tendentious is the praise of spontaneous action that supposedly characterized the urban insurrection in Beijing, a false premise based on ignorance of the facts of the case. Ignoring the actual circumstances, the tautology Grossberg indulges in to convey what he thinks is profound — "it was the fact of belonging that constituted their belonging together" — serves as proof that anomie, ephemeral accidents, an anarchistic valorization of the happenstance and contingent all acquire foundational import that becomes a warrant for novelty in cs.

The cult of vernacular experience substitutes for all-rounded historical analysis. Perhaps the style of adhoc extrapolation of the significance of a major historical event may not be as trivializing as the prodigious dissertations written on pop stars, TV talk shows, public spectacles (sports, media events), and beauty pageants that argue that such commercial icons and rituals are counterhegemonic ruses to overthrow the system. Or, more soberly, what harm can a treatise on Dali among the dolphins in Disneyland do? Nothing except that they legitimize the way things are: cash registers ring merrily while service workers in hotels, restaurants, and carnival grounds sweat it out for corporate capital and its instrumentalities to reproduce themselves and, with it, the unequal division of labor and the theft of social wealth amassed on the damaged bodies of millions of workers, peasants, women, and children around the world.

Now, surely, cs from the outset aspired to displace the centrality of victimization with the praxis of resistance, opposition, and people's democratic initiatives. From object to subject — this underlines the trajectory of the critique of determinism and the search for new forms of subjectivity launched by Williams, Thompson, and Hall. But on the way to utopian pleasure and empowerment of the fissured subject, its own internal contradictions exploded. Relativism and nominalism undermined the goal of integrating theory and practice. The imperative of rhetorical mastery, compounded with the individualist ethos of "free-trade" theorizing for privileged academics, channeled any oppositional or critical impulses into the invention of apologias for neoliberal multiculturalism. Cultural Studies becomes a scholastic game for careerists accumulating venal symbolic hoards.

At this point, we need to scrutinize the more insidious irony at work in CS when poststructuralist ideas of resistance become a framework for describing the ordinary practices of exploited people. Sheer heterogeneity reflecting the fragmentation of commodity culture infects the subject to the point where everything becomes relative. Nietzschean perspectivism prohibits the critic of Cartesian rationality from appealing to a normative framework for criticizing that rationality and its power. Through the social conditions of fragmentation and dispersal, power, discursive and otherwise, prevails (Dunn 1998). Can a positivist description of epistemic structures be conjoined with "modalities of moral self-constitution" (Dews 1995, 234) to offset the preponderance of institutional power? Can ethnographic verisimilitude dear to the connoisseurs of the particular discover the "weak links" in the social structures that repress the human potential?

Accidents of Necessity

With the deepening crisis of the global market system in the seventies and eighties marked by populist authoritarianism (Thatcher, Reagan), ludic pragmatism and poststructuralist nominalism have begun to dictate and narrow the parameters of intellectual exchange. Anti-Marxism culminates in the blanket prohibition against essentialism, teleology, metanarratives, and all claims to find truth with historical grounding; in fact, "totalizing" comprehension is equated with totalitarianism. Since the invocation of material conditions summed up in the term *political economy* is stigmatized as terrorism of the left and branded as "political correctness," CS practitioners are often left with the choice of doing positivist ethnography intended to validate any popular activity as somehow authentic and liberating.

One illustration may be cited here. Abandoning critique and exploration of possibilities negated by the market system, John Fiske celebrates bricolage as the mark of popular creativity. He extols the ethnography of an extradiscursive activity of producing quilts, diaries, or furniture arrangement, as well as routine practices of daily life. One example is the urban poor's employment of television to "enrich and further densify the texture" of quotidian life. Another example is the use of photographs, plastic flowers, and other commodities in which "lost kinship webs are reasserted, reformed through bricolage" (1992, 156). The logic of this pattern of accomodation is spelled out by Fiske in this way: "The construction, occupation, and ownership of one's own space/setting within their place/arena, the weaving of one's own richly textured life within the constraints of economic deprivation and oppression, are not just ways of controlling some of the conditions of social existence; they are also ways of constructing, and therefore exerting some control over, social identities and social relations" (1992, 160). Coping and other forms of daily adjustment to the dictates of the social order are taken as life-enhancing indices of agency. Everyday life thus becomes validated as affording scenarios for performing the ludic politics of cultural difference.

Clearly, this "take" on CS is both disingenuous and self-incriminating. It actually abstains from any task of "empowering" the oppressed and exploited by confining popular creativity to accomodation to the status quo by means of an "everyday tactical dissembling" now described as politically progressive. The model of peasant resistance cited by Fiske and other ethnographers of this persuasion reveals their conformist bias and defeatist inclination. This approach resembles the aleatory "matterism" of Foucault and his followers that Teresa Ebert condemns as obscuring the material relations in which discourses and practices are produced, an influential "protocol of ludic reading — this genealogy or eventalization — to mask the rigid divisions of class struggle" (1996, 228; see also Cotter 1996).

The stress on consumption and leisure over production/work may acount for the hermeneutic turn in CS. It may also explain the emphasis on random, arbitrary differences over determinate social practices with ascertainable intentionalities. Symbolic representation often becomes privileged apart from concrete structures of domination. But CS's shifting of the point of gravity toward gender and race, away from class and nation, sheds light on the downgrading of the political economy of cultural practice. Ignoring the processes of commodity production and exchange, the international division of labor, unequal trade, and racialized labor market, CS rejects the problem of "false consciousness," of ideology in general. It casts all popular practice as positive resistance to domination, trivializing the possibilities of revolution and emancipation. Nicholas Garnham correctly insists that CS should focus on the core characteristics of the capitalist mode of production — waged labor and commodity exchange as necessary conditions of existence — if it wants its liberatory stance to signify more than a gesture of sympathy for the underdogs. Garnham argues, "One cannot understand either the genesis, forms, or stakes of the struggles around gender and race without an analysis of the political economic foundations and context of the cultural practices that constitute these struggles," conditions that "shape in determinate ways the terrain upon which cultural practices take place — the physical environment, the available material and symbolic resources, the time rhythms and spatial relations" (1999, 502). Political economy, needless to say, is a point of departure, not the dogmatic center or end-point of any CS inquiry.

Nor is this a matter of substituting an abstract schema of political economy for an exorbitant culturalism. When the sphere of culture becomes inflated and universalized to function also as politics — call it *cultural politics* or subaltern resistance — then cultural studies becomes nothing else but an apology for commodity fetishism. This also applies to the aestheticization of all practices in ethnographic cultural studies like those of Fiske, Clifford, Grossberg, and other scholars, in which culture immediately becomes oppositional so that ideological struggle within it is elided. Actuality and possibility are conflated, resulting in a conservative standpoint (for a philosophical framework, see Jameson 1995; Hebdige 1993). Francis Mulhern warns us against this trend: "There is no space, and in fact no need, for struggle if all popular culture, abstracted from 'high' culture and from the historical realities of inequality and domination, is already active and critical, if television and shopping are already theaters of subversion" (40). Celebrating the market in "lifestyles," commodified recreation, and subsistence activity, cs abandons critique and submits to the dictates of what W. F. Haug (1999) calls "commodity aesthetics."

Deployed in cultural inquiry, the concept of everyday life can be articulated in either a pragmatic and reformist direction, as Fiske does, or in a historical-materialist one, as exemplified by Henri Lefebvre and Agnes Heller. In her book *Everyday Life*, Heller points out that "the use of means of consumption is determined by custom and tradition. . . . I construe 'consumption' as the appropriation of any meaningful object in which the key role is played by the relay of social meaning (or social import). . . . In the mere use of things, man (as person) can only realize himself via moral mediation" (1984, 149–50). Precisely here lies the problem of ethnographic Cultural Studies that evacuates any reference to historical "organic" structures in favor of the "slice of life" empiricism: the "moral mediation" of the Western commentator insinuates itself to endow recorded performances and scenes with meaning and import, a significance larger than the semantic horizon of particular routine details of lived experience. We are back to the problem of authority and explanatory validity that has afflicted Cultural Studies when it rejected a dialectical mediation of structure and experience.

Voyeuristic Ruptures

Let us now consider anthropology's refraction of cs. In our postcolonial millennium, one would have expected that a new sensorium of spatiality would compensate for the damage wrought by temporal distancing on colonized indigenous peoples. Johannes Fabian (1983) has demonstrated how the denial of coevalness and the scientistic cartography of progress legitimized Europe's "civilizing mission" over the "barbaric" natives. The ideal of progress served to apologize for the genocide of "peoples without history," justifying by extension the white supremacist evangelism of cs itself and its postcolonial hubris. But now, if the metropole is becoming a wasteland, why not travel to the periphery?

One example of this is James Clifford's intriguing essay "Traveling Cultures." Clifford is engaged in exploring and purportedly displacing "exoticist anthropological forms" inhabiting the domain of comparative Cultural Studies: the diverse, interconnected histories of travel and displacement, exile, diaspora, tourism, and immigration. While preoccupied with the theme of intercultural hermeneutics, "how cultural analysis constitutes its objects — societies, traditions, communities, identities — in spatial terms and through specific spatial practices of research" (1992, 97), Clifford is arguably intent on rehabilitating neocolonial anthropology.

The technique of salvaging what is useful can be an astute exercise in self-reflexivity. One strategy for retooling anthropology pivots around the effort to redefine "fieldwork" as less a concrete place of research than a methodological ideal, a communicative competence. The issue of representation is, for Clifford, concerned with "the portrayal and understanding of local/global historical encounters, co-productions, dominations, and resistances, [consequently] one needs to focus on hybrid, cosmopolitan experiences as much as on rooted native ones." Clifford expands on this topic:

> In tipping the balance toward traveling as I am doing here, the "chronotope" of culture (a setting or scene organizing time and space in representable whole form) comes to resemble as much a site of travel encounters as of residence, less a tent in a village or a controlled laboratory or a site of initiation and inhabitation, and more like a hotel lobby, ship, or bus. If we rethink culture and its science, anthropology, in terms of travel, then the organic, naturalizing bias of the term culture — seen as a rooted body that grows, lives, dies, etc. — is questioned. Constructed and disputed *historicities*, sites of displacement, interference, and interaction, come more sharply into view. (1992, 101)

Not a believer in nomadology or nominalism, Clifford seems earnest in proving that he can discriminate between the privileged and the disadvantaged, between the missionary West and subjugated natives, between oppressor and oppressed. He disavows linear history and its telos of progress. But he is passionately driven to do comparisons and analogies. He states that while there is no ground of equivalence between Alexander von Humboldt traveling through South America as a scientist and the Asian indentured laborer in California, "there is at least a basis for comparison and (problematic) translation" (1992, 107).

230

He believes that a comparative cultural studies would be interested in knowledge of the Asian laborer's view of "The New World" as a potential complement or critique of Von Humboldt's. But what is the basis for such comparisons?

Clifford favors itineraries, returns, and detours, "a history of locations and a location of histories." He is obsessed with migration, exile, transitions, diasporas, movements here and there. Borderlands fascinate him, cities where artists sojourn and pass through. But what is peculiar is that the cities he concentrates on are European ones, Paris in particular, "a site of cultural creation," where Alejo Carpentier, Aimé Césaire, and a host of African and Latin American intellectuals learned a "postcolonial habitus," a "discrepant cosmopolitanism." Symptomatic of an aesthetic-driven agenda, Clifford does not mention Ho Chi Minh, Chou En-lai, or Frantz Fanon who also traveled through Paris, literally and metaphorically: Ho and Chou witnessed and rejected the Eurocentric chauvinism of the French communists while Fanon experienced the gamut of racism in his encounter with psychoanalysis and existentialism. Unbeknownst to Clifford, the problematic of travel thus contains the positive in the negative, opposites uniting and separating in diremptive motion. Contrast Clifford's exhibitionist travelog with a historical-materialist delineation of places by David Harvey. Adopting the framework of "militant particularism," Harvey points out that the "dialectics of space and place" implies a process of remembering activities of "place creation and dissolution" (1996, 29) rooted in class consciousness and political action — "structures of feeling" (Raymond Williams's term) without which encyclopedic travel, albeit sophisticated and anti-ethnocentric, is nothing but blind and empty motion of atoms in space.

Clifford's broad agenda is "to rethink cultures as sites of dwelling *and* travel" (105). In a time when transnational capital, with its new modalities of "flexible accumulation" and niche marketing, is uprooting millions of "third-world" peoples and converting them into "transnational" workers, Clifford has the leisure to craft a strategy of aestheticizing this planned mobility for a refurbished ethnography of cultural mapping. An obvious symptom of this aestheticizing of migration is his agreement with cs practitioners who believe in the extinction of the nation-state. For example, he agrees with the sociologist Orlando Patterson's idea of a postnational environment in the United States, a country now possessing "borderland culture areas, populated by strong, di-asporic ethnicities unevenly assimilated" into the dominant culture. No mention here of the role of "buffer races," labor-market segmenta-tion, pauperization of gendered labor, and so on (Martin and Schumann 1996; Hoogvelt 1997). Instead, Clifford emphasizes that "travel," en-compassing the historical resonance of other terms like *migration, pil-grimage, safari*, and so on, is a translation term to be used "for com-parison in a strategic and contingent way" (1992, 110). Dense with connotations of gender, class, and race, "travel" harbors a "certain literariness" that allows semiotic free play. But of course, the play of representations, images, and texts inventoried by the ethnographer is always contrived and classified by the power of authorities who also command material, political, and economic resources/properties.

Postmodernist CS scholars make the familiar idealist move of proj-ecting into the object of inquiry a particular "way of understanding" (Eagleton 2000, 219) that, contrary to their original motivation, be-comes spontaneous dogma. While Clifford urges self-critical awareness that we are using "compromised, historically encumbered tools," he himself (like his fellow anthropologist Constable; see my afterword) does not reflect deeply enough on his own spatial politics. As a result, his survey flattens contradictions of class, nationality, race, and gender into a homogeneous cluster whose utility as ethnographic source mate-rial for knowledge is its most indispensable virtue. Significantly he treats tourism as something marginal, when in fact tourism, a form of commodified travel, reveals the function of travel as an allegory of bourgeois modernity, not a form of raw experience or unmediated con-sciousness but a virtual translation of socioeconomic institutions.

It is not irrelevant to remark that Clifford's "travel" as a pedagogical technique requires the acquisition and deployment of substantial cul-tural capital. Travel becomes a means of exchanging knowledge, osten-sibly for enriching knowledge of one's self, but ultimately for reaffirm-ing mastery of the few privileged Westerners able to engage in leisurely self-reflection. Travel seeks to domesticate Otherness (personified here by migrants, exotic cultures, diasporic artists, and intellectuals). In this connection, John Frow points out the dangers entailed by the ideology of travel when he comments on the touristic role of the Other:

> The commodification of reciprocal bonds, of the environment, and of culture are moments of that logic of contemporary capital which extends private appropriation and ownership from material to immaterial resources, and whose paradigm case is the commodification of information. . . . The logic of tourism [as of travel considered as a form of aestheticized knowledge] is that of a relentless extension of commodity relations and the consequent inequalities of power between centre and periphery, First and Third Worlds, developed and underdeveloped regions, metropolis and countryside. Promising an explosion of modernity, it brings about structural underdevelopment. (1997, 100–1)

The seeming equalization of societies imposed by Clifford's spatial politics of translation may impress those who are already die-hard crusaders of business pluralism. But I think it is one-sided and misleading in trying to remedy the chaotic fragmentation of life in late capitalism by detaching culture from its contradiction-filled matrix. Its project of breaking down national boundaries, like the aim of technocratic modernization theory still sponsored by the World Bank/International Monetary Fund, is premised on that same reality of unequal development that reproduces center and periphery under the aegis of universalized capital accumulation. As Doris Sommer remarks, "Time-lag decries inequalities, against the drone of pluralism and multiculturalism" (1996, 78). Postmodernist travel underwrites such inequality and reinforces the asymmetry of the globalized status quo.

Schizoid Mobility

Postmodernist anthropology has made a crucial intervention in CS by proposing a freewheeling ethnography in opposition to bureaucratized, cybercultural development discourse. One of the most militant proponents is Arturo Escobar who rejects World Bank/International Monetary Fund modernizing formulas. He argues for "a new reading of popular practices and of the reappropriation by popular actors of the space of hegemonic sociocultural production" (1995, 223), in short, for ethnographies of cultural difference and local alternatives that would serve as a transformative force for refiguring the third world. But such countermodernist alternatives suffer from the very same neoliberal assumptions that vitiate Clifford's project. Vernacular experience by itself cannot offset the inroads of the coercive "free market."

With the abandonment of metanarratives, teleology, and any provisional working conception of social totality, ludic CS practitioners have succumbed to relativist and nominalist paralysis. Their pretense to radicalism has been compromised by an indiscriminate self-serving, sometimes cynical, stance. In order to salvage some claim to intelligibility, if not "truthfulness," they resort to "thick description" (according to Clifford Geertz), ethnographic notations of exotic cultural performances (with emphasis on bodily pleasure, performative desire, subjectivity), and playful speculations on surrealist contingencies that produce "truth-effects." In his engaging survey of the field, Fred Inglis jettisons "analysis of institutional power" for what he considers the more suitable terrain for CS: the study of language games. While upholding Wittgenstein's stress on "how we mean anything" (1993, 87), Inglis fetishizes methodology, even though he still clings to a residual "reference" (in Frege's construal) underlying the polysemy of "sense." Consequently he endorses Geertz's essay on the Balinese cockfight as "our model" for CS.

Aesthetics trumps epistemology in the process of hierarchical discrimination. Geertz's fieldwork artifice/artifact, however, is seriously flawed by the problems of translation when it claims to register "the social history of the moral imagination." The confinement to narrow empirical environments and uncriticized common sense — the postmodernist dilation on surface, spatial intensity, and the eternal present — returns us to the limits of functionalist empiricism that deconstruction vowed to transcend in its initial appearance. Vincent Crapanzano's comment on Geertz is scrupulously on target: Geertz "offers no understanding of the native from the native's point of view, . . . no specifiable evidence for his attributions of intention, his assertions of subjectivity, his declarations of experience" (1992, 67). Erasing completely any historical perspective — for example, Indonesia as a necolonial formation subject to U.S. imperial diktat — Geertz's ethnography (according to Crapanzano) presents "little more than projections or blurrings" of the American anthropologist's constructions of constructions.

Interpretation needs to be grounded in social reality. Cultural Studies as an emancipatory discipline producing testable knowledge cannot go beyond textualism without rejecting methodological individualism and its framework of idealist metaphysics. Linguistic analysis needs to be supplemented with a critique of ideological structures. Instead of hypostatizing the arbitrary character of the sign, Anthony Giddens reminds us, we should develop instead "a theory of codes, and of code production, grounded in a broader theory of social practice, and reconnected to hermeneutics" (1986, 48). This has been cogently argued by previous materialist critiques of poststructuralist deconstruction (see Wolin 1992; Hodge 1995; McNally 1999).

On balance, cs has accomplished its initial aims. One can say that there already exists a consensual appreciation of cs's call to valorize the texts and practices of everyday life — the populist agenda of mainstream academic cs — as an antidote to bourgeois elitism and the commodification of high art. But the substitution of a populist program to validate routine behavior as in itself a form of resistance or transgression trivializes the call to pay attention to the intentionalities of subaltern actors and local knowledges. Despite its virtues of empathy and sensitivity to nuanced textures, ethnographies of quotidian life are plagued with errors: they confuse social structure with visible social relations (Godelier 1977). The ethnographic cult of intertextuality mistakes interdependence for causality, focusing on the specific gravity and efficacity of fragments. Further, postmodernist ethnographers unwittingly focus on a normative equilibrium of details, thus occluding contradictions that defy closure. They substitute a mere succession of events and density of circumstances for historical change; in fact, history is converted into Heideggerian temporality, flux, and process of "worlding," substituting itself for a historically informed critique (Bloch 1985). Ethnography of this kind that mirrors its condition of possibility cannot resolve the problems brought about by new forms of reification and inequality of power/resources brought about by the protracted historical crisis of globalized capital.

The difficulties of salvaging the old humanistic disciplines like anthropology have been acknowledged by mainstream cs scholars. The problem is associated with the postmodernist dogma on the "celebration of a radically relativized Difference," the "effectivity of surfaces" predicated on "unity in difference." Such formalist concepts replicate the anarchy of the market, anomie, and alienation (Jameson 1998a). To remedy this predicament, Slack and Whitt have proposed an "ecocul-tural alternative" that tries to mediate between a holistic ecosystem and the integrity of constituent individuals that are supposed to over-determine the whole. But this alternative still clings to a dualistic meta-physics, assuming that "life is conducted in discursive conditions not of our own making" (1992, 585). The CS program centering on biotic interdependence, with an eclectic bricolage of various pragmatic strate-gies for survival, is charged with abundant moral messages. But un-fortunately it lacks a history in which subject and object dialectically interact. Silent on the contradictions destabilizing the welfare-state con-sensus in advanced capitalist societies, ecoculturalism colludes in re-producing social inequality. Echoing Frankfurt critical theory's attack on instrumentalism, it dismisses the complicity of the systemic ac-cumulation of capital by a moralistic attack on fascism. Its communal utopianism renders the whole program a panacea for the neoliberal's guilt-stricken conscience.

I am only rehearsing here a judgment already elaborated by others (see Katz 1995–96; O'Connor 1996, 1999). Implemented in a dispersed, eclectic manner, CS works to help capitalism manage the ongoing crisis of the old humanist subject by what Samir Amin calls "culturalist strate-gies" (1998, 66) impotent to challenge the havoc wrought by the univer-salizing effects of finance capital in its new forms. Because cultural practice is conceived as inherently indeterminate, contingent, infinitely plural, and shifting, CS cannot theorize how new identities or subject positions can really transform social institutions. These identities begin and end with the testimony of everyday experience taken as irreducible and meaningful in itself, unmediated by any normative critical frame-work. Defined as one-dimensional and atomized aspects of identity, the categories of race, class, and gender are mechanically repeated without any determinate content. Instead of being viewed as new forms of col-lective labor power that intensify the contradictions in racialized bour-geois polities, CS regards class, race, and gender as abstract counters — so many incommensurable language games, articulations of the flux of some ubiquitous power that remains enigmatic, eventually assuming the guise of the incomprehensible postmodern "sublime."

It is not just a matter of shifting the focus from the now disreputable metanarratives of modernity to the quotidian habitus of postmodern consumers. The collapse of CS's radical challenge to the reign of capital stems chiefly from the nominalist subjectivism and discursivism adopted from poststructuralist doctrines. Critique is abandoned for a rhetorical assertion that certain practices, which turn out to be simply survival techniques, are inherently emancipatory or liberating. The reduction of history to a series of conjunctural moments, of identity to temporary positionalities, and positionalities to symbolic chains of equivalence, has eliminated not just lived experience but also the determinants of location and the geopolitics of place. More starkly, it has expunged class struggle. While postmodernist simulacra, pastiche, and extraterritoriality have compelled us to pay more attention to surfaces and spatial dispositions, this has not translated into a serious engagement with the geopolitics of the "global assembly line," NAFTA and MASSTRICHT, the internationalization of migrant labor comprised primarily of women of color, and other mutations of the global marketplace.

Counterintuitive Inscriptions

An alternative can be sketched here as a heuristic provocation. Of various possible routes, I can point to one rather obscure counterexample to Clifford's style of doing CS that is fully conscious of the internal contradictions that define any historical moment. This example takes into account the political economy of cultural practice and production, apprehending culture as an ensemble of agencies that produce and reproduce the totality of social relations with its specific hegemonic articulation. What Jameson suggested as a cognitive mapping based on the imperative "simultaneously to grasp culture in and for itself, but also in relationship to its outside, its content, its context, and its space of intervention and of effectivity" (1995, 47), has been pursued with lucid and impassioned eloquence by Jan Myrdal and Gun Kessle in their now classic ethico-political intervention, *Angkor: An Essay on Art and Imperialism.*

Myrdal and Kessle, committed Swedish intellectuals, traveled through Vietnam and Cambodia in the days of heavy U.S. bombing of the region in the late sixties. They preface their historical and topographical survey of the architectural ruins at Angkor, Cambodia, by transvaluing their experience into social awareness and transformative critique:

You stand face to face with the stone faces of Angkor. Beyond a border there is a war. But when you yourself face this stone then the "beauty" becomes a concrete reality. These faces of stone were hewn by sweating men in a bloody time of repression and revolt.

To write about Jayavarman VII and get beaten up by the cops; to stand in the midst of the dirt and violence writing fiction; to collect money for the striking mine-workers and lecture on Strindberg; to publish the secret Swedish army regulations on the use of gas against "rioting" strikers and to demand back all of history and all the millennia — that is to take part in the razing of the load-bearing walls of imperialism.

To write on Angkor is a necessary part of the struggle for liberation. (1970, 4–5)

For Myrdal and Kessle, culture as a mode of production is articulated in the way that Japan during the conference I mentioned at the outset articulated itself for me as a place of collision and confrontation, not a place through which one simply travels. Unlike Clifford, our joint authors do comparative cultural studies by juxtaposing testimonies and ethnographic accounts of Western travelers and the sites surrounding Angkor. They not only discuss climate, local history, topography, and tribal customs and rituals but also carry out a subtle analogizing of distant events: twelfth-century Angkor Vat interfaced with the Italian Renaissance, Hellenism, Count Gobineau, Livingstone, and of course French colonialism. André Malraux (famous author of *Les conquerants* and *La voie royale* set in Indo-China) is inserted here as someone who plundered the temple of Banteay Srei in December 1923 but was later acquitted because the monuments were not considered "protected" by the colonial government. This militant ethnography is guided by a consistent historicizing of social forms and cultural practices, thus materializing the nuanced coevalness of cultures, times, and places for judgment. Alterity is not fetishized but rather rendered concrete and practical within a project of building solidarity with anti-imperialist forces.

What distinguishes Myrdal and Kessle's travel through history and a concrete geopolitical space is not its erudition or its meticulous scrutiny of how culture and power are imbricated. Rather, it lies in the dialectical intelligibility of its discourse. This depends on its inquiry into both "the causally generated presentation of social objects and their explanatory critique — in terms of their conditions of being, both those which are historically specific and praxis-dependent and those which genuinely are not" (Bhaskar 1983, 128). While respecting the relative autonomy of art, Myrdal and Kessle situate Angkor in a constellation of political, economic, and ideological forces that determined its history. It is a mode of CS that proceeds from the materiality of signification to the political constitution of subjectivities, sublating rhetoric and textuality into a field of conflicting forces where control/access to knowledge and resources are at stake both for past and present protagonists. Mindful of the people's war of national liberation against the West often inspired by Marxism-Leninism, these European observers implicate themselves in what they are studying: they question the ideal of detachment and neutrality. They are partisans of the popular forces that built Angkor in the past and those fighting imperialist bombs at the time of their writing.

Partisanship demands sensitivity to relations, processes, movements. Employing a dialectical method of analyzing the unity of opposites, Myrdal and Kessle are grappling with symptoms of reification in the discourse of bourgeois aesthetics and history. They succeed in penetrating the surface of empirical data, of personal experience, to register the movement of conflicting tendencies. Surfaces reveal fissures, underneath the joints are rhizomatic cracks. What caused Angkor's decline? Not wars or shifts in religion, as the official textbooks say, but instead the internal contradictions immanent in society:

> Angkor perished. But Cambodia survived. The rulers vanished. But not the people. The whole history of Angkor was a history of incessant revolts, of unending social struggle. . . . Angkor grew up as a centralized state, in which, by exploiting new techniques, oligarchy has been able, at the people's expense, to create for itself immeasurable wealth. This state existed in a chronic state of war. Just as the temples were not just religion or mere ostentatious waste, but the very mechanism by which the oligarchy could absorb the people's labor, so these wars were an inevitable form in which the state's organization could exist.
>
> The most comprehensive building period in Angkor's history coincided with — and was an expression of — the inner crisis which shook the state. . . . With Angkor as with the Roman Empire, the internal contradictions tore the state asunder. . . . This social collapse [of the nobles

and wealthy merchants] — the collapse of intensive irrigational agriculture (thus of the centralized state) — was a liberation. (1970, 158, 164)

In bold strokes, Myrdal and Kessle delineate the pattern of dialectical exchange between milieu and art, between objective constraints and subjective capacities, ideas and material culture, in order to mobilize an audience for anti-imperialist intervention.

What Myrdal and Kessle exemplify is not wholly alien to CS's original project. Orthodox CS experts have repeatedly stressed the uniqueness of CS in bridging theory and material culture, contextualizing intellectual work with real social and political problems, with cultural and political power and struggle. At present, the question of AIDS, for example, is an urgent testing ground for ideological contestation: "What cultural studies must do, and has the capacity to do, is to articulate insights about the constitutive and political nature of representation itself, about its complexities, about the effects of language, about textuality as a site of life and death" (Grossberg et al. 1992, 7). This certainly responds to local academic needs. But is that all the strategic intervention CS can do?

The limits of CS stem from the lack of an alternative, counterhegemonic view of capitalist society. Conjunctural analysis and the theory of articulation are privileged because it is "embedded, descriptive, and historically and contextually specific." Myrdal and Kessle go beyond the conjunctural by transposing the lessons of the past of Angkor into the war-torn landscape of Vietnam in the sixties. They emphasize the need to grasp the historical relations of political forces in order to act intelligently and effectively. They understand Lenin's insight that national liberation struggles (such as those of the Vietnamese and Cambodian peoples; see chapter 8 below on Fanon) are forms of revolutionary subjectivity generated by capital's uneven and combined development (Lowy 1981; K. Anderson 1995). From this perspective, the stone temples of Angkor should not be read simply as symbols of gods or abstract ideas; rather they embodied power. Myrdal and Kessle assert these challenging propositions:

> All aesthetic problems connected with Angkor are wrongly put . . . unless connected with the hierarchy of social classes. . . . Prayers and ceremonies. Sacred texts and learned men. All were merely the form in

which the rice crop was collected from the peasants and distributed among the rulers. . . . The construction of these immense temples was conditional upon the majority of the people being called brute beasts.

In the night, when Gun slept and the fan squealed, I thought of Manhattan. Of Paris. And London. Walk down these streets a thousand years from now. How much will remain? (1970, 167)

Myrdal and Kessle's writing, to my mind, exemplifies a form of CS that intervenes across the boundaries of popular and elite cultures. While dealing with the fabled ruins of an Asian kingdom studied by art historians and anthropologists, Myrdal and Kessle succeed in making its history intelligible for lay persons without any prerequisite of technical knowledge. What is required is a knowledge of how culture is tied with human labor and the organization of social energies, the entire "field of cultural production" (Bourdieu 1993). Canonical CS today avoids talk of exploitation of labor, property relations, and the whole field of political economy that embraces the conditions of possibility for both elite and popular culture; for overlapping residual, dominant, and emergent tendencies in the realm of ideological class struggle.

Investments and Disavowals

What needs more critical engagement is the task of how this mediation of history and textuality, as shown in Angkor, can be accomplished in Cultural Studies. Antony Easthope's guidebook *Literary into Cultural Studies* is one such illustration. In the process of formulating his approach, Easthope demonstrates that the discipline of literary studies no longer exists as such; it has evolved into Cultural Studies as soon as it attends to "the materiality of its own construction as a discourse of knowledge" (1991, 174). This has been foreseen by literary scholars like Jeffrey Peck, for example, who envisaged the reconstruction of literary scholarship as a "critique of institutions and disciplines" (1985, 52), a view inspired by the work of Edward Said. Said's redefinition of culture refines those of Williams and Hoggart by accentuating the problem of power, ethnicity, and identity: "culture" signifies "an environment, process, and hegemony in which individuals (in their private circumstances) and their works are embedded, as well as overseen at the top by a whole series of methodological attitudes," including "the range of meanings and ideas conveyed by the phrases belonging to or in a place, being at home in a place" (1983, 8). This is a considerable amplification of experience compared to which the revitalization of aesthetics or the endorsement of rarefied biography (by Fred Inglis, for example) is a return to the iniquitous realm of a feudal division of labor.

I venture a provisional conclusion here. The crisis of contemporary cultural studies inheres in its historical origin from contradictions in social relations tied to changing modes of production. Disjunctures between social actors/agents and the material circumstances pervaded by class, gender, race, nationality, and other categorizing frames of experience have reproduced the classic problem of subject/object dualism in epistemology and ethics. Consequently, the politics of culture tends to be viewed either from an idealist and subjectivist optic, or a deterministic prism. What results in intellectual practice is either the voluntarist ideal of the "civilizing mission" or the bureaucratic-technocratic resignation of the modernizing expert whose patron-saint is Max Weber (E. Wood 1995). Having forsworn historical materialism and dialectics, cs succumbs to the miasmic polarities of metaphysical idealism.

We confront a familiar dilemma. How do we mediate the antinomies of thought that reflect in oblique ways the real-life historical contradictions in which the thinkers are embedded? Do we suspend our inquiry until we resolve first those contradictions, or do we need to register impulses of change in paradigm-shifts that catalyze problem-solving strategies? Indeed, the educator needs to be educated; theory and practice needs to be synthesized.

Unless we wrestle with both horns (philosophical realism or idealism) of the dilemma anchored in the historical process, we will end up in the "vertiginous abyss" of textual and discursive speculation. Not a salutary prospect, by any means. For praxis-oriented practitioners in cs, I would recommend as a way out of this impasse the practice of David Harvey in his recent work, *Justice, Nature and the Geography of Difference*. In chapter 12 of his book, Harvey uses a historical event — the fire that gutted the Imperial Foods plant in Hamlet, North Carolina, on Sepember 3, 1991, killed twenty-five, and seriously injured fifty-six of two hundred workers — as a point of departure for his research program. In his account, Harvey not only presents a "thick description" of the political and economic circumstances surrounding the tragic event but also explores the question of social justice and "the political geography of difference" — notably, issues of race/ethnicity and gender — in its embeddedness in place and modalities of cultural discourse and expression. Harvey modifies the genre of traditional ethnography by interrogating its hidden assumptions, articulating the organic "permanences" of U.S. social history with the conjunctural differences of racism, sexism, and national oppression specific to North Carolina and to U.S. capitalism within the global parameters of systemic crisis. I believe that Harvey's methodology of dialectical linkages of several levels of analysis conforms to the spirit of Gramsci's magisterial vision of "critical understanding of oneself" (1957, 69) founded on the moment of "catharsis" as the passage from the base to the superstructures (Gramsci 1971, 181), the union of theory and practice, attained through stages of mediating elements of social life and directed to fashioning a coherent and critical comprehension of history and one's place in it. Without this informing vision, CS cannot claim to be emancipatory or liberating — except in a gestural self-serving sense.

Problematizing CS entails a reinscription of such dichotomies as elite/popular in the dialectical coupling of mode of production/social formation. Notwithstanding all the talk about intervention, CS reveals its own compromised situation when Grossberg and colleagues pontificate: "Cultural studies does not require us to repudiate elite cultural forms — or simply to acknowledge, with Bourdieu, that distinctions between elite and popular cultural forms are themselves the products of relations of power. Rather, cultural studies requires us to identify the operation of specific practices, of how they continuously reinscribe the line between legitimate and popular culture, and of what they accomplish in specific contexts" (1992, 13). Apropos of this formalism, Easthope remarks that "it would be a form of logocentrism, the old vision of speculative rationalism, to believe that an intellectual procedure necessarily leads to a particular politics" (1991, 178). Evidently CS cannot operate as an autonomous institutional force separate from the demands of the ideological-political field. Just as "reason develops and transforms itself in the practical field" (Godelier 1977), CS acquires value-filled import in engagement with crucial public issues affecting entire peoples and societies, as Patrick Brantlinger ably demonstrated in his synoptic survey of cs, *Crusoe's Footprints* (1990). The contexts are decisive, as Ioan Davies (1995) has shown in the case of Canada and in the person of Kenyan novelist Ngugi W'a Thiongo; and Kuan-Hsing Chen, Jon Stratton, and Ien Ang for the rest of the world (1996; for the Australian scene, see G. Turner 1992; for Taiwan, see Liao 1999).

Proposals for renewing cs usually invoke a pastiche of topics such as sameness-in-difference, multidimensionality, return to the "cultural-in-the-economic" (Morley 1998, 49), syncretizing racialized ethnicities, "deracinated subaltern subjects, heterodox traditions" (Leitch 1994, 182), postnationalist ethics of hybridity, transcultural cosmopolitanism, and the like. For a start, I would like to endorse Barbara Epstein's always timely advice: "In the United States it is impossible to take our understanding of race, gender, or questions of social division and disintegration further without acknowledging the fact of class polarization" (1995, 136). Space constraints prevent me from being able to elaborate further my view that a historicist "cultural materialism" first outlined by Williams (who is discussed in the next chapter) can be renewed by recovering and adapting to new contexts the principles of "national liberation struggles" espoused by Frantz Fanon, C. L. R. James, Lu Hsun, Amilcar Cabral, Che Guevara, Aimé Césaire, and others. Cultural Studies practiced by those committed intellectuals can be a revolutionary way out of the current impasse.

Besides denaturalizing cs, we need therefore to historicize its thematics, methods, and objectives. Mindful of Williams's advice to think through the history of conflicted ideological formations, Hall recently urged the concentration of cs on problems of "racism today in its complex structures and dynamics" arising from "the terrifying, internal fear of living with *difference*" (1992, 17). Obviously the resurgence of racism in the United Kingdom and elsewhere in the last two decades precipitated this call to arms. There is no cause for premature alarm — unless apocalyptic investments persist in attributing a messianic mission to cs in the hope of revitalizing a civic but still patriotic humanism beloved by Rorty and fellow neopragmatists. Jameson in fact celebrates the utopianism of cs as a "project to constitute a historic bloc" (1995, 251) of progressive academics. However, because of its current fixation on articulation, contingency, indeterminacy, and local power resistance, cs will continue to perform at best a polite and loyal-opposition role, reinforcing that affirmative culture that Herbert Marcuse once described as the realm of freedom and happiness — "universally obligatory, eternally better and more valuable world that must be unconditionally affirmed: a world essentially different from the factual world of the daily struggle for existence, yet realisable by every individual for himself 'from within,' without any transformation of the state of fact" (1968b, 95). Unwittingly, mainstream CS promotes this affirmative culture offering temporary anodyne to the inhabitants of an administered racial polity. Far from the cacophonous din of Disneyland surrounding Dali's enigmatic masterpieces in St. Petersburg, Florida, this veritable utopia is the not so clandestine object of desire for the contemporary high priests of Cultural Studies whose complicity with predatory capital, no doubt unpremeditated and even resisted, will surely be the object of "enormous condescension by posterity."

CHAPTER 7

Postcolonial Criticism and

the Vicissitudes of Uneven Development

It is important for us to identify the new victims and the new victimizers in the neocolonial era — for we do not live in a postcolonial era as the postmodernists claim. We must struggle together both locally and globally. The local struggle must be combined with global or international struggle and solidarity. We must fight on all fronts. . . . We must carry on a continuous resistance, a continuous dissidence, which will forge the way to a better future for all the peoples of the world. — Nawal El Saadawi, *The Nawal El Saadawi Reader*

The masses are the torch-bearers of culture; they are the source of culture and, at the same time, the one entity truly capable of preserving and creating it — of making history. — Amilcar Cabral, *Return to the Source*

From 1996 to 1998, we celebrated in the Philippines and here in the United States the one-hundred-year anniversary of the Philippine revolution against Spain. December 10, 1998, denotes the centennial of the Treaty of Paris marking the end of the Spanish-American War, an event that ushered in the carnage of the Philippine-American War from 1899 to 1903 — the "first Vietnam," one historian believes — and the extirpation of numerous peasant revolts, as well as the colonial conquest of Cuba and the annexation of Puerto Rico; the latter two events still haunt us not just with mnemonic spectres but with the lived experience of pain, denials, and ordeals of servitude. We can never completely "postalize" these *Nachträglich* repercussions because to do so would just confirm the reality — Puerto Rico is recognized by the world as an anachronistic U.S. colony, and Fidel Castro's Cuba (like North Korea and other anathematized "rogue" states) will not go away like a bad dream, even though Washington hopes they will fade away like the Sandinistas, Maurice Bishop's "New Jewel Movement," the FMLN of El Salvador, Kim Il Sung, Amilcar Cabral, Che Guevara, and others who have now dissolved into the "posthistorical" folds of the "New World Order." The categories of "nation" and "class," not to mention "revolution," have been banished from the postcolonial lexicon. Unfortunately, the Pinochets and Suhartos of this world are still around — and their victims will not allow them their solipsistic retirement.

Postcolonial theory warns us not to engage in the "politics of blame" and praise. Indeed, can I as a neocolonial intellectual speak and discriminate as to who is guilty and who is innocent? Complexity and various rhetorical and ethical refinements will be sacrificed. Given the hybridity, creolization, syncretism, ambivalence, and just the sheer all-encompassing heterogeneity of relations between the postcolonized and the former colonizers, I would in fact be guilty of some cardinal sins: totalization, imposition of metanarratives, universalization, and so on. Despite the interstitial locus of enunciation, I would plead guilty to reiterating a commonplace generalization here: the Spanish-American War established the geopolitical place of the United States as an imperial power whose apogee after World War II, in the pax Americana of the Cold War, persists although in an attenuated but more insidious form, enabling the rise of neocolonial states like the Philippines, Taiwan, South Korea, and others in Africa and Latin America. The postcolonial position of genuine sovereignty for many peoples is still germinal, the embryo of wish-fulfillment.

Let me post a few reminders. After the end of Francis Fukuyama's history, in the wake of the Gulf War, the Chiapas revolt in Mexico, and Japan's recession, the "Asian Tigers" — in particular South Korea and Thailand — collapsed, and Indonesia soon unraveled. At about this period of cataclysm, Brazil was saved by the International Monetary Fund. Spasmodic ups and downs in the stock markets, currency devaluations, and capital flight from the peripheral "emerging market" economies plague the globalized "free market" despite "structural adjustment programs" imposed by the World Bank/International Monetary Fund. Loan defaults, production cutbacks, mass layoffs, and bankruptcies are rocking the whole planet. A new world depression (read: the cyclical crisis of transnational capital) seems brewing. Globalization is on the rampage — what else is new?

In November 1999, an international conference on "Alternatives to Globalization" was held in the Philippines with delegates from thirty-one countries. What is meant by globalization? In brief, it is the neo-liberal ideology of the free market operating within the racialized polities of nation-states trumpeted as the only way to economic growth and social progress everywhere. It is the general offensive of monopoly capital (transnational corporations, or TNCs) to maximize the extraction of profit and accelerate capital accumulation everywhere, particularly through the use of modern technology (such as robotics, computerized communication, and other ways of buying/selling information), and, more importantly, through the political dikta of liberalization, deregulation, and privatization mediated through the triad multilateral institutions: the IMF/WB, and World Trade Organization (Noumoff 1999; Larsen and Petras 2000). Supposed to refurbish the old nostrum of "modernization," globalization enables rapid economic restructuring, centralization of capital, takeover and control of production resources in undeveloped societies and weak nation-states by TNCs based in the industrialized metropoles (Europe, Japan, North America). The conference ended with a resolution that reads in part:

> Globalization has worsened the effects of the destructive paradigm of "growth and development." Instead of economic prosperity and social stability that it promised for all nations, globalization has brought about economic turmoil, political and social tension, and widespread devastation to the world's people and resources. . . . The gap between the rich and poor in all nations, industrial and non-industrial alike, and between the rich and poor countries is widening rather than narrowing. . . .
>
> Everywhere globalization is eroding the gains of social movements in all aspects (political, social and cultural). There is a general regression of democracy, as economic impositions by states entail increasing human rights violations, not only of economic, social and cultural rights, but of political and civil rights as well. In the third world, as the majority of the people are marginalized economically, they are also disempowered politically. (*Cyberdyaryo*, 12 Nov. 1998)

No doubt, from the postcolonial orthodoxy deriving its imprimatur from the founding scriptures of Edward Said and his disciples, that resolution will be dismissed as "old-hat" radicalism vitiated with tired Marxist clichés and reductionist excesses. But surely, the owl of Minerva has not flown yet over postcolonial theory's territory to bring this tiding of disaster and awaken the epigones from premature dogmatic slumber. Corporate ideologues and their sponsors are keeping vigil. While global unemployment has gone beyond 40 percent and 90 percent of the world's inhabitants suffer from poverty, do we still dare not whisper the tabooed words "finance capital"? This new stage of capitalism is characterized by speculation in the money market, monetary equivalence superimposed on land values, space, and so on — in brief, by the intensification of the forces of reification that have generated precisely those telltale affects of contingency, indeterminacy, ambivalence, borderline crossings, displacements, dislocations, transcultural negotiations, and diasporic exchanges whose fragments are being continually plotted by postcolonial theory (Jameson 1998). Such theory turns out to be a shamanistic reading of symptoms. Indeed, the repertoire of postcolonial tropes condense with uncanny prescience the superficies of globalized financial transactions — except that the aficionados of this language-game pride themselves in disavowing any knowledge of the historical determinants of their performance. The warning one should heed is: You might ignore globalized finance capital, but it will surely not ignore you.

Loss of critical reflexivity is the price one pays for fetishizing discourse and the deterritorialized psyche. One more warning should suffice. Recall an event not as recent as the unconscionable "killing fields" of Kosovo and East Timor but equally instructive. Retaliating for the bombing of its embassies in Kenya and Tanzania in August 1998, the United States unleashed a barrage of deadly Tomahawk missiles into Afghanistan and Sudan, two of the rogue states declared to be harboring terrorists, aka Islamic fundamentalists, hostile to the United States and its Western allies. This in a time of the "New World Order," when (according to Wall Street pundits) history ended with the demise of the Soviet Union and the worldwide triumph of profit making. But aren't we in a postality epoch where colonialism and capitalism have both been superseded, where universalizing paradigms and metanarratives have gone the way of dinosaurs?

Telltale Dossier

Let us begin with a truism of radical historiography. Capitalism as a world system has developed unevenly, with the operations of the "free market" being determined by the unplanned but (after analysis) "lawful" tendencies of the accumulation of surplus value. With the rise of merchant capital, diverse modes of production with varying temporalities and "superstructural" effects have since then reconfigured the planet. In a new cartography, we find metropolitan centers subordinating peripheral territories and peoples. Colonialism and later finance-capitalism (imperialism) compressed time and space, sharply juxtaposing a variety of cultures linked to discrepant economies and polities, with the colonizing center dictating the rigorous measure of modernity. After World War II, the accelerated migration of former colonial subjects into the metropoles together with the refinement of technologies of communication and foreign investment heightened the spectacle of heterogeneous languages and practices coexisting with the homogenizing scenarios of everyday life in both center and margin. I consider postcolonialism as the cultural logic of this mixture and multilayering of forms taken as the distinctive ethos of late modernity, a logic distanced from its grounding in the unsynchronized interaction between colonial powers and colonized subalterns.

Let us take the example of Homi Bhabha, the most celebrated exponent of postcolonial orthodoxy. Bhabha has given ontological priority to the phenomenon of cultural difference between colonized and colonizer. The articulation of such difference in "in-between" spaces allegedly produces hybridization of identities: "It is in the emergence of the interstices — the overlap and displacement of domains of difference — that the intersubjective and collective experiences of nationness, community interest, or cultural value are negotiated" (Bhabha 1994a, 1–2). Since (following Wallerstein 1991) the regime of capital accumulation ethnicizes peoples to promote labor segmentation, hybridity and other differential phenomena result. But for Bhabha, ambivalence arises from the poststructuralist *"différance* of writing" that informs any cultural performance. Such performances are found in certain privileged positionalities and experiences: "the history of postcolonial migration, the narratives of cultural and political diaspora, the major social displacements of peasants and aboriginal communities, the poetics of exile, the grim prose of political and economic refugees" (1994a, 5).

Objections have been raised to such exorbitant inferences. Callinicos calls Bhabha's approach "an idealist reduction of the social to the semiotic" (1995, 111). Indeterminacy, interruption of the signifying chain, aporia, endless displacements, and tergiversations characterize postcolonial literary theory and practice. Aijaz Ahmad (1996) points to the ambiguity of historical references in postcolonial discourse. In the realm of floating signifiers and the language metaphor, the objective asymmetry of power and resources between hegemonic blocs and subaltern groups (racialized minorities in the metropoles and in the "third world"), as well as the attendant conflicts, disappear.

Clearly this fixation on the manifestations of "unevenness" has undergone fetishization, divorced from its concrete social determinations. What postcolonial theory and its variants (minority discourse, border matterisms, transpostalities of all kinds) seem to carry out in the name of individualist resistance is hyperbolic mimicry — the symptomatic effects of colonization in various forms of "orientalisms" and strategies of adaptations and co-optations — unconnected with the network of instrumentalities underpinning them.

Tropology supersedes critical diagnosis. We are told that the figures of difference, fragmentation, liminality, and diaspora (which Lawrence Grossberg [1996] considers the principles of identity for postmodern Cultural Studies, of which postcolonialism is a subspecies) are modes of regulating the social relations of production, in particular the division of global social labor and its reproduction. But postcolonial critics not only remove them from their circumstantial grounds, from their historical contexts; they also treat them as autonomous phenomena separate from the structures of cultural production and political legitimation in late-modern societies. They become autonomous signifiers of value and meaning removed from historical anchoring. In Henri Lefebvre's words, "Each of these 'moments' of the real [that is, hybridity, fragmentation, and so on], once isolated and hypostatized, becomes the negator of the other moments and then the negator of itself. Limited and transposed into a form, the content becomes oppressive and destructive of its own reality" (1968, 167).

Postcolonialism, in my view, is guilty of what it claims to repudiate: mystification and moralism. Postcolonial criticism ultimately tries to reify certain transitory practices, styles, modalities of thought and expression that were originally attempts to resolve specific historical contradictions in the ongoing crisis of transnational capitalism. Cultural difference is the rebarbative result of colonialism that can be ventriloquized in plural ways. Unevenness is no longer an abstract categorizing term but rather an empirical description that affords the subaltern's newly discovered agency some space for the display of libertarian astuteness. What Georg Lukács (1971) calls "ethical utopianism," the lapse into subjectivism, afflicts postcolonial discourse because it denies the internally complex determinants that are its condition of possibility. This mediation of the hybrid, interstitial, and borderline experience with the concrete totality of the social formation is rejected as "essentialism" or "totalization," hence the only alternative is opportunism or anarchist posturing, more self-destructive because devoid of Nietzsche's anti-bourgeois critique.

In the textual practice of Bhabha, Spivak, and other epigones, one can discern how postcolonial theory occludes its own historical determinacy by deploying psychoanalytic and linguistic frameworks that take market/commodity relations for granted. It also takes for granted the assumptions of neoliberalism as normative and natural. We can problematize postcolonialism's claim to be liberatory — Bhabha speaks of "visions of community" via an "equivocal" articulation of power — by valorizing its partisanship for the "disjunctive borderline temporalities" of marginalized cultures as itself an intermediary link to the totality's project of extending the freedom of the gendered, stratified subject to its erstwhile "subjects" (preponderantly, people of color), this time under the aegis of a more tolerant multiculturalism that recognizes "the outside of the inside," the part in the whole. The tyranny of the marketplace is thereby reaffirmed. Absent the dialectic of part to whole that historical materialism considers a springboard for theorizing the possibilities of change and the sublation of historically specific contradictions, postcolonial orthodoxy dissolves mediations and generates exactly the predicament that it claims to prevent: the antinomy of transcendentalizing idealism and mechanical determinism.

Heterodox Scruples

By all indications, postcolonial orthodoxy expressed in the writings of Bhabha, Spivak, and their followers would register protest against a revanchist U.S. imperialism. At the same time it would condemn the totalizing philosophy of Osama bin Laden and the Manichean strategy of those ethno-fundamentalists who reject the creolized reality of societies victimized by transnational corporations. Lest I be accused of caricaturing postcolonialists, I refer my readers to the judicious appraisal of this newly institutionalized discourse by Arif Dirlik, Aijaz Ahmad, Neil Lazarus, Benita Parry, and others. Dirlik, for instance, points out the mystification of the relations of culture and power when postcolonial critics concentrate on Eurocentric ideology and foundationalism as their main target. The now scriptural text *The Empire Writes Back* (Ashcroft et al. 1989) privileges the hermeneutics of colonial discourse as a desideratum of this new scholastic mind-set. The aura of the "interstitial" and hybrid preempts any untranslatable resistance, discursive or otherwise, from the subaltern natives (Schulze-Engler 1998). Among other scholars cited by Dirlik, O'Hanlon and Washbrook bewail the conservative and authoritarian nature of the solutions offered by postcolonial theory to the problems of the contemporary world: "methodological individualism, the depoliticising insulation of social from material domains, a view of social relations that is in practice extremely voluntaristic, the refusal of any kind of programmatic politics" (Dirlik 1997, 66). From another stance, Aijaz Ahmad (1995) considers the doctrine of the postcolonial transhistoricity of colonialism as an ideological alibi to expunge "determinate histories" and determinate structures of power, releasing them from accountability. One German scholar, noting how this proliferation of differences inaugurates new hegemonies, recently asked: "Where is the protest against SAP (Structural Adjustment Programs) universalism?" (Stummer 1998, 33).

I suspect that this veritable academic industry is now unstoppable — think of the expanding archive of postcolonial discourse, from Said's classic *Orientalism* to Spivak and Bhabha's voluminous essays to the ripostes such as Aijaz Ahmad's *In Theory*, Arif Dirlik's *The Postcolonial Aura*, and provocative essays in two recent anthologies, *Post-Colonial America* edited by C. Richard King, and *Postcolonial Theory and the United States* edited by Amritjit Singh and Peter Schmidt, among others. In the last two years, aside from my work, three books have come out that inventory this field of power with fatigue-inducing redundancy: Bart Moore-Gilbert, *Postcolonial Theory* (1997); Leela Gandhi, *Postcolonial Theory* (1998); and Ania Loomba, *Colonialism/Postcolonialism* (1998). Institutionalization, together with the canonization of (in Moore-Gilbert's phrase) the "Holy Trinity" of Said, Spivak, and Bhabha, have generated the routine repertoire of rituals, clichés, formulae, platitudes, mixed with "received" common sense rehashed in the doxology of Establishment pragmatism. Said himself begs to be excluded from this enterprise when he remarks in a recent interview that postcolonialism is really a "misnomer," and that he is more concerned with neocolonialism, "the workings of the IMF/World Bank" (1998, 82).

Common among the aforementioned three books is the positive appraisal of the ideology of difference. Recognition of Otherness, decolonizing the ethnocentric gaze, radical indeterminacy immanent in hybridity, diaspora, heterogeneity, exile, displacement, dislocation, border crossing, and so on, constitute the recurrent themes, motifs, and archetypal topoi of postcolonial discourse. There are of course the classics: Said's *Orientalism*, Fanon's *Black Face/White Masks*, Spivak's "Can the Subaltern Speak?" and (as the contrapuntal voice, Ahmad's *In Theory*), together with the key texts of Salman Rushdie, Wilson Harris, Jean Rhys, and a few Africans. Leela Gandhi eulogizes the "analytic versatility and theoretical resilience" of the postcolonial practitioners. Ania Loomba's survey provides ample philological background, with a show of painstaking evenhandedness toward adversaries of postcolonial orthodoxy. However, like Gandhi, she subscribes to the general condemnation of Marxism as guilty of economism, totalization, humanism, teleology, neglect of nonclass differences (gender, sexuality, race), and other minor crimes. Unlike Gandhi, however, Loomba is not sanguine about globalization. She concurs with Dipesh Chakrabarty's aim of "provincializing Europe" (1995, 255), but her own endorsement of "empirical specificity" returns us to the affirmation of particularism with which she finds fault. Shades of melancholic irony in a peculiarly imploding Leibnizian conceit!

A nuanced dialogue between Marxism and poststructuralism recommended by Loomba seems to be attempted by Bart Moore-Gilbert in his detailed inventory of the writings of Said, Spivak, and Bhabha. However, his concluding judgment that there is a fit between postcolonial theory and postcolonial criticism (for example, the affinities between Bhabha and Wilson Harris's ideas) and that we need to apply Spivak's nostrum of "strategic essentialism," with qualifications, are anticlimactially disappointing. With some reservations, Moore-Gilbert also supports Laclau and Mouffe's strategy of multiple positioning or "equivalential articulation." He commends Ranajit Guha's liberal pluralism: "It seems to me that a choice between the predominant paradigms, or an attempted synthesis of them, is perhaps equally unnecessary if one applies an historical and differential perspective to the question of the heterogeneity of the 'postcolonial.'. . . Because postcolonial histories, and their presents, are so varied, no one definition of the 'postcolonial' can claim to be correct, at the expense of all the others, and consequently a variety of interrelated models of identity, positionality and cultural/critical practice are both possible and necessary" (1997, 203). Not to worry; we are all cosmopolitan and catholic in taste. This is obviously a species of agnostic high-mindedness, at best an old-fashioned eclecticism sported by debonair gentlemen of letters whiling away time in the English countryside. Moore-Gilbert tries to be tactful, lucid, and impartial — at the cost of tolerating the differential politics of finance capital to ride roughshod over millions in the so-called postcolonial South. In our three authors, as well as in postcolonial mimicry in general, a crippling category mistake is made by confusing culture with ideology, thus forfeiting any attempt to do what Ella Shohat calls us to do: "to interrogate the concept of the 'post-colonial' and contextualize it historically, geopolitically, and culturally" (1991, 111). Ato Quayson also calls for "a commitment to integrate the analysis into a larger [ethical and political] affirmative project" (2000, 155). Or else, there is only the ideology of the enemy to be exorcised for being reductive, deterministic, essentialist, and so on.

The paralysis and inconsequentiality of postcolonial theory and criticism on the face of globalized capitalism are patently clear not to warrant rehearsing anymore the objections of Ahmad, Dirlik, and others. This is not just because this genre is devoted to specialized studies on widow-burning or British colonization of the Indian subcontinent, Australia, Canada, and South Africa. The explanation is more than theoretical or discursive. Robert Young, the editor of the new magazine *Interventions: The International Journal of Postcolonial Studies*, put his finger on its symptomatology: "The rise of postcolonial studies coincided with the end of Marxism as the defining political, cultural and economic objective of much of the third world" (1998, 8–9). This diagnosis is more wishful thinking than a factual statement. To be sure, the "third world" as a homogenized entity never claimed to elevate Marxism as its all-encompassing objective; no one does this, anyway. Another agenda, one suspects, lurks in the background.

Postcolonialism seems to require a post-Marxism as "supplement," a prophylactic clearing of the ground. What is meant by post-Marxism or the "end of Marxism" is really the reconfiguration of the international class struggle between the imperial metropoles and the revolting masses of the periphery. It signifies the end of the bourgeois national project initiated by the Bandung Conference led by Nehru, Nasser, and Sukarno (A. Ahmad 1995). This project of postcolonial states modernizing on the basis of anticommunism and pragmatic philosophy, reliance on Soviet military support, and cynical playing of the "American card," collapsed with the bankruptcy of most neocolonial regimes that succumbed to World Bank/IMF "structural adjustment programs" and conditionalities. The killing of Salvador Allende in 1974 signaled the close of an epoch in which "national liberation" struggles, inspired with ideals learned from the Marxist tradition, led the anticolonial processes that led to the victories of Mao, Ho Chi Minh, Amilcar Cabral, and the Sandinistas, notwithstanding the reversals witnessed afterward. With the neoconservative offensive carried out by Thatcher and Reagan, we see the emergence of various postmodernist trends with their reformist and antirevolutionary program (Lazarus 1991). In this context, postcolonial theory with its nominalist/relativist orientation appears to be invariably parasitic on the larger cultural terrain of comparative, interdisciplinary, and area studies in the Western academy.

In brief, without too much sociological analysis of the position of diasporic intellectuals in North America and Europe, one can say that postcolonial discourse accompanies the restoration of the periphery of postcolonial societies to a comprador role — for those that have evolved to a more competitive stage of capitalist development. The new "third world" that postcolonialism addresses refers to those countries that have gained sufficient industrial modernization; this includes the big countries of Latin America, India, East Asia (China, South Korea, Taiwan), Eastern Europe, and the former USSR. A new fourth world has appeared comprised of most countries in Africa and the Arab world, including many that have not embarked on any sustained program of industrialization: sub-Saharan Africa, the West Indies, Central America, Bangladesh, and Indonesia (Amin 1994). Most of these remain neo-colonized by the consortia of finance capital under the WB/IMF aegis. Postcolonial legitimacy stems from this new form of national differentiation in the world system of globalized transnational capital.

Alternative Routes

Postcolonial normativity inheres in its claim to discover complexity and difference hitherto submerged by totalizing axioms. The principle of uneven and combined development, as adumbrated by Marx and Engels, Lenin, Trotsky, and others in the socialist tradition, renders all the rhetoric of ambivalence, syncretism, and hybridity redundant. But this principle has been ignored or neglected because a linear teleological narrative of social evolution has been ascribed to classical Marxism, conflating it with ideas of unidirectional progress and developmentalism from Jean Bodin to W. W. Rostow, and the gurus of modernization theory (Patterson 1997). I want to elaborate on this distortion of Marx's position because it functions as the crucial basis for arguing the alternative rationality of unpredictable social change offered by postcolonial theory. The metaphysical idealism underlying postcolonial dogma, its hostility to historical materialism (the dialectical theory of comprehensive social transformation), and its complicity with the "New World Order" managed by finance capital can be made transparent by juxtaposing it with Marx's thesis of uneven and unsynchronized process of development in specific social formations.

   In essence, the most blatant flaw of postcolonial orthodoxy (I use the rubric to designate the practice of Establishment critics mobilizing a poststructuralist organon) lies in its refusal to grasp the category of multiple modernities in all its ramifications, both the regulated and the disarticulated aspects. A mechanistic formula is substituted for a dialectical analytic of historical motion. Consequently, in the process of a wide-ranging critique of selected Enlightenment principles by postcolonial critics, the antithesis of capitalism — proletarian revolution and the socialist principles first expounded by Marx and Engels — is dissolved in the logic of the global system of capital without further discrimination. The obsession to do away with totality, foundations, universals, and systemic analysis leads to a mechanical reification of ideas and terminology, as well as the bracketing of the experiences they refer to, culminating in a general relativism, skepticism, and nominalism — even nihilism — that undercuts the postcolonial claim to truth, plausibility, or moral high ground (see Habermas 1987; Dews 1995; Callinicos 1989).

A typical exercise in repudiating a historical materialist approach can be seen in Dipesh Chakrabarty's objection to the institutional history in which Europe operates as "the sovereign theoretical subject." Modernity — "the meta-narrative of the nation state" — is understood as European imperialism in collusion with third-world nationalisms. At stake is the question of a history of India written from the subaltern (peasantry) point of view. Chakrabarty calls for "radical critique and transcendence of liberalism (i.e., of the bureaucratic construction of citizenship, modern state, and bourgeois privacy that classical political philosophy has produced)" (1995, 386), a call that he believes finds resonance in Marx, poststructuralism, and feminist philosophy. While he seeks to provincialize Europe by demonstrating the limits of Enlightenment rationalism (its coercive violence suppressed the heterogeneity of other cultures and civilizations), he also rejects cultural relativism and nativist histories.

Chakrabarty's obsession is to unmask, demystify, or deconstruct the themes of citizenship and the modern state as though they were permanent, transhistorical, and ubiquitous. In the end, Chakrabarty negotiates for a compromise he labels a "politics of despair": "I ask for a history that deliberately makes visible, within the very structure of its narrative forms, its own repressive strategies and practices, the part it plays in collusion with the narratives of citizenships in assimilating to the projects of the modern state all other possibilities of human solidarity." His intent is to unfold a hypothetical world "where collectivities are defined neither by the rituals of citizenship nor by the nightmare of 'tradition' that 'modernity' creates" (1995, 388). Not to worry. The dreams of repressed subalternity in India and elsewhere await a Foucauldean genealogical excavation that elite academics such as Partha Chatterjee, Gyan Prakash, and others have already begun. By contrast, the status quo of existing property relations and asymmetries of actual power relations (articulating class, gender, locality, religion) in India remain untouched.

Central to the postcolonial malaise is the belief that history or historical narratives of colonized peoples by Europeans have been permanently damaged, hence they are useless for recovering native or indigenous originality. Eurocentric knowledge (whether expressed by Cecil Rhodes or Joseph Conrad, by Fray Bartolome de las Casas or W. E. B. Du Bois) can never disclose the truth about the colonized. Following Lyotard, only local narratives can have validity from now on. Unless postcolonial historians naively believe they can return to a past where tribal narratives ran parallel and never intersected, the notions of locality and place are unintelligible outside of a wider global space from which they can be identified. What is missing in the critique of Eurocentric history is a dialectical comprehension of such relations — the relation between Europe and its Others — that precisely constitute the problem of one-sidedness, falsity, distortion, and all the evils that postcolonials discern in modernity (including Marxism as a peculiarly European invention). Coeval modernities need to be theorized within a differentiated, not centralized, ontology of determinate and concrete social formations if we don't want to relapse into Heideggerian metaphysics.

In 1878, Marx wrote a letter to a Russian journal, complaining about a certain tendency that mistakenly elevated his hypothesis about capitalist development in Western Europe to a "suprahistorical theory." He wanted to correct the misapplication to Russia of his idea of the transition from feudalism to capitalism given in *Capital* : the emergence of capitalism premised on the expropriation of the agricultural producers can occur only when empirical preconditions exist. Russia will tend to become capitalist only if it has transformed the bulk of the peasantry into proletarians. Marx explains that this did not happen in Roman times when the means of production of the plebians or free peasants were expropriated; they became "not wage workers but an idle mob more abject than those who were called 'poor whites' in the southern United States"; what followed was not a capitalist but rather a slave mode of production. Marx objects to the premature generalization of his thought-experiment and extrapolation:

> [My critic] absolutely insists on transforming my historical sketch of the genesis of capitalism in Western Europe into a historico-philosophical theory of the general course fatally imposed on all peoples, whatever the historical circumstances in which they find themselves placed, in order to arrive ultimately at this economic formation that ensures, together with the greatest expansion of the productive powers of social labor, the most complete development of man. But I beg his pardon. (It does me both too much honor and too much discredit.) [Here follows the instance of the Roman plebians.] Thus events that are strikingly analogous, but taking place in different historical milieu, lead to totally disparate results. By studying each of these developments separately, and then comparing them, one can easily discover the key to this phenomenon, but one will never arrive there with the master key of a historico-philosophical theory whose supreme virtue consists in being supra-historical. (1982, 109–10)

From the viewpoint of critical realism, events cannot be judged in themselves apart from the the milieu of worldly circumstances. It is clear that there is no "master key" to unlocking all phenomena — which is not to say that one doesn't need a provisional framework or speculative guidelines for gathering data, testing and evaluating them through some principle of falsifiability or verification, and finally formulating general albeit tentative observations. I think Marx was disclaiming neither the validity of the notion of primitive accumulation he outlined, nor the scheme of historical development enunciated in the "preface" to *A Contribution to the Critique of Political Economy* (1859). The fundamental thesis on the contradiction between the forces of production and the relations of production, manifest in class struggles and in the global phenomenon of uneven development, has served as a fertile paradigm or framework of inquiry in which to explore hitherto unresolved problems of social change and historical trajectories.

"Oriental" Borderlands

There are at least two examples in Marx's theoretical practice that evince a sensitivity to the seemingly unpredictable motions of diverse collectivities. The first deals with the subject of the Asiatic mode of production that departs from the teleological cast of Marx's theory of transition from the ancient and feudal to the capitalist mode of production. No necessary succession is implied in the unfolding of the transition sequence. Because the socioeconomic specificity of Asiatic formations has led to a notion of despotic and stagnant societies quite inferior to their dynamic Western counterparts, the notion has become controversial. Karl Wittfogel's book *Oriental Despotism*, which examined the hydraulic economy of China and diverse societies under a centralized "patrimonial" bureaucracy (inspired by Max Weber's studies), however, became a weapon in the Cold War against Stalinism and other "third-world" revolutionary projects.

Marx and Engels first became interested in investigating non-European societies when they engaged in journalistic criticisms of British foreign policy in 1853. They noted that despotic authoritarian rule characterized certain societies where the state management of public works (irrigation) predominated together with the self-sufficient isolated village community, as in ancient China. Overall, stagnation prevailed. In *Grundrisse*, Marx emphasized the fact of the communal ownership of land that functioned as the stable basis for the unity of autarchic formations embodied by the state. In *Capital*, Marx presented the Asiatic mode as a system founded on the social relations of the self-sufficient village anchored to the unity of handicrafts and agriculture. The "secret of the unchangingness of Asiatic society" rested on the absence of private property (which precluded the rise of social classes as agents of change), the simplicity of production methods, and the communal appropriation of the product. It is of course questionable how autonomous self-sufficient villages could coexist with the powerful interventions by absolutist states whose origin also needs to be elucidated.

From a Weberian perspective, the stationary Asiatic mode displayed a lack of civil society and the dominance of a centralized state apparatus. Some scholars have claimed that Marx and Engels justified the "progressive" role of British imperialism in creating private property in land and thus destroying the stationary Asiatic mode. This modernizing effect, carried out through the railway system, free press, modern army, and means of communication (all technological determinants incorporated into social relations) has been used to apologize for, if not legitimize, imperial expansion as the only way of exploding an otherwise inert backward formation. Here is Marx's own "apologia" for British rule in India: "England, it is true, in causing a social revolution in Hindustan, was actuated only by the vilest interests, and was stupid in her manner of enforcing them. But that is not the question. The question is: Can mankind fulfill its destiny without a fundamental revolution in the social state of Asia? If not, whatever may have been the crimes of England, she was the unconscious tool of history in bringing about that revolution" (1959, 480–81)

Faced by the "cunning of Reason" (to use the Hegelian phrase), Marx counsels us to put aside "whatever bitterness the spectacle of the crumbling of an ancient world may have for our personal feelings" because we, tutored in Enlightenment wisdom, are also aware of the advances made possible by the modern suzerain's cruelty: the destruction of barbarian egoism, the Oriental despotism that "restrained the human mind within the smallest possible compass, making it the unresisting tool of superstition, enslaving it beneath traditional rules, depriving it of all grandeur and historical energies" (1959, 480). Postcolonial skeptics condemn this narrative schema as reductive and positivistic. To my mind, however, it is the most graphic triangulation of opposites, ruptures, and contradictions that epitomizes the genuinely dialectical vicissitudes of history apprehended by Marx in his survey of historically specific milieus and conjunctures.

The other example catalyzed by the discovery of the Asiatic mode of production is the possibility of a noncapitalist road to communism exemplified by Russia in the nineteenth century. In the midst of revolutionary struggles in Russia, Marx revised his early conception of Russia as "semi-Asiatic" after anatomizing the nature of the Russian mir. Could it provide the foundation for socialism or arrest its advent? Marx and Engels held that it could provided that capitalist relations of production do not strangle the whole countryside and that working-class revolutions in Europe would coincide with any vast social change in Russia.

Plekhanov disagreed with this, but it only proved that there is no unilinear paradigm or an evolutionary mechanistic formula that would
dictate how stages of development would unfold. It was Stalin who
decreed in 1931 that Asian societies were subsumed under the categories of slavery or feudalism, thus pursuing the path of Western development from primitive communism and then sequentially to slave, feudal,
capitalist, and socialist stages. But, of course, that is not the end of the
story.

It was the return of a serious concern with non-European routes to
modernity in the sixties (such as the Asiatic mode and the Russian
commune) that spurred discussions over dependency, uneven development, world-systems theory, the specificity and complexity of "third-
world" societies, and African socialism. The theoretical liabilities of
Orientalism incurred by the Asiatic mode have been spelled out by
Bryan Turner: "Its theoretical function was not to analyse Asiatic society but to explain the rise of capitalism in Europe within a comparative
framework. Hence Asiatic society was defined as a series of gaps — the
missing middle class, the absent city, the absence of private property, the
lack of bourgeois institutions — which thereby accounted for the dyna-
mism of Europe" (1983, 36). Nonetheless, the notion functioned as a
heuristic tool that Marx deployed to get rid of any teleological determinism or evolutionary monism in his historical investigations.

On the pivotal significance of these socioeconomic formations, Eric
Hobsbawm calls attention to the implicit thesis of human individualiza-
tion through the historical process, via exchange conceived in terms of
reciprocal interactions. In the course of demarcating the precapitalist
Formen — before full-fledged commodity production set in — Marx revealed his commitment to an emancipatory vision. Whether in ancient
Greek and Roman, Asiatic, or Germanic versions, these tribal communities contrasted favorably with the bourgeois epoch because "man
always appears . . . as the aim of production, not production as the
human goal." Marx continues, "In fact, however, when the narrow
bourgeois form has been peeled away, what is wealth if not the universality of needs, capacities, enjoyments, productive powers, etc. of individuals, produced in universal exchange?" In effect, the totality of
human development, "the absolute elaboration of his creative dispositions" and human powers, signifies a "situation where man does not

reproduce himself in any determined form, but produces his totality" (1965, 84–85). Informed by this synthesizing impulse in which dealienation of labor becomes the aim of revolutionary praxis, Marx's method does not degenerate into the aleatory reflex that vitiates postcolonial discourse. Marx's empathetic understanding of the past in their uniqueness, which postcolonial hermeneutics inflates into an axiom of incommensurability, does not preclude a synoptic, all-encompassing apprehension; in fact, it presupposes that petrified continuum that, as Walter Benjamin puts it, must be blasted apart to release the forces of change.

In this context Marx seized the moment of "the break-up of the old village communes" in India by British imperialism as a disastrous event pregnant with its contrary. It is progressive in the sense that it releases or unfolds human potential. By contrast, Marx believed (as expressed in a letter to Vera Zasulich in 1881) that if the Russian village commune was left free to pursue its "spontaneous development," then it could be the point of departure for "social regeneration in Russia." This shows that Marx, far from being a determinist, posited the dialectical-materialist view that the peasantry can acquire a communist consciousness, depending on which aspects (the collectivist or privative) of the mir would be enhanced by a changing historical environment (Levine 1978, 175). This anticipates what Mao, Cabral, and others have recognized in appraising the conjuncture of forces in any contested situation, namely, "the sovereignty of the human factor in revolutionary warfare" (Ahmad 1971, 147).

Dialectics eschews any one-sided abstract mode of judgment. George Lichtheim reflects that Marx's ideas on the various forms of social metabolism that are crystallized in different stages of society illustrates the modes in which humans individualize themselves through the historical process of "evolving various forms of communal and private property, i.e., various ways of organizing his social intercourse with nature and the — natural or artificial — preconditions of work. . . . The forcible disruption of the Indian or Chinese village community by European capital completes the process by rendering it truly global" (1967, 85). To be sure, a revolutionary Marxist position does not prescribe a causal monism or a freewheeling causal pluralism. It registers the play of chance and necessity, of contradictions in the process of unfolding: "Structural principles must be complemented by, or even include, notions of individual action, natural causes, and 'accidental circumstances.' . . . Nevertheless, material and social relations can be long-term, effective real structures that set firm limits to the nature and degree of practical effect that accident and even agency have" (McLennan 1981, 234). In other words, Marxism views the world not as a closed totality but as an "open, structured whole, with irreducible differences" (Haug 1984, 16) comprehended dialectically.

I have dwelt at length on this topic because of the postcolonial critic's insistence that the method of historical materialism is fatally compromised by its Enlightenment provenance. If Marx is a Eurocentric apologist for the "civilizing mission" of imperialism, then we should have nothing to do with his indictment of capitalism and advocacy of socialist revolution. It might be instructive to note that the charge of Eurocentrism leveled against Marx does not permit a nuanced and rigorous appraisal of his critique of bourgeois philosophy; the polemic of Eurocentrism does not distinguish the nature of capitalist modernity as a specific epochal form, one which is constituted by the complex, uneven relation between colonizer and colonized. Capitalism disappears when all of modernity, both positive and negative elements, becomes ascribed to a geopolitical region (the metropole vis-à-vis the periphery) that cannot be divorced from the world-system of which it is an integral part.

Samir Amin has perspicaciously described the historical genealogy of Eurocentrism in the drive of capital to subordinate everything to exchange value, to accumulation, hence the need for standardization. But this drive to uniformity also precipitates its opposite, unequal accumulation between nation-states and the impoverishment of the masses. For Amin, the most explosive contradiction generated by transnational capital inheres in the centers/peripheries polarization and its corollary, the "imperialist dimension of capitalist expansion" (1989, 141). Affirmation of cultural difference and other interstitial by-products of the center/periphery dynamic evades a critique of economism and reproduces itself as an inverted Eurocentrism that cannot resolve the crisis of inequality. A genuine universalism cannot emerge from incommensurable and provincialized cultures, no matter how valorized as singular or cosmopolitan; the impasse can be broken only by a popular-democratic breakthrough instanced by national liberation struggles.

Toward Regrounding

We are inhabiting today a "New World Order" in which, to quote Ellen Meiksins Wood (1998), capitalism has universalized itself, subjugating everyone to the logic of capital accumulation. Can assertions of singularities suffice to offset, sidetrack, or neutralize the totalizing logic of commodification? Can a rejection of the Enlightenment paradigm of autonomous monads, the "Leibnizian conceit" (Harvey 1996), free the subaltern from colonial tutelage? Given the fact that global cities like New York and London are "the spaces of postcolonialism and indeed contain conditions for the formation of a postcolonialist discourse" (Sassen 1998, 361), how can this discourse take into account the disarticulated and unsynchronized alignment of forces in the neocolonized, still colonized (for example, Puerto Rico, Hawai'i), and recolonized geopolitical South?

It is not exorbitant to state that today all social relations and practices, as well as the process of social transformation, labor under the imperatives of accumulation, commodification, and profit maximization. Postcolonial tropes of irony, pastiche, and fragmentation are unable to offer frames of intelligibility that can analyze and critique the internal contradictions embedded in the reality and ideology of the "free market." Driven by a pragmatic empiricism, postcolonialism cannot offer the organon for an accurate "cognitive mapping" of all those trends that marked the breakdown of developmentalism, modernization theory, and other theoretical solutions to the crisis of monopoly capital since the Bolshevik Revolution of 1917 up to the scrapping of the Bretton Woods agreement and a unitary monetary system. As many have noted, postcolonialism, its logic and rhetoric, coincides suspiciously with the anarchic "free market" and the predatory logic of capital on a global scale. Bound by its problematic, the postcolonial critic cannot even entertain the crucial question that Amin poses: "How can we develop the productive forces without letting commodity relations gain ground?" (1977, 101).

There have been many explanations for those inadequacies. Amin (1998) locates it in postcolonialism's rejection of modernity, the meta-narrative of emancipation and convivial democracy. The excesses of instrumental reason are ascribed to the teleology of progress instead of the logic of capitalism and its presuppositions (private property, entrepreneurship, wage labor, technological improvement, laws of the market). The conflation of Enlightenment ideals with the telos of utilitarian capitalism and its encapsulation in the historiographic fortunes of modernity have led to a nominalist conception of subjectivity and agency. Disavowing modernity and the principle of collective human agency — humans make their own history under determinate historical conditions — postcolonialism submits to the neoliberal cosmos of fragmentation, individualist warfare, schizoid monads, and a regime of indeterminacy and contingency. This ironic turn damages postcolonialism's claim to liberate humanity from determinisms and essentialisms of all kinds.

I think the fundamental error may be traced to two sources whose historical matrix I have alluded to earlier. We have, first, the inability to conceptualize mediation or connections in a dialectical manner, substituting instead a seriality of differences whose equivalence remains unpredictable; and second, entailed by the first premise, the incapacity to conceive of the conjunctural moment of society as inscribed in the nonsynchronous development of the world system. Uneven development involves the inescapable polarization of the world into peripheral and central economies, tied with the intrinsic contradiction between labor and capital and the international division of labor whose boundaries were first laid by the history of European colonialism and later adjusted by monopoly capital. Why theorize mediation and uneven development in a precise historicized fashion? Because our intent is to "master" and so escape the "nightmare of history and to win a measure of control over the supposedly blind and natural 'laws' of socioeconomic fatality." As Fredric Jameson suggests, historical reconstruction, "the positing of global characterizations and hypotheses, the abstraction from the 'blooming, buzzing' confusion of immediacy, was always a radical intervention in the here-and-now and the promise of resistance to its blind fatalities" (2000, 35).

From a historical-materialist perspective, the dynamic process of social reality cannnot be grasped without comprehending the manifold internal relations and linkages that constitute the totality of its objective determinations. Several levels of abstraction have to be clarified, among which is the relation between the knowing subject and the surrounding world (both nature and the built environment) — knowledge of which is desired. Truth in this tradition comes from human practice, the intermediary between consciousness and its object; and it is human labor (knowing and making as a theorized synthesis) that unites theory and practice. As Lenin puts it, everything is mediated and connected by transitions that unite opposites, "transitions of every determination, quality, feature, side, property, into every other" so that "the individual exists only in the connection that leads to the universal" (1963, 132). The reciprocal interaction of various levels of formal abstractions has been elaborated by Bertell Ollman under the categories of "metamorphosis" and "contradictions." These levels of abstract mediation, however, need to be transcoded into their concrete manifestation without necessarily succumbing to the one-sided immediacy of pragmatism. Otherwise, what Fabian (1983) calls the "allochronic orientation of Eurocentric thought" with its taxonomic, noncoeval representation of Others would continue to prevail.

What is required next is to confront the second-order mediations that are historically specific and transcendable, namely, the market, money, private property, the transformation and subordination of use-value to exchange value — in short, the sources of alienation and perversion, what Istvan Meszaros (1983a, 1983b) calls "productive self-mediation" of individuals in social life. Alienation in the occupied territories can only be resolved in the colonized people's conquest of full sovereignty, "the socialization of the principal means of production," and reproduction in a socialist transformation. Indeed, poststructuralist thought hypostatizes this historical phenomenon of reification into the nihilism of modernity, converting mediation (transition) into serial negation and occluding its prefigurative aspect. Contradiction, sublation, and overdetermination do not figure as meaningful concepts in postcolonial theorizing.

Without a concept of totality, however, the notion of mediation remains vacuous and useless. All determination is mediation, Roy Bhaskar reminds us in his magisterial study *Dialectic* (1993). Totality in its historical concreteness becomes accessible to us in the concept of uneven development and its corollary ideas of overdetermination and underdetermination. Totality is discernible in the coexistence of various modes of production in a specific social formation, in the asymmetrical world-system of periphery and core societies. We have come to accept as a commonplace the differential rhythm of development of diverse societies, with the uneven pace attributed to the presence or absence of cumulative growth in the use of production techniques, labor organization, and so on, as shown by Marx's inquiry into the developments in Russia and Asia. It is indeed difficult to explain how the old imperial polities of Britain and France were superseded by Germany and the United States, and how West Germany and Japan have attained dominance today.

Uneven development results from the peculiar combination of many factors that have marked societies as peripheral or central (Novack 1966; Lowy 1981). In many societies shaped by colonial conquest and protracted subjugation, uneven and combined development may be perceived in the copresence of a modern sector (usually foreign dominated or managed by the state) and a traditional sector characterized by precapitalist modes of production and ruled by a coalition of merchant capitalist and feudal/tributary ruling classes. In these formations, we find a lack of cumulative growth, backward agriculture limited by the lack of an internal market, with the accumulated money capital diverted from whatever industrial enterprises there are into speculative activities in real estate, usury, and hoarding (Mandel 1983). This space of aporias and antinomies serves as the ideal habitat for "magic realism" and wild amorphous fantasies (Borges, Cortázar), as well as all those converging flows and permanences described as hybrid, creolized, syncretic, ambivalent, and so on, which postcolonial criticism have labored so hard to fetishize as permanent, ever-recurring, and ineluctable qualities (San Juan 1998a).

Said's Exemplum

Despite its orthodoxy, postcolonial idealism has protean incarnations. Instead of inquiring into the mystification of the "geography of difference" (Harvey 1996), I would like to comment briefly on Edward Said's contribution to this field, especially its refusal of a historical-materialist framework and its indulgence in "ethical utopianism." Given his influential work *Orientalism* (1978), Said deserves to be called the originator and patron-saint of postcolonial theory and criticism. References to him abound in the writings of Spivak and Bhabha and assorted Australian and Canadian exponents. The anti-Marxism of postcolonial theory may be attributed partly to Said's eclecticism, his belief that American left criticism is marginal, and his skewed or tendentious reading of Marxism framed within Cold War anticommunism and the model of "actually existing socialism." Given his generous latitude for fellow-travelers, Francis Mulhern includes in a recent anthology of Marxist literary criticism Said's essay on Jane Austen, even though its inferred "moral geography" supposedly "reinserts the humane traditions of English culture in their ambiguous role in the unfolding of Britain's colonial history" (1992, 97).

To be sure, Said has contributed his share to the salutary revisions of the vulgar Marxism that Fredric Jameson, Alan Wald, Terry Eagleton, and others have judged as a bourgeois perversion. But Said has certainly not revitalized historical materialism for revolutionary socialist goals. Nor can one claim that he intended to do so. Many other critics, especially Aijaz Ahmad, have pointed out the weaknesses and lacunae in Said's interpretation and rather opportunistic use of a version of dogmatic Marxism. In general, I think the excerpting and tokenizing of Marxist thinkers by postcolonial orthodoxy may explain its reputed radicalism; this putative solidarity, according to fellow-travelers, gives it a sanction to condemn its systemic excesses, reductionism, and so on (usually, of course, attributed to former Soviet Union dogmatism) under the guise of sympathy and knowledgeability about it.

I am reminded of a former colleague who, in the turbulence of the sixties, always warned me to beware of Marxists because he was a former Trotskyite in the forties. The sociologist Bryan Turner also reminds us of Said's adoption of a deconstructive strategy derived from Michel Foucault and Martin Heidegger whose anti-Marxism needs no elaboration. We find in Said not only romantic anarchism but a cavalier textualism that, although qualified by historical references, confuses "the materiality of social relations with an alleged materiality of the context" and leads to a "vicious solipsism" (B. Turner 1992, 7).

Drawing from the observations of Maxime Rodinson and Sadek Jalal el-Azm, Samir Amin (1989) has remarked on Said's provincialism and his inability to explain the historical sources of Eurocentric prejudice.

Said warns against the alibi of comprador nationalism that perpetuates colonial servility. But his cartography of "liberation" gravitating around cultural representations fails to grapple with institutional practices and structures of imperial domination, with the modes of dependent production and social reproduction. Evinced in the silence over revolutionary nationalists like Mao Zedong, Ho Chi Minh, and Che Guevara, and other leaders of "people's war," Said's contrapuntal method negotiates a compromise with the modernizing side of imperialism by completely erasing the participation of the masses of peasants and workers — the bearers of an egalitarian banner of social revolution. In short, Said evades the central question of a counterhegemonic, national-popular strategy of social transformation.

In *Culture and Imperialism*, Said uses Gramsci and C. L. R. James, among others in the Marxist tradition, to give an aura of leftism to his text. Gramsci is referred to in connection with an intellectual vocation, with Yeats's poetry, with the Indian Subaltern Studies. But it is in the way Said appropriates and refunctions Gramsci's notion of hegemony that is symptomatic of a co-optative project. Said first demarcates Gramsci from Lukács; the latter belongs to the Hegelian tradition, Gramsci to the "Vichian, Crocean departure from it" (49) so that Lukács attends more to temporality, while Gramsci to social history and actuality grasped in geographical terms. This is evidenced by Gramsci's use of such words as "terrain," "territory," "blocks," and "region," in his essay "Some Aspects of the Southern Question." But obviously Gramsci's concept of space is precisely historicized to those places in southern Italy left out of the main capitalist trend of industrialization because of the stranglehold of the landlord class and its traditional intellectuals like Croce. Clearly Gramsci's conceptualization of topography is historical, not just temporal; the meridional environment is such because of the political subordination of the agrarian economy to the financial power of the Italian bourgeoisie in the North, not simply because of mere cultural backwardness.

The problem Gramsci is grappling with in that text is the workerist sectarianism of the Italian Socialist Party. He is proposing a united-front policy in which the proletariat will demonstrate its hegemonic capacity by incorporating the demands and needs of the peasantry into its national-popular program of action. The prerequisite for this is the recognition of the historically uneven development of the Italian social formation. Profoundly conscious of uneven capitalist development, Gramsci posits the task of revolutionary intellectuals as a systematic attempt to propagate the philosophy of praxis, Marxism, on the terrain where cosmopolitan bourgeois ideas supported by the Catholic Church are dominant. The organic intellectual of the proletariat would assume this pedagogical and agitational role, helping to integrate the Italian South with the national-popular agenda of the leading class, the proletariat. Analogies to dependency theory or to the world-system paradigm may not be quite appropriate.

Said's problematic departs from Gramsci's orientation. Instead of historicizing the fact of geopolitical discordance, Said hypostatizes it and, contrary to his initial motivation, focuses on the temporal (in effect, existential) dimension of cultural progress. But what is revealing is Said's enlargement of the intellectual's role that, in retrospect, anticipates that reserved for the postcolonial mediator: "Gramsci also understands that in the extended time span during which the coral-like formation of a culture occurs, one needs 'breaks of an organic kind.' Gobetti represents one such break, a fissure that opened up within the cultural structures that supported and occluded the north-south discrepancy for so long in Italian history" (1993, 50). What distinguishes Gramsci's type of intellectual from Said's is that the former is class-rooted but upholds a universalizing mission, whereas the latter resembles more the floating petit bourgeois artists of the metropolitan literary salons. Consequently Said conceives of the intellectual outside of the hegemonic struggles of the major social classes, aggrandizing its function in a way that is antithetical to Gramsci's vision. The "Gobetti factor," that is, the intellectual who (in Said's words) "furnishes the link between disparate, apparently autonomous regions of human history," is the model of the diasporic intellectual who will link comparative literature and imperial geography, harmonizing alterities and flattening out contradictions.

What has happened here is typical of Said's methodology. The vocation of the postcolonial intellectual as middleman-facilitator of colonized subalterns and Western imperial power is thus legitimized by the illicit subsumption, if not perversion, of Gramsci's idea of how organic intellectuals can work to promote the worker-peasant alliance within an all-encompassing socialist program. Said's circumstantial intelligence ascribes a "spatial consciousness" to Gramsci's reading of the "Southern question" in order to "reinterpret the Western cultural archive as if fractured geographically by the activated imperial divide" (50). But instead of calling for a united front of the Western proletariat and the "peasantry" of the "third world," Said reverts to a purely academic exercise in contrapuntal reading of the Western canon. For Said, then, Gramsci's insights can rationalize the academic business of interpreting English novels in the context of "the specific history of colonization, resistance, and finally native nationalism," without questioning the ideological-political framework of the expansive imperial archive.

Said's "solidarity" with Marxism consists then in selective deployment of concepts to advance a deconstructive brief. In *Orientalism*, for example, he cites Gramsci's distinction between civil and political society in which culture, located in civil society, is taken as the chief instrument for inducing consent and building hegemony. Consequently the state disappears since hegemony becomes culturalized. Culture divorced from political economy offers then the framework of intelligibility for understanding the social division of labor, property relations, and the power structure. The mechanisms of injustice and exploitation are thus occluded. In *The World, the Text, and the Critic*, Said performs a desecularizing move of interpretation. He converts Gramsci into a philosophical idealist, a pluralist who assigns culture to "some large intellectual endeavor — systems and currents of thought — connected in complex ways to doing things, to accomplishing certain things, to force, to social class and economic production, to diffusing ideas, values, and world pictures" (1983, 170). Gramsci, for Said, privileges intellectual elaboration as "the central cultural activity," as "the material making a society a society." The strength of Western culture, based on "its variety, its heterogeneous plurality," accounts for "the strength of the modern Western State" (1983, 171). In effect, Said has made Gramsci a disciple of Croce and Hegel.

I submit that the Gramscian concept of hegemony cannot be reduced to the domain of culture or superstructure that guarantees the reproduction of the social relations, the state, and everything else. All relations of social forces are conditioned by the material contradictions in the social formation, hence the hegemonic apparatus of state plus civil society in Gramsci should be grasped within the political economy of social relations. I endorse Christine Buci-Glucksmann's reading of Gramsci: "The hegemonic apparatus turns out to be a constitutive part of the relations of production as 'ideological social' relations, in the distinction made by Lenin. Practical ideologies and modes of living and feeling have their roots in the economic base: the relation between *civilta* and production is a pivotal point in Gramsci's whole problematic of capitalism, and of socialism too" (1980, 89). In addition, for Gramsci, civil society cannot be fully grasped separate from its internal relations with political society since civil society involves the linkage between class relations in the economy and the explicitly political aspect of the primary agent of coercion, the state. The dual perspective of consent/coercion unites political and civil societies in Gramsci's extended or integral state, "the unified site in which Western bourgeois classes have established their social power as 'hegemony protected by the armour of coercion'" (Rupert 1993, 79).

Culture and governance interact in the struggle for hegemony. Construing Gramsci more rigorously, I argue that proletarian counterhegemony takes place in the integral state grasped as "the entire complex of practical and theoretical activities with which the ruling class not only justifies and maintains its dominance, but manages to win the active consent of those over whom it rules" (Said 1971, 244). Given this misreading of Gramsci, it is not suprising that Said is unable to propose alternatives to the hegemonic discourse of *Orientalism*. Dennis Porter comments, "Because [Said] overlooks the potential contradiction between discourse theory and Gramscian hegemony, he fails to historicize adequately the texts he cites and summarizes, finding always the same triumphant discourse where several are frequently in conflict" (1994, 160). This leads us then to Said's eclectic libertarianism, which hardens into orthodoxy as the Bandung "third worldism" of the sixties and the dependency neoliberalism of the seventies mutates into the postmodernist reaction of the eighties and nineties.

Inventory of the Palimpsest

A consensus on the postcolonial track record has been slowly crystallizing. Frank Schulze-Engler (1998) has called into question the dehistoricizing framework of the scriptural text, *The Empire Writes Back* by the Australians Bill Ashcroft, Gareth Griffiths, and Helen Tiffin. Neil Larsen (1999) noted trenchantly the theoretical impoverishment and anachronism of postcolonial critics. In a critique of Establishment post-colonial criticism, Arif Dirlik (1997) has called our attention to its fetishism of hybridity, the rejection of the categories of class and nation, and the antifoundationalist rejection of history — in short, its basic anti-revolutionary norm and motivation. He indicts it for not only betraying its radical origin but also rejecting "the possibility of imagining a world beyond the present" (2000, 16). Postcolonialism's complicity with sta-tus quo reification and commodity-fetishism has also been examined by Callinicos, Eagleton, and others. Said (1994) endorses Bhabha's blanket pronunciation on the hybridity of all cultures. The celebration of multi-plicity, difference, and syncretism at the end of *Culture and Imperialism* occurs within the field of a pluralist global market that can tolerate Said's ethical protest. Despite this moralizing, Dirlik contends, Said's lack of a dialectical method explains why he has failed to take into account the "Oriental's participation in the unfolding of the discourse of the Orient" (1997, 118; see also Chen Xiaomei 1994) and heed the imperative of historicizing capitalist modernity and its commodification of all cultural artifacts and practices.

Other commentaries elaborate on similar tendencies. An admirer of Said, Frederick Buell aptly describes Said's stance: "Said tries to bridge both positions [that of Sara Suleri and Benita Parry], advanc-ing, for example, his vision of a vehemently antinationalist, yet ardently anti-imperialist, Fanon for the present era, and eschewing a 'politics of blame,' advocating compassion, and seeking to forge 'new align-ments . . . across borders, types, nations, and essences' at the same time as he writes an extended indictment of imperial culture" (1994, 237). Fanon is refunctioned to legitimize an academic regime of compromise and multiculturalism — a perfect description of the middleman nego-tiator. By contrast, Mas'ud Zavarzadeh locates Said's pragmatic neo-humanism in the horizon of post-al theory, "a utopian theory of entre-preneurial individuality and agency, . . . a voluntarism unburdened by history" (1995, 7).

Evidence that points to Said's limitation as marked by the negation of a dialectical-materialist theorization of history may be found in his treatment of C. L. R. James. Suffice it here to note that for Said James's achievement in *The Black Jacobins* is comparable to that of the petit bourgeois nationalist George Antonius, author of *The Arab Awakening*: both allegedly stood within the fold of the Western cultural tradition, "however much they articulate the adversarial experience of colonial and/or non-Western peoples" (1994, 248). In effect, both Antonius and James, like Ranajit Guha, resemble Said, or are mirror-images of Said's postcolonial persona. James has metamorphosed into a model of the assimilationist immigrant. According to Said, James "saw the central pattern of politics and history in linear terms . . . and his basic metaphor is that of a voyage taken by ideas and people; those who were slaves and subservient classes could first become the immigrants and then the principal intellectuals of a diverse new society" (1994, 253).

The reason why postcolonial thinking like Said's cannot go beyond the limits of a liberal mentality arises from the peculiar condition of diasporic intellectuals, the political conjuncture of the United States in the eighties and nineties, and the global power alignment. Peter Gran, Arif Dirlik, Neil Lazarus, and others have discussed the historical conjunctures — in Said's case, the Palestinian struggle within the Cold War framework, the poststructuralist trend, and so on — that partly explain the rise of a conservative postcolonial consensus. The general socio-historical template of "uneven and combined development" has been articulated fully by, among others, Michael Löwy (1981), Neil Smith (1984), and David Harvey (1996), a materialist foundation for liberation struggles light-years removed from Nietzschean genealogy, which is Said's preferred epistemological mode of inquiry (in spite of the uneasy marriage of Foucault and a modified Gramsci (Porter 1994). Said's ethical utopianism preempts a dialectical approach to the fundamental condition of late modernity: reification (the effect of universal commodity-fetishism and the circulation of exchange values) on a global scale.

Ultimately, Said's muted anti-Marxism is premised on the choice of a "liberationist" perspective. Nicos Poulantzas (1978) and Alex Callinicos (1989) have already exposed the antinomies and paradoxes of this anarchist illusion. In this perspective, power/desire determines the trajectory of societies; any claim to knowledge and truth — truth is, for Said, "a function of learned judgment," of institutionalized discourses — can only be a form of ideological maneuver since history and any of the "grand metanarratives" are suspected of being nothing but totalizing blackmail. While Said's ambition to liberate Europe's silent Others from the imperial will-to-knowledge/power, to give them voice or the right of representation is exceptional vis-à-vis Baudrillard's cynicism and the nihilism of cyborg prophets, this attempt undercuts itself by revindicating a liberal brand of humanism on which capital relies for its aesthetic and ethical legitimation. This middleman position stems from a revolt against the subordination of use-value to exchange value. It springs from the failure to grasp the contradictions inherent in the system of commodity production, in the logic of imperialism as such (Haug 1986).

But the key to this strategy of humanist recuperation lies in the absence in Said's thinking of the category of a differentiated totality that underlies historical development, the principle of a Marxist critique of imperialism. This totality, in Mezsaros's words, is "a structured and historically determined overall complex" (1983b, 480) embodied in the processual mediations and passages of concrete life. Distinctions can be meaningful only within an integral unity, a synapse of internal relations in historical motion. In Marxist thought, Harvey explains, "Difference is given in this scheme of things by the perspective on the totality, not by supposing some clearly defined, isolated entity that is a totality in itself" (1996, 71) — an ontological shift that sets the historical-materialist optic apart from postmodernist textualism and its fetishism of the local and heterogeneous, with its antifoundationalist retreat into the obscurantism of Lacanian psychology. Despite Said's stress on worldliness and the secular density of experience, it is striking that he has no dialectical grasp of the structure of a multilayered totality such as finance capital, imperialism in its several stages, and so on. Said aims for "emancipation" and "enlightenment," but he confesses that "the transnational capitalism of global finance" is "relatively irrational and very difficult to comprehend" (1994, 24) — a difficulty that Said mystifies the more by judging it irrational. By contrast, we need to acknowledge the value of Said's commitment to the vocation of secular humanism (included in the response to his critics in the 1994 *Social Text* symposium), condensed in the rubrics of "enlightenment" and "liberation," as against the hedonist vogue around Lyotard and other therapy-driven post-alities.

One of his commentators, Mary Louise Pratt, has correctly put a finger on the symptomatic absence in Said of any critique of *neocoloni-alism* since this historical phenomenon marks the limits of postcolonial theory. Pratt argues, "This difference in chronology with respect to colonization and decolonization seems to be one of the main reasons the Americas have remained almost entirely off the map of the colonial discourse movement and colonial studies in general" (1994, 4). U.S. neocolonialism, in particular, is the "missing link" in Said's fugal chart-ing of modern imperialism. Remarkable too, in this context, is the ab-sence of references to the struggles of the "internal colonies" of the United States, in particular, the Puerto Rican dilemma, the Hawai'i sovereignty struggle, and raging conflicts over Affirmative Action, "un-documented aliens," among others. I don't have to dilate on the fact that postcolonial criticism has been unable to pay serious attention to the current crises in Afghanistan, East Timor, Myanmar, Colombia, Iraq, and other societies suffering from attacks by the United States/IMF/WB on their sovereignties.

This inability to challenge neocolonialism results from the failure to grasp the import of uneven and combined development globally. This in turn may be ascribed to an idealist metaphysics that overvalorizes the intervention of the diasporic intellectual in political struggle. Such a brand of intellectualism, or theoreticism, if you like, arrogates all agency to borderland scholastics who seek to negotiate a zone of recon-ciliation between the bourgeois-comprador nationalism of neocolo-nized nation-states and the cosmopolitan "high culture" of the metro-poles. Hence, despite the mention of Cabral or Fanon, Said discounts organized mass struggles as the other pole of a dialectical totality. He has nothing to say about the praxis of revolutionary transformation, about cultural literacy (emphasized by Paulo Freire), and all those "sub-jective factors" that Michael Löwy believes are necessary to thwart bureaucratic despotism: "the participatory character of the revolution-ary process, the democratic outlook of the socialist vanguard, the de-gree of proletarian self-activity and popular self-organization" (1981, 230). But those factors are remote when you conceive of decolonization merely as "the process of unlearning historically determined habits of privilege and privation" (Mohanty 1995, 110) and postcolonial criti-cism as concerned chiefly with "the multiplication of identities and the intersection" of any number of identity ascriptions (Hutcheon 1995, 11).

Lest the reader construe this view of Said as sectarian polemics, I reiterate my esteem for Said's substantive contribution to the critique of imperialism in our day and age, and for his militant stand againt U.S. military interventions. This critique derives from ecumenical, not sectarian, sources, as inspired precisely by Gramsci's notion of counterhegemony. I agree with Said's defense of certain universal ideals of the Enlightenment in opposition to the "provincial atavism" exemplified by Rorty, Butler, and other celebrities. Said's affiliation with Noam Chomsky and Raymond Williams, both partisans of an anti-imperialist platform, needs to be remembered. How then should we explain Said's calculated distance from them? Confessing his Palestinian sense of being "rootless and deracinated," Said conveys to us both nostalgically and prophetically the varying significance of habitat and collective memory. Perhaps Glenn Bowman explains better than anyone else the logic behind Said's use of Foucault and Gramsci, constructed narratives and objectivist decription, and their productive tensions, and his role as bearing witness and testimony to a specific historical experience. Glossing Said's *After the Last Sky*, Bowman perceives in the world Said depicts no room for Fawaz Turki's revolutionary internationalism or Rajah Shehadeh's militant solidarity: "Said's 'Palestinian' is a composite of the Palestinians he knows, and these are persons who, caught in the web of exile amid the anomic milieus of the late capitalist world, find occasional but brief respites from alienation in the celebration of an identity set off against that world" (1994, 152). This organic matrix of his sensibility, a disposition to rebel against oppression, suffice to illuminate both the assets and vulnerabilities of Said's politics of resistance.

Visionary Initiative

An alternative to Said may be found in the Marxist-Leninist critique of imperial modernization. To appreciate this alternative, we need to grasp uneven and combined development via a rigorous dialectical assessment of imperialism such as that propounded by Gramsci, C. L. R.

James, Walter Rodney, Amilcar Cabral, Ho Chi Minh, and others in the periphery. Lenin remedied the classical limitation of the Second International by integrating in his idea of world revolution the revolt of the industrial working class in Europe with the mass uprisings of small colonized nations, as well as peasant revolts against landowners. Lenin's post–1914 writings — the *Hegel Notebooks*, the article "The Socialist Revolution and the Right of Nations to Self-determination," and so on — theorized how the "particular" of national liberation movements can, under certain conditions, become the road to the universal of socialism. In this discourse, mediation assumes the form of contradiction between oppressed peoples in the colonies and oppressor nations. As Kevin Anderson clarifies the crux, "Lenin's theory of imperialism has become dialectical in the sense of pointing not only to the economic side of imperialism but also to a new revolutionary subject arising from within global imperialism: national liberation movements" (1995, 142). Unless we can improve on Lenin's theory of national liberation with its dialectical-materialist method, we will only be indulging in verbal magic and wish-fulfillments that mimic Bhabha, Appadurai, and other ventriloquists.

As for the historical realization of the Leninist fusion of theory and praxis, I can only dwell briefly on the enduring example of Amilcar Cabral and his achievement. In what way does Cabral supersede the formulaic version of decolonization as a valorization of syncretism and transculturation of symptomatic traumas?

Some distinctive qualities of Cabral's thought need to be underscored. Cabral's theory of national revolution is a creative application of Marxism as a dialectical theory of action in which history generates the unforeseen within the parameters of what objectively exists. Cabral understood the Marxist insight that "the process of history seeks itself and proves itself in praxis" (Lefebvre 1969, 162). He theorized national liberation in his concrete milieu (the Portuguese colonies of Guinea Bissau and Cape Verde islands) through the paradigm of interacting modes of production in history. Cabral insisted on the centrality of the level of productive forces as the "true and permanent driving power of history" (1973, 42). Imperialist rule deprived the colonized peoples of agency, the vocation of shaping their own history. Since imperialist domination negated "the historical process of the dominated people by means of violently usurping the free operation of the process of development of the productive forces, the goal of decolonization is "the liberation of the process of development of national productive forces" (1973, 43). The struggle for national liberation is not simply a cultural fact but also a cultural factor generating new forms and content in the process (Cabral 1979, 211).

For Cabral, culture is the key constituent of the productive forces in society. Culture becomes the decisive element in grasping the dialectic of subjective and objective forces, the contradiction between the productive forces and the production relations, as well as the uneven terrain of class struggles: "Culture is simultaneously the fruit of a people's history and a determinant of history, by the positive or negative influence which it exerts on the evolution of relationships between man and his environment, among men or groups of men within a society, as well as among different societies" (1973, 41). But Cabral urges a concrete differentiation of tendencies and possibilities: "Nor must we forget that culture, both as a cause and an effect of history, includes essential and secondary elements, strengths and weaknesses, merits and defects, positive and negative aspects, factors both for progress and stagnation or regression, contradictions, conflicts. . . . Culture develops unevenly at the level of a continent, a 'race,' even a community" (1979, 210, 212). If liberation is an act of culture, it is also a struggle to shape a richer culture that is simultaneously "popular, national, scientific and universal."

Framed within a nonsynchronous grid of forces, Cabral conceives of national liberation as a wide-ranging transformation of the combined political, economic, and cultural institutions and practices of the colonized society. It is not narrowly culturalist or merely superstructural because culture refers to the "dynamic synthesis of the material and spiritual historical reality of a society." In a broad sense, it is the recovery of specific African forms of subjectivity, a "regaining of the historical personality of the people, its return to history through the destruction of imperialist domination." This recovery is staged as a popular cultural renaissance with the party as the chief pedagogical agency wielding the "weapon of theory," the organized political expression of a national-popular culture in the making. This renaissance for Cabral occurred in the praxis of the liberated zones controlled by the PAIGC (African Party for the Independence of Guinea and Cape Verde) where the culture-changing processes of criticism and self-criticism, democratic discussion, teaching, and learning from the participants were encouraged and institutionalized. This will recall Marx's dialectical thesis of an alternative to unilinear evolutionism of the Russian village commune: if the subjective force of the peasantry acquires consciousness and organized identity, the objective situation can be transformed in a liberatory direction (Hudis 1983). In the context of the African Gold Goast, C. L. R. James reprised the Leninist thesis of revolution as the objective process of the "movement of a people finding themselves and creating a new social order," the basis of unity being the actual conditions in which the people live (1992, 351).

Cabral was called by his people *Fundador da Nacionalidade*, Founder of the Nationality, not Founder of the Nation. This is because, to quote Basil Davidson, "the nation was and is a collectivity and necessarily founds itself, but [Cabral was the] founder of the process whereby this collectivity could (and does) identify itself and continue to build its postcolonial culture" (1986, 39). Cabral also believed that "the dialectical nature of identity lies in the fact that it both *identifies* and *distinguishes*" (1979, 208). Seizing the strategic initiative, he exhorted his partisans, "converted" intellectuals, to engage in a synthesizing pedagogical task cognizant of the uneven ideological strata of a disintegrated polity: "Every responsible worker and every militant of our Party, every element of the population in our land in Guinea and Cape Verde, should be aware that our struggle is not only waged on the political level and on the military level. Our struggle — our resistance — must be waged on all levels of the life of our people. We must destroy everything the enemy can use to continue their domination over our people, but at the same time we must be able to construct everything that is needed to create a new life in our land" (quoted in Cohen 1998, 44). Cabral thus combined national and social elements into an insurrectionary movement in which the partisan unit, no longer a local entity, but rather a "body of permanent and mobile cadres around whom the local force is formed" (Hosbawm 1973, 166), became the germ of the "new life," the embryonic nationality becoming the nation.

Concretizing selected themes in Fanon's philosophy, Cabral's Marxism is unique in its context. Cabral focused on the potential nation as "a form of revolutionary collective subjectivity" mediating actual classes, sectors, and groups into a "nation-for-itself" that can reclaim the "in-alienable right of every people to have their own history" based on its right to control "the process of development of national productive forces." Cabral located the roots of this subjectivity in the resistance of the masses that was "protracted and multiple," a dissidence "only pos-sible because by preserving their culture and their identity, the masses retain consciousness of their individual and collective dignity despite the vexations, humiliations and cruelties they are exposed to" (1979, 209). That notion of integral "dignity" energizes Cabral's "weapon of theory." As Timothy Luke acutely remarked, Cabral valued the "eman-cipatory forms of collective subjectivity" in the colonized subjects and so promoted "the politically organized and scientifically rationalized *reconstitution* of the traditional African peoples' history-making and culture-building capacities" (1990, 191). In that spirit Cabral urged his activists: "I am asking you to accomplish things on your own initiative because everybody must participate in the struggle" (Chaliand 1969, 68). Neil Lazarus (1999) emphasizes the significance of Cabral's idea of the nation as the privileged site where the universalist thinking of "con-verted" intellectuals blends with popular consciousness, where local knowledge fuses with the principles of national and social revolution. Cabral's originality thus lies in his recognizing that the nation-in-itself immanent in the daily lives of the African peoples can be transformed into a nation-for-itself, this latter concept denoting the peoples' exercise of their historical right of self-determination through the mediation of the national liberation movement, with the PAIGC as an educational organizing force that seeks to articulate the national-popular will.

Fully informed by a knowledge of class/racial oppression in the African continent, Cabral's project concerns the shaping of a nation in the course of the anti-imperialist struggle. Comprised of numerous ethnic groups living apart, highly fragmented by more than a dozen languages, customs, and traditions, Guinea-Bissau and Cape Verde did not fulfill the orthodox qualifications of a nation laid down by Stalin: "a stable community of people formed on the basis of a common lan-guage, territory, economic life and psychological make-up manifested in the common culture" (1973, 68). Cabral's exceptional contribution consists in articulating the nation-in-process (of transition from po-tentiality to actuality) in the struggle against Portuguese colonialism.

The project of the party he founded, the PAIGC, aimed to generate national awareness by mass mobilization of the peasants in conjunction with the petty bourgeoisie, the embryonic proletariat, and the declassed youth. Through skillfull organization and painstaking ideological education, the PAIGC converted the cultural resistance of the tribal villages into a dynamic force capable of defeating a technologically sophisticated enemy.

Cabral's point of departure was the actuality of the balance of political forces in the Portuguese colonies. He confronted the paradoxical phenomenon of the indigenous petty bourgeoisie beginning to acquire a consciousness of totality by their systematic comparison of the various parts of colonized society. He urged this sector to commit class suicide in order to unite with the peasantry (workers then constituted a tiny minority; a national bourgeoisie did not exist), but Cabral had no illusions that such alliances would spontaneously firm up in a postcolonial environment. He stated before his assassination on 20 January 1973: "You know who is capable of taking control of the state apparatus after independence. . . . The African petty bourgeoisie has to be the inheritor of state power, although I wish I could be wrong. The moment national liberation comes and the petty bourgeoisie takes power we enter, or rather return, to history and the internal contradictions break out again" (Davidson 1969, 134). Cabral envisaged the dangers of reifying postcolonial culture as an interstitial space of contestation devoid of any outside from which critique can be formulated. Contradictions persist even in transitory class alliances (the famous unity of opposites in Lenin's discourse), hence the need to calculate the stages of the struggle that demand strategic revisions and tactical alterations, while keeping in mind a constant theme: "The masses keep intact the sense of their individual and collective dignity" (1973, 69). The axiom of uneven and combined development rules out the postcolonial obsession with contingency and incommensurability that prevents collective acts of self-determination. Cabral upheld the antipostcolonial belief of the "supremacy of social life over individual life," of "society as a higher form of life" (1979, 208), which in effect contradicts the neo-Kantian attribution of moral agency to bourgeois individuals, a criterion that "postpositivist realists" (Mohanty 1995) and assorted disciples of postcolonial theory espouse.

No Final Reckoning

Remembering Cabral's example is one way of repairing the damage inflicted by postcolonialist amnesia. Notwithstanding the resurgence of anti-imperialist insurgency in "third-world" neocolonies like Colombia, the Philippines, and Mexico, the moment of the PAIGC and its counterparts (the Nicaraguan Sandinistas, for example) might be deemed irretrievably remote from our present disputes. However, the formerly subjugated peoples of color grudgingly acknowledged by Western humanism (following Kant's axiom of rational autonomy and Adam Smith's notion of the "free market") cannot be pacified simply by ascribing the burden of scarcity to the fluctuating international division of labor. The postcolonial cult of the Leibnizian conceit in which alterity and marginality acquire subversive entitlement has helped contain the principles of national liberation by an aestheticizing maneuver analogous to what Neil Larsen discerned in Cultural Studies: "a subtle transfer of emancipatory aims from the process of objective social transformation to the properly 'cultural' task of intervention in the 'subject'-forming play of discourse(s)" (1995, 201). But as long as capitalism begets polarizing trends in all social formations, there will always exist residual and emergent agencies challenging the reign of "the law of value" and postmodern barbarism (Amin 1998).

We cannot return wholesale to the classic period of national liberation struggles indexed by the names of Cabral, Ho Chi Minh, Che Guevara, Fanon, and others. My purpose in bringing up Cabral is simply to refute the argument that historical-materialist thinking is useless in grasping the complexity of colonialism and its aftermath. Would shifting our emphasis then on studying the subaltern mind remedy the inadequacies and limitations of postcolonial theory? I might interpolate here the view of two Australian scholars, Jon Stratton and Ien Ang, who believe that the limits of the postcolonial/diasporic trajectory can be made up by the voices of the indigenous subalterns within the context of the "relativization of all discursive self/other positionings within the Anglophone cultural studies community" (1996, 386). This intervention in the site of textual-discursive representation is to be welcomed, but the problem of articulating a counterhegemonic strategy focusing on the "weak links" (where the IMF/World Bank's "structural conditional-ities" continue to wreak havoc) remains on the agenda.

Finally, I want to situate postcolonialism as a symptomatic recupera-tion of finance capital, at best the imaginary resolution of contradictions between exploited South and exploiting North, within the altered geo-political alignments of the world-system. Within its epochal time pe-riod, the "third world" was a viable conceptualization of the national-democratic struggles that led to the independence of India, Ghana, the Philippines, Egypt, Indonesia, and other colonized territories after World War II. The radical leaders of these postcolonial states fashioned the Bandung coalition of nonaligned states that gave a semblance of unity to the "third world." However, white supremacy led by the U.S. bourgeoisie during the cold war continued until the challenge in Viet-nam, Cuba, Ghana, and elsewhere. The last expression of "third-world" solidarity, the demand for a "New International Economic Order" staged in the United Nations, came in the wake of the oil crisis of 1973; but the OPEC nations, with their political liabilities, could not lead the "third world" of poor, dependent nations against U.S. realpolitik. Not-withstanding the debacle in Vietnam and the series of armed interven-tions in the Caribbean and elsewhere, U.S. supremacy was maintained throughout the seventies and eighties by economic-cum-military force. This mode of winning consent from the "third world" applied monetar-ist policies that caused lower export earnings and high interest rates, reducing these nations to dependencies of finance capital represented by the IMF/WB and Western/Japanese financial consortia. The defeat of the "third-world" alliance in 1982 allowed the U.S.-led Western bloc to exploit "international civil society" into a campaign against global Keynesianism. From 1984 to the nineties, however, global Reaganom-ics, the instability of the financial markets, the fall of the dollar, worsen-ing U.S. deficit, and so on, mounted a serious challenge to the U.S. maintenance of global hegemony in spite of its military advantage. Despite the success, and somewhat precipitous collapse, of the Asian newly industrializing countries, the "third world" as an independent actor, with its own singular interests and aspirations, has virtually dis-appeared from the world scene. What compensates for this eclipse — such a qualification is required, given the storms brewing in Colombia, Mexico (Chiapas), the Philippines, Palestine, and elsewhere — is postcolonial discourse, with its stress on shifting positionalities, ambivalence, heterogeneity, and so on. With this privileging of contrapuntal flux, hybridity, and fragmentation, the postcolonial critic's sophisticated opposition to finance capital can only serve as a comprador-like vehicle, much like messianic religion, for soothing the anguish of the oppressed and promising a utopia of "cultural compassion" and polyglossic conversations with Butler, Rorty, and their simulated clones. Postcolonialism dovetails with "commodity aesthetics" (Haug 1986) in reinforcing individualist ressentiment and the forces of reification. It helps the system to divide the ruled according to race, ethnicity, gender, sexuality, religion, and so on. Its provenance owes more to finance capital than has been heretofore acknowledged, its counterrevolutionary impulse masked by the carnivalesque regime of simulacra and seductive promises that tries but fails to repress, I daresay, the labor of the "old mole" burrowing underground. This underground labor (explored in the next chapter) proceeds without interruption. For wherever neocolonialism (Woddis 1972) prevails, the ideals and principles of national liberation crafted by "the wretched of the earth" will continue to thrive.

CHAPTER 8

For a Permanent Cultural Revolution

From Raymond Williams to Frantz Fanon

Thus precisely in labor where there seemed to be merely some outsider's mind and ideas involved, the bondsman [slave] becomes aware, through this re-discovery of himself by himself, of having and being a "mind of his own." —G. W. F. Hegel, *The Phenomenology of Spirit*

It is solely by risking life that freedom is obtained. . . . Human reality in-itself-for-itself can be achieved only through conflict and through the risk that conflict implies. . . . How then can one be deaf to that voice rolling down the stage of history: "What matters is not to know the world but to change it"? —Frantz Fanon, *The Wretched of the Earth*

In this epoch of capitalist triumphalism, the last thought on the minds of most arbiters of public taste and opinion would be a radical change in their sensibility or worldview, less a paradigm-shift than a thorough "overhaul" or "brainwashing." The last term easily evokes nightmares of secret-police lobotomy occurring in the Soviet Union or China at the peak of the Cold War. In fact, the dreaded phrase "cultural revolution" is automatically associated with the Great Proletarian Cultural Revolution of 1967–1968 launched by Mao Tse-tung to counter bureaucratic habits and ideological vestiges from China's bourgeois/feudal heritage. What is really meant by "cultural revolution"?

Here is an easy definition from a genteel reference book, Roger Scruton's *A Dictionary of Political Thought*: "Term introduced by Lenin, in a crucial emendation of Marxist revolutionary theory, to indicate the fact and the ideal of a revolution in consciousness which both facilitates and is faciliated by the revolutionary transformation of the social and economic basis of society. Revolution requires the fulfillment of both 'objective conditions' (material transformation), and 'subjective conditions' (the way in which social reality is perceived)" (1982, 109). What is key here is the reconfiguration of subjectivity predicated on the dissolution of "the habits and artifacts of bourgeois culture," the cultural buttresses of the old economic order. While the description alludes to Gramsci's notion of hegemony as a corollary idea foregrounding struggle between cultures, Scruton tends to rarefy the phenomenon and erase the political dimension. In contrast, the *Dictionary of Philosophy* (circa 1980) of Soviet Union academicians shifts emphasis to the matter of agency. Enabled by political and social transformations during a time of radical changes, cultural revolution is a "result of the take-over of power by the people and the transfer of all material and spiritual values into their hands." Fundamental to a cultural revolution, the Soviet authors add, is the reconstruction of the educational system as a prerequisite to "make the best achievements of culture available to the masses, thereby assuring their direct participation in managing economic, social, and political affairs, creating a socialist intelligentsia, and forming a new, socialist culture" (1984, 94).

Both Scruton and the Soviet dictionary assume that revolution involves a cultural supplement without which the process remains truncated or abortive. Questions arise immediately: Where does the old culture end and the new culture begin? When do we know when old habits and values have mutated or been replaced by new ones? If culture is assigned chiefly to the spiritual and psychological domain, how are changes in that domain registered in the public realm? One resource to help us clarify these questions and provide answers is the rich body of reflections on this subject by Raymond Williams, arguably the most provocative originator of Cultural Studies. Before surveying that, I would like to interpose here a gloss on the theme of "cultural revolution" by the most audacious Marxist theoretician of our time, Fredric Jameson.

In his pathbreaking *The Political Unconscious*, Jameson sketched the terminal horizon of a historical-materialist hermeneutic of cultural practice. Graduating from the levels of apprehending the existence of social classes and then of modes of production, we reach the ultimate object of study, *"cultural revolution*, that moment in which the coexistence of various modes of production becomes visibly antagonistic, their contradictions moving to the very center of political, social, and historical life" (1981, 95). Jameson illustrates how every transition from one dominant mode of production to another — how, for instance, the bourgeois cultural revolution entailed the dismantling of values, discourses, habits, and daily space of the ancien regime to allow the emergence of the life-forms and value systems of capitalist market society — epitomizes a vast historical rhythm in which the slow permanent conflicts between various coexisting modes of production in every social formation erupt to the surface of everyday life in the form of such rapid punctual phases of transition.

The task of cultural and social analysis, then, is to rewrite the materials of cultural and literary history in the form of this new "text" or object of study called "cultural revolution" in order that this continuous phenomenon "can be apprehended and read as the deeper and more permanent constitutive structure in which the empirical textual objects know intelligibility" (1981, 97). Jameson believes that this new object of study, the "ideology of form" that embodies a synthesis of varied sign systems coexisting in both a given artistic mode and the relevant social formation, can help establish a new framework for the humanities in which culture can be comprehended on a dialectical-materialist basis. Before applying this insight to Frantz Fanon's seminal views on "national culture" and decolonization, I would like to survey Williams's ideas on the society-culture linkage and its utility in helping to refine the arsenal of historical-materialist cultural praxis.

Lessons from the Borderland

In our generally retrograde milieu, it might be anachronistic to try to resuscitate any interest in what my daughter calls another "dead white male." Williams, now a legendary founding figure (with Richard Hoggart and E. P. Thompson), of the institutionalized thing called Cultural Studies (CS), was certainly white and male and is now physically dead. But it seems that his specter still haunts everyone, including those suspicious and hostile, as is evident in the first biography (1995) of him written by Fred Inglis and in the first American collection of critical

essays on him, *Views Beyond the Border Country*, edited by Dennis
Dworkin and Leslie Roman (1993). In a retrospective assessment, "Cultural Studies and its Theoretical Legacies," Stuart Hall warned of the
profound danger of the institutionalization of Cultural Studies as a discipline replete with protocols and ultimatums. Conceding that questions
of power are always discursive and lodged in representations, he adds,
"Nevertheless, there are ways of constituting power as an easy floating
signifier which just leaves the crude exercise and connections of power
and culture altogether emptied of any signification." This provides a
clue as to why Williams's "cultural materialism" may still be instructive to guard against the postalizing of a still inchoate vocation.

What Perry Anderson calls the "exorbitation" of the sign, the reduction of everything to language games and texts, may be easily cited as
the reason why CS need not frighten anyone today. More fashionable is
Stuart Hall's method of articulation and its reworking by Laclau and
Mouffe into the rhetoric of indeterminacy and contingency that then
serves as dogmatic premises for Bhabha and the postcolonial scribes.
Anyone caught "totalizing" or rehearsing "grand metanarratives" of
Eurocentric vintage can be flunked, denied tenure, ostracized. But the
new conformism that claims to be more radical than anything proves, on
closer examination, to be just an application of the old paradigm of
close New Critical reading — a more sophisticated encoding/decoding
exercise — to shopping malls, television and film, museums, rituals high
and low, and the practices of everyday life. The hermeneutics of Lyotard, Baudrillard, de Certeau, Clifford, and so on is now in vogue.
The "linguistic turn" in the seventies, together with the uncritical appropriation of Althusser, Gramsci, Bakhtin, Saussure, and so on, may
be responsible for the return of formalism in new guises. Could this
have been anticipated if Williams's road of the "long revolution" were
followed?

I want to offer hypothetical answers by way of tracing in a schematic
fashion Williams's trajectory as a theoretician of mutations, discontinuities, and linkages. In his first important work, *Culture and Society*,
Williams reviewed the mainly conservative English tradition of social
thought. The appeal of this work today depends on how one appreciates
its deployment of culture, culture conceived as ideals of perfection
removed from material social life, as a critique of specific large-scale

changes involving industry, democracy, class, and art. In a class-divided society, "culture" was opposed to business, urban massification, and possessive individualism. In his conclusion, Williams diagnosed the ethos of service deriving from a feudal, hierarchical worldview contradistinguished from the ethos of solidarity with roots in the great achievements of working-class culture. The idea of a "common culture" ("common" here signifying full democratic participation and equality, not homogenized uniformity) is based on the unacknowledged but extraordinary creativity of millions of working men and women embodied in the collective democratic institutions of trade unions, cooperatives, and other grassroots resources of self-empowerment.

It is in his major statement of principles, *The Long Revolution*, that Williams attacks head-on the liberal bourgeois tradition (from Locke and Hobbes to the utilitarians) by a new theorizing of culture. Culture is not just "a whole way of life," but the differentiated totality and dynamics of social practices in history. Art and literature cannot be privileged since they are "part of the general process which creates conventions and institutions, through which the meanings that are valued by the community are shared and made active." Williams proposes a relational and processual view of culture that breaks down the confines separating literature, culture, politics, and everyday life in general. He emphasizes connections, dissonance, and interactive negotiations, unfolding the conflicts implicated in patterns of learning and communication:

> Since our way of seeing things is literally our way of living, the process of communication is in fact the process of community: the sharing of common meanings, and thence common activities and purposes; the offering, reception and comparison of new meanings, leading to tensions and achievements of growth and change. . . . If art is part of society, there is no solid whole, outside it, to which, by the form of our question we concede priority. The art is there, as an activity, with the production, the trading, the politics, the raising of families. To study the relations adequately we must study them actively, seeing all activities as particular and contemporary forms of human energy. (1961, 55)

The stress on culture as a constellation of activities, forms of the disposition of human energy, is crucial here. This is meant to resolve the subject-object dualism that plagues the thought of Kant, Weber, and other idealists. It is also designed to mediate the discrepancy between consciousness and the external world that underpins the abstract rationalism and empiricism of bourgeois thought. Generally, Williams approaches culture "as the signifying system through which necessarily (though among other means) a social order is communicated, reproduced, experienced, and explored" (1981, 13). Culture, then, is not solely equivalent to high art, rare artifacts, or stereotyped representations. It encompasses both articulated expression and their experiential matrices, the rich and volatile conjunctures of these polarities.

Williams's strategy seeks to problematize the consensual individualist ethos of late capitalism. His theory of culture is totalizing in that it includes the thinker or observer's presence as reference point in its critical gaze. It concentrates on networks of relationships to "discover the nature of the organization which is the complex of these relationships," the patterns and their interface that reveal unexpected identities and correspondences, discontinuities, dispersals, and so on. Williams's emphasis on pattern and organization — not on "lived experience," as the received opinion alleges — may be explained by his goal of subverting the legitimacy of a "free enterprise" gendered, racialized polity (conceived as a collection of monadic individuals with natural rights) and its market-centered system of beliefs — in short, the structures of reification that Georg Lukács diagnosed in his now classic treatise, *History and Class Consciousness* (1971).

The critic's education presents us with a model of reflexive inquiry. In a 1981 lecture, "Crisis in English Studies," Williams confessed that much of his earlier literary criticism can be read as compatible with the dominant paradigm established by Leavis and later sanctioned by the academy. The break came with his major work, *The Country and the City* (begun in 1965, published in 1973). Not only did he locate certain forms of writing in their historical background — nothing new — but reinscribed them "within an active, conflicting historical process in which the very forms are created by social relations which are sometimes evident and sometimes occluded" (1984, 209). Alongside his pathbreaking work on communications, technologies, and cultural forms, Williams finessed his theoretical stance called "cultural materialism" (not, as some say, "critical realism") that, he asserts, "is the analysis of all forms of signification, including quite centrally writing, within the actual means and conditions of their production" (1984, 210).

In a well-known essay, "Cultural Studies: Two Paradigms" (1980), Stuart Hall labels Williams's theory "culturalism." We are given to understand that its practitioners, Williams and E. P. Thompson, focus their attention on experience and sensuous human praxis. In antithesis, the structuralists (Hall among them) direct their attention to ideology and determinate conditions, the articulation of autonomous spheres of the social field, in order to elucidate the immanent relation between power and knowledge. The term *culturalism* then applies to the analysis of "the production (rather than only the reproduction) of meanings and values by specific social formations, [and his focus] on the centrality of language and communication as formative social forces, and on the complex interaction both of institutions and forms and of social relationships and formal conventions." These preoccupations are manifest in *The Long Revolution*, *Modern Tragedy*, *The English Novel from Dickens to Lawrence*, *Orwell*, and other texts of the sixties and early seventies. The rubric "culturalism" is not only misleading but partial and distorting. In a 1976 essay, Williams designates his approach (more fully elaborated in *Marxism and Literature* and in *Culture*) as consistently materialist, dialectical, and historicizing (not historicist in the sense of epistemological relativism). He upholds "a theory of culture as a (social and material) productive process and of specific practices, of 'arts,' as social uses of material means of production (from language as material 'practical consciousness' to the specific technologies of writing and forms of writing, through to mechanical and electronic communications systems) . . . a theory of the historical variations of cultural process, which then necessarily connects (has to be connected) with a more general social, historical and political theory" (1980, 243–44).

We have now traveled far away from the alleged "whole way of life" definition inferred from the earlier work, far from "culturalism" or an imputed "radical empiricism." As the entry in *Keywords* (1983 edition) indicates, Williams discriminates between the two senses, or more precisely, usages of experience: first, past experience as lessons reflected on, analyzed, and evaluated; and second, present experience as immediate and authentic ground for all reasoning and analysis. Williams inflects his discourse with the contextualizing of "experience" joined with experiment and innovation, full and active awareness, contrasted to "experience" as the product of social conditions or systems of belief, evidence of conditions that need to be tried and tested.

Primacy in the later Williams's thinking is now placed on culture as social and material practices, no longer based on raw, unmediated experience but rather on the given character of processes of production that make up the whole fabric of society. The ensemble of productive processes constitutes the multilayered social totality in motion, with determinations that are orchestrated by varying historical circumstances. Note that cultural practices are not entirely or essentially discursive. Means and values are produced within and by specific social formations, with language and other means of communication as central formative forces. There is thus a complex interaction of institutions, forms, conventions, and intellectual formations in which political and economic questions are deeply imbricated. Now, one might ask, where in this "theory of specificities of material production within historical materialism" — Williams's description — can we encounter and grapple with the reality of power, domination and subordination, and the potential for decisive social transformation?

Right from the start of his engagement with the failure of orthodox British Marxism in *Culture and Society* up to the pivotal 1973 essay, "Base and Superstructure in Marxist Cultural Theory," Williams was concerned with power, that is, with the problematic of determination and causality. This entails the corollary question of intention and ethico-political agency. After disposing of the fetishism of the monadic subject (with the additional help of Lukács and Goldmann's critique of the positivist anatomy of consciousness), Williams grappled with the category of subjectivity within the general framework of a reconstituted historical materialism that he outlines in *Marxism and Literature*.

Gramsci's Intervention

It was partly through the catalyst of E. P. Thompson's criticism in the early sixties that Williams discovered Gramsci and the theory of hegemony. In his review of *The Long Revolution*, Thompson argues that any social totality is inescapably pervaded with conflict between opposed ways of life. Williams agrees. Now he interprets the "base" (in the base/superstructure paradigm of classical Marxism) differently; it is, for him, not a uniform state or a fixed technological mechanism but rather a complex of specific activities and relationships of real people charged with contradictions and variations, in short, a dynamic, open-ended process. Williams conceives of vital productive forces — humans producing and reproducing themselves through sexual relationships, labor, communication; people together making themselves and their history — as basic, not superstructural or epiphenomenal. In an unprecedented way, Williams distinguished the capitalist production of commodities with the general sense of "production of human life and powers," the socialized fashioning of full species-being, as a demarcating principle.

Criticizing Lukács's abstract idea of totality as empty of content and thus formalist, Williams refines his notion of a differentiated totality founded on conflicting social intentions, with class antagonism as the salient node: "For while it is true that any society is a complex whole of such practices, it is also true that any society has a specific organization, a specific structure, and that the principles of this organization and structure can be seen as directly related to certain social intentions, intentions by which we define the society, intentions which in all our experience have been the rule of a particular class" (1980, 36). This intentionality is given exactitude when Williams deploys Gramsci's theory of hegemony. Hegemony refers to the central system of practices, meanings, and values that are experienced as practices and appear reciprocally confirming. Hegemonic rule then translates to our experienced or lived reality invested with a sense of the absolute whereby it induces consent and thus exercises effective dominance over us. It is not an imposed ideology or manipulated set of opinions, as Althusserian and Lacanian versions tend to convey. Hegemony is, in Williams's singular rendering, the "whole body of practices and expectations; our assignments of energy, our ordinary understanding of the nature of man and his world" (1977, 110). It saturates public consciousness as the substance and limit of common sense, the "common sense" of the average citizen presented as majority consensus.

Williams prefers the speculative resourcefulness of Gramci's hegemony to Lukács's totality. One reason is that the concept of hegemony foregrounds the process of domination and subordination as well as the ruptures and dissonance implied in it. Hegemony is a way of integrating the three levels of culture Williams defined in *The Long Revolution*: lived culture of a particular time and place, recorded culture (from art to everyday acts), and culture of the selective tradition. The legitimacy or validity of any tradition depends on its being experienced, that is, incorporated into an effective, dominant culture. Such domination depends on varied mechanisms of incorporation enabled through education and other agencies that Althusser would call "ideological state apparatuses." The concept of hegemony provides the cultural analyst with a more flexible tool for grasping the complex interaction between dominant and alternative meanings, values, dispositions, and so on, as well as the process of incorporation, transmission, and compensatory displacements in the variable sites of education, family, and microsocial transactions. More importantly, it allows us to apprehend oppositional forms and dissident practices that seek to alter the prevailing social and political arrangements.

In analyzing the dynamics of hegemonic rule, Williams complicates his idea of the constitutive social process by recognizing historical variability. Society then is an order constituted by alternative, ascendant, and oppositional forms of meanings and practices (classified as "dominant," "residual," and "emergent") that coexist in specific spatiotemporal arenas of engagement. Domination, like any tradition, is a matter of conscious selection and organization. Agency asserts itself in the shaping of a selective tradition that contends with other sets of discourses and signifying acts. While discourses, representations, or symbolic systems affect agency, it is not identical with them or with their contingent articulations. This is to confuse terms of analysis with terms of substance.

What is the ethico-political consequence of this critical standpoint? Williams suggests the following line of inquiry: hegemony as a strategy of incorporation reveals the extent to which any social formation reaches into the whole range of human practices and experiences. It indicates what is known and what is knowable, given the fact that any dominant order always consciously selects and organizes, thus excluding the full range of actual and possible human practices. Williams offers us an antidote to the pleasures of what Adorno calls the "culture industry" and the seemingly seductive sublimations of Baudrillard's simulacras: "No mode of production, and therefore no dominant society or order of society, and therefore no dominant culture, in reality exhausts the full range of human practice, human energy, human intention" (Williams 1980, 43).

Agency then, creative intentionality, and choice in collective and micropolitical dimensions all operate within what Williams calls "structure of feeling," a heuristic and analytic category for measuring the distance between the actual and the possible. "Structure of feeling" names the dialectic of subject/object that transcends binary opposites, neo-Kantian dualisms, and Nietzschean voluntarism/decisionism. It is operationally linked to the notions of "knowable community" and "complex seeing" that Williams has invented as methodological guidelines to a materialist cultural analysis and program of action.

Toward Cultural Materialism

We can now rehearse the salient themes of Williams's cultural materialism. Its organizing principle can be distilled in the following statement: Williams seeks to avoid the reduction of formalist aesthetics and its postmodernist variants by always insisting on the "restoration of the whole social material process, and specifically of cultural production as social and material." One has to keep in mind the multiplicity of cultural practices embedded in intellectual formations (conscious movements and tendencies), the institutions of distribution and reception, the material means of cultural production, the social character of language, and ultimately the historical "determination" of all these diverse cultural practices. While Williams himself called his analytic method a radical semiotics — his *Keywords* is a protean exercise in historical semantics — he rejects the separation of the "social" from the "aesthetic" found in the poststructuralist fetishism of textuality deriving from a tendentious interpretation of Saussure.

Williams's orientation to signifying practice is thoroughly contextualized in the history of institutions and their corresponding network of habitus: "We can also come to see that a sign-system is itself a specific structure of social relationships: "internally," in that the signs depend on, were formed in, relationships; "externally," in that the system depends on, is formed in, the institutions that activate it (and that are then at once cultural and social and economic institutions); integrally, in that a "sign-system," properly understood, is at once a specific cultural technology and a specific form of practical consciousness: "those apparently diverse elements which are in fact unified in the material social process" (1977, 140). Language is only one of those practices implicated in the symptoms of the crisis of mobile, flexible capitalism. Faced with the ideological mystification of personal lives, Williams stressed the imperative of establishing connections by emphasizing the role of means of communication (he speaks of "productive communication") in shaping community. He opposed the formulas of "vulgar Marxism" (this version reduced culture to a simple reflection of commodity-production-for-profit) and the axioms of positivist structural-functionalism by a radical historicizing of contexts and collectivities. This did not imply a retreat to a romantic nihilism or a glorification of organic Volkgemeinschaft. Nor did he join others in the celebration of high-tech informatization and distance learning. Williams's reconstruction of historical materialism eludes such "commonsensical" reflexes.

Williams returns us to the ineluctable pressures and limits of history, the body, and physical nature in order to calculate determination, the measure of necessity. This illuminates also the differences between the hegemonic and subaltern classes. He does so not to revive mechanical determinism or arbitrary closure but, on the contrary, to recover the principle of intention. He was himself intent on carrying out a cognitive mapping of social agency and direction sedimented in specific traditions and various formations, discoverable through "structures of feeling" and "knowable communities," from a European and later global perspective. His style of doing cs can appreciate both place consciousness and the exigencies of the global imaginary.

One illustration of the attempt to recover and define agency may be found in Williams's adumbration of the "dramatized consciousness" of contemporary society transmitted by television. In "Drama in a Dramatized Society," Williams formulates the key insight that we live in a more complex, "unknowable" society: we live in enclosed rooms today, at home in our lives before the television, but "needing to watch what is happening 'out there': not out there in a particular street or a specific community but in a complex and otherwise unfocused and unfocusable national and international life" (1989b, 8–9). But the flow of experience that television provides, the representations that help make the world intelligible to its viewers, overwhelms even the last defense of privacy with official versions. In Williams's commentary on the 1972 Olympic Games in Munich, we have experience colonized with the coverage of the games as a drama of the conventional politics of nation-states. But this hegemonic version was ruptured by the hostage taking and the subsequent terror that marked the killing of eleven members of the Israeli Olympic Team and six Palestinian guerillas:

> What was shocking at Munich was that the arranged version of what the world is like was invaded by an element of what several parts of the world are actually like. It happened with a certain inevitability, because the act of arranged presentation had created a point of political pressure. . . . Is this [the official Olympic ceremonies] one of the effects of conventional, rule-contained competition: that every moment is a starting-point, with all previous history forgotten? Were there no irregulars of a score of honoured revolutions, no Narodniki, Mau Mau, Stern Gang and a thousand others, before Black September? I knew I could only mourn the 17 dead if I remembered the history which had made them victims: a continuing history, without rules. (1989b, 25)

So television precipitates a rupture but does not offer any memory or sense of responsibility. You need cultural analysis of Williams's kind to respond to a whole complex of experiences obfuscated and mystified by the conventions of television time determined by sports events, commercial advertising, and apologetic "common sense."

In another television transcribing of events, this time of the Malvinas/Falkland War, Williams apprehends motives in the media culture of distance that enables the institutions of constitutional authoritarianism to dominate. The television distancing of war, an unnecessary one, was made possible by a bureaucratic culture that had already distanced mass unemployment: "The cynical culture of late capitalism, which had used a national flag for underwear or for carrier bags, switched, as it seemed overnight, to an honorific fetishism which at the same time, though in different colours, was on the streets in Buenos Aires. . . . The sinking of a ship shocks and grieves, but is then sealed over by the dominant mood. . . . The larger argument that now needs to be started, with a patience determined by its urgency, is about the culture of distance, the latent culture of alienation, within which men and women are reduced to models, figures and the quick cry in the throat" (1989b, 19–21). Professional management of events, the distant calculating of actual experience of battles and deaths, the sanitized abstractions — these are all connected to the class and imperial system that thrives on reification and abstracted knowledge.

Anticipating the Mass Line

What are the stakes and risks of Williams's ambitious project? From *Culture and Society* (1958) to *Communications* (1962) and *Television: Technology and Culture Form* (1974) to *The Country and the City* (1973) and *Writing and Society* (1981), Williams's quest was unequivocal: the democratization of culture through mass participation in political decisions and the broadest access to education and the resources of communication. In a 1958 essay, "Culture Is Ordinary," as well as in *The Long Revolution*, Williams destroyed the rationale for the hierarchical segmentation of culture into high, middle, and mass/popular. What is ordinary about culture is its ubiquity: every society engages in finding common meanings and directions, growing through "active debate and amendment under the pressures of experience, contact, and discovery." Aside from meanings shared by all, culture also includes the arts and learning, "the special processes of discovery and creative effort" that conjoin deep personal meanings and common purpose. The task of the politically committed intellectual is to release the creative energies of millions embedded in the following values, namely, "that the ordinary people should govern; that culture and education are ordinary; that there are no masses to save, to capture, or to direct, but rather this crowded people in the course of an extraordinary rapid and confusing expansion of their lives. A writer's job is with individual meanings, and with making these meanings common. I find these meanings in the expansion, there along the journey where the necessary changes are writing themselves into the land, and where the language changes but the voice is the same" (1989c, 18).

Now this democratizing agenda has earned censure from Stuart Hall, Paul Gilroy, and others as "narrow exclusive nationalism," as perversely ethnocentric. I think this is based on a misunderstanding of Williams's idea of "a common culture." In the 1968 essay on that theme, Williams endorses the Marxist insight that in a class-divided society, "culture would have an inevitable class content and class bearing, and that in the historical development of a society, a culture will necessarily change as relations between men and classes change" (1989c, 33–34). Williams insists that culture is not the property of a privileged minority; meanings and values comprising a particular form of life arise from the common experience and activities of all. But the possibility of articulating and communicating those meanings and values are limited by the nature of the educational system, the control of work, and the private ownership of communication. The possible "community of culture" or the "community's self-realization" is limited by the class divisions of the given society compounded by racial and gender oppression.

Consequently, Williams states that he was using "the idea of the common element of the culture — its community — as a way of criticizing" the capitalist arrangement of society: "A common culture is not the general extension of what a minority mean and believe, but the creation of a condition in which the people as a whole participate in the articulation of meanings and values, and in the consequent decisions between this meaning and that, this value and that" (1989c, 36). In this vision of a society where a "mutual determination" of meanings and values takes place, Williams anticipates the risks that "common culture" may imply standardization, uniformity, mandating one standard, leveling down, in short, mediocrity, repression, and conformity.

Williams's project of an "educated and participating democracy" is so far from ethnocentrism and exclusive nationalism that it is worth quoting his credal proposition: "The idea of a common culture is in no sense the idea of a simply consenting, and certainly not of a merely conforming, society. One returns, once more, to the original emphasis of a common determination of meanings by all the people, acting sometimes as individuals, sometimes as groups, in a process which has no particular end, and which can never be supposed at any time to have finally realized itself, to have become complete. . . . In speaking of a common culture, one is asking, precisely, for that free, contributive and common process of participation in the creation of meanings and values" (1989c, 37–38). This principle of a genuinely participatory democracy underlying Williams's theory of culture allowed him to be particularly sensitive to new developments in his time such as the rise of the women's movement, racist or xenophobic reactions to the demands of ethnic communities for recognition, and ecological issues. Unless one performs a willful misreading of his substantial corpus of writings, Williams, the inaugural thinker of the New Left, cannot so easily be charged for class-reductionism and other kinds of deterministic super-stitions that he strove to identify and oppose throughout his life.

Williams's prescience also engaged with problems in the sphere of social reproduction. Long before the advent of feminism, he had al-ready stressed one of the four interlocking systems within any society as vital and necessary: "the system of generation and nurture." As Terry Eagleton remarks, Williams's novels explored the questions of family, gender, and women's work in a much more penetrating way than his criticism, although he did expose the destructiveness of male hege-mony, "the disabling notion of masculinity," in appraising the works of women novelists in *The English Novel from Dickens to Lawrence*. Wil-liams confessed, however, that other critics were better equipped to elaborate on the "repression of women's experience" in criticism than he was. He welcomed the militant women's liberation movement from the late sixties onward. He insisted, however, on contextualizing the ideological reduction of sex to consumption: "Now the contradiction of contemporary social changes has been that the unfinished attempt to liberate women and children from the traditional controls of extreme deprivation and from the reproduction of brutality within the family has itself become complicated, as every human liberation is within the capi-talist order, by imperatives which are a product of the system itself" (1979, 148–49). He also observed that "it is scarcely possible to doubt the absolute centrality of human reproduction and nurture and the un-questioned physicality of it" (1979, 147).

Locating Disenchantment

On the matter of the postmodern celebration of plurality and difference, the now notorious "politics of identity," Williams was one of the first CS pioneers who fully appreciated the affective force of place, of local bonds of place, nation, religion, and so on. He welcomed the "new social movements" involving transclass causes such as nuclear disarmament, ecology, women's liberation, and other biopolitical quality-of-life issues. Despite the retreat of many radicals to either neoliberalism or business-as-usual pragmatism, Williams adhered to the key Marxist argument that exploitation continually reproduces class consciousness and organization on a universal basis.

From the beginning, however, Williams knew that the universalization of class bonds would not be automatic and inevitably supersede other affiliations and loyalties. He grasped the dialectics of local/global long before journalists seized on the "globalization" potlatch: "I recognize the universal forms which spring from this fundamental exploitation — the system, for all its local variety, is everywhere recognizable. But the practice of fighting against it has always been entered into, or sometimes deflected by, these other kinds of more particular bonds" (1989c, 318). These affective bonds inhabit spaces-turned-into-places that Williams has configured in his social history of art forms, especially in how "the common experiences" of colonized natives with their "alienating screens of foreignness and race" are mediated through the "New Metropolis" of the imperialist system and its vicissitudes charted in *The Country and the City*.

In that book, Williams discusses how the slave trade and the exploitation of the subjugated natives in the colonies generated the idea of England as "home" and sustained the pastoral myths of country-house life. Dialectically, the sense of belonging of retired colonial businessmen and officers arose from the dispossession and deracination of slaves in the plantations and the labor of people of color in general. Williams's method of formational analysis can detect how the attractive rural mode of play in the English countryside rests on the misery and privations of the indigenous inhabitants of Africa, Asia, and Latin America. Williams appreciates the rise of new conventions in the novel (as the citations of Achebe, Wilson Harris, and other writers from India, Africa, and Asia testify) as a response to new needs and demands, with the colonial hinterland registering its presence in the effects on the sensibilities and rhythms of everyday life in the metropolis. In effect, the subaltern speaks through a rich cultural repertoire of refusal, adaptation, and resistance, with their own authentic affiliations and solidarities.

Empire is then both a literal referent and symbolic figure in Williams's discourse on war, ecology, and North-South relations in *The*

Year 2000 and his late essays on modernism and variable socialisms. Robin Blackburn reminds us that Williams grew up in a border community where farmers, agricultural laborers, teachers, preachers, and railway workers mixed. In his youth he worked in campaigns of solidarity with China and Spain; his internationalism, grounded on local attachments and personal experience in World War II, shaped his assent to popular revolts in the third world against landlord-military rule and imperialism. He recognized the tragedy and suffering in these revolutions, but he urged that we "follow the whole action: not only the evil, but the men who have fought against evil; not only the crisis but the energy released by it, the spirit learned in it" (1979, 83). For more than three decades, Williams was active in the Vietnam Solidarity Campaign, the Campaign for Nuclear Disarmament, and various coalitions against British military power responsible for the Western subjugation of people of color and their struggles for self-determination.

In a 1984 interview in *Politics and Letters*, Williams distinguishes between the reactionary nationalism of the Labour Party based on a unitary British state, and the progressive nationalism of oppressed peoples (Welsh, Scots, Irish) in colonized and other subjugated territories. Williams exposes the United Kingdom centralized nation-state as based on a spurious "English middle-class universality." He denounces the oligarchic, discriminatory character of political representation within the United Kingdom. To counter this repressive status quo, locality and other vital affiliations need to be mobilized in forging a new decentralized socialist politics that recognizes bonding mechanisms beyond national or class consciousness: "Place has been shown to be a crucial element in the bonding process — more so perhaps for the working class than the capital-owning classes — by the explosion of the international economy and the destructive effects of deindustrialization upon old communities. When capital has moved on, the importance of place is more clearly revealed" (1989c, 242). Ethnic identity, like Welsh culture, is a complex and ongoing synthesis of place, collective or popular memory, language, and meanings being fashioned from daily struggles. That insight nourishes the arguments of Williams's essays on "Welsh Culture" (1975) and "The Social Significance of 1926" (1977).

However, it must be pointed out that Williams's conception of place has nothing to do with blood-and-soil communitarianism. He invokes the women's movement as an example of popular constituencies allying together on concretely elaborated programs of action. Instead of the Labor Party's "metropolitan provincialism," Williams envisions communities of purpose grappling not just with economic goals but with the larger condition of women and families, collectivities generated from popular mobilizations in part triggered by the need for the self-definition of groups and peoples long disenfranchised and rendered anonymous by uneven capitalist development.

At this point, especially with *The Year 2000*, Williams breaks new ground. He attempts to supersede the received model between country and city as part of the spatial division of capitalist production by calling for a "new politics of equitable livelihood" within the larger framework of variable socialisms around the planet. CS now needs to include the care for the environment since pivotal social and political questions turn around the fate of nature and its interface with commercial civilization. His ecological agenda is not one-dimensional but rather dialectical, oriented to "the idea of 'livelihood' within, and yet active within, a better understood physical world and all truly necessary physical processes" (1989c, 237). In "Socialism and Ecology," Williams criticizes the orthodox Marxist attitude of mastering nature, unreservedly exhausting the nonrenewable resources for commodity production, since this instrumentalist drive of expansion is precisely the rationale of imperialism. This obsession with the conquest of nature accompanies present-day glorification of the consumption/acquisition ideal and the persistence of patriarchy. Remember that we are ourselves part of nature so that maximized and intensified production by itself will not solve poverty, alienation, and other attendant disasters. And, Williams adds, there are real material limits not derived from sociohistorical necessity.

Here the temptation is to offer individual or family solutions, the preferred attitude today, or else the appeals for sanity are addressed to the present leaders of the advanced industrial states that, in the first place, have caused the devastation. Any kind of planning for sustainable growth requires an alteration of the way production and distribution are organized, of the priorities between different forms of production; the precondition for that is fundamental changes in the social and economic institutions, in particular how political decisions are made. This applies more urgently in the international arena where the struggles over the supply and price of oil, among other commodities, determine not only the world economy but also political relations between states, including the certainty of conventional and nuclear wars mainly against formerly colonized countries where the scarce resources are found. Ultimately, ecology as the problem of resources — what Williams calls "the pressure point on the whole existing capitalist mode of production" — is a question of worldwide inequalities, a question of war or peace among nation-states. It is above all a question of the standard of life, of the overcoming of racism and the "chauvinism of the old rich countries" slandering "the leaders and movements of the poor countries who are striving to redress these major and unforgivable inequalities" (1989c, 225). It concerns the goal of promoting "actual self-governing societies."

Trajectories Unraveled

Toward the end of his life, Williams delivered two lectures, one on the "uses of cultural theory" and the other on the "future of cultural studies" vis-à-vis the neoconservative resurgence in European politics. Such theoretical extrapolations from his personal engagement with the politics of cultural revolution reveal an intellect always endeavoring to match the scope of theory with the abundant richness of practice in lived experience.

Reflecting on CS's serviceability, Williams reminds us that culture as a realized signifying system is imbricated in a whole range of activities, relations, and institutions of everyday life. Cultural theory needs to be examined within concrete social and historical situations, as the Bakhtin Circle proposed. Williams underscores the need for specificity (versus the formalist analysis of autonomous elements of art and the generalized application of social categories to cultural production), the need to explore the relations among diverse and specific human activities "within describably whole historical situations which are also, as practice, changing and, in the present, changeable" (1989c, 164). Formalism (whether New Critical, structuralist, poststructuralist, and so on) is inadequate because it cannot grasp how different arts change, how this change indexes a dynamic historical process, one involving "a distinct

307

historical practice, by real agents, in complex relations with others, both diverse and varying, agents and practices." Forms need to be historicized and intentionalities socialized.

For Williams, the introduction of Gramsci's concept of hegemony and the role of intellectuals in grassroots mobilization advanced and deepened the reach of cultural theory. Culture now becomes the site of power antagonisms and differential lines of force. It is at this junction that Williams resumes the actual genealogy of CS from the debate over the "changing and contested structure of public education" and the influence of the new media (television, film) that was drastically revising "all received definitions of majority or popular cultural enterprise." The influence of Saussure, Freud, and others who valorized the text and the language-paradigm above all strikes Williams as damaging in that it negated the necessary task of an all-sided cultural analysis, namely, "the identification of the matrix of any formation . . . the analysis of specific relationships through which works are made and move." Cultural Studies examines the socially and historically specifiable agency of the work's making, "an agency that has to include both content and intention, in relative degrees of determinacy, yet is only fully available as agency in both its internal (textual) and social and historical (in the full sense, formal) specificities" (1989c, 172). For this task, Williams recommends Bakhtin's concept of the artwork as indissociable from the multivalence of social language with its complex range of agencies and intentions — analytic, interpretive, creative, and emancipatory.

Cultural Studies is engaged not just with particular works or texts but with institutions and formations of intellectuals (in the broad sense). And this requires historical and structural analysis to determine purposes, intentions, and consequences. This is where Williams grapples with ideology and the problematic of determination. An instructive exhibit here is his commentary on "Advertising: The Magic System" (originally part of *The Long Revolution* but published separately). Williams analyzes advertising, the official art of modern capitalist society, as a form of communication shaped by converging social, economic, and cultural forces. Advertising, for Williams, is a cultural pattern that responds to the need for objects to "be validated, if only in fantasy, by association with social and personal meanings" that are not directly available or easily discoverable in the routines of ordinary life. This system of magical inducements and satisfactions is a market mechanism that, in the service of profit making, functionally obscures the choice that humans ought to make between being a consumer and being a user. Within a system where only a minority makes the major social decisions, consumption — humans as consumers — is offered as the "commanding social purpose." But many social needs (for hospitals, schools, quiet) cannot be answered by the consumer ideal because consumption is always an individual activity.

A critique of the totality (production/reproduction nexus) would endow CS with the rudiments of a social conscience. To satisfy the range of basic social needs, Williams insists, we need to question "the autonomy of the economic system, in its actual setting of priorities." The consumption ideal is fostered by advertising. Advertising "operates to preserve the consumption ideal from the criticism inexorably made of it by experience" (1980, 188). The magical aura of advertising conceals the real sources of satisfaction for human needs because, according to Williams, "their discovery would involve radical change in the whole common way of life." Advertising is a symptom of "the social failure to find means of public information and decision over a wide range of economic life." Williams particularizes this failure in the fact that the dominant values and meanings do not give any answers or means of negotiating the problems of death, loneliness, frustration, the need for identity and love and respect, so that what advertising as organized fantasy does is to bind "the weakness to the condition which has created it." This analysis of advertising as a form of communication that now deeply contaminates political propaganda and the formation of public opinion leads to a deliberate critique: the contradiction of capitalism (between controlling minority and widely "expectant" majority) is what demands resolution if this ideology is to be broken. Williams's critique aims to mobilize the ethical will and political agency of everyone for reasoned initiatives and collective intervention.

This central idea of agency subtends Williams's mature version of CS. The most decisive strategy in cultural analysis, he writes, lies in "the exploration and specification of distinguishable cultural formations" for which he devised the concepts of "structure of feeling" (a heuristic category mediating lived experience with articulated ideas and institutions), complex seeing, knowable communities, emergent/residual/

dominant tendencies, and so on. We discover agency as we describe significant relations in movement, in tension and contraction with major institutions; "the extending and interpenetrating activity of artistic forms and actual or desired social relations." A specifying formal analysis combines with a generalizing social-empirical analysis to yield practicable knowledge: "It is the steady discovery of genuine formations which are simultaneously artistic forms and social locations, with all the properly cultural evidence of identification and presentation, local stance and organization, intention and interrelation with others, moving as evidently in one direction — the actual works — as in the other: the specific response to the society" (1989c, 175). Williams reaffirms the vocation of cultural analysis: the understanding of an intellectual or artistic project in the context of its formation. Project and formation are, to him, "different ways of materializing ... of describing, what is in fact a common disposition of energy and direction" (1989c, 151). Process, structure, direction: these three key elements of the project interact to chart the research trajectory of CS.

The future of CS, for Williams, is intimately connected to the uses of theory he surveyed. It is connected to a particular reading of the nature of our contemporary situation. The intent of cultural studies cannot be divorced from the crisis of the late-bourgeois world, one of whose symptoms is the habit of distance enforced by the consumption ideal. At no time in history has the need for representation and identification been so demanding as in our dramatized and spectatorial milieu (Williams's version of Guy Debord's "society of the spectacle"). One response to the overall crisis is Williams's choice of formulating a definition of drama as an intricate set of practices that include incorporated rhythms of residual systems and exploratory rhythms of emergent identifications. In his 1974 inaugural lecture as professor of drama, Williams presents a theory of drama that can stand as an allegory for the "structure of feeling" that prefigures crisis as rupture, metamorphosis, renewal, change. It can serve as a model for what exactly CS is trying to accomplish in divergent contexts:

> Drama is a special kind of use of quite general processes of presentation, representation, signification. . . . Drama is a precise separation of certain common modes for new and specific ends. It is neither ritual

which discloses the God, nor myth which requires and sustains repetition. It is specific, active, interactive composition: an action not an act; an open practice that has been deliberately abstracted from temporary practical or magical ends; a complex opening of ritual to public and variable action; a moving beyond myth to dramatic versions of myth and history. . . . The drama of any period, including our own, is an intricate set of practices of which some are incorporated — the known rhythms and movements of a residual but still active system — and some are exploratory — the difficult rhythms and movements of an emergent representation, rearrangement, new identification. (1984, 15–16)

This "active variable experimental drama" appears in periods of crisis and change, when a given social order is tested by experience, unfolding breaks, alternatives, possibilities. Commenting on Rudolf Bahro's notion of "surplus consciousness," Williams syncopated his sense of drama with Brecht's "complex seeing" to produce the subjunctive mode of cultural analysis that is Williams's unique contribution.

Viewed from the subjunctive, not pejoratively utopian, angle, the project of cs is in principle not only oppositional but liberatory. It is to bring to as many people as possible "that dimension of human and social knowledge and critical possibility" denied to them by a world of market priorities and bureaucratic abstractions. In the light of that goal, the pedagogy of cs is shaped "by the acceptance and the possibility of broader common relationships, in a shared search for emancipation" from the alienating world of capitalist production to what Williams calls the "new orientation of livelihood: of practical, self-managing, self-renewing societies, in which people care first for each other, in a living world." In short, cs aims to promote genuine democracy in which "the systems of production and communication are rooted in the satisfaction of human needs and the development of human capacities."

I want to sum up Williams's most substantial and enduring contributions to cs as a developing field of political and intellectual concern regularly contoured by historical pressures and exigencies, by intellectual disputes and sociopolitical events:

1. The idea of culture as social processes and practices that are thoroughly grounded in material social relations — in the systems of main-

tenance (economics), decision (politics), learning and communication (culture), generation and nurture (the domain of social reproduction) — must be the controlling principle of any progressive and emancipatory program of action.

2. The historicizing of all cultural practices and processes stems from a need to grasp the the ideology and politics of class-divided societies in late capitalism, a fact that also illuminates North-South inequalities, ecological imbalances, and racial-ethnic conflicts that are the precipitating condition of wars. Cultural Studies needs to inquire into the nature, function, and future of the integral state (government plus civil society).

3. The consumptive/consumerist paradigm of capitalism and the inequalities across ethnicity, race, gender, sexuality, religion, and locality that it reproduces should be criticized by a platform based on the imperative of solidarity. Cultural Studies qualifies and counterpoints the relations of power, property, and production with activities of describing, learning, exchanging, and preserving experiences.

4. The project of cs is the production of practicable knowledge that will advance a participatory democratic interaction of diverse communities with their specific historical experiences, a goal achieved through the extension of public education and public control and access to all means of communication. Since the processes of learning and communication are integral to cs, Williams conceives of the "long" cultural revolution as committed to a radical transformation of society that will promote these values: "that [humans] should grow in capacity and power to direct their own lives — by creating democratic institutions, by bringing new sources of energy to human work, and by extending the expression and exchange of experience on which understanding depends" (1962, 125–26).

5. The importance of agency and intention. Cultural Studies matters most crucially in making its subject the arena for serious engagement with all the vital issues besetting us. We really have no choice if it is a question of nuclear war or pollution of the water we drink and the air we breathe. Resignation, neutral contemplation, and retrospective sympathy are precisely what Williams fought against throughout his life. But, of course, in any revolutionary transformation, there are always risks in negotiating constraints and pressures. Nevertheless, there are opportunities

to be seized. The intervention of CS then is "to make hope practical, rather than despair convincing" — to make the cultural revolution a permanent happening. Williams's prospectus about the larger vision and calling of CS, a topic for collective exchange and personal meditation, may be gleaned from this memorable testimony of his convictions:

> We are living through a long revolution that is simultaneously and in connected ways economic, political, and cultural and that transform people and institutions in the process of extending the transformations of nature, the forms of democratic self-governance, and the modes of education and communication. Uneven and conflicted as this process may be, enhancing its development is the main criterion of intellectual, moral and political value. . . . I believe that the system of meanings and values which a capitalist society has generated has to be defeated in general and in detail by the most sustained kinds of intellectual and educational work. . . . The task of a successful socialist movement will be one of feeling and imagination quite as much as one of fact and organization. . . . We have to learn and to teach each other the connections between a political and economic formation, a cultural and educational formation, and, perhaps hardest of all, the formations of feeling and relationship which are our immediate resources in any struggle. (1989a, 76)

Facing Emergencies

Williams's overriding stress on making connections in the context of popular democratic struggles is salutary. It corrects the objectivist determinism and subjectivist psychologizing by prefiguring the process of cultural revolution as a dialectic of modes of production operating on several levels: individual and class, social formations, ideological synthesis of overlapping stages in history. Williams's stress on formations parallels Fredric Jameson's endeavor to systematize the levels of meaning and, by extension, the diverse interpretive communities and collectivities whose fates are implicated in making sense of cultural expression. Both Williams and Jameson are responding to the destruction of culture by the capitalist reduction of cultural values and products into commodities, what Lukács in his seminal essay "The Old Culture and the New Cuture" bewailed as "the domination of the economy over the totality of life" (1973, 12), which distinguishes the singularity of bourgeois social relations. The aim of revolutionary cultural critique, then, is to expose this domination, analyze its mechanisms, and mobilize all the necessary forces to destroy the conditions that enslave people to the economy, to the system of commodity exchange.

Confronted by the crisis of bourgeois hegemony in the sixties, the French philosopher Henri Lefebvre theorized everyday life, quotidian experience, as the new site of radical transformation. The last chapter of his seminal book, *Everyday Life in the Modern World*, presents a blueprint of the progression toward "a permanent cultural revolution." Lefebvre reiterates Lukács's call for the abolition of the market and its laws so that we can "subordinate the mastery of nature to man's adaptation of his own natural and social being" (1971, 195). By discarding this concept of adaptation, radical thought has succumbed to economism where the regimentation of industrial production supersedes everything, and to utopian leftism where the law of exchange-value is transcended by pure voluntarism heedless of objective determinations. In both cases, subject and object, consciousness and the concrete environment, remained polarized and unmediated.

The alienation of everyday life, the "social territory" of controlled consumption and terror-enforced passivity," in late-modern capitalism is Lefebvre's principal object of diagnosis. He believes that this category of quotidian life has supervened over economics as the outcome of a generalized class strategy whereby "creative activity is replaced by contemplative passivity," a disposition characterized by "the voracious consumption of signs, displays, products and even works of art" (1971, 196–97). To conduct a wide-ranging revolutionary offensive, Lefebvre urges the renewal of a totalizing praxis that should distinguish the three planes of the economic, political, and cultural in their interconnections and relative autonomy. While the economic plane concerns the planned growth of industrial production to satisfy social needs, the political aspect deals with "the decay of the state" and its possible transformation. State power alone, however, cannot resolve the contradictions of progress, so it is necessary to focus our appraisal on the cultural dimension since this has acquired a massive efficacy in the context of urban reality.

Reconaissance

The perennial question resurfaces: What is to be done? Lefebvre reminds us of Lenin's recognition of the desideratum of the ideological transformation of the proletariat in the face of socialist construction in an underdeveloped milieu, especially in the aftermath of World War I and global counterrevolution. Socialism, after all, is built on the ruins and selected achievements of bourgeois and precapitalist formations. While science and rationality as well as techniques of administration are necessary for managing the state, Lefebvre also warns against the "limited rationalism of bureaucracy" and of positivist technocratic ideology, including moralism and aestheticism, and the dogmatism associated with them as part of a generalized terrorism — "the bureaucratic society of controlled consumption" — in bourgeois dispensations. A revolutionary cultural strategy opposes conformism to the status quo and calls for the transfiguration of everyday life, renewing in the process the search for a resolution of the tensions between theory and practice, basis and superstructure, knowledge and strategic action.

Lefebvre's task is double-edged: obstacles have to be cleared before the foundations are laid. After addressing the twin problems of positivist compulsion and anarchic mystification that have derailed progressive movements, Lefebvre reaffirms the need for total revolution: "One of the first and most essential conditions for the realization of a cultural revolution is that the concepts of art, creation, freedom, adaptation, style, experience, values, human being, be restored and reacquire their full significance; but such a condition can only be fulfilled after a ruthless criticism of productivist ideology, economic rationalism and economism, as well as of such myths and pseudo-concepts as participation, integration and creativity, including their practical application, has been performed" (1971, 199). Creation, Lefebvre explains, is not restricted to aesthetics; it signifies "the activity of a collectivity assuming the responsibility of its own social function and destiny — in other words for *self-administration*" (1971, 204), adapting — note Lefebvre's use of the term to link opposites — self-consciousness to the parameters of reality: body, desire, time, space. What is envisioned is a materialist hermeneutic of form already broached by Jameson and condensed here in the rediscovery of the Festival, the emblem of a reintegrated humanity freed from the tyranny of commodity-fetishism.

Instead of pursuing further Lefebvre's own fertile thought-experiments, especially in his speculations on the production of space, the city, and utopia, I would like to articulate his concept of adaptation (contraposed to the concepts of mastery and instrumental practice) with Frantz Fanon's theme of decolonization that animates an innovatively controversial allegory of national liberation.

The theory of national liberation was first systematically expounded by Lenin in his post–1914 speeches, in particular "The Socialist Revolution and the Right of Nations to Self-Determination, Theses" (April 1916), and the "Theses on the National and Colonial Questions" presented to the 1920 Second Congress of the Communist International. Lenin's originality cannot be overexaggerated. I concur with Kevin Anderson's considered opinion that Lenin was the first important Marxist thinker in the early twentieth century to grasp the emergence of a new revolutionary subject, national liberation movements "as the dialectical opposite brought onto the historic stage by the new stage of imperialism and monopoly" (1995, 144). Founded on Marx's principle of uneven development of capital around the world, Lenin's idea of national liberation movements as a form of revolutionary subjectivity follows from his analysis of imperialism and its concomitant internationalist ideal of revolution as a worldwide process. Imperialist economics harbors within itself its political contradiction: national liberation movements. In discussing the situation in Ireland, Lenin conceived of social revolution in which the salient participants are not only the industrial working class but also the peasants in the colonies whose revolts against the reactionary landlord class act as "one of the ferments" helping the socialist proletariat to make its appearance. This dialectical method of coalescing the particular and the universal informs Lenin's thought on self-determination and national-democratic revolutions in the colonies:

> While the proletariat of the advanced countries is overthrowing the bourgeoisie and repelling its attempts at counter-revolution, the undeveloped and oppressed nations do not just wait, do not cease to exist, do not disappear. . . . The social revolution can come only in the form

of an epoch in which are combined civil war by the proletariat against the bourgeoisie in the advanced countries and a whole series of democratic and revolutionary movements, including the national liberation movement, in the undeveloped, backward and oppressed nations. Why? Because capitalism develops unevenly, and objective reality gives us highly developed capitalist nations side by side with a number of economically slightly developed or totally undeveloped nations. (1960, 4)

Approaching the "national question" historically, in the epoch of imperialism, the revolt of the masses (chiefly peasants and the middle strata of petty-bourgeois intellectuals) in the colonies against imperialism and its local allies, Lenin hailed these revolts as contributing factors to the success of socialism everywhere, even where the struggle ended in failure — as in the Dublin 1916 uprising, in which the socialist leader James Connolly died for the cause of national liberation (Kiernan 1983). In this connection, the distinguished Marxist thinker Ernest Mandel counseled the international working-class movement that it is their duty "to give unconditional support to every movement and every effective mass action in the colonial and semi-colonial countries against the exploitation and oppression to which they are subjected by the imperialist powers. . . . Wars of national liberation . . . , independent of the political force which leads the oppressed people at any particular stage of the struggle, are just wars" (1979, 74).

This is the moment to reassess Fanon's own singular narrative of cultural revolution reinscribed in the all-embracing plot of national liberation. What is the "structure of feeling" embodied in this plot? Of late, while Fanon has been experiencing a postmodernist revival of sorts signaled by the appearance of several thick anthologies and new editions of his works, his thought has suffered mummification, if not perversion, via postcolonial aggrandizement. Typical of the latter is Homi Bhabha's transmogrification of Fanon's historicizing project in *Black Skin, White Masks.* In the frequently reprinted essay "Remembering Fanon: Self, Psyche and the Colonial Condition," Bhabha attempts a synthesis of Fanon's historionic yet incisive reflections on the identity of the black, specifically Antillean, people in a situation of colonial subjugation. Bhabha converts Fanon into a supreme ironist who purveys "transgressive and transitional truth" from the "uncertain interstices of historical change, from the area of ambivalence between race and sexuality" (1994b, 113). Fanon then becomes a slippery thinker who gives us no warrant for grasping the state "as a homogeneous philosophical or representational unity" and who encourages us to think of the "social" as "always an unresolved ensemble of antagonistic interlocution between positions of power and poverty, knowledge and oppression, history and fantasy, surveillance and subversion" (1994b, 122). If the concepts of the state and the social are so diffuse, enigmatic, and difficult to apprehend, then how can any kind of political strategy be crafted and implemented? What agents and forces should we unite and mobilize for cultural critique and action? Bhabha illegimitately ascribes to Fanon a hypostatization of the stage of the "Unhappy Consciousness" in Hegel's phenomenology, while occluding the initiative of the bondsman whose labor has *always already* undermined the lord's stability. Before any serious criticism of Eurocentric psychoanalysis (such as the texts of O. Mannoni) can be undertaken, we are already crippled by what Bhabha calls Fanon's "problematic of difference."

To reread *Black Skin, White Masks* without Bhabha's filtering optic is to experience a shock of recognition. Indeed, the whole thrust of Fanon's pedagogical agenda is to resist the temptation of irony and antinomies. Right in the introduction, he reveals his overarching purpose of attaining "a new humanism" by resituating the individual in

> the universality inherent in the human condition. . . . It will be seen that the black man's alienation is not an individual question. Beside phylogeny and ontogeny stands sociogeny.
>
> Reality, for once, requires a total understanding. On the objective level as on the subjective level, a solution has to be supplied. . . .
>
> The architecture of this work is rooted in the temporal. Every human problem must be considered from the standpoint of time. Ideally, the present will always contribute to the building of the future.
>
> And this future is not the future of the cosmos but rather the future of my century, my country, my existence. . . . I belong irreducibly to my time. And it is for my own time that I should live. (1967, 12–13)

In dealing with intertwined problems of sexuality, blackness, linguistic alienation, and the putative "dependency complex" of colonized peoples, Fanon's mind inveterately seeks the historically specific and concrete determinants of any existential situation. The influence of Hegel and Sartre cannot be erased. Fanon's reflections on freedom throughout the book demonstrate the power of dialectical thought to grasp the unity of contradictions, the transformation of elements into their opposite, and the imbrication of such contradictory elements and forces in historically defined stages of social systems with intricately sutured, varying modes of production. Ambivalence and irony become transitory phenomena in the law-governed play of contradictions.

Subterranean Mutations

In this appreciation of Fanon as a historical-materialist intelligence, I think we can recover elements of a theory of cultural revolution relevant to a CS project first initiated by Williams. We are thus far removed from the vacillating world of Bhabha and from the cynicism of Cold War commentators who see in Fanon the paralysis of a Manichean cosmos awaiting deliverance by a utopian-messianic judgment from somewhere. Edward Said's efforts to sketch an analogy among certain motifs in the writings of Fanon, Lukács, and Adorno is praiseworthy insofar as they underscore affinities of dialectical thought in all three; but the non-synchrony of their historical circumstances — even though both Lukács and Fanon address the phenomenon of reification and class struggle in their distinctive modalities — only reveal how each thinker cannot be divorced from their historically imposed projects and their personally chosen missions. Traveling intellectuals have no doubt historically specific trajectories, origins, and destinations.

The postmodernist aim of inventing a deconstructive reading of Fanon is a tactic of distraction, at worst an alibi for disingenuous apologetics. Fanon is used to attack socialism (in its British or European variant) for ignoring racism. Using the weapons of Otherness, essentializing identity and ambivalence ferreted out of Fanon's texts, postcolonial scholars substitute for anti-imperialist revolution a cosmopolitanism "against the grain." Caught in the old dualistic metaphysics, these expropriators of Fanon's thought cannot discern its heretical originality and versatility, as evinced in this conclusion to "On National Culture," in which Fanon envisages national liberation as the staging ground for building a universal non-Eurocentric humanist culture:

If man is known by his acts, then he will say that the most urgent thing today for the intellectual is to build up his nation. If this building up is true, that is to say if it interprets the manifest will of the people and reveals the eager African peoples, then the building of a nation is of necessity accompanied by the discovery and encouragement of universalizing values. Far from keeping aloof from other nations, therefore, it is national liberation which leads the nation to play its part on the stage of history. It is at the heart of national consciousness that international consciousness lives and grows. And this two-fold emerging is ultimately only the source of all culture. (1968, 247–48)

Three points need to be emphasized in Fanon's theory of national liberation expounded in *The Wretched of the Earth*: first, the decisive role played by the intellectual as organic "tribune of the people" (to use Lenin's phrase) whose task is to synthesize and direct the energies of the subaltern masses; second, the national-popular character of the "nation" as reflective of a coalition of diverse social forces (peasantry, intelligentsia, national bourgeoisie, declassed elements, and so on) united by a political program of overthrowing colonial rule; and third, the planetary vision of national liberation as an indivisible part of world socialist revolution designed to end imperialism, the late-modern phase of global capitalism. Founded on mobilizing the participation of the broad masses across class, gender, and sexuality, Fanon's antiracist humanism is the direct antithesis of the metropole's "civilizing mission" and its instrumental racism.

Fanon's answer to the existential question, "What does the black want?" impels him to a formidable "sociogenic critique of traditional ontology" and "European Reason" (Gordon 1999, 49). In reappraising Fanon's conceptualization of the interaction between class and nation, we need to keep in mind the cardinal axiom of dialectics. This inheres in the interpenetration of opposites and their mediations within a differentiated totality evolving within concrete historical parameters. Both voluntarist contingency and mechanical fatalism, however nuanced and sophisticated, constitute isolated moments of the dialectic whose import derives from the whole. According to Lenin, "The basis of the Marxist dialectic is that all limits in nature and in history are simultaneously determinate and mutable, and that there is *not a single* phenomenon which, under certain conditions, cannot be transformed into its opposite" (Lenin 1980, 12). Fanon's violence, apprehended as a tactic of national liberation, undergoes the rigors of this materialist dialectic. Negativity is immanent with constructive impulses. Decolonization "transforms spectators crushed with their inessentiality into privileged actors, with the grandiose glare of history's floodlights upon them. . . . Decolonization is the veritable creation of new men. But this creation owes nothing of its legitimacy to any supernatural power; the 'thing' which has been colonized becomes man during the same process by which it frees itself" (1968, 36–37). This newness, however, is neither wholly purged of the residual traits of the obsolescent archaic tributary social formation, nor freed from the dominant Manicheanism of colonial rule.

Throughout the discourse on violence, we note a pronounced tendency in Fanon to accent the unifying power of national liberation. He stresses its capacity to bring about a solid coherent community of fighters, to remove a heterogeneity founded on individualism. If there is a trace of nativist nostalgia for communal institutions whose myths and rituals sublimate the energies of the people, this impulse is harnessed to revitalizing the masses' cooperative traditions paralyzed by Manichean inertia. Fanon writes, "The immobility to which the native is condemned can only be called in question if the native decides to put an end to the history of colonization — the history of pillage — and to bring into existence the history of the nation — the history of decolonization" (1968, 51). Decolonizing violence is precisely addressed to the mystifying paralysis of colonialism. Violence has no political significance unless it is contextualized in concrete historical acts and agents with explicit political objectives. Thus, the organized violence of the masses "has all the less reason for disappearing since the reconstruction of the nation continues within the framework of cutthroat competition between capitalism and socialism."

Fanon's paramount concern is the establishment of the conditions for the education of the nation-people toward a democratic, egalitarian polity. There is no basis for anyone to label Fanon a naive nationalist. In the chapters entitled "Spontaneity: Its Strength and Weakness" and "The Pitfalls of National Consciousness," he is fully aware of the dangers of neocolonialism, the substitution of the African national bourgeoisie for the colonial bourgeoisie as the new tyrants. Organized mass struggles led by committed intellectuals are precisely designed to guard against this eventuality. Against postcolonial detractors, Neil Lazarus (1999) has perspicuously delineated the anatomy of Fanon's didactic partisan who coincides with Amilcar Cabral's responsible activists. Perhaps Fanon has overestimated the educational value of armed struggle and underestimated the legacy of colonial dehumanization:

> Even if the armed struggle has been symbolic and the nation is demobilized through a rapid movement of decolonization, the people have the time to see that the liberation has been the business of each and all and that the leader has no special merit. . . . When the people have taken violent part in the national liberation they will allow no one to set themselves up as "liberators." . . . Yesterday they were completely irresponsible; today they mean to understand everything and make all decisions. Illuminated by violence, the consciousness of the people rebels against any pacification. From now on the demagogues, the opportunists, and the magicians have a difficult task. The action which has thrown them into a hand-to-hand struggle confers upon the masses a voracious taste for the concrete. The attempt at mystification becomes, in the long run, practically impossible. (1968, 94–95)

The "voracious taste for the concrete," alas, was not sufficient to guard against populist dictators and military juntas inheriting the posts vacated by the French, British, and other European suzerains. Reality exceeds the grasp of even the most fanatical partisan of freedom.

National liberation exhibits all the complex "structure of feeling" that Williams imputes to any social movement in history, saturated with the contradictions originating from the tensions among residual, dominant, and emergent modes of production. Fanon recognized this when he estimated accurately the revolutionary potential of the proletariat in colonial Algeria and intuited the subversive élan of the peasantry, the intelligentsia, and the declassed elements. In "Critical Remarks on the National Question" (1913), Lenin pointed to the coexistence of contradictory values and attitudes in any "national culture." From this viewpoint, Fanon is correct in his class analysis of the concrete alignments of forces that can be mobilized for the phase of the national-democratic struggle, with his populist nationalism qualified by his heightened sensitivity to the racial/sexual oppression of all Africans. Moreover, Fanon transcended European philosophy (Sartre, Merleau-Ponty) by valorizing the "racial-epidermal schema" as the matrix of the racial imaginary underlying classical ontology and the phenomenological embodiment of difference (Weate 2001) found in current speculations on the body and desire.

There is no doubt that Fanon knew the inadequacy of populism as the antithesis of bureaucratic commandism, hence his obsessive focus on the function of intellectuals as revolutionary militants. Since Fanon is cognizant of the liability of spontaneous voluntarism, he assigns heavy responsibility to the educational program of the leadership, its skill in connecting tactics with strategy, means with ends: "The task of bringing the people to maturity will be made easier by the thoroughness of the organization and by the high intellectual level of its leaders. The force of intellect increases and becomes more elaborate as the struggle goes on. . . . Each local ebb of the tide will be used to review the question from the standpoint of *all* villages and of *all* political networks" (1968, 146). The political maturity of the masses is measured in its recognition of the "rational basis" of the rebellion whose politics — national, revolutionary, and social — are facts "which the native will now come to know exist only in action." Nigel Gibson (1999) and Tony Martin (1999) have skillfully elucidated Fanon's creative application of Marxist dialectics to calibrate the nexus between spontaneity and organization as the movement fashions the historical protagonist of national liberation. The transformation of popular consciousness in collective, informed action against colonial barbarism is what Fanon privileges, not violence per se.

Nation as Force Field

In the fashionable discourse of postmodernists, nation and nationalism are made complicit with the conduct of Western colonialism and imperialism. They become anathema to deconstructionists hostile to any revolutionary project in the "third world" inspired by emancipatory goals. This is the reason why postcolonial critics have a difficult time dealing with Fanon and his engagement with decolonizing violence as a strategic response of subjugated peoples to the inhumane violence of colonial

323

racism and imperial subjugation. Fanon's conceptualization of a national culture is the direct antithesis to any culturalist syndrome, in fact an antidote to it, because he emphasizes the organic integration of cultural action with a systematic program of subverting colonialism: "A national culture is the whole body of efforts made by a people in the sphere of thought to describe, justify and praise the action through which that people has created itself and keeps itself in existence" (1968, 155). Discourse and power are articulated by Fanon in the dialectics of practice inscribed in the specific historical conditions of their effectivity. Fanon's universalist-critical theory of national liberation proves itself a true "concrete universal" in that it incorporates via a dialectical sublation the richness of the particulars embodied in the Algerian revolution.

Given his historicizing method, Fanon refuses any demarcation of culture from politics and economics. Liberation is always tied to the question of property relations, the social division of labor, and the process of social reproduction — all these transvalued by the imperative of the revolutionary transformation of colonial relations. Opposed to Fanon's denunciation of "abstract populism," Said and Bhabha fetishize an abstract "people" on liminal, borderline spaces. Such recuperation of colonial hegemony via a "third space" or contrapuntal passage of negotiation reveals the comprador character of postcolonial theories of translation and cultural exchange. Transcultural syncretism devised to abolish the nation substitutes for anti-imperialist revolution a pragmatic modus vivendi of opportunist compromises.

An analogous charge can be leveled at Edward Said's reading of Fanon's "liberationist" critique. Said locates violence in nationalist movements (unless it is "critical") since they deny the heterogeneity of precolonial societies by romanticizing the past. For Said, a liberationist populism is preferable to nativism and the fanatical cult of "minor differences." Said presents us a hypothetical dilemma: "Fanon's notion was that unless national consciousness at its moment of success was somehow changed into social consciousness, the future would not hold liberation but an extension of imperialism" (1993, 323). Said thus posits a spurious antithesis between the project of national self-determination and a vague notion of social liberation. For Said, nationalism is always a tool of the hegemonic oppressor and holds no socially emancipatory potential. Said's answer evacuates Fanon's popular-democratic nationalism of all social content, postulating an entirely abstract divide between a nationalist program and a socially radical one. For Said, the violence of anticolonial movements becomes symptomatic of a profound colonial malaise.

National liberation and social justice via class struggle are interdependent. As Leopoldo Marmora observes, "While classes, in order to become predominant, have to constitute themselves as national classes, the nation arises from class struggle" (1984, 113). The populardemocratic aspiration for self-determination contains both national and social dimensions. In "On Violence," Fanon invoked the ideal of decolonizing freedom as the legitimizing rationale of mass popular revolution. It is force deployed to accomplish the political agenda of overthrowing colonial domination and bourgeois property relations. Violence here becomes intelligible as an expression of subaltern agency and its creative potential. Its meaning is crystallized in the will of the collective agent, in the movement of seizing the historical moment to realize the human potential (Lukács 2000). If rights are violated and the violence of the violator (for example, the state) held responsible, can the concept of rights be associated with peoples and their national identities? Or is the authority of the state to exercise violence derived from the nation/people? Here we need to ascertain the distinction between the state as an instrument of class interest and the nation/people as the matrix of sovereignty. The authority of the state as regulative juridical organ and administrative apparatus with a monopoly of coercive force derives from its historical origin in enforcing bourgeois rights of freedom and equality against the absolutist monarchy. National identity is used by the state to legitimize its actions within a delimited territory, to insure mobilization and coordination of policy (Held 1992). Formally structured as a *Rechststaat*, the bourgeois nation-state functions to insure the self-reproduction of capital through market forces and the continuous commodification of labor power (Jessop 1982). Fanon understands that national liberation challenges the global conditions guaranteeing valorization and realization of capital, conditions in which the internationalization and nationalization of the circuits of capital are enforced by hegemonic nation-states.

We are thus faced with the notion of structural violence attached to the bourgeois state as opposed to the intentionalist mode of violence as an expression of subject/agency such as the collectivity of the people. Violence is thus inscribed in the dialectic of identity and Otherness, with the bourgeois state's coherence depending on the subordination (if not consent) of workers and other subalterns.

Exorcising Corporeal Maledictions

Revolutionary praxis (the overthrow of the colonial order) worthy of the name is not just a matter of deceptive misrecognition of the subaltern voice. It is an educational project of transformation, a process of reciprocal learning between the masses and their chosen leaders. National liberation belongs to the genre of cultural revolution. It designates a process of transformation in which the rudimentary elements of democratic and socialist culture of the working masses are nurtured to resist the dominant "national culture" of the settler colonizers who rule by force/suasion and through the collaboration of the entrenched landlord class, the clergy, and the local bourgeoisie. Of course, this process pursues a zigzag line, with mistakes and setbacks, depending on the international alignment of forces; but the goal of participatory democracy and conquest of a people's dignity are what validate and make intelligible the whole undertaking.

What has hitherto been neglected in Fanon studies is the failure to specify the historically specific mode of mediation between the evolving nation-people and the vanguard leadership, the moment of hegemony (the exception is Sekyi-Otu 1996). Perhaps Fanon has elided the question in his desire to conflate the national aspect with the continental (African) drive of decolonization. He deploys the Guinean poet Keita Fodeba's art to allegorize the predicament of embattled African communities, their wrestling with the historicity of pain and desire. We can observe his calculated maneuver to conjugate the territorial sphere of the nation with the hemispheric totality of the African continent in such passages:

> The responsibility of the native man of culture is not a responsibility vis-à-vis his national culture, but a global responsibility with regard to the totality of the nation, whose culture merely, after all, represents one aspect of that nation. The cultured native should not concern himself

with choosing the level on which he wishes to fight or the sector where he decides to give battle for his nation. To fight for national culture means in the first place to fight for the liberation of the nation, that material keystone which makes the building of a culture possible. . . . A national culture is not a folklore, nor an abstract populism that believes it can discover the people's true nature. It is not made up of the inert dregs of gratuitous actions, that is to say actions which are less and less attached to the ever-present reality of the people. A national culture is the whole body of efforts made by a people in the sphere of thought to describe, justify, and praise the action through which that people has created itself and keeps itself in existence. A national culture in under-developed countries should therefore take its place at the very heart of the struggle for freedom which these countries are carrying on. . . .

National consciousness, which is not nationalism, is the only thing that will give us an international dimension. The problem of national consciousness and of national culture takes on in Africa a special dimension. . . . The responsibility of the African as regards national culture is also a responsibility with regard to African Negro culture. This joint responsibility is not the fact of a metaphysical principle but the awareness of a simple rule which wills that every independent nation in an Africa where colonialism is still entrenched is an encircled nation, a nation which is fragile and in permanent danger. (1968, 232–33, 247)

We know of course that Fanon carried out diplomatic missions for the Algerian FLN (Front de Liberation Nationale) in which building solidarity with other African nation-states was his main charge; see his contributions to the FLN organ, *El Moudjahid*, for example, "Unity and Effective Solidarity Are the Conditions for African Liberation" (January 5, 1960). The influential essay "On National Culture" was delivered to an international Congress of Black Writers and Artists in Rome in 1959, which Fanon attended as part of the Antilles delegation even while working as an FLN militant. Before he died in 1961, he was aware of the "new ratio of forces on an international scale" (Hansen 1999). But in addition to this pressure we need to clarify the missing link between nation and race, namely, class consciousness distilled through a counterhegemonic strategy.

It seems to me that Fanon's dilemma stems from discursively performing an unmediated leap to the utopian level of the hemispheric "new man" shorn of the residues or vestiges of the old. A certain prophetic impatience accents his premature subsumption of the territorially demarcated nation into the hemispheric or continental domain of the struggle. While Fanon is careful to advise us that "there can be no two cultures which are completely identical," he immediately qualifies that with the statement: "No one can truly wish for the spread of African culture if he does not give practical support to the creation of the conditions necessary for the existence of that culture; in other words, to the liberation of the whole continent" (1968, 234–35). Fanon's historical materialism anchors him to determinate locations (what Williams calls "cultural formations"): "Negritude therefore finds its first limitation in the phenomena which take account of the formation of the historical character of men. . . . Every culture is first and foremost national" (1968, 216). But how is the national also at the same time continental or hemispheric? The totality that subsumes both is European racism.

Race consciousness has certainly eclipsed class consciousness in the Manichean world of African settler colonies. This is because the division of labor and property relations are starkly marked: exploited natives have been racialized, with the categories of race and class dissolving into each other. Omitting the dialectical mediation between the national/popular sphere in which the intellectual acquires organic purposiveness and the continental arena in which racism and racializing ideology holds unchallenged ascendancy, Fanon downgrades the class question as pivotal to the composition of the vanguard leadership and the orchestration of short-range and maximum goals of the national-democratic revolution. Or, to put it another way, I think Fanon was convinced that the "pitfalls of national consciousness" can be remedied by universalizing the Algerian quest for national autonomy into a continental African social if not socialist revolution. But unfortunately such a move sacrifices concrete uniqueness into an abstract indeterminate totality, something like a "bad infinite" bedeviling a Hegelian "unhappy consciousness."

One can easily impute this elision of the class question in Fanon's discourse to the urgency of the demands for unity across classes in the mobilization against racialized colonial brutality. This is not to say that

Fanon was unaware of class antagonisms pervading the diverse modes of production fused in the colonial social formation. But what is the internal linkage between class and race? Bertell Ollman suggests that "though racial and sexual differences obviously existed before the onset of class society, it is only with the division between those who produce wealth and those who direct its production that these differences become the basis of the distinctive forms of oppression associated with racism and patriarchy" (1993, 30). Racism and sexism are thus modalities in which class oppression manifests itself with peculiarities contingent on specific times and places. If I may venture a hypothesis: the primacy of the rhetorical/polemical attention to racism, that is, to the colonial ideology of racial subordination of the whole African continent, preoccupied Fanon to the point where the substantive analysis of uneven development of capitalism was intermittently overshadowed. Fanon understood that the liberation of one national territory was not enough to eliminate a European racism shrouding the whole continent. The intellectual priority to combat racism became a pragmatic necessity. In short, cultural revolution, which for Fanon is equivalent to the struggle for freedom and the material conditions necessary to live in dignity, in one territorially bounded nation-state such as Algeria or Senegal will not suffice to get rid of a hemispheric evil. Cultural revolution — see Fanon's references to Dien Bien Phu, Madagascar, the Korean and Indo-Chinese wars — must be continental, if not global, embracing not only Africa but the Caribbean, Asia, and Latin America as well.

Cultural revolution in Fanonian discourse is a species of national liberation. It incorporates the antagonisms of incompatible modes of production that Jameson construed as the deep subtext of all narratives of revolutionary social transformation. It embraces Lefebvre's idea of adaptation of nature and society to human species-needs as well as Lukács's attack on the commodified and reifying "culture" of late capitalism. For Fanon, the Manichean apparatus of segregation and immobility operated not only in urban compartmentalization but also in the "dispersed" Algerian family described in *A Dying Colonialism* (1965). National liberation particularizes Williams's heuristic concept of "structure of feeling" that orchestrates lived experience with institutions and traditions. Fanon's idea of cultural revolution opens the space for resistances, transgressions, and challenges to the power/knowledge Leviathan of consumerism, "commodity aesthetics" (Haug 2000), and pluralist co-optation in the global arena.

Fanon adds something new, something missing from previous historical-materialist perspectives I have surveyed here. While Fanon's "subject-object dialectic" locates its center of gravity in the germination of the organic revolutionary intellectual-militant, the historic agency for national liberation, its novelty lies in taking account of a new pattern of racism that infects "the social constellation, the cultural whole." The key text here is Fanon's "Racism and Culture" (1967b; see San Juan 1999c). Lewis R. Gordon (1997) has already given us a trenchant interpretation of Fanon's critique of ontological racism. My argument here is that the critique of racism needs to be framed by the theory of national liberation. Against the foundational principle that culture is by definition a dynamic structure, "permeated by spontaneous, generous, fertile lines of force," Fanon sketches a narrative of decolonization — the matrix of emancipatory plots and subplots elaborated in *The Wretched of the Earth* — that culminates in protracted cultural revolution whose denouement is a concrete universality, a point of departure arising from "this decision to recognize and accept the reciprocal relativism of different cultures, once the colonial status is irreversibly excluded" (1967b, 44). In his unrelenting critique of the ideology of racism, the encounter with the colonial and neocolonial legitimation crisis, Fanon demonstrates the mediated articulation of the categories of class, nation, gender, and race that we need today in confronting the hierarchization of cultural differences — a postcolonial regime — in the globalized marketplace.

Afterword

> If the way that I have shown to lead to this seems to be very arduous, yet it
> can be discovered. And indeed it must be arduous, since it is found so
> rarely. For how could it happen that, if salvation were ready at hand and
> could be found without great labor, it is neglected by almost all? But all
> excellent things are as difficult as they are rare.
> — Benedict de Spinoza, *Ethics*

With the end of the Cold War and the globalization of a "free-market"
regime, a new "cultural war" has erupted in the United States, an
ideological-political conflict symptomatic of the organic crisis of capitalism as a historical stage of sociality and human development. I
am not alluding here to Samuel Huntington's "war of civilizations,"
the replacement of class struggle with the clash between the Islamic/
Confucian axis and a monolithic Western dispensation. If by "culture"
we mean the "public, standardized values of a community that mediate
the experience of individuals" (Douglas 1966, 39), the war involves
antagonistic sets of norms, values, and beliefs expressed in institutional
and discursive systems open to differing critiques and interpretations.
The existing maps of meaning that make the world intelligible, maps
objectified in patterns of social organization and relationship, are being
discarded, reinvented, and reassessed in the interminable search for
order in a chaotic interregnum. In any case, history has certainly not
ended with the demise of archaic utopias and the triumph of the free-
market neoliberal gospel.

What has flared up is the long-buried antagonism between different
worldviews and frames of knowledge-production. In scholastic circles,
we observe the confrontation of two irreconcilable positions: one that

claims the priority of a "common culture," call it liberal or civic nationalism, as the foundation for the solidarity of citizens; and another that regards racism or a racializing logic as inherent in the sociopolitical constitution of the United States, a historical *episteme* undercutting the universalizing rhetoric of its proclaimed democratic ideals and principles (Perea 1998). Attempts to mediate the dispute, whether through the artifice of a "multicultural nationalism" or a postethnic cosmopolitanism (Hollinger 1998), have only muddled the precise distinctions laid out by the various protagonists. Multiculturalism, inflected in terms of cultural literacy, canon revision, the debate between Eurocentrism versus Afrocentrism, and other issues reviewed in the previous chapters, has become the major site of philosophical contestation. It has become a field of power in which the exercise of symbolic violence (Bourdieu and Wacquant 1992) preempts the functioning of communicative rationality and supplements the coercive surveillance of citizen-subjects.

Redeeming the Unread

A drive toward uniform standards informs the goal of Establishment thinkers who want to mediate contradictory paradigms in the "culture wars." The literary critic E. D. Hirsch gained a certain notoriety by producing his *Dictionary of Cultural Literacy* (1993) premised on the notion of a common knowledge of certain items as a necessary requisite for a "truly functional literacy." According to Hirsch, the hegemonic national language and culture on which "the unity and effectiveness" of the nation-state depends needs to be transmitted in the schools to insure "national communication" among a diverse population divided by ethnicity, party affiliation, generation, locality, and so on. This communication among "strangers," Hirsch argues, repudiates conventional interpretations and induces us to acquiesce to an avowedly conservative, traditional curriculum: "We help people in the underclass rise economically by teaching them how to communicate effectively beyond a narrow social sphere, and that can only be accomplished by teaching them shared, traditional literate culture. Thus the inherent conservatism of literacy leads to an unavoidable paradox: the social goals of liberalism require educational conservatism. We only make social and economic progress by teaching everyone to read and communicate, which means teaching myths and facts that are predominantly traditional" (1993, xv). Certain assumptions underlying Hirsch's plea for conservatism — that the existence of the underclass is caused by illiteracy, that reading/ communication skills require canonical material — expose their hidden logic when Hirsch attacks multicultural antielitists as elitist themselves; having enjoyed a traditional education themselves, these "self-appointed protectors of minority cultures" are guilty of condemning disadvantaged minorities to illiteracy.

What is at stake is the imperative to regulate citizens' conduct by policing their minds and sanitizing their sentiments. Hirsch then concludes by asserting that the debate is less ideological and more empirical or pragmatic, hence the debate over multiculturalism should be replaced with a statistical test of utility concerning multicultural versus conservative pedagogy. In short, what would be more efficacious as an instrument in sustaining the status quo? Hirsch opines that "ideological partisanship on the subject of national literacy is more empirical than ideological." And since the major ideological commitment to universal literacy has already been made, what is left now for us to examine is "reality," not "ideology." Hirsch thus implicitly accuses those who construe "reality" deviantly as engaging in "ideological" debate, hence his circular argument that reality is nothing but the hierarchical order of race and class we inhabit.

We are witnessing not just another local retrograde trend confined to the United States. The current controversy over multiculturalism as political doctrine or pedagogical stance has moved beyond national borders in line with the explosion of ethnic and racially motivated conflicts in Europe, Africa, and around the world. Take the observations of popularizer Alvin Toffler in *Powershift* (1990). Toffler calls attention to the contemporary resurgence of identity politics accompanied with xenophobia and new varieties of racist violence worldwide. But for Toffler this is an ineluctable result of new information technologies and the predominance of knowledge/power complexes that we have no means of controlling. Meanwhile, reactionary publicists like Dinesh D'Souza continue to attack exponents of cultural pluralism and Boasian cultural relativism for trying to destroy Western civilization. Reacting to the vogue of multicultural education, proponents of a neoconservative American Studies discipline decry intellectuals of color for being divisive, subjective, and covertly anti-American. The liberal expert Peter Rose could not help recapitulating Arthur Schlesinger Jr.'s attack against tribal separatists apotheosizing ethnicity and against particularists who romanticize their own group and demonize others, thus allowing "pluribus" to overrule the "unum" (1997, 250). In contrast to Rose's subsumption of diversity in nationhood, Henry Giroux calls for a "democratic pluralization of cultural identities" to rectify an illusory dissolution of class, and in the process recover the knowledge (absent or suppressed) that the American national identity has been constructed "within the unequal distribution of resources" (1996b, 200–1). Multiculturalism may just be a euphemism for imperial white supremacy.

Crossing the Barricades

Certain questions epitomize the pros and cons of the debate on multiculturalism in the ongoing "Culture Wars" which I rehearsed in chapters 4 and 5. Allow me to recapitulate the nodal points of contention in the following queries:.Is the question of ethnic difference, the politics of identity, reducible to the celebration of cultural diversity? How does a group claim to be distinctive and different? Can the expression of cultural difference be tolerated as long as it pays deference to the prior claims of civic nationalism? Does the notion of citizenship premised on the universalizing discourse of individualism resolve inequalities of class, gender, and race? If ethnicity is not primordial (as Clifford Geertz contends) but rather a strategic choice (as John Rex and others argue), will reforms of the now obsolescent "welfare state" curtail institutional racism and racist violence? With the demise of liberal programs of amelioration and safety nets, will "ethnicity" still function as before by legitimizing stratification and inequality as a result of disparate cultural norms and folkways?

In almost every occasion, we encounter the belief that the present culture wars will persist because we don't share a "common culture" — shared values, symbols, and rituals that inform the "imagined national community." Communalism is then presented as an alternative to the atomistic and competitive liberalism of "rights." The magic word *community* compensates for the lack of organic cohesion or authentically shared values among heterogeneous groups. A clarification should be interpolated here. The doctrine of a need for a shared value system or dominant ideology to legitimize the social order originates from Talcott Parson's misreading of Durkheim's notion of "collective consciousness" (Featherstone 1991). Such collective consciousness is embodied in culture defined as "an historically created system of explicit and implicit designs for living, which tends to be shared by all or specially designated members of a group at a specified point in time" (Kluckhohn and Kelley 1945, 98). Community and commonality thus need to be historicized and their distribution of power and resources fully articulated.

Given these time-space coordinates of "designs for living," it is untenable to posit a homogeneous culture dominating a complex society. Instead of fixing on the abstract and large cultural configuration at play in any society, we should conceive of historically specific cultures that stand to one another in relations of domination and subordination, in struggle with one another. One might recall that Raymond Williams once suggested that we construe any social formation as comprised of stratified layers of dominant, residual, and emergent cultures in varying degrees of tension with one another. The authors of the influential book *Resistance Through Rituals* proposed an analogous approach: "We must move at once to the determining relationships of domination and subordination in which these configurations stand; to the processes of incorporation and resistance which define the cultural dialectic between them; and to the institutions which transmit and reproduce 'the culture' (i.e. the dominant culture) in its dominant or hegemonic form" (1976, 12–13).

A historical-materialist frame of interpretation may enable us to appreciate what is involved in the struggle over classification and delimitation of social space and the fields of power. In a polity (such as the United States) configured by a long history of divisions along class, gender, race, nationality, and locality, the claim that there is a single moral consensus, "habits of the heart," or communitas can only be a claim for the ascendancy of a particular ruling group. And it is around the moral-intellectual leadership of a social bloc, which translates into effective hegemony, that hierarchy and stratification, along with the norms and rules that constitute canons and disciplinary regimes, become legitimized. This is also the locus of struggle over who defines the nation, authorizes the criteria of citizenship, and sanctions violence.

335

Liberal pluralism and its variants obfuscate this hegemonic process conducted via wars of position and maneuver. Establishment pluralism exalts diversity, multiple identities, as "a condition of human existence rather than as the effect of an enunciation of difference that constitutes hierarchies and asymmetries of power" (Scott 1992, 14). From this pluralist perspective, group differences and discrete ethnic identities are cognized in a static categorizing grid; that is to say, they are not examined relationally or dialectically as, in Joan Scott's words, "interconnected structures or systems created through repreated processes of the enunciation of difference" (1992, 17). Cultural pluralism then legitimates and reinforces the status quo of differential power based on asymmetrical positioning in social space and on unequal property relations.

Viewed from this angle, the "common culture" interpellates individuals and articulates them in a commonality of monadic identities. Instead of a composite identity overdetermined by manifold lines of interests and affiliations, one acquires an identity defined by this shared heritage with its naturalized closure and its exclusivist fiat. Implicit here is the constitutive role of the market, specifically the buying and selling of labor as commodity, which guarantees and is predicated on individual rights, the foundation of bourgeois civil law and procedural liberty. Thus, if the "common culture" of Hirsch, Schlesinger, and others is affirmed by the status quo in education, workplace, family, and other institutional matrices of subjectivity, then there will be no room for encountering, much less recognizing, the dignity and integrity of uncommon texts, expressive practices, and deviant expressions of people of color within and outside the North American continent. This is so given the fact that, to paraphrase George Lipsitz's (1998) thesis, the racial polity's ruinous pathology in the "possessive investment in whiteness" perpetuates the absence of mutuality, responsibility, and justice. We should then disabuse ourselves that there is equality of cultures and genuine toleration of differences in a class/race/gender-polarized society. No doubt, culture wars (both of position and maneuver) will continue until the present hegemonic order is transformed and antagonisms sublated to another level where a more democratic resolution can be realized.

Alternative views and dissenting arguments are available. In his book *Ethnocriticism* (1992), for example, Arnold Krupat pleads for a Bakhtinian mode of deconstructing all dichotomized paradigms of us/them, all Manichean engines of Othering. He endorses Bakhtin's view that cultures, like languages, are never pure or monolithic but heteroglossic and polyvocal; our speech and by extension our designs for living are never entirely and exclusively our own. All cultures inhabit the borderland between ourselves and the others. Thus a genuinely multicultural studies would, in Krupat's words, engage "the other in such a way as to provoke an interrogation of and a challenge to what we take as ours" (1992, 237). The Others then assume the roles of the selves that we have denied and repressed to be what we are.

While sympathetic to such a view, in my article "Problematizing Multiculturalism and the 'Common Culture'" (1994; also in San Juan 1995), I expressed reservations about the possible co-optative and compromising effect of the liberal brand of "multiculturalism" commodified by the globalized marketplace. Its answer to inequalities of power and privilege is to add and relativize Others' modalities of interaction without altering the underlying hierarchy of status and class. This pragmatic species of multiculturalism, color-blind and gender-blind, elides the actual differences in systemic power relations immanent in the lived experiences of communities, peoples, and nations. In fact it apologizes for the institutionalized racism, sexism, heterosexism, and overall class exploitation that prevail, sanctioned by the instrumentalities of government and the realpolitik of international agencies.

One can of course discriminate among varieties of "multiculturalisms" — from conservative to liberal, left-liberal, critical, or resistance multiculturalism (see Goldberg 1994). It is not the best polemical strategy to reduce the wide spectrum of positions to the usual binary or Manichean formula. Nor is it judicious to multiply positions in a permanent state of deferment, flux, or "suspension of disbelief." Nonetheless, the "politics of difference" and identity operating in the United States reifies "superstructural" differences into almost intractable social and political disjunctions, rendering dialogue and communication among groups impossible.

Confronting this quandary, we need to return to our point of departure: the historicity of the racial polity and the dialectics of race and class. Hazel Carby warns us that "because the politics of difference work with concepts of diversity rather than structures of dominance, race is a marginalized concept" (1990, 85) replaced by ethnic pluralism. Instead of revealing the structures of power at work in the racialization of a social order, "a social formation structured in dominance by the politics of race," academic multiculturalism fosters ethnic separatisms among the oppressed in the guise of celebrating the virtues of every ethnic group and culture. As Carby elaborates:

> By insisting that "culture" denotes antagonistic relations of domination and subordination, this perspective undermines the pluralistic notion of compatibility inherent in multiculturalism, the idea of a homogeneous national culture (innocent of class or gender differences) into which other equally generalized Caribbean or Asian cultures can be integrated. The paradigm of multiculturalism actually excludes the concept of dominant and subordinate cultures — either indigenous or migrant — and fails to recognize that the existence of racism relates to the possession and exercise of politico-economic control and authority and also to forms of resistance to the power of dominant social groups. (quoted in San Juan 1992, 128–29)

In effect, an integrative liberal version of multiculturalism can celebrate (in order to fossilize) differences within an imagined national community. Cultural autonomy may hide or ignore structural inequalities under the umbrella of a refurbished "humanitarian" civilization. Multiculturalism thus legitimizes pluralist stratification, exploitation, and oppression in the process of capital accumulation here and worldwide (Davis 1996; Appelbaum 1996). One recent comment by a British sociologist offers the always timely caveat that informing the logic of the formation of Western multiculturalism is "the political irreducibility of racialization" (Hesse 1997, 377).

Illusions of Transparency

At this point I want to comment on a typical scholastic diagnosis of the malaise afflicting metropolitan societies on the verge of falling down the fabled multicultural abyss. Symptomatic of the failure to discern cultures interlocked within any historical conjuncture is George Steiner's provocative homage to Eurocentric civilization, *In Bluebeard's Castle*. At the height of the worldwide revolt against U.S. aggression in Indo-

338

China, Steiner bewails the barbarism he sees coexisting with beneficent material progress and visions of an "ontological utopia." Bourgeois culture damaged by ennui and corrupted by an obsession with ethical absolutes could lead only to glorifying an aesthetics of violence, guilt, and genocide (the carnage of World War I and the holocaust of World War II). For Steiner, what destroyed the "critical mass of genetic material and diversity needed to keep a civilization engaged" were the methodical repetitiveness of mass industry and urban crowding — a familiar theme for fans of Frankfurt Critical Theory. He harps on "biosociology" and historical genetics as the key to explain the "destruction of inner forms," "touchstones of order and of that unbroken continuum of intellectual power" he ascribes to European and Anglo-Saxon man. Ambivalence, however, explains social injustice, violence, and the cruelty of European civilization that has produced dazzling literary, artistic, and philosophic achievements surpassing those of primitive shamans, the "myth-enclosed stasis of the savage," the "drum taps and Javanese bells" (1971, 65, 67). The shadow of Joseph Conrad's Mr. Kurtz seems to be hovering and floating around here.

How then can the Others be recognized by the imperial European self? Surveying the rest of the planet from the "manifest centers of philosophic, scientific, poetic force" found "within the Mediterranean, North European, Anglo-Saxon racial and geographical matrix," Steiner reserves for himself one certainty amid the general skepticism of his milieu: the empathy needed to share an alien worldview, appreciated as "the rules of consciousness of a colored or 'third-world' culture," is limited to a few. Steiner is of the conviction that multicultural democracy is a "false situation," a deception: "Nearly all the Western gurus and publicists who proclaim the new penitential ecumenism, who profess to be brothers under the skin with the roused, vengeful soul of Asia or Africa, are living a rhetorical lie" (1971, 66). Partially prophetic words, indeed, in 1971. There is no choice then but to return to the European past.

Steiner's essentially moralizing concept of a "post-culture" resuscitates the twin rationality and barbarism of the past and seeks to restore white-supremacist hegemony that has suffered an irreversible decline. After all, the paradox obtains: refined and scrupulous intelligence can coexist with "barbaric, politically sadistic behavior" in the same individual. While puzzling over the "dialectically paradoxical and paro-distic relations between culture and society," Steiner does not waste time relegating the non-Western two-thirds of humanity to oblivion.

Steiner's theory of culture, whose conditions of possibility include a reason and political will vulnerable to "nostalgias for destruction" and horrendous barbarism, succumbs to an ironic paralysis brought about by the collapse of "hierarchized, definitional value-gradients." He protests the advent of a relativistic anthropology, and eclectic "countercultures" signifying "sociophysiological metamorphoses" not yet adequately grasped. Culture, in Steiner's comprehension, ultimately concerns a hierarchy of classic elite values and order, the "creation of the gifted few" (1971, 77, 87), the "truths and beauties" achieved in the tradition of the cultural sensibility. In the end, Steiner opts for a "gamble on transcendence," a "religious" way out of the crisis of late capitalism. So much for the "post-culture" of the privileged man-of-letters in the imperial academy.

The primacy of racism and racialization is acknowledged by the social-democratic critics of multicultural education in the United States who nonetheless insist on commonality. Todd Gitlin, a venerable vet-eran of the "New Left," agrees that race is the origin or template of most identity quarrels today. Race is tied to the unbridled market that "fuels fantasies of a 'moral community' surrounded by fortifications" (1995, 235). However, he deplores the mind-set of identity politics, the obses-sion with cultural identity at the expense of political citizenship. While asserting that "growing inequality erodes social solidarity," Gitlin also believes that there is "no necessary contradiction between a recognition of difference and the affirmation of common rights" (1995, 225, 228). In rebuttal, Robin Kelley upbraids Gitlin for losing sight of the fact that "sexual identities and practices are lived through race and class and can only be understood historically," so that anti-immigrant sentiment, for example, is not just about class anger: "It's about dark people, whether some invisible Pacific Rim empire run by 'sneaky Orientals' or 'wet-backs'" (2000, 333–34). Support for marjoritarian positions, given the current rightist hegemony, is equivalent to rallying around the national-ism and chauvinism of the corporate elite.

Actually, the paradox that Gitlin offers, the proposition that com-monality is needed to recognize diversity, is nothing new. It is implicit in the Establishment version of multiculturalism as pluralism with a more nuanced, sophisticated tolerance of differences. The French philosopher Colette Guillaumin has elucidated the axiomatic presence of hierarchy underneath or behind the egalitarian articulation of difference in democratic regimes. What exactly is the ideological significance of this paradox? Guillaumin explains: "To speak of 'difference' is to articulate a rule, a law, a norm — briefly, an absolute which would be the measure, the origin, the fixed point of a relationship, by which the 'rest' would be defined. . . . It is quite simply the statement of the effects of a power relationship. . . . [Difference presupposes] a source of evaluation, a point of reference, an *origin of the definition*. . . . The definition is seen for what it is: a fact of dependence and a fact of domination" (1995, 250–51). It is clear, then, that the marker of difference is diacritical, with opposites coexisting in suspended tension. Is there a way of untangling this web of interdependencies to seize an opportunity for mass intervention? Before reflecting on this crux, and on why generic multiculturalism itself has become a "buzzword" of contention if not opprobrium, allow me to note that the antagonisms among variegated worldviews and life-forms have been going on since the monotheists battled the polytheists in ancient Egypt, and even before that. In clarifying why cultural identity has suddenly become salient in the terrain of multiple social antagonisms, however, it would be useful to invoke here again Gramsci's ideas about ideological disputes functioning as synecdoches for deeper, protracted systemic conflicts.

Hegemony is the key concept that unlocks the political ambiguity of multiculturalism within the analytic framework of mapping the relations of social forces in any given conjuncture. Gramsci postulated that hegemony (political and intellectual leadership) in most societies is realized through a combination of peaceful incremental reforms (voluntary consent from the majority) and violent struggles (coercive domination). He distinguished between a war of maneuver in which the dominated masses confront head-on the central fortress of the state and a war of position in which the partisans occupy trenches found in civil society that surround and penetrate the coercive state apparatuses. These trenches refer to agencies and institutions that generate and maintain consensus. Specific circumstances dictate which mode of struggle, or what combination of the two, is appropriate to attain hegemony, that is, the consensual submission of the masses to power. Placed in Bourdieu's framework, hegemony incorporates the working of symbolic violence shown in the "transfiguration of relations of domination and subordination into affective relations, the transformation of power into charisma" (1998, 102). Culture wars are thus engagements for ideological-moral positions that at some point will generate qualitative changes in the terms of engagement and thus alter the balance of power in favor of one social bloc against another. In modern industrial formations, the struggle is not just to occupy city hall, as it were, but also (from a radical democratic point of view) transform the relations of power, their bases and modality, on both material and symbolic levels.

Interrogating Exceptionalism

At this juncture, we may ask: In what way can culture be conceived as a site for such maneuver and positioning? How and why has culture been subsumed into the tropology of war? And what exactly is the politics of multicultural projects and practices?

In the first decades of the twenty-first century, the population of the United States will be comprised mainly of people of color: Latinos, African Americans, Asian/Pacific Islanders, American Indians, and other diasporic or refugee settlers. This would mean that the global majority of people of color from the continents of Africa, Asia/Oceania, and Latin America would become predominant in a racial polity that since World War II has symbolized Western hegemony over the planet. In the event that the former numerical minority becomes the majority, would the existing power relations and social divisions today be fundamentally changed? How would this affect the production, circulation, and allocation of material wealth and symbolic capital? So far, though, the status quo remains unchanged. In fact, the civil rights gains of the fifties and sixties — in particular, affirmative action that benefited chiefly white women — are being rolled back, slandered, gutted, and even erased from memory.

Persistence and discontinuity are syncopated in any moment of change. The neoconservative agenda of salvaging the idea of Western civilization as a sacred legacy transcending history and mutable social relations is still being implemented today. Newt Gingrich, one of the stalwart upholders of "white supremacy" culture, once proclaimed that the United States will disintegrate "if we allow the multicultural model of a multilingual America to become dominant" (quoted in Patterson 1997, 12). In my book *Racial Formations/Critical Transformations*, I suggested that the critique of hegemony — how the U.S. social order is constituted and maintained — should precede any exploration of one's racial or ethnic identity. This is because one's place can be discovered and assayed only in the field of multiple relationships, the totality of socioeconomic relations; that is, "cultures cannot be thought in their social or anthropological diversity except by comparison with universals," and the identity of each culture is always recognized as "containing a value that, as such, is universal" (Balibar 1995, 174).

There is general consensus in metropolitan culture for certain ideals now widely subscribed to: freedom, equality, justice, welfare, democracy, and respect for individual rights. Foremost in the order of value is the dignity of persons as against the instrumentality of things, but this dignity — I express a minoritarian stand — can only be realized in equality of conditions and fair treatment for communities whose distinctive particularities have been denied by the hegemonic order. To express it another way: the affirmation of cultural identity in the late-capitalist milieu of alienation and reification is a principled position required to attain "the moral equality of persons." For Andrew Levine, this movement for racial/ethnic autonomy can be "at best, only a strategic programme or a (pluralist) complement to an essentially universalistic vision" (1988, 236) noted above. My view is that the struggles for redistribution and for recognition, while analytically separable, are interdependent and mutually enabling. As David Harvey (1996) noted, the politics of otherness, identity, and difference cannot be divorced from the constraints of material circumstances and the imperatives of a wide-ranging political project of popular-democratic empowerment.

One of the central protagonists in the debate, the Canadian philosopher Charles Taylor, contends that behind the culture wars is the more fundamental conflict encapsulated by the rubric of "politics of recognition." Proceeding historically, Taylor traces this politics to the modern concept of individual dignity, in a universalist and egalitarian sense, at the heart of the Western heritage from the Enlightenment and the bourgeois revolution. Romanticism (Rousseau and Herder) contributed the

343

ideal of authenticity, which replaced the aristocratic concept of honor: "Being true to myself means being true to my own originality, which is something only I can articulate and discover. In articulating it, I am also defining myself. I am realizing a potentiality that is properly my own" (Taylor 1994, 31). Because human life is fundamentally relational or dialogical, this authentic identity is realized in the public sphere as the politics of equal and reciprocal recognition. The problem arises in the public sphere in our liberal construal: a politics of universalism privileges the equal dignity of all citizens, the equalization of rights and entitlements. This ignores the historical specificity of groups that have been denied reciprocity, in short, collectivities (women, racialized communities, and so on) excluded, marginalized, discriminated, and oppressed across time and space. Are all cultures and their group embodiments equal?

Taylor, who is sympathetic to the dilemma of the French-speaking people of Quebec, believes that there is no universal standard yet that can be used to answer the question. In search of a compromise between the homogenizing demand for recognition of equal worth and the "self-immurement within ethnocentric standards," Taylor resorts to a hope in the meeting or encounter of incommensurable horizons of meanings and values peculiar to each culture. The presumption that all cultures are of equal value, Taylor concludes, requires of us "not peremptory and inauthentic judgments of equal value, but a willingness to be open to comparative cultural study of the kind that must displace our horizons in the resulting fusions. It requires above all an admission that we are very far away from that ultimate horizon from which the relative worth of different cultures might be evident" (1994, 73). To close the distance, Edward Said, for example, recommends "the intellectual and interpretive vocation to make connections . . . to see complementarity and interdependence." This is a version of the hermeneutic circle opening up to the *Novum*, the unthought or unsaid, the utopian future in the present.

Now the protagonists of our present culture wars fall into two camps: the communitarians like Taylor who question the ethical neutrality of law in a liberal polity and who want the state to promote a specific conception of the good life, and liberals like Rawls and Dworkin, and by extension Richard Rorty and any number of Establishment pragmatists who opt for the majoritarian consensus. Meanwhile, there are some who believe that a multiculturalist program can coexist with the movement for political and economic democracy. But such a program suppresses the historical genealogy of the incorporation of racialized groups in the U.S. socioeconomic formation (sketched in the Introduction) together with the legal-ideological apparatuses that continue to reproduce the unequal distribution of power and resources. Culturalism results from the erasure of differential histories of peoples. Based on current trends, ethnic mobilization (interethnic strife in Los Angeles and other highly segregated cities) will continue as long as class consciousness is negated by an ideology of "possessive individualism" and as long as the alienation of labor power and the reification of social relations persist.

Appearances are not what they seem, to repeat a platitude. A multiethnic liberal society that recognizes formally the equality of cultures (as Taylor contends) may in fact effectively conceal existing material injustices (gender inequality, for one) as well as the repression of individual rights — an ironic situation, indeed, for transnational entrepreneurs who claim that the next millenium (contrary to the futurologists) will transcend ethnic particularisms and local differences in favor of a globalized, supranational, universal culture. In fact, the pursuit of the ideals of rationality (in economics, for instance) and of individual liberty requires material inequality for its fulfillment (Woodiwiss 1990).

It may be instructive here to quote Jurgen Habermas on the linkage between cultural identity and rights in civil society. He asks, "Does not the recognition of cultural forms of life and traditions that have been marginalized, whether in the context of a majority culture or in a Eurocentric global society, require guarantees of status and survival — in other words, some kind of collective rights that shatter the outmoded self-understanding of the democratic constitutional state, which is tailored to individual rights and in that sense is "liberal" (1994, 109)? Habermas believes that there is an internal connection between individual rights of private persons and the public autonomy of citizens; if the system of rights is to be actualized democratically, then citizens' autonomy must be activated to take account of the social and cultural differences that contextualize such autonomy. The liberal theory of rights, the establishment of normative rules of behavior, is influenced by the society's political goals and thus expresses a particular cultural form of life, the self-understanding of a collectivity; that is, the ascriptive net-work of traditions, intersubjectively shared contexts of life and experi-ence. This self-understanding changes when the social makeup of the population changes; historical circumstances alter the persons involved in the dialogue that shapes the discourse of identity. Such ethical-political decisions of a nation of citizens embody a conception of the social good and a desired form of authenticity that can exclude and discriminate Others. What sparks culture wars then, to follow Haber-mas's reasoning, "is not the ethical neutrality of the legal order but rather the fact that every legal community and every democratic process for actualizing basic rights is inevitably permeated by ethics" (1994, 125–26). But ethics for whom? In relation to what needs and aspira-tions? In what kind of habitat?

Reconfigurations

In the globalized environment of profit making and renewed ethnic conflicts around the world, we are faced with ethical/moral questions that cannot be divorced from the political economy of relations among groups, nation-states, regional alliances, and so on. With migration (ref-ugees, diasporic movements, genocidal expulsion) as the salient fact of this century, the dialectics of Othering has become more vexed and fraught. The politics of cultural difference, or what Stuart Hall (1998) calls the "pluralization of cultural difference," has intertwined pro-cesses of racialization and ethnicization that need to be finely discrimi-nated. Ideas of postcolonial syncretism and hybridity cannot account for the forced diaspora of millions of migrant workers (for example, eight million Filipino Overseas Contract Workers spread around the world) whose transnational vicissitudes the conventional theories of migration cannot fully make sense of. We need to theorize more adequately these new developments if we are not simply going to surrender to the apolo-getics of "the end of history" or the triumph of laissez-faire market liberalism — a sure-fire recipe for ecological planetary disaster.

Many observers have suggested that the multiculturalist problematic should be seen as capital's scheme of peacefully managing the crisis of race, ethnicity, gender, and labor in the North, a way of neutralizing the perennial conflicts in the system (Palumbo-Liu 1995). By containing diversity in a common grid, multiculturalism preserves the ethnocentric paradigm of commodity relations that generate particularisms in the experience of life-worlds within transnational capitalism. Cultural difference sells. Of relevance to this new phenomenon is Slavoj Žižek's essay "Multiculturalism, Or, the Cultural Logic of Multinational Capitalism," in which he points out that "postmodern racism is the symptom of multiculturalist late capitalism" (1997, 37). The inherent contradiction of the liberal democratic project, for Žižek, lies in its objectification of the Other, reducing the others — minorities, strangers, immigrants, undocumented aliens, refugees, and so on — into folkloric spectacles or objects, the "ethnic Thing" supposedly liberated from the transnational market and the reign of commodity-fetishism. Against the radical chic of postmodernist nihilism, Žižek formulates one of the most powerful critiques of multiculturalism as a historical phenomenon in this cogent insight:

> And, of course, the ideal form of ideology of this global capitalism is multiculturalism, the attitude which, from a kind of empty global position, treats each local culture the way the colonizer treats colonized people — as "natives" whose mores are to be carefully studied and "respected." That is to say, the relationship between traditional imperialist colonialism and global capitalist self-colonization is exactly the same as the relationship between Western cultural imperialism and multiculturalism: in the same way that global capitalism involves the paradox of colonization without the colonizing Nation-State metropole, multiculturalism involves patronizing Eurocentrist distance and/or respect for local cultures without roots in one's own particular culture. In other words, multiculturalism is a disavowed, inverted, self-referential form of racism, a "racism with a distance" — it "respects" the Other's identity, conceiving the Other as a self-enclosed "authentic" community towards which he, the multiculturalist, maintains a distance rendered possible by his privileged universal position. Multiculturalism is a racism which empties its own position of all positive content (the multiculturalist is not a direct racist, he doesn't oppose to the Other the particular values of his own culture), but nonetheless retains this position as the privileged empty point of universality from which one is able

to appreciate (and depreciate) properly other particular cultures — the multiculturalist respect for the Other's specificity is the very form of asserting one's own superiority. . . .

The conclusion to be drawn is thus that the problematic of multiculturalism — the hybrid coexistence of diverse cultural life-worlds — which imposes itself today is the form of appearance of its opposite, of the massive presence of capitalism as universal world system: it bears witness to the unprecedented homogenization of the contemporary world. It is effectively as if, since the horizon of social imagination no longer allows us to entertain the idea of an eventual demise of capitalism — since, as we might put it, everybody silently accepts that capitalism is here to stay — critical energy has found a substitute outlet in fighting for cultural differences which leave the basic homogeneity of the capitalist world-system intact. (1997, 44, 46)

I suggest that we meditate at length on Žižek's critique of liberal, neopragmatic multiculturalism before we celebrate its putative virtues and lament the pathos of its inadequacies. "Corporate national populism" deploying notions of cultural/ethnic absolutism can advance their postmodern agendas for racial apartheid by mobilizing multiculturalist rhetoric and policy strategies (Solomos and Beck 1996). Only a creative, militant historical-materialist critique can enable us to distinguish and evaluate the overdetermined trajectories and tendencies in the raging "PC/culture wars" from whose effects none of us is immune.

Discriminating Nation/State

Even as the skirmishes between the universalists and the localists in North America stir up more substantive controversies in tandem with inane posturing, globalization marches on without scruples. Not only TV advertisements (Benetton, Coca-Cola) blend multihued faces of ethnic models, the procession of women of color to the global cities and newly industrializing countries serves to foster the scrambling, if not miscegenation, of populations. Given the rapid migrant flows, the vogue of clichés like "transmigrant" and "transcultural" tends to conceal the rapacious operations of transnational business and promote wrongheaded notions about the disappearance of the nation-state, the loss of national identity, and so on. Are we now all citizens of the world, as Goethe and the Enlightenment philosophes once dreamed of becoming?

It has become axiomatic for post-ality thinkers to condemn the nation and its corollary terms *nationalism* and *nation-state* as the classic evils of modern industrial society. The nation-state, its reality if not its concept, has become a kind of malignant paradox, if not a sinister conundrum. It is often linked to violence and the terror of "ethnic cleansing." Despite this the United Nations and the interstate system still function as seemingly viable institutions of everyday life. How do we explain this situation?

Let us review the inventory of charges made against the nation-state. Typically described in normative terms as a vital necessity of modern life, the nation-state has employed violence to accomplish questionable ends. Its disciplinary apparatus is indicted for committing unprecedented barbarism. Examples of disasters brought about by the nation-state are the extermination of indigenous peoples in colonized territories by "civilizing" nations, the Nazi genocidal "holocaust" of Jews, and most recently the "ethnic cleansing" in the former Yugoslavia, Ruwanda, East Timor, and so on. Echoing Elie Kedourie, Partha Chatterjee, and others, Alfred Cobban (1994) believes that the theory of nationalism has proved one of the most potent agencies of destruction in the modern world. In certain cases, nationalism mobilized by states competing against other states has become synonymous with totalitarianism and fascism. Charles Tilly (1975), Michael Howard (1991), and other historians concur in the opinion that war and the military machine are principal determinants in the shaping of nation states. In *The Nation-State and Violence*, Anthony Giddens defines nationalism as "the cultural sensibility of sovereignty" (note the fusion of culture and politics) that unleashes administrative power within a clearly demarcated territory, "the bounded nation-state" (1985, 219). Although it is allegedly becoming obsolete under the pressure of globalization, the nation-state is considered by "legal modernists" (Berman 1995) as the prime source of violence against citizens and entire peoples.

Postmodernist critiques of the nation (often sutured with the colonialist/imperialist state) locate the evil in its ideological nature. This primarily concerns the nation as the source of identity for modern individuals via citizenship or national belonging, converting natal filiation (kinship) into political affiliation. Identity implies definition by negation, inclusion based on exclusion underwritten by a positivist logic of representation (Balibar and Wallerstein 1991). But these critiques seem to forget that the nation is a creation of the modern capitalist state, that is, a historical artifice or invention.

It is a truism that the nation and its corollary problematic, nationalism, presupposes the imperative of hierarchization and asymmetry of power in a political economy of commodity-exchange. Founded on socially constructed myths or traditions, the nation is posited by its proponents as a normal state of affairs used to legitimize the control and domination of one group over others. Such ideology has to be deconstructed and exposed as contingent on the changing grid of social relations. Postcolonial theory claims to expose the artificial and arbitrary nature of the nation: "This myth of nationhood, masked by ideology, perpetuates nationalism, in which specific identifiers are employed to create exclusive and homogeneous conceptions of national traditions" (Ashcroft et al. 1998, 150). Such signifiers of homogeneity not only fail to represent the diversity of the actual "nation" but also serve to impose the interests of a section of the community as the general interest. But this is not all. In the effort to make this universalizing intent prevail, the instrumentalities of state power — the military and police, religious and educational institutions, judiciary and legal apparatuses — are deployed. Hence, from this orthodox postcolonial perspective, the nation-state and its ideology of nationalism are alleged to have become the chief source of violence and conflict since the French Revolution.

Mainstream social science regards violence as a species of force that violates, breaks, or destroys a normative state of affairs. It is coercion *tout court*. Violence is often used to designate power devoid of legitimacy or legally sanctioned authority. Should violence as an expression of physical force always be justified by political reason in order to be meaningful and therefore acceptable? If such a force is used by a state, an inherited political organ legitimized by "the people" or "the nation," should we not distinguish between state-defined purposes and in what specific way nationalism or nation-making identity is involved in those state actions? State violence and assertion of national identity need not be automatically conflated so as to implicate nationalism — whose nationalism? — in all class/state actions in every historical period, for such a move would be an absolutist censure of violence bereft of intentionality — in order words, violence construed as merely physical force akin to tidal waves, earthquakes, volcanic eruptions, and so on.

Violence, in my view, signifies a political force that demands dialectical triangulation in order to grasp how nation and state are implicated in it. A historical-materialist historicization of this phenomenon is needed to determine the complicity of individual states and nations in specific outbreaks of violence. But postcolonialists like Homi Bhabha (1990) resort to a questionable use of the discursive performativity of language to ascribe a semiotic indeterminacy to the nation, reducing to a formula of hybridity and liminality the multifarious narratives of nations/peoples. History is reduced to the ambiguities of culture and the play of textualities, ruling out critique and political intervention.

In this light, what makes the postcolonialist argument flawed becomes clear in the fallacies of its non-sequitur reasoning. It is perhaps easy to expose the contingent nature of the nation once its historical condition of possibility is pointed out. But it is more difficult to contend that once its socially contrived scaffolding is revealed, then the nation-state and its capacity to mobilize and apply the means of violence can be restricted, if not curtailed. We can pose this question at this point: Can one seriously claim that once the British state is shown to rest on the myth of the Magna Carta or the U.S. government on the covenant of the Founding Fathers to uphold the interests of every citizen — except of course African slaves and other nonwhite peoples — then one has undermined the power of the British or American nation-state? Not that this is an otiose and naive task. Debunking has been the classic move of those protesting against an unjust status quo purporting to be the permanent and transcendental condition for everyone.

But the weapon of criticism, as Marx once said, needs to be reinforced by the principled criticism of weapons. If we want to guard against committing the same absolutism or essentialism of the imperial nationalists, we need a historicizing strategy of ascertaining how force — the energy of social collectivities — turns into violence for the creation or destruction of social orders and singular life-forms. Violence sanctioned by the authority of the agent becomes political power. Understood as embodying "the pathos of an elemental force," the insurrec-

351

tionary movements of nationalities has been deemed the source of a vital and primordial energy that feeds "the legal Modernist composite of primitivism and experimentalism," a fusion of "radical discontinuity and reciprocal facilitation" (Berman 1995, 238).

The question of the violence of the nation-state thus hinges on the linkage between the categories "nation" and "state." A prior distinction perhaps needs to be made between "nation" and "society"; while the former "may be ordered, the [latter] orders itself" (Brown 1986). Most historical accounts remind us that the modern nation-state has a beginning — and consequently, it is often forgotten — and an ending. But the analytic and structural distinction between the referents of nation (local groups, community, domicile, or belonging) and state (governance, machinery of sanctioning laws, disciplinary codes, military) is often elided because the force of nationalism is often conflated with the violence of the state apparatuses, an error compounded by ignoring the social classes involved in each sphere. This is the lesson of Marx and Lenin's necessary discrimination between oppressor and oppressed nations — a nation that oppresses another cannot really claim to be free. Often the symptom of this fundamental error is indexed by the formula of counterpointing the state to civil society, obfuscating the symbiosis and synergy between them. This error may be traced partly to the Hobbesian conflation of state and society in order to regulate the anarchy of the market and of brutish individualism violating civil contracts (Ollman 1993).

Given the rejection of a materialist analysis of the contradictions in any social formation, postcolonial critics in particular find themselves utterly at a loss in making coherent sense when dealing with nationalism. Representations of the historicity of the nation in the modern period give way to a Nietzschean will to invent reality as polysemic discourse, a product of enunciatory and performative acts. Postcolonialism resorts to a pluralist, if not equivocating, stance. It sees nationalism as "an extremely contentious site" in which notions of self-determination and identity collide with notions of domination and exclusion. Such oppositions, however, prove unmanageable indeed if a mechanical idealist perspective is employed. Such a view leads to an irresolvable muddle in which nation-states as instruments for the extraction of surplus value (profit) and "free" exchange of commodities also become violent agencies preventing "free" action in a global marketplace that crosses national boundaries. Averse to empirical grounding, postcolonialism regards nationalist ideology as the cause of individual and state competition for goods and resources in the "free market," with this market conceived as a creation of ideology. I cite one postcolonial authority that attributes violence to the nation-state, on the one hand, and liberal disposition to the nation, on the other:

> The complex and powerful operation of the idea of a nation can be seen also in the great twentieth-century phenomenon of global capitalism, where the "free market" between nations, epitomized in the emergence of multinational companies, maintains a complex, problematic relationship with the idea of nations as natural and immutable formations based on shared collective values. Modern nations such as the United States, with their multi-ethnic composition, require the acceptance of an overarching national ideology (*in pluribus unum*). But global capitalism also requires that the individual be free to act in an economic realm that crosses and nullifies these boundaries and identities. (Ashcroft et al. 1998, 151)

It is misleading and foolish then to label the slogan "one in many" as the U.S. national ideology. Officially the consensual ideology of the U.S. is neoliberal pluralism, or possessive individualism, centered on the right of property ownership — right to own, buy, or sell commodities (such as labor power). Utilitarian doctrine underwrites an acquisitive, entrepreneurial individualism that fits perfectly with mass consumerism and the gospel of the unregulated market. It is within this framework that we can comprehend how the ruling bourgeoisie of each sovereign state utilizes nationalist sentiment and the violence of the state apparatuses to impose their will. Consequently, the belief that the nation-state simultaneously prohibits economic freedom and promotes multinational companies actually occludes the source of political and juridical violence — for example, the war against Serbia by NATO (an expedient coalition of nation-states led by the United States), or the stigmatization of rogue and "terrorist" states (North Korea, Iran, Iraq, Afghanistan) by the normative standards of hegemonic capitalism. The source of political violence — and I am speaking of that kind where collective energy and intentionality are involved — is the competitive drive for accumulation in the world market system where the propertied class is the key actor mobilizing, apart from technological weapons, its symbolic capital made up of ethnic loyalties and nationalist imaginaries.

Lacking any historical anchorage, the argument of postcolonial theory generates inconsistencies due to an exorbitant culturalism. Because they disregard the historical genealogy of the nation-state discussed by Gellner, Anderson, Smith (1971), and others, postcolonial critics uphold the sphere of culture as the decisive force in configuring social formations. Not that culture is irrelevant in explaining political antagonisms. Rather, it is erroneous when such antagonisms are translated into nothing but the tensions of cultural differences. The dogma of cultural difference (for Charles Taylor, the need and demand for recognition in a modern politics of identity; discussed in chapters 1 to 5) becomes the key to explaining colonialism, racism, and postcolonial society. Ambivalence, hybridity, and interstitial or liminal space become privileged signifiers over homogenizing symbols and icons whose "authority of cultural synthesis" is the target of attack. Ideology and discursive performances serve as the primary field of analysis against "localized materialism" and vulgar Marxism.

Violence in postcolonial discourse is thus located in ideas and cultural forces that unify, synthesize, or generalize a range of experiences; such forces suppress difference or negate multiple "others" not subsumed within totalities such as nation, class, gender, and so on. While some culturalist critics allow for different versions of the historic form of the nation, the reductive dualism of their thinking manifests a distinct bias for a liberal framework of analysis: the choice is either a nation based on an exclusionary myth of national unity centered on abstractions such as race, religion, or ethnic singularity; or a nation upholding plurality and multiculturalism (for example, Canada or the United States). This fashionable vogue of pluralism and culturalism has already been proved inutile in confronting inequalities of class, gender, and "race." Moreover, it cannot explain the appeal of nationalism as a means of reconciling the antagonistic needs for order and autonomy (A. Smith 1979) in the face of mechanistic bureaucratism and the anarchic market of atomized consumers.

The most flagrant evidence of the constrained parameters of this culturalist diagnosis of nation/nationalism may be found in its construal of racist ideology as "the construction and naturalization of an unequal form of intercultural relations" (Ashcroft et al. 1998, 46). If racism occurs only or chiefly on the level of "intercultural relations," from this constricted optic, the other parts of a given social formation (political, economic) become superfluous and marginal. Politics is then reduced to an epiphenomenal manifestation of discourse and language games.

A virtuoso application of a culturalist contextualism may be illustrated by the legal scholar Rosemary Coombe, who defends the right of the Canadian First Nations to claim "ownership" rights to certain cultural property. Coombe correctly rejects the standard procedure of universalizing the Lockean concept of property and its rationale, possessive individualism, which underlies the Western idea of authorship and authentic artifacts. She writes, "By representing cultures in the image of the undivided possessive individual, we obscure people's historical agency and transformations, their internal differences, the productivity of intercultural contact, and the ability of peoples to culturally express their position in a wider world" (1995, 264). Although Coombe calls attention to structures of power and the systemic legacies of exclusion, the call remains abstract and consequently trivializing. Above all, it obscures the reality and effect of material inequities. The postmodernist leitmotif of domination and exclusion mystifies the operations of corporate capitalism and its current political suppression of the indigenous struggles for self-determination. Coombe ignores precisely those "internal differences" and their contradictory motion that give concrete specificity to the experiences of embattled groups such as the First Nations. Here ironically the postmodernist inflection of the nation evokes the strategy of bourgeois nationalism to erase class, gender, and other differences ostensibly in the name of contextual nuances and refined distinctions.

Notwithstanding her partisanship for the oppressed, Coombe condemns "cultural nationalism" as an expression of possessive individualism and its idealist metaphysics. But her method of empiricist contextualism contradicts any emancipatory move by the First Nations at self-determination. It hides the global asymmetry of power, the dynamics of exploitative production relations, and the hierarchy of states in the geopolitical struggle for world hegemony. We have not transcended identity politics and the injustice of cultural appropriation be-

355

cause the strategy of contextualism reproduces the condition for refusing to attack the causes of class exploitation and racial violence. Despite gestures of repudiating domination and exclusion, postmodernist contextualism mimics the moralizing rhetoric of UN humanitarianism that cannot, for the present, move beyond reformism since it continues to operate within the framework of the transnational corporate globalized market. Such a framework is never subjected to critical interrogation.

The Minotaur Returns

We can resolve the initial paradox of the nation, a Janus-faced phenomenon (Nairn 1977), by considering the following historical background. The idea of state-initiated violence (as opposed to communal ethnic-motivated violence) performs a heuristic role in the task of historicizing any existing state authority and questioning the peaceful normalcy of the status quo. The prevailing social order is then exposed as artificial and contingent; what is deemed normal or natural reveals itself as an instrument of partial interests. But the relative permanence of certain institutional bodies and their effects need to be acknowledged in calculating political strategies. The long duration of collective and individual memories exerts its influence through the mediation of what Pierre Bourdieu calls "habitus" (1993). We begin to understand that the state's hierarchical structure is made possible because of the institutionalized violence that privileges the hegemony (moral and intellectual leadership crafted via negotiating compromises) of a bloc of classes over competing blocs and their alternative programs. Hegemony is always underwritten by coercion (open or covert, subtle or crude) in varying proportions and contingencies. The demarcated territory claimed by a state in rivalry with other states becomes for Max Weber one major pretext for the state monopoly of legitimate violence in order to defend private property and promote the overseas interests of the domestic business class (Krader 1968).

Georges Sorel argued for the demystificatory use of violence in his *Reflections on Violence* (1972). Sorel believed that the only way to expose the illusion of a peaceful and just bourgeois order is to propagate the myth of the general strike. Through strategic, organized violence, the proletariat is bound to succeed in releasing vast social energies hitherto repressed and directing them to the project of radical social transformation. This is still confined within the boundaries of the national entity. Open violence or war purges the body politic of hatred, prejudice, deceptions, and so on. Proletarian violence destroys bourgeois mystification and the nationalist ethos affiliated with it. Sorel's syndicalist politics of violence tries to convert force as a means to a political and social end, the process of the general strike. This politics of organized mass violence appeals to a utopian vision that displaces the means-ends rationality of bourgeois society in the fusion of force with pleasure realizable in a just, egalitarian order.

The classical Marxist view of violence rejects the mechanical calculation of means-ends that undermines the logic of Blanquist and Sorelian conceptions of social change. Marx disavowed utopian socialism in favor of the overthrow of the bourgeoisie through a combination of violent and peaceful means. Instrumentalism is subordinated to a narrative of emancipation from class bondage. The objective of emancipating labor associated with the laboring nation/people requires the exposure of commodity-fetishism and the ideology of equal exchange of values in the market. Reification and alienation in social relations account for the bourgeois state's ascendancy. Where the state bureaucracy supporting the bourgeoisie and the standing army do not dominate the state apparatus completely (a rare case) or has been weakened, as in the case of the monarchy and the Russian bourgeoisie at the time of the Bolshevik Revolution in 1917, the working class might attain their goal of class liberation by peaceful means; but in most cases, "the lever of the revolution will have to be force" harnessed by the masses unified by class consciousness and popular solidarity.

Based on their historical investigations, Marx and Engels understood the role of violence as the midwife in the birth of a new social order within the old framework of the nation-state. In his later years Engels speculated that with the changes in the ideological situation of the classes in any national territory, "a real victory of an insurrection over the military in street fighting is one of the rarest exceptions." In an unusual historic conjuncture, however, the Bolshevik Revolution mobilized mass strikes and thus disproved Engels. Nevertheless, Marx's "analytical universality," to use John Dunn's (1979, 78) phrase, remains valid in deploying the concept of totality to comprehend the nexus of state, class, and nation. We can rehearse here the issues that need to be examined from the viewpoint of totality: Was Lenin's "dictatorship of the proletariat" an imposition of state violence, or the coercive rule of the people against the class enemy? If it is an instrumental means of the new proletarian state, did it implicate the nation? Is violence here both structured into the state system of apparatuses and inscribed in the collective agency of the working masses cognized as the nation? Is the political authority invoked by the proletarian state embodied in the class interest of all those exploited by capital (in both periphery and center) ascendant over all? Marxists critical of the Leninist interpretation denounce the use of state violence as an anarchist deviation, an arbitrary application of force. They affirm instead the law-governed historical process that will inevitably transform capitalism into socialism, whatever the subjective intentions of the political protagonists involved. Such teleological fatalism, however, rules out the intervention of a class-for-itself freed from ideological blinders and uniting all the oppressed with its moral-intellectual leadership, the cardinal axiom of socialist revolution.

Rationalist thinkers for their part reject violence as an end in itself while accepting the force of the market as normal and natural. This is epitomized by legal thinkers who contend that primordial nationalist claims should be regulated by autonomous international law, "the domain of the *metajuridique*" (Berman 1995). By identifying nationalism as a primitive elemental force outside the jurisdiction of positive law, the modernist legal scholar is alleged to be receptive to its experimental creativity so that new legal techniques are devised to regulate the destabilization of Europe — and, for that matter, its colonial empires — by "separatist nationalisms." The aim is to pacify the subalterns and oppressed classes by juridical and culturalist prophylactic.

As I have noted above in dealing with Fanon's work, the nature of violence in the process of decolonization cannot be grasped by such dualistic metaphysics epitomized in the binarism of passion-versus-law. What is needed is the application of a historical-materialist critique to the complex problem of national self-determination. Marxists like Lenin and Rosa Luxemburg, despite their differences, stress the combination of knowledge and practice in analyzing the balance of political

358

forces. They contend that class struggle is a form of knowledge/action, the civil war of political groups, which can synthesize wars of position (legal, peaceful reforms) and the war of maneuver (organized frontal assault by armed masses, to use Gramsci's terminology) in the transformation of social relations in any particular nation. Violence itself can become a creative force insofar as it reveals the class bias of the bourgeois/colonial state and serves to accelerate the emergence of class consciousness and organized popular solidarity. Insofar as the force of nation/national identity distracts and prohibits the development of class consciousness, then it becomes useless for socialist transformation. In colonized societies, however, nationalism coincides with the converging class consciousness of workers, peasants, and the masses of subjugated natives that constitute the political force par excellence in harnessing violence for emancipatory goals.

Escape from the Labyrinth

From the historical-materialist perspective then, violence cannot be identified with the nation or nation-state per se under all circumstances. We need to distinguish between the two positions — the postmodernist one of indiscriminate attack on all totalities (such as class, nation, and so on) premised on a syllogistic Kantian means-ends rationality, and the historical-materialist one where means/ends are dialectically calibrated in historically inventive modalities — to illuminate the problem of violence in this new millennium. The impasse between these two positions reflects the relation of unceasing antagonism between the bourgeoisie and the nationalities they exploit in the world system of commodity-exchange and accumulation.

On another level, the impasse may be viewed as a theoretical crux. It signifies the antinomy between agency and structure, the intentionalist-nominalist pragmatism of liberals and the structuralist views of historical materialists. The former looks at the nation as always implicated in the state while the latter considers the nation as historically separate and contingent on the vicissitudes of class warfare. One way of trying to elucidate this contradiction is by examining Walter Benjamin's argument in his "Critique of Violence."

Taking Sorel as one point of departure, Benjamin considers the use of violence as a means for establishing governance. Law is opposed to divine violence grasped as fate and the providential reign of justice. Bound up with violence, law is cognized as power, a power considered as a means of establishing order within a national boundary. The abolition of state power is the aim of revolutionary violence that operates beyond the reach of law-making force, an aspiration for justice that would spell the end of class society. Proletarian revolution resolves the means-ends instrumentalism of bourgeois politics. Violence becomes problematic when fate/justice, once deemed providential, eludes our grasp with the Babel of differences blocking communication and also aggrandizing particularisms found below the level of the nation-form and its international, not to say cosmopolitan, possibilities.

Violence is only physical force divorced from its juridical potency. Benjamin's thesis may be more unequivocal than the academically fashionable Foucauldian view of subsuming violence in power relations. It takes a more scrupulous appraisal of the sectarian limitations as well as empowering possibilities of violence in the context of class antagonisms. While the issue of nationalist violence is not explicitly addressed in his essay, Benjamin seeks to explore the function of violence as a creator and preserver of law, a factor intricately involved in the substance of normative processes. Benjamin writes, "Lawmaking is powermaking, and, to that extent, an immediate manifestation of violence. Justice is the principle of all divine end making, power the principle of all mythical lawmaking" (1978, 295). Lawmaking mythical violence can be contested only by divine power, which today, according to Benjamin, is manifested in "educative power, which in its perfected form stands outside the law." Benjamin is not entirely clear about this "educative power," but I think it can only designate the influence of the family and other agencies in civil society not regulated by the traditional state apparatuses. In another sense, Benjamin alludes to "the proper sphere of understanding, language," which makes possible the peaceful resolution of conflicts. Since language is intimately linked with the national community, national consciousness contradicts the disruptive effects of violence in its capacity to resolve antagonisms.

Benjamin goes on to investigate violence embodied in the state (as contradistinguished from the national community) through a process of demystification. Critique begins by disclosing the idea of its development, its trajectory of ruptures and mutations, which in turn exposes the fact that all social contract depends on a lie, on fiction. "Justice, the criterion of ends," supersedes legality, "the criterion of means." Justice is the reign of communication that, because it excludes lying, excludes violence. In effect, violence is the mediation that enables state power to prevail. It cannot be eliminated by counterviolence that simply inverts it. Only the educative power of language, communication associated with the national collectivity, can do away with the need to lie. But since the social contract displaces justice as the end of life with legality connected with the state, and law is required as an instrument to enforce the contract, violence continues to be a recurrent phenomenon in a commodity-centered society.

Benjamin is silent about the nation and the efficacy of popular sovereignty in this text. His realism seeks to clarify the historic collusion between law, violence, and the state. He wants to resolve the philosophical dualism of means and ends that has bedeviled liberal rationalism and its inheritors, pragmatism and assorted postmodernist nominalisms. His realism strives to subordinate the instrumentality of violence to law, but eventually he dismisses law as incapable of realizing justice. But we may ask: How can justice — the quest for identity without exclusion/ inclusion, without alterity — be achieved in history if it becomes some kind of intervention by a transcendent power into the secular domain of class struggle? How can justice be attained as an ideal effect of communication? Perhaps through language as mediated in the nation-form, in the web of discourse configuring the nation as a community of speakers (San Juan 2000b), the nation as the performance of groups unified under the aegis of struggle against oppression and exploitation?

Benjamin's speculation on the reconciling charisma of language seems utopian in the pejorative sense. Peoples speaking the same language (for example, Northern Ireland, Colombia, North and South Korea) continue to be locked in internecine conflict. If violence is inescapable in the present milieu of reification and commodity-fetishism, then how can we use it to promote dialogue and enhance the resources of the oppressed for liberation? In a seminal essay on "Nationalism and

Modernity," Charles Taylor underscores the modernity of nationalism in opposition to those who condemn it as atavistic tribalism or a regression to primordial barbarism. In the context of modernization, Taylor resituates violence in the framework of the struggle for recognition — nationalism "as a call to difference, . . . lived in the register of threatened dignity, and constructing a new, categorical identity as the bearer of that dignity" (1999, 240).

What needs to be stressed here is the philosophical underpinning of the struggle for recognition and recovery of dignity. It invokes clearly the Hegelian paradigm of the relation between lord and bondsman in *The Phenomenology of Mind*. In this struggle, the possibility of violence mediates the individual's discovery of his finite and limited existence, his vulnerability, and his need for community. Piotr Hoffman's gloss underlines the Hegelian motif of freedom as risk: "Violence . . . is the necessary condition of my emergence as a universal, communal being . . . for I can find common ground with the other only insofar as both of us can endure the mortal danger of the struggle and can thus think independently of a blind attachment to our particular selves" (1989, 145). Since the nation evokes sacrifice, the warrior's death on the battlefield, honor, self-transcendence, destiny, the state seeks to mobilize such nation-centered feelings and emotions to legitimize itself as a wider, more inclusive, and less artificial reality to attain its own accumulative goals. Weber reminds us, "For the state is the highest power organization on earth, it has power over life and death. . . . A mistake comes in, however, when one speaks of the state alone and not of the nation" (quoted in Poggi 1978, 101).

The nationalist struggle for recognition and the violence of anti-colonial revolutions thus acquire a substantial complexity in the context of modernity, the fact of uneven development, and the vicissitudes of capitalist crisis. In any case, whatever the moral puzzles entailed by the plural genealogies of the nation-state, it is clear that a dogmatic pacifism is no answer to an effective comprehension of the real world and purposeful intervention in it. Given the continued existence of nation-states amid the increasing power of transnational corporations in a geopolitical arena of sharpening rivalry, can we choose between a "just" and an "unjust" war when nuclear weapons that can destroy the whole planet are involved? Violence on such a scale obviously requires the dialectical transcendence of the system of nation-states in the interest of planetary justice and survival.

Overall, the question of violence cannot be answered within the framework of the realpolitik of the past but only within the framework of nation-states living in mutual reciprocity. Causality, however, has to be ascertained and responsibility assigned even if the nation is construed as "an interpretive construct" (Arnason 1990, 230). My view is that the hegemonic bloc of classes using the capitalist state machinery is the crux of the problem. If nations have been manipulated by states dominated by possessive/acquisitive classes that have undertaken and continue to undertake colonial and imperial conquests, then the future of humanity and all living organisms on earth can be insured only by eliminating those classes that are the origin of state violence. The nation-form can then be reconstituted and transcended to insure that it will not generate reasons or opportunities for state violence to recur. That will be the challenge for future revolutionaries.

Excavations in the Boondocks

Whatever the rumor about the demise of the nation-state, agencies that assume its healthy existence are busy: the World Trade Organization, NATO, the United Nations, the World Bank and IMF, and other consortia are all exerting pressures and influence everywhere. Citizenship cards, passports, customs gatekeepers, and border patrols are still mundane regularities. Saskia Sassen has described the advent of the global city as a sign of the "incipient unbundling of the exclusive territoriality of the nation-state." At the same, however, she adds that what we see looming in the horizon is the "transnational geography of centrality . . . consisting of multiple linkages and strategic concentrations of material infrastructure," a "grid of sites and linkages" (1998, 214) between North and South still comprised of nation-states. What has not escaped the most pachydermous epigones of Baudrillard or Rorty who have not been distracted by the Gulf War or the fighting in Bosnia and Kosovo are the frequency and volume of labor migration, flows of bodies of color (including mail-order brides, children, and the syndicated traffic in prostitutes), in consonance with the flight of labor-intensive industries to far-flung industrial zones in Mexico, Thailand, the Philippines, Haiti, and

China. Such bodies are not the performative parodists of Judith Butler in quest of pleasure or the aesthetically fashioned selves idealized by the later Foucault.

Culture wars are being conducted by other means through the transport and exchange of bodies of color in the international bazaars. And the scaling of bodies proceeds according to corporeal differences (sex, race, age, physical capacity). Other diasporas — in addition to the historic ones of the Jews, Africans, Chinese, Irish, Palestinians, and so on — are in the making. The editors of *The South Atlantic Quarterly* special issue on "diaspora and immigration" celebrate the political and cultural experiences of these diasporic cohorts who can "teach us how to think about our destiny and how to articulate the unity of science with the diversity of knowledges as we confront the politics of difference" (Mudimbe and Engel 1999, 6). Unity, diversity, politics of difference — the contours and direction of diasporas are conceived as the arena of conflict among disparate philosophical/ideological standpoints. Contesting the European discourse on modernity and pleading for "the inescapability and legitimate value of mutation, hybridity, and intermixture" (1993, 223), Paul Gilroy has drawn up the trope of the "Black Atlantic" on the basis of the "temporal and ontological rupture of the middle passage." Neither the Jewish nor the African diasporas can of course be held up as inviolable archetypes if we want to pursue an "infinite process of identity construction." My interest here, however, is to inquire into how the specific historical contingencies of the Filipino diaspora-in-the-making can problematize this infinitude of identity formation in the context of Fanon's principle of national liberation discussed in the previous chapter.

Postmodern CS from the industrial North is now replicating McKinley's gunboat policy of "Benevolent Assimilation" at the turn of the century. Its missionary task is to discover how without their knowing it Filipina domestics are becoming cosmopolitans while working as maids (more exactly, domestic slaves), empowering themselves by devious tactics of evasion, accommodation, and making do. Obviously this task of euphemizing or naturalizing servitude benefits the privileged few, the modern slave masters. This is not due to a primordial irony in the nature of constructing their identity that, according to Ernesto Laclau, "presupposes the constitutive split" between the content and the function of identification as such since they — like most modern subjects — are "the empty places of an absent fullness" (1994, 36). Signifiers of lack, these women from poverty-stricken regions in the Philippines are presumably longing for a plenitude symbolized by a stable, prosperous homeland/ family that, according to postcolonial theory, is forever deferred, if not evacuated. Though these maids possess faculties of resourcefulness and ingenuity, experts are needed for them to acquire self-reflexive agency, to know that their very presence in such lands as Kuwait, Milan, Los Angeles, Taipeh, Singapore, and London and the cultural politics they spontaneously create are "complexly mediated and transformed by memory, fantasy and desire" (Hall 1992, 254). The time of labor has annihilated indeed the spaces of the body, home, community, and nation.

Space-time particulars are needed if we want to ascertain the "power-geometry" (Massey 1993) that scales diasporic existence. I might state at the outset an open secret: the annual remittance of billions of dollars by Filipino workers abroad suffices to keep the Philippine economy afloat and support the luxury and privileges of less than 1 percent of the people, the Filipino oligarchy. Since the seventies, Filipino bodies have been the No. 1 Filipino export, and their corpses (about five or six re-turn in coffins daily) are becoming a serious item in the import ledger. In 1998 alone, according to the Commission on Filipinos Overseas, 755,000 Filipinos found work abroad, sending home a total of P7.5 billion. Throughout the nineties, the average total of migrant workers is about one million a year; they remit more than 5 percent of the national GNP, not to mention the millions of pesos collected by the Philippine government in myriad taxes and fees. Hence these overseas cohorts are glorified as "modern heroes," "*mga bagong bayani*" (the "new he-roes"), the most famous of whom are Flor Contemplacion who was falsely accused and hanged in Singapore, and Sarah Balabagan, flogged in Saudi Arabia for defending herself against her rapist-employer.

This is an unprecedented and mind-boggling phenomenon. More than one thousand concerned Filipino American students made this the central topic of the 1997 FIND CONFERENCE at SUNY-Binghamton where I was the invited keynote speaker. These concerned youth were bothered by the reputation of the Filipina/o as the "domestic help" or glorified servant of the world. How did Filipinas/os come to find them-selves dispersed and scattered to the four corners of the earth? What are

365

we doing about it? In general, what is the meaning and import of this unprecedented traffic, millions of Filipinas/os in motion and in transit around the planet?

Lifting the Embargo

There are at present more than 100,000 Filipina domestics (also known as "Overseas Contract Workers") in Hong Kong today, employed under terrible conditions. News reports of brutal and inhumane treatment, slavery, rape, suicide, and murder suffered by these workers abound. The reason why thousands of college-educated women continue to travel to Hong Kong, even as the procession of coffins of their sisters greet them at the ports of embarkation, is not a mystery.

Suffice it here to cite the context of this labor diaspora: the accelerated impoverishment of millions of Filipino citizens, the oppressive unjust system (a neocolonial dependency of the United States and the corporate power-elite) managed by compradors, landlords, and bureaucrat-capitalists who foster emigration to relieve unemployment and defuse mass unrest, combined with the economic enticements in Hong Kong and other newly industrializing countries, and so on — all these comprise the parameters for this transnational phenomenon. The convergence of complex factors, including the internal conditions in the Philippines, has been carefully delineated by, among others, Saskia Sassen (1998), Bridget Anderson (2000), Delia Aguilar (2000), and Grace Chang (2000). We may cite, in particular, the devalorization of women's labor in global cities, the shrinking status of sovereignty for peripheral nation-states, and the new saliency of human rights in a feminist analytic of the "New World Order." In addition to the rampant pillage of the national treasury by corrupt Filipino compradors, bureaucrat-capitalists, and landlords, the plunder of the economy by transnational companies has been worsened by the "structural conditionalities" imposed by the World Bank and International Monetary Fund. Disaggregation of the economy has registered in the disintegration of ordinary Filipino lives due to forced migration because of lack of employment, recruiting appeals of governments and business agencies, and the dissolution of the homeland as psychic and physical anchorage in the vortex of the rapid circulation of capital.

In general, imperialism and the anarchy of the "free market" engender incongruities, nonsynchronies, the Other inscribed in the liminal space of subjugated territory. Capital accumulation is the matrix of unequal power (Hymer 1975; Harvey 1996) between metropolis and colonies. The historical reality of uneven cultural development in a U.S. colonial and, later, neocolonial society like the Philippines is evident in the visible Americanization of schooling, mass media, sports, music, and diverse channels of mass communication (advertisements, TV and films, cyberspace). Backwardness now helps hi-tech corporate business. Since the seventies, globalization has concentrated on the exploitation of local tastes and idioms for niche marketing while the impact of the Filipino diaspora in the huge flow of remittances from OCWs (Overseas Contract Workers) has accentuated the discrepancy between metropolitan wealth and neocolonial poverty, with the consumerist habitus made egregiously flagrant in the conspicuous consumption of domestic helpers returning from the Middle East, Europe, Hong Kong, Japan, and other places with *balikbayan* boxes. Unbeknownst to observers of this postmodern "cargo cult," coffins of these dead workers (one of them martyred in Singapore, Flor Contemplacion, achieved the status of national saint) arrive in Manila at the rate of five or six a day without too much fanfare.

Notwithstanding this massive research into the structural and historical background of these "new heroes" (as President Corazon Aquino once called the domestics), a recent ethnographic account of the lives of Filipina maids celebrates their newfound subjectivity within various disciplinary regimes. Deploying Foucault's notion of "localized power," the American anthropologist Nicole Constable seeks "to situate Filipina domestic workers *within* the field of power, not as equal players but as participants" (1999, 11). Ambivalence characterizes the narratives of these women: they resist oppression at the same time as they "participate in their own subordination." And how is their agency manifested? How else but in their consuming power? Consider this spectacle: during their Sundays off, Filipina maids gather in certain places like the food restaurants of the Central District in Hong Kong and demand prompt service or complain to the managers if they are not attended to properly. They can also exercise agency at McDonald's if they ask for extra condiments or napkins. Apart from these anecdotal examples, the fact that these maids were able to negotiate their way through a bewildering array of institutions in order to secure their jobs is testimony to what Constable calls "the subtler and more complex forms of power, discipline and resistance in their everyday lives" (1999, 202). According to one reviewer, this scholarly attempt to ferret out signs of tension or conflict in the routine lives of domestics obfuscates the larger context that defines the subordination of these women and the instrumentalities that reproduce their subjugation. Functionalism has given way to neopositivism. Constable shares Foucault's dilemma of ascribing resistance to subjects while devaluing history as "meaningless kaleidoscopic changes of shape in discourse totalities" (Habermas 1987, 277).

Nor is Constable alone in this quite trendy vocation. Donna Haraway, among others, has earlier urged CS to abandon the politics of representation that allegedly objectifies and disempowers whatever it represents. She wants us to choose instead local struggles for strategic articulations that are always impermanent, vulnerable, and contingent. This precept forbids the critique of ideology — how can one distinguish truth from falsehood since there are only "truth effects" contrived by power? This populist and often demagogic stance promotes "a radical skepticism" (Brantlinger 1990, 102) that cannot discriminate truth-claims or establish a basis for sustained and organized political action.

The most flagrant erasure in Constable's postmodernist inventory of episodes is the unequal relation between the Philippines and a peripheral capitalist city like Hong Kong, a relation enabled by the continuing neocolonial domination of Filipinos by Western corporate interests led by the United States. But this microphysics of learning how to survive performed by Filipino maids cannot exonerate the ethnographist from complicity with this strategy of displacing causality (a technique of inversion also found in mainstream historians of the Philippines such as Glenn May, David Steinberg, Stanley Karnow) and apologizing for the victims by oblique patronage. Anne Lacsamana pronounces a felicitous verdict on this specimen of CS: "To dismiss the broader history of Filipino OCWs in favor of more trivial pursuits (such as watching them eat at a fast food restaurant) reenacts a Western superiority that has already created (and is responsible for) many of the social, economic, and political woes that continue to plague the country" (1998, 42).

Deracinated Trauma

Now the largest cohort in the Asian American group, Filipinos have now become the newest diasporic community in the whole world. UN statistics indicate that Filipinos make up the newest diasporic assemblage in the world: eight million Filipino migrant workers (out of eighty million citizens), mostly female domestic help and semiskilled labor. They endure poorly paid employment under substandard conditions, with few or null rights, in the Middle East, Asia, Europe, North America, and elsewhere. Diasporic groups are historically defined not only by a homeland but also by a desire for eventual return and a collective identity centered on myths and memories of the homeland. The Filipino diaspora, however, is different. Since the homeland has been long colonized by Western powers (Spain, United States) and remains neocolonized despite formal or nominal independence, the Filipino identification is not with a fully defined nation but with regions, localities, and communities of languages and traditions. Perceived as Others, they are lumped with familiar aliens: Chinese, Mexicans, Japanese, Indonesians, and so on. Where is the nation alluded to in passports and other identification papers? How do we conceive of this "Filipino" nation, given the preemptive impact of U.S. colonization and now, on top of the persistent neocolonizing pressure, the usurping force of abstractive, quantifying capital?

According to orthodox immigration theory, "push" and "pull" factors combine to explain the phenomenon of Overseas Contract Workers. Do we resign ourselves to this easy schematic formulation? Poverty and injustice, to be sure, have driven most Filipinos to seek work abroad, sublimating the desire to return by remittances to their families; occasional visits and other means of communication defer the eventual homecoming. Anomie and isolation quarantine their movements. Some resort to amphibious subterfuges; others feign compliance, killing time. Many resort to schizoid fantasies while a few deploy temporizing tactics. If the return is postponed, are modes of adaptation and temporary domicile in nonnative grounds the feasible alternatives?

The reality of "foreignness" cannot be eluded. Alienation, brutal treatment, and racist violence prevent their permanent resettlement in the "receiving societies," except where Filipino communities (as in the United States and Canada, for example) have been given legal access to citizenship rights. Individuals, however, have to go through abrasive screening and tests. During political crisis in the Philippines, Filipino overseas workers mobilize themselves for support of local and nation-wide resistance against imperial domination and local tyranny. Because the putative "Filipino" nation is in the process of formation in the neocolony and abroad, overseas Filipino workers have been considered transnationals or transmigrants — a paradoxical turn since the existence of the nation is problematic, and the "trans" label a chimera. This diaspora then faces the ineluctable hurdles of racism, ethnic exclusion, and inferiorization. Can Filipino migrant labor mount resistance against globalized exploitation? Can the Filipino diaspora expose also the limits of genetic and/or procedural notions of citizenship? In what way can the Filipino diaspora serve as a paradigm for analyzing and critically unsettling the corporate globalization of labor and the reification of identities in the new millennium?

As a point of departure for future inquiry, we might situate the Filipino diaspora within its Asian American configuration — since the author is based here in this racial polity. His intervention proceeds from a concrete historic staging ground. First, a definition of *diaspora*: according to Milton Esman, the term refers to "a minority ethnic group of migrant origin which maintains sentimental or material links with its land of origin" (1996, 316). Either because of social exclusion, internal cohesion, or other geopolitical factors, these communities are never assimilated into the host society; but they develop in time a diasporic consciousness that enacts "a collective sharing space with others, devoid of exclusivist and dominating power," a sensibility endowed with "species-wide care" that thrives on cultural difference (Boyarin and Boyarin 1995, 325). Unlike peoples who have been conquered, annexed, enslaved, or coerced in some other way, diasporas are voluntary movements of people from place to place, although such migrations may also betray symptoms of compulsion if analyzed within a global political economy of labor and interstate political rivalries. Wallerstein (1995) feels that these labor migrants can challenge transnational corporations by overloading the system with "free movement," at the same time that they try to retain for themselves more of the surplus value they produce. But are such movements really free? And if they are cheap labor totally contingent on the unpredictable fortunes of business, isn't the expectation of their rebelliousness exorbitant? Like ethnicity, diaspora that is fashioned by determinate historical causes has tended to take on "the 'natural' appearance of an autonomous force, a 'principle' capable of determining the course of social action" (Comaroff and Comaroff 1992). Like racism and nationalism, diaspora presents multiform physiognomies open to various interpretations and articulations. Historical precedents may provide clues of what's to come.

Let us consider one late-modern interpretation of diaspora. For David Palumbo-Liu, the concept of *diaspora* performs a strategic function. It probably endows the slash in the rubric "Asian/American" with an uncanny performative resonance. Palumbo-Liu contends that diaspora affords a space for the reinvention of identity free from naturalized categories but (if I may underscore here) not from borders, state apparatuses, and other worldly imperatives. Although remarking that the concept of diaspora as an "enabling fiction" affords us "the ideological purchase different articulations of the term allow," Palumbo-Liu doesn't — if I'm not mistaken — completely succumb to the rebarbative postcolonialist babble about contingency ruling over all. I want to quote a passage from his book, *Asian/American*, that might afford parameters for the random reflections here apropos of the theme and discourse of Filipino diaspora:

> "Diaspora" does not consist in the *fact* of leaving Home, but in having that factuality available to representation *as such* — we come to "know" diaspora only as it is psychically identified in a narrative form that discloses the various ideological investments. . . . It is that narrative form that locates the representation of diaspora in its particular chronotope. This spatiotemporal construct approximates a psychic experience particularly linked to material history. It is only after the diasporic comes into contact with the material history of its new location that a particular discourse is enabled that seeks to mark a distance, a relation, both within and outside that constellation of contingency. (1999, 355)

Like the words "hybridity," border crossing, ambivalence, subaltern, transculturation, and so on, the term *diaspora* has now become chic in polite conversations. A recent conference at the University of Minnesota on "Race, Ethnicity, and Migration" lists as first of the topics one can engage with, "Diaspora and diasporic identities," followed by "Genocide, ethnic cleansing, and forced migration." One indeed dreads to encounter in this context such buzzwords as "post-nation," "alterity," or ludic *"différance"* now overshadowed by "globalization" and everything prefixed with "trans-". In fact I myself used the word "diaspora" as part of the title of my book, *From Exile to Diaspora: Versions of the Filipino Experience in the United States* (1998b). Diaspora enacts a mimicry of itself, dispersing its members around in a kaleidoscope of simulations and simulacras borne by the flow of goods, money, labor, and so on, in the international commodity chain.

Let me interject a personal note: I have lived in the United States for about forty years now (the greater part of my life), with frequent visits to the Philippines without too many balikbayan boxes, unfortunately. And in my various travels I have encountered Filipinos in many parts of the world. In the early eighties I was surprised to meet compatriots at the footsteps of the post office in Tripoli, Libya, and later on in the streets and squares of London, Edinburgh, Spain, Italy, Tokyo, Taiwan, Hong Kong, and other places. Have I then stumbled onto some unheard-of enigmatic scandal known as a "Filipino diaspora"? Or have I surreptitiously constructed this, dare I say, "reality" and ongoing experience of about eight million Filipinos around the planet? Not to speak of millions of displaced indigenous peoples in the Philippines itself, an archipelago of 700 islands, "one of the world's most strategically important land masses," according to geographer George Demko.

For those not familiar with my other writings critical of poststructuralist approaches (San Juan 1996; 1998a), I want to state outright that I consider such views about the Filipino diaspora half-truths closer to rumor, if not sheer mystifications. Spurious distinctions about cognition and perception concerning ethnic identity will remain vacuous if they do not take into account the reality of imperial world-systemic changes. Lacking any dialectical-materialist analysis of the dynamics of colonialism and imperialism that connect the Philippines and its peoples with the United States and the rest of the world, conventional studies on Filipino immigration and resettlement are all scholastic games, at best disingenuous exercises in chauvinist or white-supremacist apologetics. This is because they rely on concepts and methodologies that conceal unequal power relations — that is, relations of subordination and domination, racial exclusion, marginalization, sexism, gender inferiorization, as well as national subalternity, and other forms of discrimination. Lest people be misled by academic gossip, I am proposing here neither an economistic and deterministic approach, nor a historicist one with a monolithic Enlightenment metanarrative, teleology, and essentialist or ethnocentric agenda. Far from it. What is intriguing are the dynamics of symbolic violence (Bourdieu 1991) and the naturalization of social constructs and beliefs that are dramatized in the figures of diasporic happenings.

Retrospective Marginalia

The testimony of diasporic narratives when read symptomatically may prove to be a useful pedagogical device to make sense of the experiences of Filipina migrant workers. Stuart Hall, a diasporic intellectual from the Caribbean, believes that "identity shifts with the way in which we think and hear them and experience them," conveyed by "stories which change with historical circumstances" (1995, 8). A historical resume at this juncture would be useful in apprehending the contour and trajectory of these identity shifts. This will disrupt the postcolonial impasse born from the crisis of bourgeois metaphysics and situate postcolonial difference in the Philippine context. Let me refresh the reader's memory with some textbook commonplaces. Some nativist compatriots in the United States, eager to preempt the Pilgrims in New England, consider the fugitive "Manillamen" of the seventeenth century who escaped from the galleon trade, fled their Spanish masters in Mexico, and found their way to Louisiana, as the first Filipino Americans. But their settlement disappeared quickly in a few years, blown away by fortune and ill winds. There was no significant group of inhabitants from the Philippine Islands in the North American continent or anywhere else — except for a few student enclaves in Spain in the latter half of the nineteenth century — until the annexation and colonization of the Philippines by the United States in 1898 as part of the spoils of the Spanish-American War. This transpired after the genocidal Filipino-American War of 1899–1903.

With the exclusion of Chinese and Japanese workers by a barrage of

immigration laws from 1882 to 1924, the recruitment of Filipino labor
for the Hawaii plantations began in earnest in 1907 and continued without letup until 1935, when immigration was cut to fifty a year. From the
twenties to the thirties, Filipino contract labor in the United States
totalled about half a million. Most of these workers eventually settled in
the U.S. mainland rather than return to their native villages. If there is a
collective trauma or primal scenario of loss to which postcolonial critics
would gesture, it would be nothing else but the destruction of the institutions of Filipino sovereignty established by the Philippine revolution of
1896–1898 and the suppression of about a million rebellious bodies by
the U.S. military forces during the Filipino-American War. We are still
living with the legacy of this defeat and occupation, this time in a
neocolonial outpost enjoying mock-sovereignty.

There was no real Filipino diaspora before the Marcos dictatorship in
the seventies and eighties. It was only after the utter devastation of the
Philippines in World War II, and the worsening of socioeconomic conditions from the late sixties to the present, that Filipinos began to leave
in droves. During the Marcos martial-law regime, the functionality of
ocws was constructed and/or discovered by the elite and its hegemonic
patrons as a response to both local and global conditions. The export of
bodies became the prime local industry designed to relieve widespread
immiseration and curb mounting revolts from the majority of impoverished citizens. From the Aquino to the present Arroyo regime, ocw
productivity serves to keep the rotten system afloat. "Overseas Filipino
Workers" is now a category of citizens in the Philippines and in so-
called receiving societies like Japan, Taiwan, Hong Kong, Middle Eastern kingdoms, Iraq, and assorted European states — including Spain,
Greece, and Yugoslavia.

It is now a banal truism that globalization has facilitated the mobility
of goods, services, information, ideas, millions of domestics, and a few
hundred "symbolic analysts" headed for Silicon Valley. The anthropologist James Clifford has invented the trope of contemporary traveling
cultures — a version of the cargo cults — borne by nomadic or diasporic
intellectuals. Globalization has proceeded to the extent that in our
reconfigured landscapes, according to the experts in interstitial loci,
boundaries have shifted, borders disappeared, and everyone has become
transculturized. Americanization, or Disneyfication, has spread phys-

ically and in cyberspace. There is also the parachuting transmigrants that Aihwa Ong (1999) has described, as well as mutations of expatriates, refugees, and exiles — including our own Filipino TNTs (an indigenized form of hide-and-seek, according to our vernacular spies), our Filipinized version of "undocumented aliens" and cyborgesque next-of-kin.

Given these transformations, the reality and idea of the nation as well as of national sovereignty have become the burning issues of theoretical speculation. Linked to that are concepts of identity and its attendant politics of difference, notions of citizenship, nationality, cosmopolitanism, belonging, human rights, and so on. It is in this milieu of globalization (aka neoimperialism), where ethnic conflicts, religious fanaticisms, and universal commodification coexist in a compressed time-space locus within the postmodern axis (Harvey 1989) that we should situate the predicament of the Filipino diaspora and its vicissitudes.

Instead of pronouncing here any *obiter dicta* on this topic, I would like to tease out certain questions on the historical and ideological specificity of this unprecedented scattering of a people around the planet. One way of doing this is by interrogating certain themes and notions presented by James Clifford (1997) as springboards for further exchange. Clifford proposes "an ideal type" of diaspora based on the archetypal Jewish original. The main features of this ideal type are: (1) dispersal from an originary habitat, (2) myths and memories of the homeland, (3) alienation in the host country, (4) desire for eventual return, (5) ongoing support for the homeland, and (6) a collective identity defined by the relationship to the homeland. Responding to the globalization process I mentioned earlier, Clifford espouses a decentered network, a constellation of separate members. He rejects teleologies of origin and return because he perceives multiple transnational connections that provide a range of experiences to dispersed communities; these experiences depend on the ever-changing possibilities, obstacles, openings, antagonisms, and connections in the host countries.

Given the various histories of peoples' uprooting and removal, segregation and confinement, none of which coincide, diaspora is for Clifford the site of contingency par excellence. He envisages a "polythetic field of diasporic forms" articulating variegated discourses of travels, homes, memories, and transnational connections. Clifford conceives of diaspora as a "loosely coherent, adaptive constellation of responses to dwelling-in-displacement," hence his ideal is that of a tribal cosmopolitanism, a postmodern version of the old cosmopolitanism of tribal groups shaped by travel, spiritual quest, trade, exploration, warfare, labor migrancy, and political alliances that transcend the subtler sublimations of apartheid. Can Filipinos be conceived of as tribal cosmopolitans who, although prostituted and quarantined and stigmatized, can still assert their integrity and dignity in their beleaguered enclaves?

Deterritorialized Rhizome

At first glance, the Filipino genre of diaspora exhibits a peculiar configuration. Symptomatic of a disaggregated socioeconomic formation are the narratives spun around the trauma of dislocation undergone by more than eight million OCWs, mostly women. This severe hemorrhage of labor-power, the massive export of educated women whose skills have been downgraded to quasi-slavish domestic help, issues from a diseased body politic. The marks of the disease are the impoverishment of 75 percent of the population, widespread corruption by a moribund oligarchy, criminality, military/police atrocities, and the intensifying insurgency of peasants, women, workers, and indigenous communities.

The network of the patriarchal family and semifeudal civil society unravels when women from all sectors (except the very rich) alienate their "free labor" in the world market. While the prime commodity remains labor-power (singularly measured here in both time and space especially for live-in help), OCWs find themselves frozen in a tributary status between serfhood and stifling petty-bourgeois households. Bridget Anderson (2000) has cogently demonstrated how the international labor market consistently racializes the selling of Filipina/o selfhood; thus not only gender and class but, more decisively, "racial identities" conditioned by immigrant status, inferior nationality, and so on, are reproduced through the combined exploitation and oppression taking place in the employer's household. Except for the carceral condition of "hospitality" entertainers (modern versions of the "comfort women" in World War II) in Japan and elsewhere overseen by gangsters, most Filipinas function as indentured servants akin to those in colonial settler societies in seventeenth century Virginia, Australia, Jamaica, and elsewhere. But unlike those societies, the Middle East, Canada, Hong Kong, Singapore, and other receiving countries operate as part of the transnationalized political economy of global capitalism. These indentured cohorts are witness to the dismemberment of the emergent Filipino nation and the scattering of its parts to the metropoles of the North, the Middle East, and certain prosperous cities in the South.

Postcolonial disjunctures are reproduced by acts of revolt and sustained resistance. Such acts constitute a bad example for metropolitan citizens of industrialized states with live-in Filipina maids, or those who enjoy the benefits of sweatshops with millions of "third-world" workers. Institutional racism still prevents them from uniting with their victims. While it would be exorbitant to claim that global capitalism has been dealt a blow by Filipina agencies of coping and life maintenance, I would suggest here that this mode of representation (as exemplified by literary works like "Arrivederci" by Fanny Garcia, Ricardo Lee's play *Pitik-Bulag sa Buwan ng Pebrero*, and numerous feature films and documentaries), which I would categorize as a type of allegorical realism grounded in the confluence of vernacular poetics and selective borrowings from the Western avant-garde (Brecht, Neruda, Mayakovsky), enables us to grasp the synthesizing virtue of Filipino nationalism as it inhabits diasporic subjects. Perhaps this virtue manifests itself only as a potential reservoir of energies that can be mobilized in crisis situations; still, the cultural and ideological resistance of neocolonized Filipinos overseas testifies to its immanent presence in what Lenin called "the weak links" of the imperialist chain around the planet, not only in the peripheral dependencies but also in the nomadic embodiments of the margins now transposed to the centers of empire.

My first thesis on the phenomenon of the Filipino dismemberment is this: Given that the Philippine habitat has never cohered as a genuinely independent nation — national autonomy continues to escape the nation-people in a neocolonial setup — Filipinos are dispersed from family or kinship webs in villages, towns, or provincial regions first, and loosely from an inchoate, even "refeudalized," nation-state. This dispersal is primarily due to economic coercion and disenfranchisement under the retrogressive regime of comprador-bureaucratic (not welfare-state) capitalism; migration is seen as freedom to seek one's fortune, experience the pleasure of adventure, libidinal games of resistance, and other illusions of transcendence. So the origin to which one returns is not properly a nation-state but rather a village, a quasi-primordial community, kinship network, or even a ritual family; the state is viewed in fact as a corrupt exploiter, not representative of the masses, a comprador agent of transnational corporations and Western (specifically U.S.) powers.

Second thesis: What are the myths enabling a cathexis of the homeland? They derive from assorted childhood memories and folklore together with customary practices surrounding municipal and religious celebrations; at best, there may be signs of a residual affective tie to national heroes like Rizal, Bonifacio, and latter-day celebrities such as singers, movie stars, athletes, and so on. Indigenous food, dances, and music can be acquired as commodities whose presence temporarily heals the trauma of removal; family reunification can resolve the psychic damage of loss of status or alienation. In short, rootedness in autochtonous habitat does not exert a commanding sway, experienced only as a nostalgic mood. Meanwhile, language, religion, kinship, the aura of family rituals, and common experiences in school or workplace function invariably as the organic bonds of community.

Third thesis: Alienation in the host country is what unites Filipinos, a shared history of colonial and racial subordination, marginalization, and struggles for cultural survival through hybrid forms of resistance and political rebellion. This is what may replace the nonexistent nation/ homeland, absent the liberation of the Filipino nation. In the thirties, Carlos Bulosan once observed that "it is a crime to be a Filipino in America." Years of union struggle and political organizing in interethnic coalitions have blurred, if not erased, that stigma. Accomplishments in the civil rights struggles of the sixties have provided nourishment for ethnic pride. And, on the other side, impulses of assimilationism via the "model minority" umbrella have aroused a passion for multiculturalism divorced from any urge to disinvest in the "possessive investment in whiteness" (Lipsitz 1998). But compared to the Japanese or Indian Americans, Filipino Americans as a whole have not made it; the exceptions prove the rule. Andrew Cunanan, the serial killer who slew the famous Versace, is the specter that continues to haunt "melting pot" Filipino Americanists who continue to blabber about the "forgotten Filipino" in the hope of being awarded a share of the obsolescent welfare-state pie. Dispossession of sovereignty leads to shipwreck, natives drifting rudderless or marooned on islands all over the planet. Via strategies of community preservation and other schemes of defining the locality of the community in historical contexts of displacement, the Filipino diaspora defers its return — unless and until there is a Filipino nation that they can identify with. This will continue in places where there is no hope of permanent resettlement as citizens or bonafide residents (as in Japan, Hong Kong, Taiwan, Singapore, and elsewhere).

Fourth thesis: Some Filipinos in their old age may desire eventual return only when they are economically secure. In general, Filipinos will not return to the site of misery and oppression — to poverty, exploitation, humiliated status, unemployment, hunger, and lack of dignity. Of course, some are forcibly returned: deported or dead. But ocws would rather move their kin and parents to their place of employment, preferably in countries where family reunification is allowed, as in the United States, Italy, Canada, and so on. Or even in places of suffering and humiliation, provided there is some hope or illusion of future improvement. Devolution to kinship seems a protection against racist violence and unrelenting commodification.

Fifth thesis: Ongoing support for nationalist struggles at home is sporadic and intermittent during times of retrenchment and revitalized apartheid. Do we see any mass protests and collective indignation here at the Visiting Forces Agreement, for example, and the recent invasion of the country by several thousand U.S. Marines in joint U.S.-Philippines military exercises? During the Marcos dictatorship, the politicized generation of Filipino American youth here was able to mobilize a large segment of the community to support the national-democratic mass struggles, including the armed combatants of the New People's Army (led by the Communist Party of the Philippines), against U.S.-supported authoritarian rule. Filipino nationalism blossomed in the late sixties and seventies, but suffered attenuation when it got re-channeled to support the elite populism of Aquino and Ramos, the lumpen populism of Estrada, and now the mendacious Arroyo regime. This precarious balance of class forces at this conjuncture is subject to the shifts in political mobilization and calculation, hence the intervention of Filipino agencies with emancipatory goals and socialist principles is crucial and strategically necessary.

Sixth thesis: In this time of emergency, the Filipino collective identity is in crisis and in a stage of formation and elaboration. The Filipino diasporic consciousness is an odd species, a singular genre: it is not obsessed with a physical return to roots or to land where common sacrifices (to echo Ernest Renan) are remembered and celebrated. It is tied more to a symbolic homeland indexed by kinship or particularistic traditions that it tries to transplant abroad in diverse localities. So, in the moment of Babylonian captivity, dwelling in "Egypt" or its modern surrogates, building public spheres of solidarity to sustain identities outside the national time/space "in order to live inside, with a difference" may be the most viable route (or root) of Filipinos in motion— the collectivity in transit, although this is subject to the revolutionary transformations emerging in the Philippine countryside and cities. It is susceptible also to other radical changes in the geopolitical rivalry of metropolitan powers based on nation-states. There is indeed deferral, postponement, or waiting—but history moves on in the battlefields of Luzon, Visayas, and Mindanao where a people's war rooted in a durable revolutionary tradition rages on. This drama of a national-democratic revolution will not allow the Filipino diaspora to slumber in the consumerist paradises of Los Angeles, New York, Chicago, San Francisco, or Seattle. It will certainly disturb the peace of those benefiting from the labor and sacrifices of overseas Filipino workers who experience the repetition-compulsion of globalized trade and endure the recursive traumas of displacement and dispossession.

Caught in the crosscurrents of global upheavals, I can only conclude with a provisional and indeed temporizing epilogue—if I may beg leave from those Filipina bodies (at least five a day arrive at the Manila International Airport) in coffins heading home: Filipinos in the United States (and elsewhere, given the still hegemonic Western dispensation)—if I may quote the closing lines of my article in the Internet cyberspace on Filipino Americans—are neither "oriental" nor "hispanic," despite their looks and names. They might be syncretic or hybrid subjects with suspect loyalties. They cannot be called fashionable "transnationals" because of racialized, ascribed markers (physical appearance, accent, peculiar nonwhite folkways, and other group idiosyncracies) that are needed to sustain and reproduce white supremacy in this racial polity. Ultimately, Filipino agency in the era of global capitalism depends not only on the vicissitudes of social transformation in the

United States but, in a dialectical sense, on the fate of the struggle for autonomy and popular-democratic sovereignty in the Philippines where *balikbayans* still practice, although with increasing trepidation interrupted by fits of amnesia, the speech-acts and durable performances of *pakikibaka, pakikiramay, at pakikipagkapwa-tao.*

Left untranslated, those phrases from the "Filipino" vernacular address a gradually vanishing audience. Indeed, this book itself may just be a wayward apostrophe to a vanished dreamworld — a liberated homeland, a phantasmagoric refuge — evoking the utopias and archaic golden ages of myths and legends. But wherever it is, this homeland will surely be inhabited by a new collectivity as befits a new objective reality to which Susan Buck-Morss, in her elegiac paean to the catastrophe that overtook mass utopia, alludes: "the geographical mixing of people and things, global webs that disseminate meanings, electronic prostheses of the human body, new arrangements of the human sensorium. Such imaginings, freed from the constraints of bounded spaces and from the dictates of unilinear time, might dream of becoming, in Lenin's words, 'as radical as reality itself'" (2000, 278). That destination become destiny was already approximated by Marx in his view that "the coincidence of the changing of circumstances and of human activity or self-changing can be conceived and rationally understood only as revolutionary practice" (Fischer 1996, 170). Or, to translate in the proverbial idiom warranted by the experience of all diasporic bodies and ventriloquized by the Angel of History surveying the ruins before and after: *De te fabula.*

Works Cited

Agoncillo, Teodoro, and M. Guerrero. 1970. *History of the Filipino People.* Quezon City: R. P. Garcia Publishing Co.

Aguilar, Delia. 2000. *Globalization, Labor, and Women.* No. 9 of *Working Papers Series on Historical Systems, Peoples and Cultures.* Bowling Green, Ill.: Bowling Green State University.

Ahmad, Aijaz. 1992. *Theory: Classes, Nations, Literatures.* London: Verso.

———. 1995. Post-Colonialism: What's in a Name? In *Late Imperial Culture,* ed. Roman de la Campa, E. Ann Kaplan, and Michael Sprinker. London: Verso.

———. 1996. The Politics of Literary Postcoloniality. *Race and Class* 36.3: 1–20.

Ahmad, Eqbal. 1971. Revolutionary Warfare and Counterinsurgency. In *National Liberation,* ed. Norman Miller and Roderick Aya. New York: Free Press.

———. 1980. *Political Culture and Foreign Policy.* Washington, D.C.: Institute for Policy Studies.

Alcoff, Linda. 1991. The Problem of Speaking for Others. *Cultural Critique* (winter): 5–29.

Alexander, Jeffrey. 1992. Citizen and Enemy as Symbolic Classification: On the Polarizing Discourse of Civil Society. In *Cultivating Differences,* ed. Michelle Lamont and Marcel Founier. Chicago: University of Chicago Press.

Alexander, Neville. 1985. Nation and Ethnicity. In *Sow the Wind.* Johannesberg, South Africa: Skotaville Press.

Alter, Jonathan. 1995. Jumping to Conclusions. *Newsweek,* 1 May, 55.

Amin, Samir. 1977. *Imperialism and Unequal Development.* New York: Monthly Review Press.

———. 1989. *Eurocentrism.* New York: Monthly Review Press.

———. 1994. *Re-Reading the Postwar Period.* New York: Monthly Review Press.

———. 1998. *Spectres of Capitalism.* New York: Monthly Review Press.

————. 2000. The Political Economy of the Twentieth Century. *Monthly Review* 52 (June): 1–17. Also published as "Not a Happy Ending." *Al-Ahram* 30 Dec.–5 Jan. 1999/2000).

Andersen, Christopher. 1991. *Madonna Unauthorized*. New York: Dell.

Anderson, Benedict. 1991. *Imagined Communities*. London: Verso.

Anderson, Bridget. 2000. *Doing the Dirty Work?: The Global Politics of Domestic Labour*. London: Zed Press.

Anderson, Kevin. 1995. *Lenin, Hegel and Western Marxism*. Urbana: University of Illinois Press.

Anthias, Floya, and Nira Yuval-Davis. 1994. Women and the Nation-State. In *Nationalism*, ed. John Hutchinson and Anthony D. Smith. New York: Oxford University Press.

Appelbaum, Richard P. 1996. Multiculturalism and Flexibility: Some New Directions in Global Capitalism. In *Mapping Multiculturalism*, ed. Avery Gordon and Christopher Newfield. Minneapolis: University of Minnesota Press.

Arnason, Johann. 1990. Nationalism, Globalization and Modernity. In *Global Culture*, ed. Mike Featherstone. London: Sage Publications.

Aronowitz, Stanley. 1970. *Honor America*. New York: Times Change Press.

Ashcroft, Bill, Gareth Griffiths, and Helen Tiffin. 1989. *The Empire Writes Back*. London: Routledge.

————. 1998. *Key Concepts in Post-Colonial Studies*. New York: Routledge.

Bakhtin, Mikhail. 1981. *The Dialogic Imagination*. Austin: University of Texas Press.

Baldwin, James. 1988. A Talk to Teachers. In *The Graywolf Annual Five: Multicultural Literacy*, ed. Rick Simonson and Scott Walker. St. Paul, MN: Graywolf Press.

Balibar, Etienne. 1995. Culture and Identity (Working Notes). In *The Identity in Question*, ed. John Rajchman. New York: Routledge.

Balibar, Etienne, and Immanuel Wallerstein. 1991. *Race, Nation, Class: Ambiguous Identities*. London: Verso.

Banks, James A. 1991. *Teaching Strategies for Ethnic Studies*. Boston: Allyn and Bacon.

Banton, Michael. 1988. Institutional Racism. In *Dictionary of Race and Ethnic Relations*, ed. E. Ellis Cashmore. 2d ed. London: Routledge.

Banton, Michael, and Robert Miles. 1988. Racism. In *Dictionary of Race and Ethnic Relations*. London: Routledge.

Baraka, Amiri. 1998. Multinational, Multicultural America versus White Supremacy. In *Multi-America*, ed. Ishmael Reed. New York: Penguin Books.

Baron, Harold M. 1985. Racism Transformed: The Implications of the 1960s. *Review of Radical Political Economics* 17, no. 3: 10–33.

Barthes, Roland. 1972. *Mythologies*. New York: Hill and Wang.

———. 1981. *Camera Lucida*. New York: Hill and Wang.

Bastide, Roger. 1972. Dusky Venus, Black Apollo. In *Race and Social Difference*, ed. Paul Baxter and Basil Sansom. London: Penguin.

Baudrillard, Jean. 1988. *America*. London: Verso.

Benjamin, Walter. 1969. Theses on the Philosophy of History. In *Illuminations*. New York: Schocken.

———. 1978. *Reflections*. New York: Harcourt Brace Jovanovich.

Berger, John. 1999. Against the Great Defeat of the World. *Race and Class* 40, nos. 2–3: 1–4.

Berkhofer, Robert F. 1978. *The White Man's Indian*. New York: Vintage Books.

Berman, Nathaniel. 1995. Modernism, Nationalism and the Rhetoric of Reconstruction. In *After Identity: A Reader in Law and Culture*, ed. Dan Danielsen and Karen Engle. New York: Routledge.

Bernasconi, Robert. 2001. Who Invented the Concept of Race? Kant's Role in the Enlightenment Construction of Race. In *Race*, ed. R. Bernasconi. Oxford: Blackwell Publishers.

Bhabha, Homi. 1994a. *The Location of Culture*. New York: Routledge.

———. 1994b. Remembering Fanon: Self, Psyche and the Colonial Condition. In *Colonial Discourse and Post-Colonial Theory*, ed. Patrick Williams and Laura Chrisman. New York: Columbia University Press.

Bhaskar, Roy. 1983. Dialectic. In *A Dictionary of Marxist Thought*, ed. Tom Bottomore. Cambridge, Mass.: Harvard University Press.

———. 1993. *Dialectic: The Pulse of Freedom*. London: Verso.

Billig, Michael. 1995. *Banal Nationalism*. London: Sage Publications.

Black Elk. 1932. *Black Elk Speaks* (as told through John G. Neihardt). New York: Pocketbooks.

Black Radical Congress. 2001. Contemporary Police Brutality and Misconduct: A Continuation of the Legacy of Racial Violence. Press Release/Statement, February 8, 2001. ⟨http://www.blackradicalcongress.org⟩

Blauner, Robert. 1972. *Racial Oppression in America*. New York: Harper & Row.

Bloch, Maurice. 1985. *Marxism and Anthropology*. Oxford: Oxford University Press.

Bloom, Steve. 1999. *Fighting for Justice: The Case of Mumia Abu-Jamal*. New York: Prison Issues Working Group of Solidarity.

Bocock, Robert. 1986. *Hegemony*. London: Tavistock.

Bonacich, Edna. 1996. The Class Question in Global Capitalism. In *Mapping Multiculturalism*, ed. Avery Gordon and Christopher Newfield. Minneapolis: University of Minnesota Press.

————. 2000. Racism in the Deep Structure of U.S. Higher Education: When Affirmative Action is Not Enough. In *Structured Inequality in the United States*, ed. Adalberto Aguirre Jr. and David V. Baker. Englewood Cliffs, N.J.: Prentice Hall.

Boggs, Grace Lee. 1998. *Living for Change: An Autobiography*. Minneapolis: University of Minnesota Press.

————. 1999. Our Country — to Change for the Better. *Amerasia Journal* 25: xvii–xxviii.

Bonilla-Silva, Eduardo. 1999. The New Racism: Racial Structure in the United States, 1960s–1990s. In *Race, Ethnicity and Nationality in the United States*, ed. Paul Wong. Boulder, Colo.: Westview Press.

Boose, Lynda. 1993. Techno-muscularity and the "Boy Eternal": From the Quagmire to the Gulf. In *Cultures of United States Imperialism*, ed. Amy Kaplan and Donald Pease. Durham, N.C.: Duke University Press.

Boti, Marie, and Michelle Smith. 1997. Migration in Asia: Human Resources for Globalization. Montreal, Quebec, Canada. Unpublished ms. 6 pages.

Bourdieu, Pierre. 1991. *Language and Symbolic Power*. Cambridge, Mass.: Harvard University Press.

————. 1993. *The Field of Cultural Production*. New York: Columbia University Press.

————. 1998a. *Acts of Resistance*. New York: New Press.

————. 1998b. *Practical Reason*. Stanford, Calif.: Stanford University Press.

————. 1999. Structures, Habitus, Practices. In *Contemporary Social Theory*, ed. Anthony Elliot. Malden, Mass.: Blackwell.

————. 2000. *Pascalian Meditations*. Trans. Richard Nice. Stanford, Calif.: Stanford University Press.

Bourdieu, Pierre, and Loic J. D. Wacquant. 1992. *An Invitation to Reflexive Sociology*. Chicago: University of Chicago Press.

Bourne, Randolph. 1997. Trans-National America. In *Identity, Community and Pluralism in American Life*, ed. William Fischer et al. New York: Oxford University Press.

Bowle, John. 1947. *Western Political Thought*. London: Methuen.

Bowman, Glenn. 1994. "A Country of Words": Conceiving the Palestinian Nation from the Position of Exile. In *The Making of Political Identities*, ed. Ernesto Laclau. London: Verso.

Bowser, Benjamin. 1995. Racism in the Modern World Community. In *Racism and Anti-Racism in World Perspective*, ed. Benjamin Bowser. Thousand Oaks, Calif.: Sage Publications.

Brantlinger, Patrick. 1990. *Crusoe's Footprints*. New York: Routledge.

Brecher, Jeremy, John Brown Childs, and Jill Cutler. 1993. *Global Visions: Beyond the New World Order*. Boston: South End Press.

Bromley, Y. V. 1974. The Term "Ethnos" and Its Definition. In *Race and Peoples: Contemporary Ethnic and Racial Problems*. Moscow: Progress Publishers.

Brown, Michael. 1986. *The Production of Society*. Totowa, N.J.: Rowman and Littlefield.

Bruin, Janet. 1996. *Root Causes of the Global Crisis*. Manila, Philippines: Institute of Political Economy.

Buci-Glucksmann, Christine. 1980. *Gramsci and the State*. London: Lawrence and Wishart.

———. 1982. Hegemony and Consent: A Political Strategy. In *Approaches to Gramsci*, ed. Ann Showstack Sassoon. London: Writers and Readers.

Buck-Morss, Susan. 2000. *Dreamworld and Catastrophe*. Cambridge, Mass.: MIT Press.

Buell, Frederick. 1994. *National Culture and the New Global System*. Baltimore, Md.: Johns Hopkins University Press.

Bulosan, Carlos. 1995. *On Becoming Filipino: Selected Writings of Carlos Bulosan*, ed. E. San Juan Jr. Philadelphia, Pa.: Temple University Press.

Butler, Johnella. 1991. Ethnic Studies: A Matrix Model for the Major. *Liberal Education* 77, no. 2 (Mar.–Apr.): 26–32.

Cabezas, Amado, and Gary Kawaguchi. 1989. Race, Gender, and Class for Filipino Americans. In *A Look Beyond the Model Minority Image*, ed. Grace Yun. New York: Minority Rights Group Inc.

Cabral, Amilcar. 1973. *Return to the Source: Selected Speeches of Amilcar Cabral*. New York: Monthly Review Press.

———. 1979. The Role of Culture in the Liberation Struggle. In *Communication and Class Struggle*. Vol. 1, *Capitalism, Imperialism*. New York: International General.

Callinicos, Alex. 1982. *Is There A Future for Marxism?* Atlantic Highlands, N.J.: Humanities Press.

———. 1989. *Against Postmodernism: A Marxist Critique*. New York: St. Martin's Press.

———. 1993. *Race and Class*. London: Bookmarks.

———. 1995. Wonders Taken for Signs: Homi Bhabha's Postcolonialism. In *Post-Ality: Marxism and Postmodernism*, ed. Mas'ud Zavarzadeh, Teresa Ebert, and Donald Morton. Washington, D.C.: Maisonneuve Press.

Carby, Hazel. 1990. The Politics of Difference. *Ms.* (Sept./Oct.): 84–85.

Carr, E. H. 1961. *What is History?* New York: Vintage Books.

Carroll, Peter N., and David W. Noble. 1988. *The Free and the Unfree: A New History of the United States*. 2d ed. New York: Penguin Books.

Cashmore, Ellis. 1988. *Dictionary of Race and Ethnic Relations*. London: Routledge.

Cawelti, John. 1976. *Adventure, Mystery, and Romance*. Chicago: University of Chicago Press.

Chakrabarty, Dipesh. 1995. Postcoloniality and the Artifice of History. In *The Postcolonial Studies Reader*, ed. Bill Ashcroft, Gareth Griffiths, and Helen Tiffin. New York: Routledge.

Chaliand, Gerard. 1969. *Armed Struggle in Africa*. New York: Monthly Review Press.

Chan, Sucheng. 1991. *Asian Americans*. Boston: Twayne Publishers.

Chang, Grace. 2000. *Disposable Domestics*. Boston: South End Press.

Chang, Harry. 1985. Toward a Marxist Theory of Racism. *Review of Radical Political Economics* 17, no. 3: 34–45.

Chang, Robert S. 1995. Toward an Asian American Legal Scholarship: Critical Race Theory, Post-Structuralism, and Narrative Space. In *Critical Race Theory: The Cutting Edge*, ed. Richard Delgado. Philadelphia, Pa.: Temple University Press.

Chasin, Barbara. 1998. *Inequality and Violence in the U.S.* Amherst, N.Y.: Humanity Books.

Chavez, Linda. 1998. Civic Education in a Changing Society. In *Multiculturalism and American Democracy*, ed. Arthur Melzer et al. Lawrence: University of Kansas Press.

Chen, Kuan-Hsing. 1996. Cultural Studies and the Politics of Internationalization: An Interview with Stuart Hall. In *Stuart Hall: Critical Dialogues in Cultural Studies*, ed. David Morley and Kuan-Hsing Chen. New York: Routledge.

Chen Xiaomei. 1994. *Occidentalism: Theory of Counter-Discourse in Post-Mao China*. New York: Oxford University Press.

Cheung, King-kok. 1990. The Woman Warrior versus the Chinaman Pacific: Must a Chinese-American Critic Choose Between Feminism and Heroism? In *Conflicts in Feminism*, ed. Marianne Hirsch and Evelyn Fox Keller. New York: Routledge.

Childs, John Brown. 1993. The Value of Diversity for Global Cooperation. In *Global Visions: Beyond the New World Order*, ed. Jeremy Brecher, John Brown Childs, and Jill Cutler. Boston: South End Press.

Chin, Frank. 1976. Back Talk. In *Counterpoint: Perspectives on Asian America*, ed. Emma Gee. Los Angeles: Asian American Studies Center.

———. 1981. *The Chickencoop Chinaman and The Year of the Dragon*. Seattle: University of Washington Press.

———. 1983. Our Life is War. *Seattle Weekly*. 4 May, 28–32, 34–38.

———. 1988. *The Chinaman Pacific and Frisco R.R. Co*. Minneapolis: Coffee House Press.

———. 1991. *Donald Duk*. Minneapolis: Coffee House Press.

———. 1992. Interview. In *Race* by Studs Terkel. New York: New Press.

———. 1994. *Gunga Din Highway*. Minneapolis: Coffee House Press.

———. 1997. Rashomon Road: On the Tao to San Diego. In *MultiAmerica: Essays on Cultural Wars and Cultural Peace*, ed. Ishmael Reed. New York: Viking.

———. 1999. *Bulletproof Buddhists*. Honolulu: University of Hawaii Press.

Chomsky, Noam. 1992. *What Uncle Sam Really Wants*. Berkeley: Odonian Press.

Clark, Joe et al. 1976. Subcultures, Cultures and Class. In *Resistance Through Rituals*, ed. S. Hall and T. Jefferson. London: Hutchinson.

Clark, Lorenne. 1979. Women and Locke: Who Owns the Apples in the Garden of Eden? In *The Sexism of Social and Political Theory*, ed. Lorenne Clark and Lynda Lange. Toronto: University of Toronto Press.

Clifford, James. 1992. Traveling Cultures. In *Cultural Studies*, ed. Lawrence Grossberg, Cary Nelson, and Paula Treichler. Urbana: University of Illinois Press.

———. 1997. Diasporas. In *The Ethnicity Reader*, ed. M. Guibernau and John Rex. Cambridge: Polity Press.

Cobban, Alfred. 1994. National Self-Determination. In *Nationalism*, ed. John Hutchinson and Anthony D. Smith. New York: Oxford University Press.

Cohen, Sylvester. 1998. Amilcar Cabral: An Extraction from the Literature. *Monthly Review* (Dec.): 39–47.

Collins, Patricia Hill. 2001. Like One of the Family: Race, Ethnicity, and the Paradox of U.S. National Identity. *Ethnic and Racial Studies* (Jan.): 3–28.

Comaroff, John, and Jean Comaroff. 1992. *Ethnography and the Historical Imagination*. Boulder, Colo.: Westview Press.

Constable, Nicole. 1997. *Maid to Order in Hong Kong: Stories of Filipina Workers*. Ithaca, N.Y.: Cornell University Press.

———. 1999. At Home But Not at Home: Filipina Narratives of Ambivalent Returns. *Cultural Anthropology* 14: 203–28.

Constantino, Renato. 1970. *Dissent and Counter-Consciousness*. Quezon City, Philippines: Malaya Books.

———. 1975. *The Philippines: A Past Revisited*. Quezon City, Philippines: Tala Publishing Services.

Coombe, Rosemary. 1995. The Properties of Culture and the Politics of Possessing Identity: Native Claims in the Cultural Appropriation Controversy. In *After Identity*, ed. Dan Danielsen and Karen Engle. New York: Routledge.

Cotter, Jennifer. 1996. Dematerializing the Material: (Post)modern Cultural Studies and the Politics of Experience. *Red Orange* 1, no. 1 (May): 203–24.

Cowley, Geoffrey. 1995. It's Time to Rethink Nature and Nurture. *Newsweek*, 27 Mar., 52–53.

Cox, Oliver Cromwell. 1948. *Caste, Class and Race*. New York: Monthly Review Press.

Crapanzano, Vincent. 1992. *Hermes' Dilemma and Hamlet's Desire*. Cambridge, Mass.: Harvard University Press.

Daniels, Roger. 1993. United States Policy Towards Asian Immigrants: Contemporary Developments in Historical Perspective. *International Journal* 48: 310–34.

Davidson, Basil. 1969. *The Liberation of Guine*. New York: Penguin Books.

———. 1986. On Revolutionary Nationalism: The Legacy of Cabral. *Race and Class* xxvii, no. 3: 21–45.

Davies, Ioan. 1995. *Cultural Studies and Beyond: Fragments of Empire*. London: Routledge.

Davis, Angela. 1996. Gender, Class, and Multiculturalism: Rethinking "Race" Politics. In *Mapping Multiculturalism*, ed. Avery Gordon and Christopher Newfield. Minneapolis: University of Minnesota Press.

———. 1998. *The Angela Davis Reader*. New York: Blackwell.

Davis, Horace. 1978. *Toward a Marxist Theory of Nationalism*. New York: Monthly Review Press.

Davis, Mike. 1992. In Los Angeles, Burning All Illusions. *The Nation*, 1 June, 743–46.

Davis, Robert Murray. 1995. Gunga Din Highway. *World Literature Today* 69 (spring): 360–61.

Delgado, Richard, ed. 1995. *Critical Race Theory: The Cutting Edge*. Philadelphia, Pa.: Temple University Press.

Demko, George. 1992. *Why in the World: Adventures in Geography*. New York: Anchor Books.

Denis, Manuel Maldonado. 1982. National Liberation: Categorical Imperative for the Peoples of Our America. *Tricontinental* 82: 8–15.

Dews, Peter. 1995. *Logics of Disintegration*. London: Verso.

Dinnerstein, Leonard, Roger Nichols, and David Reimer. 1996. *Natives and Strangers*. New York: Oxford University Press.

Dirlik, Arif. 1997. *The Postcolonial Aura*. Boulder, Colo.: Westview Press.

———. 2000. *Postmodernity's Histories*. New York: Rowman and Littlefield.

Douglas, Mary. 1966. *Purity and Danger*. London: Routledge.

D'Souza, Dinesh. 1991. *Illiberal Education*. New York: Free Press.

Dudley, William, ed. 1997. *Asian Americans: Opposing Viewpoints*. San Diego, Calif.: Greenhaven Press, Inc.

Dunn, John. 1979. *Western Political Theory in the Face of the Future*. Cambridge: Cambridge University Press.

Dunn, Robert G. 1998. *Identity Crises: A Social Critique of Postmodernity*. Minneapolis: University of Minnesota Press.

Dyson, Michael Eric. 1997. *Race Rules*. New York: Vintage Books.

Dworkin, Dennis, and Leslie G. Roman. 1993. *Views Beyond the Border Country*. New York: Routledge.

Eagleton, Terry. 1991. *Ideology: An Introduction*. London: Verso.

——. 2000. *The Idea of Culture*. Oxford: Blackwell.

Easthope, Antony. 1991. *Literary Into Cultural Studies*. New York: Routledge.

Ebert, Teresa. 1996. *Ludic Feminism and After*. Ann Arbor: University of Michigan Press.

——. 2000. *Globalization, Class and Cynical Reason*. Vol. 15 of *Working Papers in Cultural Studies, Ethnicity and Race Relations*, ed. E. San Juan Jr. Pullman: Department of Comparative American Cultures, Washington State University.

Edelman, Bernard. 1979. *Ownership of the Image*. London: Routledge and Kegan Paul.

Edwards, Richard, Michael Reich, and Thomas Weisskopf, eds. 1972. *The Capitalist System*. Englewood Cliffs, N.J.: Prentice-Hall, Inc.

Eisenstein, Zillah. 1994. *The Color of Gender: Reimaging Democracy*. Berkeley: University of California Press.

El Saadawi, Nawal. 1997. *The Nawal El Saadawi Reader*. London and New York: Zed Books.

Ellwood, Wayne, ed. 1999. *The A to Z of World Development*. Oxford: The New Internationalist.

Enloe, Cynthia. 1989. *Bananas, Beaches and Bases*. Berkeley: University of California Press.

——. 1993. *The Morning After*. Berkeley: University of California Press.

Epstein, Barbara. 1995. Postwar Panics and the Crisis of Masculinity. In *Marxism in the Postmodern Age*, ed. Antonio Callari, Stephen Cullenberg, and Carole Biewener. New York: Guilford Press.

Escobar, Arturo. 1995. *Encountering Development*. Princeton, N.J.: Princeton University Press.

Esman, Milton. 1996. Diasporas and International Relations. In *Ethnicity*, ed. John Hutchins and Anthony Smith. New York: Oxford University Press.

Essed, Philomena. 1991. *Everyday Racism*. Newbury Park, Calif.: Sage Publications.

Fabian, Johannes. 1983. *Time and the Other*. New York: Columbia University Press.

Fanon, Frantz. 1965. *A Dying Colonialism*. Trans. Haakon Chevalier. New York: Grove Press.

———. 1967a. *Black Skin, White Masks*. Trans. Charles Markmann. New York: Grove Press.

———. 1967b. *Toward the African Revolution*. New York: Grove Press.

———. 1968. *The Wretched of the Earth*. Trans. Constance Farrington. New York: Grove Press.

Feagin, Joe R. 1997. Old Poison in New Bottles: The Deep Roots of Modern Nativism. In *Critical White Studies*, ed. Richard Delgado and Jean Stefancic. Philadelphia: Temple University Press.

Featherstone, Mike, ed. 1990. *Global Culture*. London: Sage Publications.

———. 1991. *Consumer Culture and Postmodernism*. London: Sage Publications.

Fischer, Ernst. 1996. *How to Read Karl Marx*. New York: Monthly Review Press.

Fiske, John. 1992. Cultural Studies and the Culture of Everyday Life. In *Cultural Studies*, ed. Lawrence Grossberg et al. New York: Routledge.

———. 1993. Madonna. In *Ways of Reading*, ed. David Bartholomae and Anthony Petrosky. New York: Bedford Books.

Fox-Genovese, Elizabeth. 1995. Between Elitism and Populism: Whither Comparative Literature? In *Comparative Literature in the Age of Multiculturalism*, ed. Charles Bernheimer. Baltimore, Md.: Johns Hopkins University Press.

Francisco, Luzviminda. 1987. The Philippine American War. In *The Philippines Reader*, ed. D. B. Schirmer and S. Shalom. Boston: South End Press.

Fraser, Nancy. 1995. From Redistribution to Recognition? Dilemmas of Justice in a "Post-Socialist" Age. *New Left Review* 212 (July–Aug.): 68–93.

———. 1997. *Justice Interruptus*. New York: Routledge.

Fredrickson, George. 2000. *The Comparative Imagination*. Berkeley: University of California Press.

Freedman, Carl. 1992. Louisiana Duce: Notes Toward a Systematic Analysis of Postmodern Fascism in America. *Rethinking Marxism* 5, no. 1 (spring): 20–31.

Frow, John. 1997. *Time and Commodity Culture*. Oxford: Clarendon Press.

Galeano, Eduardo. 1973. *Open Veins of Latin America*. New York: Monthly Review Press.

Gandhi, Leela. 1998. *Postcolonial Theory*. New York: Columbia University Press.

Gans, Herbert. 1996. Symbolic Ethnicity. In *Ethnicity*, ed. John Hutchins and Anthony Smith. New York: Oxford University Press.

Garcia, Fanny. 1994. Arrivederci. In *Ang Silid na Mahiwaga*, ed. Soledad Reyes. Pasig, Rizal: Anvil Publishing Co.

Garnham, Nicholas. 1999. Political Economy and Cultural Studies. In *The Cultural Studies Reader*. 2d ed. New York: Routledge.

Gates, Henry Louis Jr. 1992. "Ethnic and Minority" Studies. In *Introduction to Scholarship in Modern Languages and Literatures*, ed. Joseph Gibaldi. New York: Modern Language Association of America.

Geertz, Clifford. 1993. "Ethnic Conflict": Three Alternative Terms. *Common Knowledge* (winter): 54–64.

Gellner, Ernest. 1983. *Nations and Nationalism*. Ithaca, N.Y.: Cornell University Press.

Gibson, Nigel C. 1999. Radical Mutations: Fanon's Untidy Dialectic of History. In *Rethinking Fanon*, ed. Nigel Gibson. Amherst, N.Y.: Humanity Books.

Giddens, Anthony. 1979. *Central Problems in Social Theory*. Berkeley: University of California Press.

———. 1984. *The Constitution of Society: Outline of the Theory of Structuration*. Cambridge: Polity Press.

———. 1985. *The Nation-State and Violence*. Cambridge: Polity Press.

———. 1987. *Social Theory and Modern Sociology*. Stanford, Calif.: Stanford University Press.

Gilroy, Paul. 1993. *The Black Atlantic*. Cambridge, Mass.: Harvard University Press.

Giroux, Henry. 1995. National Identity and the Politics of Multiculturalism. *College Literature* 22 (June): 42–57.

———. 1996a. *Fugitive Cultures: Race, Violence and Youth*. New York: Routledge.

———. 1996b. Pedagogy and Radical Democracy in the Age of "Political Correctness." In *Radical Democracy*, ed. David Trend. New York: Routledge.

Gitlin, Todd. 1995. *The Twilight of Common Dreams*. New York: Henry Holt and Co.

Glazer, Nathan, and Daniel P. Moynihan. 1975. *Ethnicity: Theory and Experience*. Cambridge, Mass.: Harvard University Press.

Gleason, Philip. 1980. American Identity and Americanization. In *Harvard Encyclopedia of American Ethnic Groups*, ed. Stephan Thernstrom. Cambridge, Mass.: Harvard University Press.

Godelier, Maurice. 1977. *Perspectives in Marxist Anthropology*. London: Cambridge University Press.

Goffman, Erving. 1963. *Stigma: Notes on the Management of Spoiled Identity*. New York: Simon & Schuster.

Goldberg, David Theo. 1993. *Racist Culture*. Cambridge, Mass.: Blackwell.

———, ed. 1994. *Multiculturalism: A Critical Reader*. Cambridge, Mass.: Blackwell.

Goldfield, Michael. 1991. The Color of Politics in the United States: White Supremacy as the Main Explanation for the Peculiarities of American Politics from Colonial Times to the Present. In *The Bounds of Race*, ed. Dominick Lacapra. Ithaca, N.Y.: Cornell University Press.

———. 1997. *The Color of Politics*. New York: New Press.

Gonzales, Juan L. 1993. *Racial and Ethnic Groups in America*. Dubuque, Iowa: Kendall Hunt Publishing Co.

Gooding-Williams, Robert. 2001. Race, Multiculturalism and Democracy. In *Race*, ed. Robert Bernasconi. Oxford: Blackwell Publishers.

Gordon, Lewis. 1997. *Her Majesty's Other Children*. Lanham, Md.: Rowman and Littlefield.

———. 1999. Fanon, Philosophy, and Racism. In *Racism and Philosophy*, ed. Susan Babbit and Sue Campbell. New York: Cornell University Press.

Gotanda, Neil. 1995. Critical Legal Studies, Critical Race Theory and Asian American Studies. *Amerasia Journal* 21, nos. 1–2: 127–36.

———. 1996. Multiculturalism and Racial Stratification. In *Mapping Multiculturalism*, ed. Avery Gordon and Christopher Newfield. New York: Routledge.

Gould, Stephen Jay. 1996. The Geometer of Race. In *Race and Ethnic Relations 96/97*, ed. John A. Kromkowski. Guilford, Conn.: Dushkin Publishing Group.

Graff, Gerald. 1992. *Beyond the Culture Wars*. New York: W. W. Norton.

Gramsci, Antonio. 1957. *The Modern Prince and Other Writings*. New York: International Publishers.

———. 1971. *Selections from the Prison Notebooks*. New York: International Publishers.

Gran, Peter. 1993. Race and Racism in the Modern World: How It Works in Different Hegemonies. *Transforming Anthropology* 5, nos. 1–2: 8–14.

———. 1996. *Beyond Eurocentrism: A New View of Modern World History*. Syracuse, N.Y.: Syracuse University Press.

———. 1999. Subaltern Studies as Praxis in India and in the United States. *Working Papers in Cultural Studies, Ethnicity and Race Relations #4*, ed. E. San Juan Jr. Pullman: Department of Comparative American Cultures, Washington State University.

Grandin, G., and F. Goldman. 1999. Bitter Fruit for Rigoberta. *The Nation*, 8 Feb.: 25–8.

Greenblatt, Stephen. 1994. Culture. In *Critical Terms for Literary Study*, ed. Frank Lentricchia and Thomas McLaughlin. Chicago: University of Chicago Press.

Greene, Felix. 1970. *The Enemy: What Every American Should Know About Imperialism*. New York: Random House.

Greer, Colin. 1984. The Ethnic Question. In *The 60s Without Apology*, ed. Sohnya Sayres et al. Minneapolis: University of Minnesota Press.

Grossberg, Lawrence. 1996. Identity and Cultural Studies: Is That All There Is? In *Questions of Cultural Identity*, ed. Stuart Hall and Paul du Gay. London: Sage Publishers.

Grossberg, Lawrence, Cary Nelson, and Paula Treichler, eds. 1992. Cultural Studies: An Introduction. In *Cultural Studies*. New York: Routledge.

Gruenbaum, Ellen. 1996. The Cultural Debate Over Female Circumcision: The Sudanese are Arguing This One Out For Themselves. *Medical Anthropology Quarterly* 10, no. 4: 455–75.

Guattari, Felix, and Toni Negri. 1990. *Communists Like Us*. New York: Semiotext(e) Foreign Agents Series.

Guerrero, M. Anette Jaimes. 1996. Academic Apartheid: American Indian Studies and Multiculturalism. In *Mapping Multiculturalism*, ed. Avery Gordon and Christopher Newfield. Minneapolis: University of Minnesota Press.

Guillaumin, Colette. 1995. *Racism, Sexism, Power and Ideology*. London: Routledge.

Guinier, Lani. 1995. Groups, Representation, and Race-Conscious Districting: A Case of the Emperor's Clothes. In *Critical Race Theory*, ed. Kimberle Crenshaw et al. New York: New Press.

Gutierrez, Ramon. 1994. Ethnic Studies: Its Evolution in American Colleges and Universities. In *Multiculturalism: A Critical Reader*, ed. David Goldberg. Cambridge, Mass.: Blackwell.

Habermas, Jurgen. 1987. *The Philosophical Discourse of Modernity*. Cambridge, Mass.: MIT Press.

———. 1994. Struggles for Recognition in the Democratic Constitutional State. In *Multiculturalism*, ed. Amy Gutman. Princeton, N.J.: Princeton University Press.

Hall, Stuart. 1980. Race, Articulation and Societies Structured in Dominance. In *Sociological Theories: Race and Colonialism*. Paris: UNESCO.

———. 1986. Gramsci's Relevance for the Study of Race and Ethnicity. *Journal of Communication Inquiry* 10, no. 2: 5–27.

———. 1992a. New Ethnicities. In *Race, Culture and Difference*, ed. James Donald and Ali Rattansi. London: Sage.

———. 1992b. Race, Culture, and Communications: Looking Backward and Forward at Cultural Studies. *Rethinking Marxism* 5, no. 1 (spring): 10–18.

———. 1996a. *Critical Dialogues in Cultural Studies*, ed. David Morley and Kuan-Hsing Chen. New York: Routledge.

——. 1996b. On Postmodernism and Articulation: An Interview with Lawrence Grossberg. In *Critical Dialogues in Cultural Studies*. Ed. David Morley and Kuan-Hsing Chen. New York: Routledge.

——. 1998. Subjects in History: Making Diasporic Identities. In *The House that Race Built*, ed. Wahneema Lubiano. New York: Vintage Books.

Hall, Stuart, and T. Jefferson, eds. 1976. *Resistance Through Rituals*. London: Hutchinson.

Handlin, Oscar. 1957. *Race and Nationality in American Life*. Boston: Little Brown & Co.

——. 1959. *Immigration as a Factor in American History*. New York: Prentice Hall.

Hansen, Emmanuel. 1999. Frantz Fanon: Portrait of a Revolutionary. In *Rethinking Fanon*, ed. Nigel Gibson. Amherst, N.Y.: Humanity Books.

Haraway, Donna. 1992. The Promises of Monsters: A Regenerative Politics for Inappropriate/d Others. In *Cultural Studies*, ed. Lawrence Grossberg et al. New York: Routledge.

Harris, Alice Kessler. 1992. Multiculturalism Can Strengthen, Not Undermine A Common Culture. *The Chronicle for Higher Education*. 21 Oct.: B3, B7.

Harvey, David. 1989. *The Condition of Postmodernity*. London: Blackwell.

——. 1996. *Justice, Nature and the Geography of Difference*. Malden, Mass.: Blackwell.

——. 2000. *Spaces of Hope*. Berkeley: University of California Press.

Haug, Frigga. 1992. *Beyond Female Masochism*. New York: Verso.

Haug, Wolfgang Fritz. 1984. Learning the Dialectics of Marxism. In *Rethinking Marx*, ed. Sakari Hanninen and Leena Paldan. New York: International General.

——. 1986. *Critique of Commodity Aesthetics*. Oxford: Polity Press.

——. 1987. *Commodity Aesthetics, Ideology and Culture*. New York: International General.

——. 2000. Commodity Aesthetics. *Working Papers in Cultural Studies, Ethnicity and Race Relations #15*, ed. E. San Juan Jr. Pullman: Department of Comparative American Cultures, Washington State University.

Hebdige, Dick. 1979. *Subculture: The Meaning of Style*. London: Methuen.

——. 1993. From Culture to Hegemony. In *The Cultural Studies Reader*, ed. Simon During. New York: Routledge.

Held, David. 1992. The Development of the Modern State. In *Formations of Modernity*, ed. Stuart Hall and Bram Gieben. Cambridge: Polity Press.

Heller, Agnes. 1984. *Everyday Life*. New York: Routledge and Kegan Paul.

——. 1999. *A Theory of Modernity*. Oxford: Blackwell Publishers.

Hernton, Calvin. 1965. *Sex and Race in America*. New York: Anchor Books.

Hesse, Barnor. 1997. It's Your World: Discrepant M/Multiculturalisms. *Social Identities* 3, no. 3 (Oct.): 375–94.

Higham, John. 1971. *Strangers in the Land.* New York: Atheneum.

Hirsch, E. D. 1993. The Theory Behind the Dictionary: Cultural Literacy and Education. In *The Dictionary of Cultural Literacy*, ed. E. D. Hirsch, Joseph F. Kett, and James Trefill. Boston: Houghton Mifflin Co.

Hobsbawm, E. J. 1973. *Revolutions.* New York: New American Library.

Hodge, Bob. 1995. Labor Theory of Language: Postmodernism and a Marxist Science of Language. In *Post-Ality: Marxism and Postmodernism*, ed. Mas'ud Zavarzadeh et al. Washington, D.C.: Maisonneuve Press.

Hoffman, Piotr. 1989. *Violence in Modern Philosophy.* Chicago: University of Chicago Press.

Hollinger, David A. 1998. Nationalism, Cosmopolitanism, and the United States. In *Immigration and Citizenship*, ed. Noah Pickus. Lanham, Md.: Rowman and Littlefield.

Hongo, Garrett. 1998. Culture Wars in Asian America. In *The Social Construction of Race and Ethnicity in the United States*, ed. Joan Ferrante and Prince Brown Jr. New York: Longman.

Hoogvelt, Ankie. 1997. *Globalization and the Postcolonial World.* Baltimore, Md.: Johns Hopkins University Press.

Horowitz, Irving Louis. 1977. *Ideology and Utopia in the United States 1956–1976.* New York: Harper Torchbooks.

Horsman, Reginald. 1981. *Race and Manifest Destiny: The Origins of American Racial Anglo-Saxonism.* Cambridge, Mass.: Harvard University Press.

Howard, Dick. 1977. *The Marxian Legacy.* New York: Urizen Books.

Howard, Michael. 1991. *The Lessons of History.* Oxford: Oxford University Press.

Hu-DeHart, Evelyn. 1995. The Undermining of Ethnic Studies. *The Chronicle of Higher Education*, 20 Oct., sec. 2.

———. 1999. Introduction: Asian American Formations in the Age of Globalization. In *Across the Pacific: Asian Americans and Globalization.* New York: Asia Society.

Hudis, Peter. 1983. *Marx and the Third World.* Detroit, Mich.: News and Letters Committees.

Hughes, Robert. 1993. *Culture of Complaint.* New York: Warner Books.

Hutcheon, Linda. 1995. Introduction: Complexities Abounding. *PMLA* (Jan.): 7–16.

Hymer, S. 1975. The Multinational Corporation and the Law of Uneven Development. In *International Firms and Modern Imperialism*, ed. Hugo Radice. Baltimore, Md.: Penguin Books.

Ignatiev, Noel. 1994. Treason to Whiteness is Loyalty to Humanity. *Utne Reader*, Nov.–Dec., 82–86.

Ileto, Reynaldo. 1998. *Filipinos and Their Revolution*. Quezon City, Philippines: Ateneo de Manila University Press.

Inglis, Fred. 1993. *Cultural Studies*. Oxford: Blackwell.

———. 1995. *Raymond Williams*. New York: Routledge.

Isikoff, Michael. 1995. To Be or Not to Be. *Newsweek*, 23 Jan., 64–67.

Jackson, George L. 1972. *Blood in My Eye*. New York: Bantam Books.

Jacobs, Ronald N. 1998. The Racial Discourse of Civil Society: The Rodney King Affair and the County of Los Angeles. In *Real Civil Societies*, ed. Jeffrey C. Alexander. London: Sage.

Jacoby, Russell. 1994a. *Dogmatic Wisdom*. New York: Anchor Books.

———. 1994b. The Myth of Multiculturalism. *New Left Review* 208 (Nov.–Dec.): 121–26.

James, C. L. R. 1992. *The C. L. R. James Reader*. Oxford: Blackwell Publishers.

Jameson, Fredric. 1981. *The Political Unconscious*. Ithaca, N.Y.: Cornell University Press.

———. 1991. Thoughts on the Late War. *Social Text* 28: 142–46.

———. 1995. On Cultural Studies. In *The Identity in Question*, ed. John Rajchman. New York: Routledge.

———. 1998a. *The Cultural Turn*. London: Verso.

———. 1998b. *Brecht and Method*. London: Verso.

———. 2000. *The Jameson Reader*, ed. Michael Hardt and Kathi Weeks. Oxford: Blackwell.

Janiewski, Dolores. 1995. Gendering, Racializing and Classifying: Settler Colonization in the United States, 1590–1990. *Unsettling Settler Societies*, ed. Daiva Stasiulis and Nira Yuval-Davis. London: Sage Publications.

Jefferson, Thomas. [1815] 1998. Letter from Thomas Jefferson: Virginia's Definition of a Mulatto. In *The Social Construction of Race and Ethnicity in the United States*, ed. Joan Ferrante and Prince Brown Jr. New York: Longman.

Jenkins, Richard. 1986. Social Anthropological Models of Inter-Ethnic Relations. In *Theories of Race and Ethnic Relations*, ed. John Rex and David Mason. New York: Cambridge University Press.

Jessop, Bob. 1982. *The Capitalist State*. New York: New York University Press.

Johnson, Chalmers. 2001. Blowback. *The Nation* 273, no. 11 (October 15): 13–15.

Johnson, Richard. 1996. What is Cultural Studies Anyway? In *What Is Cultural Studies?*, ed. John Storey. London: Arnold.

Johnston, David Cay. 1999. Gap Between Rich and Poor Found Substantially Wider. *The New York Times*, 5 Sept.: 14–15.

Jones, Gareth Stedman. 1970. The Specificity of US Imperialism. *New Left Review* 60 (Mar.–Apr.): 59–86.

Kammen, Michael. 1991. *Mystics Chords of Memory*. New York: Alfred A. Knopf.

Kaplan, Amy. 1993. Black and Blue on San Juan Hill. *Cultures of United States Imperialism*. Durham, N.C.: Duke University Press.

———. 2000. Romancing the Empire: The Embodiment of American Masculinity in the Popular Historical Novel of the 1890s. In *Postcolonial Theory and the United States*, ed. Amritjit Singh and Peter Schmidt. Jackson: University of Mississippi.

Karnow, Stanley. 1989. *In Our Image*. New York: Random House.

Karnow, Stanley, and Nancy Yoshihara. 1992. *Asian Americans in Transition*. New York: The Asia Society.

Katz, Adam. 1995–1996. Postmodern Cultural Studies: A Critique. *The Alternative Orange* 5, no. 1 (fall/winter): 56–70.

Kelley, Robin D. G. 2000. Identity Politics and Class Struggle. In *Race and Ethnicity in the United States*, ed. Stephen Steinberg. Oxford: Blackwell Publishers.

Khare, R. S. 1991. The Other's Double — The Anthropologist's Bracketed Self: Notes on Cultural Representation and Privileged Discourse. *New Literary History* 23: 1–23.

Kiernan, V. G. 1983. Nationalism. In *A Dictionary of Marxist Thought*, ed. Tom Bottomore. Cambridge, Mass.: Harvard University Press.

Kitano, Harry, and Roger Daniels. 1998. *Asian Americans: Emerging Minorities*. Englewood Cliffs, N.J.: Prentice-Hall.

Kluckhohn, C., and W. H. Kelley. 1945. The Concept of Culture. In *The Science of Man in the World Crisis*. New York: Columbia University Press.

Kochiyama, Yuri. 1998. Yuri Kochiyama: With Justice in Her Heart. *Revolutionary Worker* 986 (13 Dec.): 1–2.

Kolko, Gabriel. 1976. *Main Currents in Modern American History*. New York: Pantheon Books.

Krader, Lawrence. 1968. *Formation of the State*. Englewood Cliffs, N.J.: Prentice Hall.

———. 1972. *The Ethnological Notebooks of Karl Marx*. Asem, Netherlands: Van Gorcum.

Krupat, Arnold. 1992. *Ethnocriticism*. Berkeley: University of California Press.

———. 1996. *The Turn to the Native*. Lincoln: University of Nebraska Press.

Kymlicka, Will. 1997. Ethnicity in the USA. In *The Ethnicity Reader*, ed. Montserrat Guibernau and John Rex. Cambridge: Polity Press.

Laclau, Ernesto, and Chantal Mouffe. 1985. *Hegemony and Socialist Strategy*. London: Verso.

———. 1994. Minding the Gap. In *The Making of Political Identities*. London: Verso.

Lacsamana, Anne. 1998. Academic Imperialism and the Limits of Postmodernist Discourse: An Examination of Nicole Constable's *Maid to Order in Hong Kong: Stories of Filipina Workers*. *Amerasia Journal* 24, no. 3 (winter): 37–42.

Larrain, Jorge. 1995. Identity, the Other, and Postmodernism. In *Post-Ality: Marxism and Postmodernism*, ed. Mas'ud Zavarzaedh, Teresa Ebert, and Donald Morton. Washington, D.C.: Maisonneuve Press.

Larsen, Neil. 1995. *Reading North by South*. Minneapolis: University of Minnesota Press.

———. 1996. Negativities of the Popular: C. L. R. James and the Limits of "Cultural Studies." *Rethinking C. L. R. James*, ed. Grant Farred. Cambridge, Mass.: Blackwell.

———. 1999. DetermiNation: Postcolonialism, Poststructuralism and the Problem of Ideology. In *The Pre-Occupation of Post-Colonial Studies*, ed. Kalpana Seshadri-Crooks and Fawzia Afzal-Khan. Durham, N.C.: Duke University Press.

Larsen, Neil, and James Petras. 2000. Globalization: Theory, Politics, Ideology. *Working Papers in Cultural Studies #22*, ed. E. San Juan Jr. Pullman: Department of Comparative American Cultures, Washington State University.

Lasch, Christopher. 1979. *The Culture of Narcissism*. New York: Norton.

Lazarus, Neil. 1991. Doubting the New World Order: Marxism, Realism, and the Claims of Postmodernist Social Theory. *Differences* 3, no. 3: 94–138.

———. 1998–1999. Charting Globalization. *Race and Class* 40 (Oct.–Mar.): 91–110.

———. 1999. *Nationalism and Cultural Practice in the Postcolonial World*. New York: Cambridge University Press.

Lears, T. J. Jackson. 1981. *No Place of Grace*. New York: Pantheon.

Lee, Jayne Chong-Soon. 1995. "Navigating the Topology of Race." *Critical Race Theory*, ed. Kimberle Crenshaw, Neil Gotanda, Gary Peller, and Kendall Thomas. New York: New Press.

Lee, Rachel. 1999. Asian American Cultural Production in Asian-Pacific Perspective. *Boundary* 2 (summer): 231–54.

Lefebvre, Henri. 1968. *Dialectical Materialism*. Trans. John Sturrock. London: Jonathan Cape.

———. 1969. *The Sociology of Marx*. New York: Vintage Books.

———. 1971. *Everyday Life in the Modern World*. Trans. Sacha Rabinovich. New York: Harper and Row.

Leitch, Vincent. 1994. Cultural Studies. In *The Johns Hopkins Guide to Literary Theory and Criticism*, ed. Michael Groden and Martin Kreiswrith. Baltimore, Md.: Johns Hopkins University Press.

Leiwei Li, David. 1991. The Formation of Frank Chin and Formations of Chinese American Literature. *Asian Americans: Comparative and Global Perspectives*, ed. Shirley Hune et al. Pullman: Washington State University Press.

Lenin, Vladimir. 1960. *Lenin on the National Liberation Movement*. Peking: Foreign Language Press.

———. 1963. The Unity and Conflict of Opposites. *Reader in Marxist Philosophy*, ed. Howard Selsam and Harry Martel. New York: International Publishers.

———. 1968. *National Liberation, Socialism and Imperialism*. New York: International Publishers.

———. 1970. *On Culture and Cultural Revolution*. Moscow: Progress Publishers.

———. 1980. *On the Question of Dialectics*. Moscow: Progress Publishers.

Lerner, Max. 1987. *America As a Civilization*. New York: Henry Holt and Co.

Levine, Andrew. 1988. *Arguing for Socialism*. London: Verso.

Levine, Norman. 1978. Dialectical Materialism and the Mir. In *Marx: Sociology/Social Change/Capitalism*, ed. Donald McQuarie. New York: Quartet Books.

Liao, Ping-hui. 1999. Postcolonial Studies in Taiwan: Issues in Critical Debates. *Postcolonial Studies* 2, no. 2: 199–211.

Lichtenberg, Judith. 1999. How Liberal Can Nationalism Be? In *Theorizing Nationalism*, ed. Ronald Beiner. New York: State University of New York Press.

Lichtheim, George. 1967. *The Concept of Ideology and Other Essays*. New York: Vintage Books.

Lipset, Seymour M. 1960. Trends in American Society. In *An Outline of Man's Knowledge of the Modern World*, ed. Lyman Bryson. New York: Nelson Doubleday, Inc.

———. 1963. *The First New Nation*. New York: Basic Books.

Lipsitz, George. 1998. *The Possessive Investment in Whiteness*. Philadelphia, Pa.: Temple University Press.

Loewen, James W. 1995. *Lies My Teacher Told Me*. New York: Free Press.

Loomba, Ania. 1998. *Colonialism/Postcolonialism*. London: Routledge.

Lopez, Ian F. Haney. 1998. The Mean Streets of Social Race. In *The So-*

cial Construction of Race and Ethnicity in the United States. New York: Longman.

Lott, Eric. 1995. *Love and Theft*. New York: Oxford University Press.

Löwy, Michael. 1981. *The Politics of Combined and Uneven Development*. London: New Left Books.

———. 1998. *Fatherland or Mother Earth?* London: Pluto Press.

Lukács, Georg. [1968] 1971. *History and Class Consciousness*. Trans. Rodney Livingston. London: Merlin Press.

———. 1973a. *Marxism and Human Liberation*, ed. E. San Juan Jr. New York: A Delta Book.

———: 1973b. The Old Culture and the New Culture. In *Marxism and Human Liberation*, ed. E. San Juan Jr. New York: A Delta Book.

———. 1991. *The Process of Democratization*. Trans. Susanne Bernhardt and Norman Levine. Albany: State University of New York Press.

———. 2000. *Defense of History and Class Consciousness*. London: Verso.

Luke, Timothy W. 1990. *Social Theory and Modernity*. Newbury Park, Calif.: Sage Publications.

Lye, Colleen. 1995. M. Butterfly and the Rhetoric of Antiessentialism: Minority Discourse in an International Frame. In *The Ethnic Canon*, ed. David Palumbo-Liu. Minneapolis: University of Minnesota Press.

Malik, Kenan. 1996. *The Meaning of Race: Race, History and Culture in Western Society*. Basingstoke, UK: Macmillan.

Mandel, Ernest. 1979. *Introduction to Marxism*. London: Ink Links.

———. 1983. Uneven Development. In *A Dictionary of Marxist Thought*, ed. Tom Bottomore. Cambridge, Mass.: Harvard University Press.

———. 1995. The Relevance of Marxist Theory for Understanding the Present World Crisis. In *Marxism in the Postmodern Age*, ed. Antonio Callari et al. New York: Routledge.

Mantsios, Gregory. 1995. Class in America: Myths and Realities. In *Race, Class, and Gender in the United States*, ed. Paula Rothenberg. New York: St. Martin's Press.

Marable, Manning. 1983. *How Capitalism Underdeveloped Black America*. Boston: South End Press.

———. 1995. History and Black Consciousness: The Political Culture of Black America. *Monthly Review* 43 (July–Aug.): 71–87.

———. 2000. We Need a New and Critical Study of Race and Ethnicity. *The Chronicle of Higher Education*, 25 Feb., B4–B7.

Marcuse, Herbert. 1968a. *One-Dimensional Man*. London: Sphere.

———. 1968b. *Negations*. Boston: Beacon Press.

Mariategui, Jose Carlos. 1996. *The Heroic and Creative Meaning of Social-*

ism: Selected Essays of Jose Carlos Mariategui, ed. Michael Pearlman. Atlantic Highlands, N.J.: Humanities Press.

Marmora, Leopoldo. 1984. Is There a Marxist Theory of Nation? In *Rethinking Marx*, ed. Sakari Hanninen and Leena Paldan. New York: International General.

Marshall, T. H. 1950. *Citizenship and Social Class and Other Essays.* Cambridge: Cambridge University Press.

Martin, Hans Peter, and Harald Schumann. 1997. *The Global Trap*. London and New York: Zed Books.

Martin, Tony. 1999. Rescuing Fanon from the Critics. In *Rethinking Fanon*, ed. Nigel Gibson. Amherst, N.Y.: Humanity Books.

Martinez, Elizabeth. 1996. Beyond Black/White: The Racisms of Our Time. In *Multicultural Experiences, Multicultural Theories*, ed. Mary F. Rogers. New York: The McGraw-Hill Companies.

Marx, Andrew. 1980. Amilcar Cabral and Two Problems of the Guinean Revolution. *Forward Motion* (winter): 41–46.

Marx, Karl. 1965. *Pre-Capitalist Economic Formations*. New York: International Publishers.

———. 1972. *Ireland and the Irish Question*. New York: International Publishers.

———. 1982. Pathways of Social Development: A Brief Against Suprahistorical Theory. In *Introduction to the Sociology of "Developing Societies"*, ed. Hamza Alavi and Theodor Shanin. New York and London: Monthly Review Press.

Marx, Karl, and Friedrich Engels. 1959. *Basic Writings on Politics and Philosophy*. New York: Doubleday and Co.

Mason, David. 1982. After Scarman: A Note on the Concept of "Institutional Racism." *New Community* 10: 38–45.

Massey, Doreen. 1993. Politics and Space/Time. In *Place and the Politics of Identity*, ed. Michael Keith and Steve Pile. London: Routledge.

May, Glenn. 1992. *Inventing a Hero: The Posthumous Re-creation of Andres Bonifacio.* Quezon City, Philippines: New Day Press.

McCord, William. 1996. *The Dawn of the Pacific Century.* Rutgers, N.J.: Transaction Publishers.

McLaren, Peter, and Ramin Farahmandpur. 2000. Reconsidering Marx in Post-Marxist Times: A Requiem for Postmodernism? *Educational Researcher* 29, no. 3: 25–33.

McLennan, Gregor. 1981. *Marxism and the Methodologies of History*. London: Verso.

McNally, David. 1999. Language, History, and Class Struggle. *Monthly Review* 3 (July–Aug.): 13–30.

McRobbie, Angela. 1992. Post-Marxism and Cultural Studies: A Post-script. In *Cultural Studies*, ed. Lawrence Grossberg, Cary Nelson, and Paula Treichler. New York: Routledge.

McWilliams, Carey. 1973. Editorial. *The Nation*, 30 Apr., 548.

Meillassoux, Claude. 1993. Toward a Theory of the "Social Corps." In *The Curtain Rises: Rethinking Culture, Ideology, and the State in Eastern Europe*, ed. Hermine De Soto and David Anderson. New Jersey: Humanities Press.

Memmi, Albert. 2000. *Racism*. Minneapolis: University of Minnesota Press.

Menchú, Rigoberta. 1984. *I, Rigoberta Menchú*. New York: Verso.

———. 1998. *Crossing Borders*. London: Verso.

Meszaros, Istvan. 1972. *Lukács' Concept of Dialectic*. London: Merlin Press.

———. 1983a. Mediation. In *A Dictionary of Marxist Thought*, ed. Tom Bottomore. Cambridge, Mass.: Harvard University Press.

———. 1983b. Totality. In *A Dictionary of Marxist Thought*, ed. Tom Bottomore. Cambridge, Mass.: Harvard University Press.

Miles, Robert. 1986. Labour Migration, Racism and Capital Accumulation in Western Europe since 1945: An Overview. *Capital and Class* 28 (spring): 49–86.

———. 1989. *Racism*. London: Routledge.

Miles, Robert, and Rodolfo Torres. 1999. Does "Race" Matter? Transatlantic Perspectives on Racism after "Race Relations." In *Race, Identity and Citizenship: A Reader*, ed. Rodolfo Torres et al. Oxford: Blackwell.

Miller, Stuart Creighton. 1982. *"Benevolent Assimilation": The American Conquest of the Philippines 1899–1903*. New Haven, Conn.: Yale University Press.

Mills, Charles. 1999. The Racial Polity. In *Racism and Philosophy*, ed. Susan Babbit and Sue Campbell. Ithaca, N.Y.: Cornell University Press.

Min, Pyong Gap, ed. 1995. *Asian Americans: Contemporary Trends and Issues*. Thousand Oaks, Calif.: Sage Publications.

Minnerup, Gunter. 1984. Marxism and the Nation. In *Rethinking Marx*, ed. Sakari Nanninen and Leena Paldan. Berlin: Argument-Verlag.

Miyoshi, Masao. 2000. Ivory Tower in Escrow. *Boundary* 2 (spring): 7–50.

Mohanty, Satya P. 1995. Epilogue. Colonial Legacies, Multicultural Futures: Relativism, Objectivity, and the Challenge of Otherness. *PMLA* 110, no. 1 (Jan.): 108–18.

Moore-Gilbert, Bart. 1997. *Postcolonial Theory: Contexts, Practices, Politics*. London: Verso.

Morley, David. 1998. So-Called Cultural Studies: Dead Ends and Reinvented Wheels. *Cultural Studies* 12, no. 4 (Oct.): 476–97.

Morton, Donald. 1996. Literary/Cultural Studies and the Crisis of Liberalism in the U.S. Academy Today. *Red Orange* 1, no. 1 (May): 101–26.

Mosse, George L. 1985. *Nationalism and Sexuality*. New York: Howard Fertig.

Mudimbe, V. Y., and Sabine Engel. 1999. Introduction. *The South Atlantic Quarterly* (winter/spring): 1–8.

Mulhern, Francis. 1995. The Politics of Cultural Studies. *Monthly Review* (July–Aug.): 31–40.

———, ed. 1992. *Contemporary Marxist Literary Criticism*. London: Longman.

Murray, Charles. 1984. *Losing Ground*. New York: Basic Books.

Myers, Gustavus. [1943] 1960. *History of Bigotry in the United States*. New York: Capricorn Books.

Myrdal, Gunnar. 1944. *An American Dilemma*. New York: Harper and Row.

Myrdal, Jan, and Gun Kessle. 1970. *Angkor: An Essay on Art and Imperialism*. Trans. Paul Britten Austin. New York: Vintage Books.

National Asian Pacific American Legal Consortium. 1999. *1998 Audit of Violence Against Asian Pacific Americans (Sixth Annual Report)*. Washington, D.C.: NAPALC.

Needham, Joseph. May 1975. History and Human Values: A Chinese Perspective For World Science and Technology. Lecture given to the Canadian Association of Asian Studies Annual Conference.

Noumoff, Sam. 1999. Globalization and Culture. *Working Papers Series in Cultural Studies, Ethnicity, and Race Relations*, ed. E. San Juan Jr. Pullman: Department of American Comparative Cultures, Washington State University.

Novack, George. 1966. *Uneven and Combined Development in History*. New York: Merit Publishers.

Ocampo, Ambeth. 1998. *The Centennial Countdown*. Pasig, Rizal: Anvil Publishing Co.

O'Connor, Alan. 1989. *Raymond Williams: Writing, Culture, Politics*. New York: Blackwell.

———. 1996. The Problem of American Cultural Studies. *What is Cultural Studies?*, ed. John Storey. London: Arnold.

———. 1999. Who's Emma and the Limits of Cultural Studies. *Cultural Studies* 13, no. 4: 691–702.

O'Hare, William P., and Judy Felt. 1991. *Asian Americans: America's Fastest Growing Minority Group*. Washington, D.C.: Population Reference Bureau Inc.

Ohmann, Richard. 1997. English and the Cold War. In *The Cold War and the Academy*, ed. Noam Chomsky et al. New York: New Press.

———. 2000. Historical Reflections on Accountability. *Academe* (Jan.–Feb.): 24–29.

Okihiro, Gary. 1994. *Margins and Mainstreams*. Seattle: University of Washington Press.

Ollman, Bertell. 1979. *Social and Sexual Revolution*. Boston: South End Press.

———. 1993. *Dialectical Investigations*. New York: Routledge.

Omatsu, Glenn. 1994. The "Four Prisons" and the Movements of Liberation: Asian Ameican Activism from the 1960s to the 1990s. *The State of Asian America*, ed. Karin Aguilar-San Juan. Boston: South End Press.

Omi, Michael, and Howard Winant. 1986. *Racial Formation in the United States*. New York: Routledge.

Ong, Aihwa. 1999. Cultural Citizenship as Subject Making: Immigrants Negotiate Racial and Cultural Boundaries in the United States. In *Race, Identity, and Citizenship: A Reader*, ed. Rodolfo Torres, Louis Miron, and Jonathan Xavier Inda. Oxford: Blackwell.

Ong, Paul, ed. 1994. *The State of Asian Pacific America: Economic Diversity, Issues and Policies*. Los Angeles: LEAP Asian Pacific American Public Policy Institute and UCLA Asian American Studies Center.

Ong, Paul, Edna Bonacich, and Lucie Cheng, eds. 1994. *The New Asian Immigration in Los Angeles and Global Restructuring*. Philadelphia, Pa.: Temple University Press.

Ong, Paul, and John Liu. 1994. U.S. Immigration Policies and Asian Immigration. In *The New Asian Immigration in Los Angeles and Global Restructuring*, ed. Paul Ong et al. Philadelphia, Pa.: Temple University Press.

Ortega y Gasset, José. 1956. *The Dehumanization of Art*. New York: Doubleday Anchor Books.

Osborne, Peter, and Lynne Segal. 1999. Interview with Stuart Hall: Culture and Power. *Race, Identity, and Citizenship*, ed. Rodolfo Torres, Louis Miron, and Jonathan Inda. Oxford: Blackwell.

Outlaw, Lucius Jr. 1990. Toward a Critical Theory of Race. In *Anatomy of Racism*, ed. David Goldberg. Minneapolis: University of Minnesota Press.

Palumbo-Liu, David, ed. 1995. *The Ethnic Canon*. Minneapolis: University of Minnesota Press.

———. 1999. *Asian/American: Historical Crossings of a Racial Frontier*. Stanford, Calif.: Stanford University Press.

Parenti, Michael. 1989. *The Sword and the Dollar*. New York: St. Martin's Press.

———. 1994. *Land of Idols: Political Mythology in America*. New York: St. Martin's Press.

Parker, Andrew, Mary Russo, Doris Sommer, and Patricia Yaeger, eds. 1992. *Nationalisms and Sexualities*. New York: Routledge.

Patel, Dinker. 1992. Asian Americans: A Growing Force. *Race and Ethnic Relations 92/93*, ed. John Kromkowski. Guilford, Conn.: Dushkin Publishing Co.

Pateman, Carole. 1988. *The Sexual Contract*. Stanford, Calif.: Stanford University Press.

Patterson, Thomas C. 1997. *Inventing Western Civilization*. New York: Monthly Review Press.

Pease, Donald. 1993. Hiroshima, the Vietnam Veterans War Memorial, and the Gulf War: Post-National Spectacles. *Cultures of United States Imperialism*. Durham, N.C.: Duke University Press.

Peck, Jeffrey. 1985. Advanced Literary Study as Cultural Study: A Redefinition of the Discipline. *Profession 85*: 49–54.

Peller, Gary. 1995. Race Consciousness. In *After Identity*, ed. Dan Danielsen and Karen Engle. New York: Routledge.

Perea, Juan. 1998. Am I an American or Not? Reflections on Citizenship, Americanization, and Race. In *Immigration and Citizenship*. Lanham, Md.: Rowman and Littlefield.

Perlo, Victor. 1996. *Economics of Racism II*. New York: International Publishers.

Pfeffer, Richard. 1979. *Working for Capitalism*. New York: Columbia University Press.

Poggi, Gianfranco. 1978. *The Development of the Modern State*. Stanford, Calif.: Stanford University Press.

Polanyi, Karl. 1957. *The Great Transformation*. Boston: Beacon Press.

Porter, Dennis. 1994. Orientalism and its Problems. In *Colonial Discourse and Post-Colonial Theory*, ed. Patrick Williams and Laura Chrisman. New York: Columbia University Press.

Poster, Mark. 1997. *Cultural History and Postmodernity*. New York: Columbia University Press.

Poulantzas, Nicos. 1978. *State, Power, Socialism*. London: Verso.

Pratt, Mary Louise. 1994. Comment on Edward Said's *Culture and Imperialism*. *Social Text* 39: 2–10.

Quayson, Ato. 2000. *Postcolonialism: Theory, Practice or Process?* Cambridge: Polity Press.

Readings, Bill. 1996. *The University in Ruins*. Cambridge, Mass.: Harvard University Press.

Reed, Adolph Jr. 1999. *Stirrings in the Jug*. Minneapolis: University of Minnesota Press.

————. 2000. Race and Class in the Work of Oliver Cromwell Cox. *Monthly Review* 52, no. 9 (Feb.): 23–32.

Reed, Ishmael, ed. 1998. *MultiAmerica.* New York: Penguin Books.

Reiche, Reimut. 1971. *Sexuality and Class Struggle.* New York: Praeger.

Reimers, Ronald. 1992. *Still the Golden Door.* New York: Columbia University Press.

Rex, John. 1970. *Race, Colonialism and the City.* London: Oxford University Press.

————. 1986. *Race and Ethnicity.* Milton Keynes: Open University Press.

————. 1997. The Concept of a Multicultural Society. In *The Ethnicity Reader*, ed. Montserrat Guibernau and John Rex. Cambridge: Polity Press.

Ricci, Claudia. 1995. Gunga Din Highway. *New York Times Book Review*, 29 Jan.

Robbins, Bruce. 1993. *Secular Vocations.* London: Verso.

Roediger, David. 1992. *The Wages of Whiteness.* London: Verso.

Rose, Peter. 1997. *They and We: Racial and Ethnic Relations in the United States.* 5th ed. New York: McGraw-Hill.

Roseberry, William. 1996. The Unbearable Lightness of Anthropology. *Radical History Review* (spring): 9–25.

Rossi, Ino. 1983. *From the Sociology of Symbols to the Sociology of Signs.* New York: Columbia University Press.

Rupert, Mark. 1993. Alienation, Capitalism and the Inter-State System: Towards a Marxian/Gramscian Critique. In *Gramsci, Historical Materialism and International Relations*, ed. Stephen Gill. New York: Cambridge University Press.

Said, Edward. 1979. *Orientalism.* New York: Vintage Books.

————. 1983. *The World, the Text, and the Critic.* Cambridge: Harvard University Press.

————. 1994a. *Culture and Imperialism.* New York: Alfred A. Knopf.

————. 1994b. Response. *Social Text* 39: 20–24.

————. 1998. Edward Said. In Conversation with Neeladri Bhattacharya, Suvir Kaul and Ania Loomba, New Delhi, 16 December 1997. *Interventions* 1, no. 1 (Oct.): 81–96.

Saifulin, Murad, and Richard R. Dixon, eds. 1984. *Dictionary of Philosophy.* New York: International Publishers.

Salecl, Renata. 1994. The Crisis of Identity and the Struggle for New Hegemony in the Former Yugoslavia. *The Making of Political Identities*, ed. Ernesto Laclau. London: Verso.

San Juan, E. Jr. 1992. *Racial Formations/Critical Transformations.* Atlantic Highlands, N.J.: Humanities Press.

———. 1995. Beyond Ethnicity: Toward a Critique of the Hegemonic Discipline. *Explorations in Ethnic Studies* 18, no. 2 (July): 131–44.

———. 1996a. *Hegemony and Strategies of Transgression*. Albany: State University of New York Press.

———. 1996b. *The Philippine Temptation*. Philadelphia, Pa.: Temple University Press.

———. 1998a. *Beyond Postcolonial Theory*. New York: St Martin's Press.

———. 1998b. *From Exile to Diaspora*. Boulder, Colo.: Westview Press.

———. 1998c. The Symbolic Economy of Gender, Class and Nationality in Filipina Migrant Narratives. *Lila* 7: 20–41.

———. 1999a. Fanon: An Intervention Into Cultural Studies. In *Frantz Fanon: Critical Perspectives*, ed. Anthony C. Alessandri. New York: Routledge.

———. 1999b. From the Immigrant Paradigm to Transformative Critique: Asians in the Late Capitalist United States. In *Race, Ethnicity, and Nationality in the United States*, ed. Paul Wong. Boulder, Colo.: Westview Press.

———. 1999c. The Question of Race in the 21st Century. *Dialogue and Initiative* [Committees of Correspondence] (spring): 31–34.

———. 2000a. *After Postcolonialism*. Lanham, Md.: Rowman and Littlefield.

———. 2000b. Bakhtin: Uttering the "(Into)nation of the Nation/People." In *Bakhtin and the Nation*, ed. San Diego Bakhtin Circle. Lewisburg, Penn.: Bucknell University Press.

Sanoff, Alvin P. 1996. The Core of the Matter. *U.S. News & World Report*. 25 Mar.: 57–58.

Sassen, Saskia. 1998. *Globalization and Its Discontents*. New York: New Press.

Schiller, Herbert I. 1989. *Culture, Inc.: The Corporate Takeover of Public Expression*. New York: Oxford University Press.

Schirmer, Daniel Boone, and Stephen Shalom, ed. 1987. *The Philippines Reader*. Boston: South End Press.

Schlesinger, Arthur Jr. 1994. The Return to the Melting Pot. In *From Different Shores*, ed. Ronald Takaki. New York: Oxford University Press.

Schlesinger, Arthur M. Sr. 1985. What Then is the American, This New Man? In *Reflections on America and Americans*, ed. David Queen. Washington, D.C.: U.S. Information Agency.

Schneider, David. 1977. Kinship, Nationality, and Religion in American Culture: Toward a Definition of Kinship. In *Symbolic Anthropology*, ed. Janet Dolgin, David Kemnitzer, and David Schneider. New York: Columbia University Press.

Schulze-Engler, Frank. 1998. The Politics of Postcolonial Theory. In *Post-*

colonial Theory and the Emergence of a Global Society, ed. Gordon Collier et al. Frankfurt am Main: Acolit.

Scott, Joan. 1992. Multiculturalism and the Politics of Identity. *October* 61 (summer): 12–19.

Scruton, Roger. 1982. *A Dictionary of Political Thought.* New York: Hill and Wang.

Seaman, Donna. 1994. Gunga Din Highway. *Booklist* 15 (Sept.): 111.

Segal, Ronald. 1967. *The Race War.* Middlesex: Penguin Books.

Sekyi-Otu, Ato. 1996. *Fanon's Dialectic of Experience.* Cambridge, Mass.: Harvard University Press.

Shohat, Ella. 1991. Notes on the Post-Colonial. *Social Text*: 99–112.

Shumway, David R. 1994. *Creating American Civilization.* Minneapolis: University of Minnesota Press.

Sison, José Maria. 1999. *100 Years of Struggle Against US Imperialism.* Rebolusyon Series, Vol. 2, English ed. (Apr.–June): 41–49.

Sklair, Leslie. 1991. *Sociology of the Global System.* Baltimore, Md.: Johns Hopkins University Press.

Sklar, Holly. 1995. Imagine a Country. *Race, Class, and Gender in the United States*, ed. Paula Rothenberg. New York: St. Martin's Press.

Slack, Jennifer Daryl, and Laurie Anne Whitt. 1992. Ethics and Cultural Studies. In *Cultural Studies*, ed. Lawrence Grossberg, Cary Nelson, and Paula Treichler. New York: Routledge.

Slater, Philip. 1970. *The Pursuit of Loneliness.* Boston: Beacon Press.

Smedley, Audrey. 1993. *Race in North America.* Boulder, Colo.: Westview Press.

Smith, Anthony. 1971. *Theories of Nationalism.* New York: Harper Torchbooks.

———. 1979. *Nationalism in the Twentieth Century.* New York: New York University Press.

Smith, Barbara. 1998. *The Truth That Never Hurts: Writings on Race, Gender, and Freedom.* New Brunswick, N.J.: Rutgers University Press.

Smith, Barbara Herrnstein. 1992. Cult-Lit: Hirsch, Literacy, and the "National Culture." In *The Politics of Liberal Education*, ed. Darryl Gless and Barbara Herrnstein Smith. Durham, N.C.: Duke University Press.

Smith, Neil. 1984. *Uneven Development.* New York: Blackwell.

———. 1993. Homeless/Global: Scaling Places. In *Mapping the Futures*, ed. John Bird et al. London: Routledge.

Smith, Paul Chaat, and Robert Allen Warrior. 1996. *Like a Hurricane.* New York: New Press.

Sohn-Rethel, Alfred. 1978. *Intellectual and Manual Labor*. Atlantic Highlands, N.J.: Humanities Press.

Sollors, Werner. 1986. *Beyond Ethniticity: Consent and Descent in American Culture*. New York: Oxford University Press.

Solomos, John. 1986. Varieties of Marxist Conceptions of Race, Class and the State: A Critical Analysis. In *Theories of Race and Ethnic Relations*, ed. John Rex and David Mason. Cambridge: Cambridge University Press.

Solomos, John, and Les Back. 1996. *Racism and Society*. New York: St. Martin's Press.

Sommer, Doris. 1996. OUR AmeRica. In *Field Work: Sites in Literary and Cultural Studies*, ed. Marjorie Garber et al. New York: Routledge.

Sorel, Georges. [1906] 1961. *Reflections on Violence*. New York: Macmillan.

Sowell, Thomas. 1994. *Race and Culture*. New York: Basic Books.

Spears, Arthur K., ed. 1999. *Race and Ideology*. Detroit, Mich.: Wayne State University Press.

Stalin, Joseph. 1970. Marxism and the National Question. In *Selections from Lenin and J. V. Stalin on National Colonial Question*. Calcutta: Calcutta Book House.

Steinberg, Stephen. 1981. *The Ethnic Myth*. Boston: Beacon Press.

———. 1995. *Turning Back*. Boston: Beacon Press.

———. 2000. Occupational Apartheid and the Origins of Affirmative Action. In *Race and Ethnicity in the United States*, ed. Stephen Steinberg. Oxford: Blackwell Publishers.

Steiner, George. 1971. *In Bluebeard's Castle*. New Haven, Conn.: Yale University Press.

Stoler, Ann Laura. 1995. *Race and the Education of Desire*. Durham, N.C.: Duke University Press.

Stoll, David. 1999. *I, Rigoberta Menchú and the Story of All Poor Guatemalans*. Boulder, Colo.: Westview Press.

Stratton, Jon, and Ien Ang. 1996. On the Impossibility of a Global Cultural Studies: "British Cultural Studies in an 'International' Frame." In *Stuart Hall: Critical Dialogues in Cultural Studies*, ed. David Morley and Kuan-Hsing Chen. New York: Routledge.

Strinati, Dominic. 1995. *An Introduction to Theories of Popular Culture*. New York: Routledge.

Stummer, Peter. 1998. Some Pragma-Theoretical Considerations. In *Postcolonial Theory and the Emergence of a Global Society*, ed. Gordon Collier et al. Frankfurt am Main: ACOLIT.

Takaki, Ronald. 1987. Reflections on Racial Patterns in America. In *From Different Shores*, ed. Ronald Takaki. New York: Oxford University Press.

————. 1989. *Strangers from a Different Shore*. Boston: Little, Brown and Co.

————. 1994. At the End of the Century: The "Culture Wars" in the U.S. In *From Different Shores*, ed. Ronald Takaki. New York: Oxford University Press.

Tanenbaum, Leora. 1995. Gene Fools. *In These Times* 196 (6–19 Feb.): 14–17.

Taylor, Charles. 1994. The Politics of Recognition. In *Multiculturalism*, ed. Amy Gutman. Princeton, N.J.: Princeton University Press.

————. 1999. Nationalism and Modernity. In *Theorizing Nationalism*, ed. Ronald Beiner. New York: State University of New York Press.

Teitelbaum, Michael, ed. 1976. *Sex Differences*. New York: Anchor.

Therborn, Goran. 1995. Routes to/through Modernity. In *Global Modernities*, ed. Mike Featherstone et al. London: Sage Publications.

Thompson, John B. 1984. *Studies in the Theory of Ideology*. Berkeley: University of California Press.

Tilly, Charles. 1975. Western State-Making and Theories of Political Transformation. In *The Formation of National States in Western Europe*, ed. Charles Tilly. Princeton, N.J.: Princeton University Press.

Toffler, Alvin. 1990. *Powershift*. New York: Bantam.

Turner, Bryan S. 1983. Asiatic Society. In *A Dictionary of Marxist Thought*, ed. Tom Bottomore. Cambridge, Mass.: Harvard University Press.

————. 1992. *Orientalism, Postmodernism and Globalism*. New York: Routledge.

Turner, Graeme. 1992. It Works For Me: British Cultural Studies, Australian Cultural Studies, Australian Film. In *Cultural Studies*, ed. Lawrence Grossberg et al. New York: Routledge.

U.S. Commission on Civil Rights. 1992. *Civil Rights Issues Facing Asian Americans in the 1990s*. Washington, D.C.: U.S. Commission on Civil Rights.

Van den Berghe, Pierre. 1978. *Race and Racism*. New York: John Wiley.

Van Erven, Eugene. 1992. *The Playful Revolution: Theatre and Liberation in Asia*. Bloomington: Indiana University Press.

Von Senger, Harro. 1991. *The Book of Stratagems*. New York: Penguin Books.

Waller, Nicole. 1995. Past and Repast: Food as Historiography in Fae Myenne Ng's *Bone* and Frank Chin's *Donald Duk*. *Amerikastudien* 40, no. 3: 485–502.

Wallerstein, Immanuel. 1991. The Construction of Peoplehood: Racism, Nationalism, Ethnicity. In *Race, Nation, Class*, ed. Etienne Balibar and Immanuel Wallerstein. New York: Verso.

————. 1995. Revolution as Strategy and Tactics of Transformation. In *Marx-*

ism and the Postmodern Age, ed. Antonio Callari et al. New York: Guilford.

Wang, L. Ling-chi. 1995. The Structure of Dual Domination: Toward a Paradigm for the Study of the Chinese Diaspora in the United States. *Amerasia Journal* 21, nos. 1–2: 149–69.

Weate, Jeremy. 2001. Fanon, Merleu-Ponty and the Difference of Phenomenology. In *Race*, ed. Robert Bernasconi. Oxford: Blackwell Publishers.

Wellman, David. 1977. *Portraits of White Racism*. Cambridge: Cambridge University Press.

West, Cornel. 1990. *Toward A Socialist Theory of Racism*. New York: Democratic Socialists of America.

———. 1993. *Keeping Faith*. New York: Routledge.

Wilentz, Sean. 1996. Integrating Ethnicity into American Studies. *The Chronicle of Higher Education*, 29 Nov., A56.

Williams, Jenny. 1985. Redefining Institutional Racism. *Ethnic and Racial Studies* 8 (July): 323–48.

Williams, Patricia. 1995. The Obliging Shell. In *After Identity*, ed. Dan Danielsen and Karen Engle. New York: Routledge.

———. 1998. The Ethnic Scarring of American Whiteness. In *The House that Race Built*, ed. Wahneema Lubiano. New York: Vintage Books.

Williams, Raymond. [1958] 1983. *Culture and Society: 1780–1950*. New York: Columbia University Press.

———. 1961. *The Long Revolution*. New York: Columbia University Press.

———. 1962. *Communications*. London: Penguin Books.

———. 1971. *George Orwell*. New York: Columbia University Press.

———. 1973. *The Country and the City*. New York: Oxford University Press.

———. 1974. *Television: Technology and Cultural Form*. Middletown: Wesleyan University Press.

———. [1976] 1983. *Keywords*. New York: Oxford University Press.

———. 1977. *Marxism and Literature*. New York: Oxford University Press.

———. 1979. *Politics and Letters*. London: Verso.

———. 1980. *Problems in Materialism and Culture*. London: Verso.

———. 1981. *The Sociology of Culture*. New York: Schocken Books.

———. 1983. *The Year 2000*. New York: Pantheon Books.

———. 1984. *Writing in Society*. London: Verso.

———. 1989a. *The Politics of Modernism*, ed. Tony Pinkney. London: Verso.

———. 1989b. *Raymond Williams on Television*. London: Routledge.

———. 1989c. *Resources of Hope*. London: Verso.

Williams, Rhonda. 1995. Consenting to Whiteness: Reflections on Race and Marxian Theories of Discrimination. In *Marxism in the Postmodern Age*, ed. Antonio Callari et al. New York: Guilford Press.

Wilson, R. 1999. A Challenge to the Veracity of a Multicultural Icon. *The Chronicle of Higher Education*, 15 Jan., A14–16.

Winant, Howard. 1990. Postmodern Racial Politics in the United States: Difference and Inequality. *Socialist Review* 1: 121–47.

Woddis, Jack. 1972. *Introduction to Neo-Colonialism*. New York: International Publishers.

Wolfenstein, Eugene Victor. 1993. *Psychoanalytic Marxism: Groundwork*. New York: The Guilford Press.

Wolin, Richard. 1992. *The Terms of Cultural Criticism*. New York: Columbia University Press.

Wong, Sau-ling Cynthia. 1992. Ethnicizing Gender: An Exploration of Sexuality as Sign in Chinese Immigrant Literature. In *Reading the Literatures of Asian America*, ed. Shirley Geok-lin Lím and Amy Ling. Philadelphia: Temple University Press.

Woo, Deborah. 1989. The Gap Between Striving and Achieving: The Case of Asian American Women. In *Making Waves*, ed. Asian Women United of California. Boston: Beacon Press.

Wood, Ellen Meiksins. 1995. *Democracy Against Capitalism*. New York: Cambridge University Press.

———. 1998. Modernity, Postmodernity or Capitalism? In *Capitalism and the Information Age*, ed. Robert McChesney, Ellen Meiksins Wood, and John Bellamy Foster. New York: Monthly Review Press.

Wood, Paul. 1996. Commodity. In *Critical Terms for Art History*. Chicago: University of Chicago Press.

Woodiwiss, Anthony. 1990. *Social Theory After Postmodernism*. London: Pluto Press.

Wright, Richard. 1957. *White Man, Listen!* New York: Harper Perennial.

Yang, Suzanne. 1998. A Question of Accent: Ethnicity and Transference. *The Psychoanalysis of Race*. Ed. Christopher Lane. New York: Columbia University Press.

Young, Robert. 1998. Ideologies of the Postcolonial. *Interventions* 1, no. 1: 1–9.

Young-Bruehl, Elisabeth. 1996. *The Anatomy of Prejudice*. Cambridge, Mass.: Harvard University Press.

Zalin, Larry. 2000. Three Illegal Immigrants Found Dead in Cargo Container at Port. *The Daily Evergreen*, 11 Jan., 4.

Zavarzadeh, Mas'ud. 1995. Postality: The (Dis)simulation of Cybercapitalism. In *Post-Ality: Marxism and Postmodernism*, ed. Mas'ud Zavarzadeh, Teresa Ebert, and Donald Mordon. Washington, D.C.: Maisonneuve Press.

Zelinsky, Wilbur. 1988. *Nation Into State: The Shifting Symbolic Foundations of American Nationalism*. Chapel Hill: University of North Carolina Press.

Zhang, Longxi. 1988. The Myth of the Other: China in the Eyes of the West. *Critical Inquiry* 15 (autumn): 108–31.

Zinn, Howard. 1980. *A People's History of the United States*. New York: Harper & Row.

Ziff, Larzer. 1981. *Literary Democracy*. New York: Penguin Books.

Žižek, Slavoj. 1993. *Tarrying with the Negative*. Durham, N.C.: Duke University Press.

———. 1997. Multiculturalism, Or, the Cultural Logic of Multinational Capitalism. *New Left Review* 225 (Sept.–Oct.): 28–51.

Index

Miles, Robert, 31, 98, 142
Militarism, 76, 80–82
Mills, Charles, 25–26
Model minority myth, 96–97, 102–5,
124, 378
Modernity, 19, 81–82, 117, 125, 168,
177, 180–83, 212, 225, 232, 236,
240, 258–59, 263, 268, 352, 364
Modernization, 13, 72–74, 91, 99,
146, 192, 248, 257, 263, 266, 362
Moore-Gilbert, Bart, 255
Morgan, Henry Lewis, 137
Mosse, George, 81–82
Mouffe, Chantal, 218–20, 224, 255,
291
Moynihan, Daniel P., 140, 154
Mulhern, Francis, 222–23, 228, 270
Multiculturalism, 5–10, 27, 40–43,
49, 70, 90–91, 96, 101, 109–10,
135–36, 148–52, 158, 165, 169,
180, 199, 204, 252, 275, 332, 341,
347, 378
Murray, Charles, 29–30, 42, 85
Muslims, 49, 63, 193
Myrdal, Gunnar, 46, 98, 138, 158
Myrdal, Jan, 237–41
Myth, 121, 356, 378, 381

Narcissism, 73–76
Nation, 32, 37–41, 63–66, 69–71,
74–76, 79–83, 88, 139, 247, 282–
83, 320–24, 354–56, 361, 370,
375–77; Aryan, 76, 89; civic, 90
National liberation, 100, 134, 142,
239–41, 244, 256, 265, 280–87,
317–330, 364
National question, 92, 107, 281, 317
Nationalism, 15, 33–40, 54, 60–95,
124–25, 129, 141, 151, 155–57,
163, 195, 271–73, 301–2, 323,
332–34, 350, 377–79
Nation-state, 18, 31, 36, 64–66, 70,
77, 90–93, 101, 128, 141, 149, 157,
161, 170, 190, 248, 305, 348–49,
362–63, 380

Native Americans, 2, 35–37, 63, 99,
124, 142, 145, 156, 170
Nativism, 29, 40, 69–70, 82, 101
Naturalization law (1790), 144
Neocolonialism, 17–18, 160, 185,
190, 194, 247, 254, 266, 278, 287,
321, 366–69, 377
Neoconservatism, 34, 69, 83–84, 110,
136–37, 333, 342
Neoliberalism, 6, 19, 82, 96, 128, 134,
157–58, 161, 214, 217, 233, 236,
248, 257, 274, 304, 331
Neo-Marxism, 147–48
New Criticism, 176, 291
New People's Army (Philippines),
176, 193, 379
"New World Order," 1, 40, 247–49,
257, 266
Nietzsche, Friedrich, 215, 226, 276,
298, 352
Nihilism, 162, 222, 258, 268, 299, 347
Nominalism, 153, 158, 186, 190, 226,
230, 234, 256, 267, 361

Ocalan, Abdullah, 128
Ohmann, Richard, 158, 169
Oligarchy, 192, 239, 365, 376
Ollman, Bertell, 268, 329
Omatsu, Glenn, 110
Omi, Michael, 139
Ong, Aihwa, 98, 125, 131, 375
Orientalism, 99, 105, 119, 251, 263,
273–75
Ortega y Gasset, José, 180
Overseas Contract Workers (OCW),
17, 43, 126, 131, 194, 346–81. See
also Diaspora; Filipino Americans;
Filipinos

Packard, Vance, 72
Palestine, 128, 276, 279, 286, 300
Palumbo-Liu, David, 106, 371
Parsons, Talcott, 198, 335
Patriarchy, 61, 72, 78–82, 87–89, 172,
306, 329, 376

E. SAN JUAN JR. is a Fellow of the Center for the Humanities, Wesleyan University, and Director of the Philippines Cultural Studies Center. He was professor and chair of the Department of Comparative American Cultures at Washington State University and has taught at the University of California, the University of Connecticut, Brooklyn College (CUNY), the University of the Philippines, the University of Trento, Italy, and Tamkang University in Taiwan. He was a Fellow at the Institute of Humanities, University of Edinburgh, and a Fulbright Lecturer at the Ateneo de Manila University and the University of the Philippines. Among his recent books are Beyond Postcolonial Theory, Hegemony and Strategies of Transgression, From Exile to Diaspora, and After Postcolonialism: Remapping Philippines-United States Confrontations.